DATE DUE			
Apr18 77			
Apr10 78			
Aug14 78G			
Mar 16 79			
Nov 2 79			

Language in Sociocultural Change

Language in Sociocultural Change

Essays by Joshua A. Fishman

**Selected and Introduced
by Anwar S. Dil**

Stanford University Press, Stanford, California 1972

Language Science and National Development

A Series Sponsored by the
Linguistic Research Group of Pakistan

General Editor: Anwar S. Dil

Stanford University Press
Stanford, California
© 1972 by Joshua A. Fishman
Printed in the United States of America
ISBN O-8047-0816-9
LC 72-85699

Contents

Acknowledgments

The Linguistic Research Group of Pakistan and the Editor of the Language Science and National Development Series are deeply grateful to Professor Joshua A. Fishman for giving us the privilege of presenting his selected writings as the sixth volume in our series established in 1970 to commemorate the International Education Year.

We are indebted to the editors and publishers of the following publications. The ready permission on the part of the holders of the copyrights, acknowledged in each case, is a proof of the existing international cooperation and goodwill that gives hope for better collaboration among scholars of all nations for international exchange of knowledge.

The Sociology of Language. Pensiero e Linguaggio 2. 113–27 (1971), with permission of the Editor.

Planned Reinforcement of Language Maintenance in the United States: Suggestions for the Conservation of a Neglected National Resource. Language Loyalty in the United States, by Joshua A. Fishman et al. (The Hague: Mouton & Company, 1966), pp. 369–391, with permission of the publisher.

Language Maintenance in a Supra-Ethnic Age: Summary and Conclusions. Language Loyalty in the United States, by Joshua A. Fishman et al.(The Hague: Mouton & Company, 1966), pp. 392–411, with permission of the publisher.

Societal Bilingualism: Stable and Transitional. The Sociology of Language, by Joshua A. Fishman (Rowley, Mass.: Newbury House, 1972), with permission of the publisher.

The Description of Societal Bilingualism. The Description and Measurement of Bilingualism, ed. by L. G. Kelley (Toronto: University of Toronto Press, 1969), pp. 275-81, with permission of the publisher.

The Multiple Prediction of Phonological Variables in a Bilingual Speech Community; with Eleanor Herasimchuk. American Anthropologist 71, No. 4. 648-57 (1969), with permission of the American Anthropological Association.

Varieties of Ethnicity and Varieties of Language Consciousness. Monograph No. 18, Report of the Sixteenth Annual Round Table Meeting on Linguistics and Language Study (Washington, D. C.: Georgetown University Press, 1966), pp. 69-79, with permission of the publisher.

National Languages and Languages of Wider Communication in the Developing Nations. Anthropological Linguistics 11. 111-35 (1969), with permission of the Editor.

The Impact of Nationalism on Language Planning. Can Language Be Planned?, ed. by Joan Rubin and Bjorn Jernudd (Honolulu: The University Press of Hawaii, an East-West Center Book, 1971), pp. 3-20, with permission of the publisher.

The Relationship Between Micro- and Macro-Sociolinguistics in the Study of Who Speaks What Language to Whom and When. Bilingualism in the Barrio, by Joshua A. Fishman, Robert L. Cooper, Roxana Ma et al. Indiana University Language Science Monograph Series, No. 7 (Bloomington: Research Center for Language Sciences, Indiana University, 1971), pp. 583-603, with permission of the publisher.

Problems and Prospects of the Sociology of Language. Einar Haugen Festschrift, ed. by N. Hasselmo et al. (The Hague: Mouton & Company, in press), with permission of the publisher.

Socio-Cultural Organization: Language Constraints and Language Reflections. The Sociology of Language, by Joshua A. Fishman (Rowley, Mass.: Newbury House, 1972), with permission of the publisher.

The Uses of Sociolinguistics. Applications of Linguistics: Selected Papers of the Second International Congress of Applied Linguistics, ed. by G. E. Perren and J. L. M. Trim (Cambridge: Cambridge University Press, 1971), pp. 19-40, with permission of the Editors and the publisher.

What Has the Sociology of Language to Say to the Language Teacher? Functions of Language in the Classroom, ed. by Courtney Cazden, Vera John, and Dell Hymes (New York: Teachers College Press, 1972), with permission of the publisher. Copyright 1972 by Teachers College, Columbia University.

The Editor completed work on this volume during 1969-72, while he was in residence as Visiting Scholar in Linguistics at Stanford University.

He would like to record his thanks to the language scholars who have sent materials for the forthcoming volumes and others who are working with him in the preparation of further volumes in the Series. Dr. Afia Dil and Dr. Robert L. Cooper of the California State University at San Diego and Dr. Nasim Dil of the University of Texas at Austin, deserve our gratitude for help in many ways.

This volume is affectionately dedicated to M. Manuel Fishman, the author's oldest son and colleague in the quest for intergenerational communication.

EDITOR'S NOTE

These essays have been reprinted from the originals with only minor changes made in the interest of uniformity of style and appearance. A few changes in wording have been made in consultation with the author. In some cases bibliographical entries and notes have been updated. Footnotes marked by asterisks have been added by the Editor.

Introduction

Joshua A. Fishman was born in Philadelphia on July 18, 1926. He received his B. S. and M. S. degrees from the University of Pennsylvania, and his Ph.D. degree in social psychology from Columbia University in 1953. For some time he worked as a researcher for the College Entrance Examination Board, where he became Director of Research in 1957, and taught at the City College of New York. In 1958 he was appointed Associate Professor of Human Relations and Psychology at the University of Pennsylvania, where he also served as Research Director of the A. M. Greenfield Center for Human Relations. In 1960 he was invited by Yeshiva University to serve as Professor of Psychology and Sociology and Dean of the Ferkauf Graduate School of Humanities and Social Sciences. Since 1966 he has been Distinguished University Research Professor of Social Sciences at Yeshiva.

Fishman grew up in a home that emphasized the importance of preserving the Yiddish language. In high school he came in contact with Max Weinreich and his son Uriel, two outstanding scholars of Yiddish linguistics, who helped influence his choice of language in its sociocultural setting as his chief scholarly focus. His interest in sociology, psychology, and the history and philosophy of the social sciences caused him to favor a multidisciplinary approach to intellectual pursuits. His awareness of minority group problems and his concern for the underprivileged led to his conviction that knowledge must be justified by its application to the upgrading of human life. As I see it, this conviction underlies Fishman's pioneering work in the sociology of language.

It was at the University of Pennsylvania, where Fishman
was working up the first course in the sociology of language in 1958-
59, that in response to a routine questionnaire circulated by the U. S.
Census Bureau he suggested revising the language questions in the
national census for 1960. This chance occurrence began his campaign to establish the importance of collecting data on the status of
non-English languages among the different ethnic and religious groups
throughout the country. In the early 1960's Fishman gathered together a team of research associates on the Language Resources
Project at Yeshiva University and produced a comprehensive three-
volume report that not only covered the main theoretical and methodological issues of interest to social scientists, but also reviewed a
whole series of practical problems in national perspective and made
a set of workable recommendations to the federal government for
preserving the language resources of the country. Just as he completed his project Fishman was invited to spend a year (1963-64) as
a Fellow at the Center for Advanced Study in the Behavioral Sciences
at Stanford University to bring together his findings for publication
and to develop their broader implications. His Language Loyalty in
the United States was published in 1966. Hailed by one eminent
reviewer as "a great book, a chapter in the history of the American
mind, a milestone in the sociological study of languages and cultures
in contact, " this volume served as an important reference document
during the discussions and hearings preceding the passing of the
Bilingual Education Act of 1968, which has resulted in the establishment of scores of bilingual education programs throughout the United
States. The value of this volume for similar situations in other parts
of the world, especially in a number of countries in the Third World,
is just beginning to be realized.

From language maintenance and language shift to societal
bilingualism as an element of sociocultural change was a logical step.
In contrast with Einar Haugen, who had produced an exhaustive
linguistic study of immigrant bilingualism among Norwegian-Americans,
and Wallace Lambert, who was conducting controlled psycholinguistic
experiments in bilingualism in a situation of social conflict among
French- and English-speaking Canadians in Quebec, Fishman was
interested in the description and measurement of bilingualism from a
more comprehensive societal viewpoint utilizing a variety of social

science research methods. His original plan to conduct such a study
in a Hausa-speaking Nigerian community had to be given up; instead
he selected a Puerto Rican Spanish-speaking community in Jersey
City, near New York. This change turned out to be a blessing for
his students in the Language and Behavior Ph. D. program at Yeshiva
University, who could carry on in-depth background studies on different aspects of the processes of societal bilingualism as part of
their graduate training program. Robert L. Cooper and other research associates helped Fishman produce in 1968 a two-volume
report for the U. S. Office of Education. Bilingualism in the Barrio,
published in 1971, is a solid case study of bilingual behavior showing
the complementary functioning of two languages in the life of a social
group. However, its chief merit lies in identifying problems of wider
social significance through a variety of theoretical and methodological
approaches to the study of language in society.

Fishman's current international project on language planning
has been conducted in collaboration with Charles A. Ferguson of
Stanford University as a follow-up of their jointly planned conference
of November 1966 on the language problems of developing nations.
Fishman spent 1968-69 as Senior Specialist at the East-West Center
on the University of Hawaii campus, carrying out background studies
on different aspects of language planning processes. A by-product of
that period is his monograph Language and Nationalism, scheduled
for publication in 1972, which discusses language planning in socio-
historical and cross-national perspective, pointing the way to empirical description and measurement of the impact of nationalism (and
internationalism) on language behavior. Since 1969, Fishman and
his associates have been collecting language planning data in Indonesia,
India, Sweden, and Israel.

Fishman's contributions to sociolinguistic theory and to the
applied sociology of language are difficult to summarize in this brief
introduction. Besides his own research, Fishman has edited two
well-known anthologies, Readings in the Sociology of Language (1968)
and Advances in the Sociology of Language (2 volumes, 1971-72),
and written an introductory review, Sociolinguistics: A Brief Introduction (1970), which he has followed up with a more comprehensive
text entitled The Sociology of Language (1972). To students of

language science and national development, perhaps his most notable accomplishment is his solid contribution to our understanding of the social organization of language behavior through carefully selected local, national, and international case studies. In my estimation, Fishman's future work will show him in his essential role as a social thinker and philosopher of language in relation to human development, an area in which he has recently been raising a number of critical questions and attempting some bold generalizations. To the stimulating nature of his work along these lines the present volume is eloquent testimony.

Anwar S. Dil

Committee on Linguistics
Stanford University
August 14, 1972

Language in Sociocultural Change

Part I. Approach to Sociolinguistics

1 | The Sociology of Language

Man is constantly using language—spoken language, written language, printed language—and man is constantly linked to others via shared norms of behavior. The sociology of language examines the interaction between these two aspects of human behavior: use of language and the social organization of behavior. Briefly put, the sociology of language focuses upon the entire gamut of topics related to the social organization of language behavior, including not only language usage per se but also language attitudes, overt behavior toward language and toward language users.

The latter concern of the sociology of language—overt behavior toward language and toward language users—is also a concern shared by political and educational leaders in many parts of the world and is an aspect of sociolinguistics that frequently makes the headlines. Many French-Canadian university students oppose the continuation of public education in English in the Province of Quebec. Many Flemings in Belgium protest vociferously against anything less than full equality—at the very least—for Dutch in the Brussels area. Some Welsh nationalists daub out English signs along the highways in Wales and many Irish revivalists seek stronger governmental support for the restoration of Irish than that made available during half a century of Irish independence. Jews throughout the world protest the Soviet government's extermination of Yiddish writers and the forced closing of Yiddish schools, theatres and publications.

Swahili, Filippino, Indonesian, Malay and the various provincial languages of India are all being consciously expanded in vocabulary, standardized in spelling and grammar so that they can increasingly function as the exclusive languages of government and of higher

culture and technology. The successful revival and modernization of
Hebrew has encouraged other smaller language communities—the
Catalans, the Provençals, the Frisians, the Bretons—to strive to
save their ethnic mother tongues (or their traditional cultural tongues)
from oblivion. New and revised writing systems are being accepted—
and, at times, rejected—in many parts of the world by communities
that hitherto had little interest in literacy in general or in literacy in
their mother tongues in particular.

Such examples of consciously organized behavior toward
language and toward users of particular languages can be listed almost endlessly. The list becomes truly endless if we include examples from earlier periods of history, such as the displacement of
Latin as the language of religion, culture and government in Western
Christendom and the conscious cultivation of once lowly vernaculars—
first in Western Europe and then subsequently in Central, Southern
and Eastern Europe, and finally in Africa and Asia as well—as
independent languages, as languages suitable for all higher purposes,
and as languages of state-building and state-deserving nationalities.
All of these examples too feed into the broad data pool of modern
sociology of language, providing it with historical breadth and depth
in addition to its ongoing interest in current language issues throughout the world.

However, the sociology of language reaches far beyond interest in case studies and in catalogs of language conflict and language
planning in the public arena. The ultimate quest of the sociology of
language is pursued diligently in many universities and is very far
from dealing directly with headlines or news reports. One part of
this quest is concerned with describing the generally accepted social
organization of language usage within speech community (or within
speech-and-writing communities, to be more exact). This part of
the sociology of language—descriptive sociology of language—seeks
to provide an answer to the question "who speaks (or writes) what
language (or what language variety) to whom and when and to what
end?" (Fishman, in press a). Descriptive sociolinguistics tries to
disclose the language usage norms—i.e., the generally accepted and
implemented social patterns of language use and of behavior toward
language—for particular larger or smaller social networks and communities. Another part of sociolinguistics—dynamic sociology of

language—seeks to provide an answer to the question "what accounts for differential changes in the social organization of language use and behavior toward language?" Dynamic sociology of language tries to explain why and how the social organization of language use and behavior toward language have become selectively different in the same social networks or communities on two different occasions. Dynamic sociology of language also seeks to explain why and how two once similar social networks or communities have arrived at a quite different social organization of language use and behavior toward language.

Descriptive Sociology of Language

Let us look first at descriptive sociology of language, since it is the basic task of the discipline per se. Unless we can attain reliable and insightful description of any existing patterns of social organization in language use and behavior toward language it will obviously be impossible to contribute very much that is sound toward the explanation of why or how this pattern changes or remains stable. One of the basic insights of descriptive sociology of language is that members of social networks and communities do not always display either the same language usage or the same behavior toward language. Perhaps a few examples will help illustrate this crucial point.

Government functionaries in Brussels who are of Flemish origin do not always speak Dutch to each other, even when they all know Dutch very well and equally well. Not only are there occasions when they speak French to each other instead of Dutch, but there are some occasions when they speak standard Dutch and others when they use one or another regional variety of Dutch with each other. Indeed, some of them also use different varieties of French with each other as well, one variety being particularly loaded with governmental officialese, another corresponding to the non-technical conversational French of highly educated and refined circles in Belgium, and still another being not only a "more colloquial French" but the colloquial French of those who are Flemings. All in all, these several varieties of Dutch and of French constitute the linguistic repertoire of certain social networks in Brussels. The task of descriptive sociology of language is to portray the general or normative patterns of language use within a speech network or speech community so as to show the systematic nature of the alternations between one variety and another among individuals who share a repertoire of varieties (Fishman, 1970; Fishman, Cooper, Ma, et al., 1971).

However, not only multilingual speech networks or communities utilize a repertoire of language varieties. In monolingual speech communities the linguistic repertoire of particular social networks may consist of several social class varieties, or of social class and regional varieties, or, even, of social class, regional and occupational varieties of the same language. Thus, monolingual native born New Yorkers speak differently to each other on different occasions— and these differences can be pinpointed phonologically (i.e. in the way words are pronounced), lexically (i.e. in the very words that are used) and grammatically (i.e. in the systematic relationship between words). The same young man who sometimes says "I sure hope yuz guys'll shut the lights before leavin'" also is quite likely to say, or at least to write, "Kindly extinguish all illumination prior to vacating the premises." It's all a question of when to say the one and when the other, when interacting with individuals who could equally well understand both but who would consider use of the one when the other is called for as a serious faux pas.

Situational shifting

The description of societal patterns of language variety use— a variety being either a different language or a different social "dialect," or a different occupational "dialect" or a different regional "dialect"—whenever any two varieties are present in the linguistic repertoire of a social network—commonly utilizes the concept of situation. A situation is defined by the co-occurrence of two (or more) interlocutors related to each other in a particular way, communicating about a particular topic, in a particular setting. Thus, a social network or community may define a beer-party between university people as a quite different situation than a lecture involving the same people. The topics of talk in the two situations are likely to be different; their locales and times are likely to be different; and the relationships or roles of the interlocutors vis-à-vis each other are likely to be different. Any one of these differences may be sufficient for the situations to be defined as <u>sufficiently</u> different by the members of the university community to require that a different language variety be utilized in each case.

Members of social networks sharing a linguistic repertoire must (and do) know when to shift from one variety to another. One category of such shifts is that known as situational shifts. A shift in situation <u>may</u> require a shift in language variety. A shift in language variety <u>may</u> signal a shift in the relationship between co-members of a social network, or a shift in the topic and purpose of their interaction, or a shift in the privacy or locale of their interaction (Blom and Gumperz, 1968).

The careful reader will note that I have written "<u>may</u> require" and "<u>may</u> signal." Does this mean that a shift in situation does not always and invariably require a shift in language variety or that a change in language variety does not always and invariably signal a change in situation? Yes, precisely. At times, members of the same speech network or community go from one situation to another without changing from one variety to another. Thus, interaction with one's friends and with one's younger siblings—two seemingly different role relations that may well transpire in generally different settings and involve at least somewhat different topics—may still be acceptably conducted in the same variety. Thus, what is or is not a different situation with respect to language variety use is a matter of the internal social organization of particular speech networks or communities. Native members of such networks or communities slowly and unconsciously acquire <u>sociolinguistic communicative competence</u> with respect to appropriate language usage. They are not necessarily aware of the norms that guide their sociolinguistic behavior. Newcomers to such networks or communities—including sociolinguistic researchers—must discover these norms more rapidly, more painfully and, therefore, more consciously (Hymes, 1967).

One thing is clear: there are classes of occasions recognized by each speech network or community such that several seemingly different situations are classed as being of the same kind. No speech network has a linguistic repertoire which is as differentiated as the complete list of apparently different role relations, topics and locales in which its members are involved. Just <u>where the</u>

boundaries come that do differentiate between the class of situations
generally requiring one variety and another class of situations generally requiring another variety must be empirically determined by
the investigator, and constitutes one of the major tasks of descriptive
sociolinguistics. Such classes of situations are referred to as
domains. The derivation of domains and of domain appropriate usage
from the data of numerous discrete situations and the variety shifting
or non-shifting which they reveal, is a task of descriptive sociology
of language—descriptive macro-sociology of language to be exact—
which proceeds via participant observation, survey methods, experimental designs and depth interviews (Fishman, 1971).

Metaphorical switching

        The fact that co-members of the same speech networks or
speech communities also change from one variety to another without signaling any change in situation is also indicative of the categorizing in which native members so frequently and effortlessly engage.
When variety switching is fleeting and non-reciprocal it is commonly
metaphorical in nature. This means that it is utilized for purposes
of emphasis or contrast, rather than as an indication of situational
discontinuity. A switch to Cockney where Received Pronounciation
(and grammar) is called for may well elicit a brief raising of eye-
brows or a pause in the conversation—until it is clear from the
speaker's demeanor and from the fact that he has reverted to RP
that no change in situation was intended. However, such metaphorical switching can be risky. Someone might feel that Cockney for the
situation at hand is in poor taste. Metaphorical switching is a luxury
that can be afforded only by those that comfortably share not only the
same set of situational norms but also the same view as to their
inviolability. Since most of us are members of several speech networks, each with somewhat different sociolinguistic norms, the
chances that situational shifting and metaphorical switching will be
misunderstood and conflicted—particularly where the norms pertaining to variety selection have few or insufficiently powerful guardians—are obviously great (Blom and Gumperz, 1968; Kimple,
Cooper and Fishman, 1969).

A speech community maintains its sociolinguistic pattern as long as the functional differentiation of the varieties in its linguistic repertoire is systematically and widely maintained. As long as each variety is associated with a separate class of situations there is good reason and established means for retaining them all, each in its place, notwithstanding the modicum of metaphorical switching that may occur. However, two or more varieties with the same societal function become difficult to maintain and, in the end, one must either displace the other or a new functional differentiation must be arrived at between them. Let us look quickly at how such changes in linguistic repertoire or in functional allocation occur.

Dynamic Sociology of Language:
The Bases of Repertoire Change

At the very same time that a linguistic repertoire with its particular societal functional allocation of varieties exists in a particular speech community, certain of these same or very similar varieties may be found in other or neighboring speech communities in association with other functions. If the members of these speech communities are brought into greater interaction with each other, or if their relative power to influence or control one another changes sufficiently, then the societal functional allocation of linguistic repertoire of one or another or both communities is likely to undergo change. Thus, most immigrants to the United States have experienced sufficient interaction with English-speaking Americans, particularly in the work domain and in the education domain to learn English. This has also long been true for French Canadians in large industrial centers such as Montreal. Yet, how differently these two processes of linguistic repertoire change have worked out. In the United States the immigrants largely lost their mother tongues within one, two, or at most, three generations. In Montreal each new French Canadian generation starts off monolingual in French and then acquires English later in life without, however, handing on this second language to the next generation as its initial language. How can we best describe and account for this difference in outcome between two populations each of which was <u>forced</u> to acquire English for its educational and economic improvement? The difference

seems to be related to the ability of one population to maintain a certain societal functional differentiation within its linguistic repertoire
while the other was unable to do so.

Unstable bilingualism

        American immigrants needed English both as a lingua franca
because they came from so many different speech communities and
as a passport to social and economic advancement. Because of the
severe dislocation of their "old-country" rural or small town ways
(as a result of rapid exposure to American urban, industrial contexts) it quickly became impossible for them to maintain the original
home and family patterns upon which their only chance for domain
separation depended. Those whose English was better, progressed
more rapidly on the American scene and became models within the
immigrant home and within the immigrant organization and neighborhood. Thus, the home and immigrant life itself became domains of
English—particularly under the onslaught of the American school and
the Americanizing and amalgamating efforts of American churches.
As a result, children of immigrants soon became bilingual in the
family and immigrant contexts themselves. Since English was the
only language of value outside of the home and immigrant organization only the latter might have been capable of preserving the non-
English mother-tongue if they had been able to maintain themselves
as separate, self-contained domains.

        This, the immigrant speech networks could do only in those
few cases where immigrants of a single background clearly pre-
dominated (as they had for a long time in the case of German- and
Scandinavian-language islands in the Mid-West) or where their social
mobility via English was sharply restricted (as in the case of Spanish
speakers in the Southwest). Almost everywhere else, economic
advancement and the dislocation of traditional home, neighborhood
and organizational practices went hand in hand. There was no domain
in which the non-English ethnic language alone was required for
"membership" and as a result, there was no domain in which it was
retained. The non-English ethnic languages continued somewhat
longer to serve fleeting metaphorical purposes but there were soon
no situational shifts in which they were required. As a result,

children who had become bilingual in the very bosom of the family
and the immigrant neighborhood became increasingly monolingual
English speakers as they passed to and through their English-speaking
schools, their English-speaking careers and their English-speaking
neighborhoods. Such individuals raised their own children in English
(Haugen, 1953; Fishman et al. , 1966).

Stable bilingualism

        In Montreal the situation was and still is much different.
French speakers were initially exposed to English instruction and to
English job success only slowly over a long period of time. Their
elementary schools long remained entirely French (as did their
churches) and even their secondary schools (in which English instruction was offered to those rather few who were fortunate enough to
attend) were under French (and under Church) auspices. The result
was that the monolingual French-speaking child remained such as
long as his life was restricted to home, neighborhood and church.
He became increasingly bilingual as he passed through more advanced
levels of the school and work domains, but he then reverted to increasing French monolingualism if his school and work careers were
kept at lower levels or when he passed beyond their reach. As a
result, the domains of English and the domains of French were kept
functionally quite separate. Not only did the English domains reach
proportionally fewer French Canadians and not only did they reach
them more superficially, but, chronologically, the early and late
domains of the speech community's networks were basically French-
speaking (except for metaphorical purposes), thus assuring that the
next generation would be monolingual French-speaking as well
(Lieberson, 1965).

        However, something new has recently been added to the
Montreal picture. French-Canadian education expanded to the point
that it produced more well-qualified or highly qualified individuals
than could be assimilated into the various English-managed industrial,
commercial and cultural enterprises which traditionally reserved
most of their leading positions for English Canadians. As a result,
French-speaking elites have increasingly claimed and formed their
own enterprises in these domains. For them English has become

increasingly superfluous in view of its lack of domain separation and
situational need. In addition, of course, it has become symbolic of
their not being masters in their own home, and, as such, is opposed
both for general symbolic as well as for specifically functional reasons (Lieberson, 1970; Hughes, 1971).

      These two sociolinguistic patterns, the American immigrant
and the French-Canadian nationalist, have been repeated many times
in the past century. The Russification of Soviet minorities—particularly the smaller ones—whether they be immigrants to large urban
centers in other regions or inundated by Russian and various other
immigrants into their own regions (Lewis, in press), has followed
the same path as that of the Anglification of immigrants to the United
States, the Hispanization of indigenous populations moving to urban
centers throughout Latin America, or the Wolofization of diverse
Senegalese populations in Dakar. Similarly, the "indigenization" of
the domains of education, industry and government (which has previously "belonged" to English, so to speak), that has increasingly typi-
fied French-Canada, is not at all unlike the growing displacement of
English in Puerto Rico, Tanzania, India, Malaysia and the Philippines
(Epstein, 1970; Das Gupta, 1970; Ramos et al., 1967; Whiteley,
1969).

      The last four instances—Tanzania, India, Malaysia and the
Philippines—also exemplify the constantly recurring need to develop
newly promoted indigenous national languages, so that they can be
effectively and uniformly utilized in the new domains and situations
that they have won or are winning for themselves. How this process
of language planning is conducted, who accepts and who rejects the
manufactured terminologies, orthographies and grammars, whether
their differential acceptance can be influenced by differing approaches
to the implementation of language planning and language policy, these
too are parts of the sociology of language—applied sociology of language to be sure—a topic in itself and one which deserves a few words
before this review is brought to a close.

Applied Sociology of Language

      The sociology of language has applied significance for all of
the topics normally considered within the field of applied linguistics:

native language teaching, second language teaching, translation, the creation and revision of writing systems, language policy decisions, and language planning as a whole. In connection with each of these topics successful "application" depends not only on competent linguistic analysis of the languages being taught, used or developed but also (and, perhaps, even primarily) upon the social circumstances surrounding all applied efforts in connection with these languages. Similarly all branches of applied sociology stand to benefit from the sociology of language, since all of them (sociology of education, sociology of medicine, sociology of planning, industrial sociology, etc.) deal with group boundaries, role networks, role repertoires, role compartmentalization, social situations, institutional domains, etc. The confluence between applied linguistics and applied sociology is most dramatically illustrated in the context of social and national modernization, a context in which the applied sociology of language has been most actively pursued (Fishman, Ferguson, Das Gupta, 1968). Let us look at some examples.

The creation and revision of writing systems

The progress of social and national modernization depends to a large extent upon sufficiently widespread as well as sufficiently advanced literacy. However, such literacy is often impossible because writing systems as such have not yet been divised for the languages spoken natively in various larger and smaller speech communities throughout the world. However, devising a simple and technically exact system of representing spoken sounds via written symbols is not at all a sufficient step for the acceptance of this system by its intended users.

To begin with there must be some felt need for reading and writing, some actual or implied gain as a result of the acquisition of literacy and, not infrequently, an absence of major status loss to those who have hitherto been the status and power elites of the society (Garvin, 1959).

Furthermore, the purely visual aspect of writing systems is also a factor in their acceptance or rejection.

Many speech communities have insisted on indigenous writing systems unlike those of other written languages, in order to

stress their separateness from their neighbors and their independence from "big brothers" at a greater geographic distance. Others,
on the other hand, have demonstrated positive modelling (rather than
anti-modelling), or have had such modelling foisted upon them. It is
hardly accidental that the new writing systems of many North American Indian groups "look like English, " that those of Latin American
Indians "look like Spanish, " that those of Siberian peoples "look like
Russian, " etc. The determining factors of such modelling and anti-
modelling are all social and political rather than merely linguistic
and pedagogical (Fishman, Cooper, Ma, et al. , 1971).

Even more complicated, socially, than the creation of new
writing systems is the revision of old ones. Attempts to simplify
spelling or writing systems per se have been singularly ineffective
in modern times although an inordinate amount of time and effort has
gone into such attempts (Smalley, 1964). While the writing systems
for Polish, Czech and Roumanian were changed from Cyrillic to
Roman alphabets, during the nineteenth century, and while the Soviets
have changed the writing systems of many Asian nationalities (sometimes more than once within a decade or two), others have experienced far greater difficulty, even under similar authoritarian conditions. Communist Chinese plans to phoneticize the writing of
Mandarin seem to have been postponed for the indefinite future and
Soviet efforts to "declericalize" Yiddish spelling by abandoning the
four "end of word" letters of the traditional Hebrew alphabet have
also been abandoned.

In more widely participatory decision-making settings spelling reform has proved to be, if anything, even more difficult to exe-
cute. Thus, while many developing nations of an earlier period were
able to push through spelling reforms before literacy became much
more than an elitist preoccupation (e. g. nineteenth-century Germany,
post-Revolutionary USSR) neither Israel nor Indonesia nor Pakistan
nor India nor any other developing nation of today has been able to
push through the spelling or writing reforms that would make literacy
more accessible to all its citizens. Nevertheless, Norway has been
able to revise the spelling of both of its standard national languages
in modern times, albeit in an atmosphere of considerable conflict
(Haugen, 1966).

Language planning

As the above discussion reveals, it is exceedingly difficult
to come to conclusions of applied significance when entire countries
or national entities are taken as the unit of analysis, particularly
when these units are at vastly different stages of social, economic
and political development. As a result, the applied sociology of language has tended more and more toward the in-depth study of localized
cases of language planning. Focusing increasingly upon differential
reactions to centrally authorized and controlled language innovations
(whether these be orthographic or lexical, on the one hand, or the
functional reallocation of codes within a speech-and-writing community, on the other hand), such studies do not speak of success or failure as a nation-wide phenomenon but rather, of differential rates of
acceptance or rejection (cognitively, affectively and/or overtly) in
various population segments.

As a result of recent studies it is becoming increasingly
possible for language planning agencies (e.g. , for those seeking to
foster the use of recently established national languages for purposes
of higher education, government or technology) to pinpoint the particular programs, projects or products that are successful with particular target populations and those that are not. It is becoming increasingly clear that the study of role relationships, role networks, role
compartmentalization and role access in speech communities and
speech networks is a very practical matter indeed.

For only such study can demonstrate where language planning per se must leave off and where wider social planning (including
the expansion of opportunity as well as of participation in decision
making and decision evaluation) must begin (Rubin and Jernudd, 1971).
This is the stage at which the applied sociology of language now finds
itself.

NOTE

Revised and enlarged version of a lecture prepared for the Voice of
America Forum Lecture Series, George A. Miller, Rockefeller
University, Coordinator.

14   Language in Sociocultural Change

REFERENCES

Blom, J. P. and Gumperz, J. (1968), "Fattori sociali determinanti
del comportamento verbale," in P. P. Giglioli (ed.), Socio-
linguistica, special issue of the Rassegna Italiana di Socio-
logia, vol. 9, no. 2, pp. 301-328 (to appear in English as
"Social Meaning in Linguistic Structures," in J. Gumperz
and D. Hymes (eds.), Directions in Sociolinguistics, Holt,
Rinehart and Winston, in press).

Das Gupta, J. (1970), Language Conflict and National Development,
University of California Press.

Epstein, Erwin H. (ed.) (1970), Politics and Education in Puerto
Rico; A Documentary Survey of the Language Issue, Methuen;
Scarecrow.

Fishman, J. A. et al. (1966), Language Loyalty in the United States,
Mouton.

_____ Ferguson, C. A. and Das Gupta, J. (eds.) (1968), Language Problems of Developing Nations, Wiley.

_____ (1970), Sociolinguistics: A Brief Introduction, Rowley,
Newbury House.

_____ (1971), "The sociology of language: an interdisciplinary
social science approach to sociolinguistics," in J. A. Fishman (ed.), Advances in the Sociology of Language I, Mouton.

_____ (in press, a), "Domains and the relationship between
micro- and macrolinguistics," in J. Gumperz and D. Hymes
(eds.), Directions in Sociolinguistics, Holt, Rinehart and
Winston.

_____ (in press, b), "The uses of sociolinguistics," Proceedings
of the Second International Congress of Applied Linguistics,
Cambridge University Press. [In this volume pp. 305-30.]

_____ Cooper, R. L., Ma, R., et al. (1971), Bilingualism in
the Barrio, Bloomington, Indiana University Language Sciences Monographs.

Garvin, P. (1959), "The standard language problem: concepts and
methods," Anthrop. Linguistics, no. 2, pp. 28-31.

Haugen, E. (1953), The Norwegian Language in America, University
of Pennsylvania Press, 2 vols.

_____ (1966), Language Planning and Language Conflict; The
Case of Modern Norwegian, Harvard University Press.

Hughes, E. (1971), "The linguistic division of labor in Montreal,"
    Monograph Series on Languages and Linguistics, George-
    town University Press; also in J. A. Fishman (ed.),
    Advances in the Sociology of Language II, Mouton. (1972)
Hymes, D. (1967), "Models of the interaction of language and social
    setting," J. Soc. Issues, vol. 23, no. 2, pp. 8-28.
Kimple Jr., J., Cooper, R. L. and Fishman, J. A. (1969), "Lan-
    guage switching in the interpretation of conversations,"
    Lingua, vol. 23, pp. 127-34.
Lewis, G. (in press), "Language maintenance and language shift in
    the Soviet Union," Inter. Migration Rev.
Lieberson, S. (1965), "Bilingualism in Montreal: a demographic
    analysis," Amer. J. Sociol., vol. 71, pp. 10-25; also in
    J. A. Fishman (ed.), Advances in the Sociology of Language
    II, Mouton. (1972)
_____ (1970), Language and Ethnic Relations in Canada, Wiley.
Ramos, M. et al. (1967), The Determination and Implementation of
    Language Policy, Alemar-Phonnix.
Rubin, J. and Jernudd, B. (eds.) (1971), Can Language Be Planned?
    East West Center Press, Honolulu.
Smalley, W. A. (1964), Orthography Studies: Articles on New Writ-
    ing Systems, United Bible Societies.
Whiteley, W. (1969), Swahili; The Rise of a National Language,
    Methuen.

Part II. Language Maintenance and Language Shift

2 | Planned Reinforcement of Language Maintenance in the United States:

Suggestions for the Conservation of a Neglected National Resource

After many generations of neglect and apathy, American speakers of non-English languages have, of late, become objects of more positive attention than has commonly been their lot in most American communities. They have not been proclaimed national heroes, nor have they been the recipients of public or private largesse. In the eyes of the general public, they continue to be objects of curiosity in that their atypicality is obvious even if it is no longer shameful. Nevertheless, the attitude toward them has changed. They are now more frequently viewed as commanding a rare commodity, a skill which has "suddenly" become a valuable asset for the country. As a result, there have been a number of recent efforts to study the distribution of this commodity and to consider ways of safeguarding it. The Language Resources Project itself may be viewed as one such effort; there could be many more if it were fully and finally decided to pursue a consistent and effective policy of language maintenance, reinforcement, and development. Our purpose here is to indicate some possible ingredients of such a policy.

I approach this task with some ambivalence. At a professional level, most social scientists feel more comfortable with diagnosis (study design, instrument construction, data collection, data analysis, data interpretation) than with therapy (recommendations for action, planning action, involvement with action-oriented branches of government or segments of the community).[1] Our self-concepts and our professional standing as scientists and scholars are reinforced and advanced by activities removed from the work-a-day world of political pressures, social tactics, and applied activities. Since our scientific status is often relatively recent and insecure within the academic community itself, we are frequently tempted to pursue security and respectability by increasing our isolation from the complexities and the frustrations of social arenas in which our findings and theories might be put to overly demanding, time-consuming, and frustrating tests. Although it is frequently admitted that applied settings <u>can</u> provide powerful stimulation for theoretical developments, the leap from the role of scholar to that of consultant or activist is still rarely attempted among behavioral scientists, and even more rarely pursued to the point of both conceptual and pragmatic "success."[2]

As a research venture the Language Resources Project was guided by an intellectual preoccupation with language maintenance under the impact of social change in the United States. No particular attitudinal position with respect to the language maintenance efforts of American ethnic groups was necessary in order to plan, conduct, or interpret the score of interrelated studies which constituted the Project. Given necessary levels of previous training and concurrent ability, and given an interest in the topic as an area of professional promise, it was rarely necessary either to significantly depend upon or to discount personal sympathies or biases in order to proceed with the Project. This might not have been the case had we made greater use of intensive interviewing, clinical testing, or participant observation techniques. As it was, the structured and quantitative research designs that we initially imposed on ourselves usually limited the impact of values and biases toward language maintenance on the part of the Project staff. Although such biases as did exist (and they were by no means unidirectional) are, at times, apparent upon a careful reading of the reports contributed by various Project staff members, it is rarely necessary to share these biases in order to accept the data presented.

However, when one approaches the realm of recommendations and of social engineering more generally, it is impossible to disclaim the guiding role of values and biases. Recommendations with respect to social policy require a social philosophy. A social philosophy can be adopted in a role-playing sense, i.e., as a purely temporary, expedient exercise. A social philosophy can be a deeply experienced commitment derived from basic value positions pertaining to the nature of man and the meaning of life. In either case,

social philosophy results in recommendations that <u>may</u> be derived
from data but aim at goals which exist above and beyond the reaches
of data. In part, the recommendations advanced here are derived
from the point of view that language maintenance in the United States
is desirable, in that the non-English language resources of American
minority groups have already helped meet our urgent national need
for speakers of various non-English languages, and that these resources can be reinforced and developed so as to do so to a very
much greater extent in the future. The recommendations are also
derived from an awareness that while competence in two languages
can be a decided asset to those who have this command (indeed, most
language learning in schools is based on just such an assumption),
the bilingualism of hundreds of thousands of Americans is a liability
in their lives, and this for no reason inherent in the nature of bilingualism per se. It is our treatment of bilinguals and of bilingualism
that brings this sad state of affairs into being and, therefore, it is
this treatment that must be altered. Finally, in the realm of sheer
practicality, it is obvious that our national resources of native non-
English language competence are allowed—even encouraged—to
languish and disappear at the very time that unprecedented efforts
and sums are being spent to improve and increase the teaching of
"foreign" languages in the nation's schools and colleges. The recommendations aim to eliminate this wasteful ambivalence.

        At an even more basic (and less instrumental) level, language
maintenance support is advocated on the ground that our national
genius and our national promise depend upon a more conscious and a
better implemented commitment to a culturally pluralistic society.
Such support is crucial because neither a fondness for cultural quaint-
ness nor a romantic interest in cultural diversity can materially benefit language maintenance or materially alter its prospects. Only a
mobilization of sensitivity, concern, intellect, and means can accomplish this goal. Only an unembarrassed acceptance of the merits of
linguistic and cultural variations from the English-speaking norm of
American core society can bring such mobilizations into being. Just
as Dobzhansky has vigorously maintained that the merit of a society
is significantly dependent on the maintenance of the most varied pool
of genes (Dobzhansky 1956), so must there be substantial conviction
that the merit of a society—of our American society—is significantly
dependent on the appropriate maintenance of the most varied pool of
languages and cultures. In present day America such a conviction

cannot be derived from nor maintained by a tradition of permissiveness or a spirit of toleration alone. Rather, such a conviction requires that honestly pursued cross-cultural understanding, democratically pursued internal unity, deeply experienced traditional practices,
deeply valued cultural creativity, deep sensitivity to the nature of
human tragedy and human hope—that all of these be viewed as more
than romantic luxuries; indeed, that they be viewed as desiderata
that carry with them imperatives for rational action.

The recommendations that follow are offered in the hope they
will be implemented and that language maintenance will be strengthened as a result of such implementation. However, these recommendations are not necessarily derived from data reported by the Language
Resources Project. Many could have been advanced (and probably
would have been) without the data obtained from three years of concerted effort. Others, usually those oriented toward detailed alternatives or priorities, have been influenced by the data to some extent.
Nevertheless, all of the recommendations should be evaluated not so
much on the basis of accuracy of data as on the basis of extrapolations
beyond data into the realm of desirability. Certainly this is not an
unusual situation—either in the realm of national planning as a whole
or in the realm of language planning more specifically. Students of
the sociology of language have been called upon many times to depart
from exclusive attention to their basic disciplines and to enter the
realm of desirability and possibility. Not only have such students
helped create, select, standardize, and develop national (and international) languages but they have also accumulated considerable experience in the realm of planned language protection, maintenance,
and reinforcement. Whenever this is to be done, more than technical
linguistics and technical sociology are called for. Recommendations
leading to language reinforcement imply a willingness to espouse certain values, and to assist certain groups in an informed pursuit of
"the art of the possible." Language reinforcement, like all language
planning, whether in developing or in developed contexts, deals with
much more than language per se; it deals with goals and values, both
those of the planners and those of the populace.

Many American intellectuals reveal particular ambivalence
or hostility in connection with discussions—whether at a theoretical
or applied level—concerning ethnic or ethno-religious participation
in the United States. Many are themselves of second and third gen-

eration background. More than most Americans they are likely to
have been "liberated" (intellectually and overtly, if not emotionally)
from the claims and constraints of many primordial ties and biases.
As a result, they are less inclined than most to take kindly to serious
consideration of the values of ethno-religious participation, not to
mention consideration of ways and means of reinforcing such participation. To the extent that they acknowledge pervasive value commitments beyond those directly related to their own academic specialities,
these commitments usually take the form of assisting various population groups to gain liberation from constraints that impede their full
participation in higher levels of socio-cultural life. However, the
particular ethnocentric and egocentric ingredients of this value commitment usually remain unexamined. Such commitments may well
assume the complete relevance of the intellectual's own experiences
and convictions as a goal for all mankind. The very completeness of
their own divestment from ethnicity and religion may prompt all-or-
none distinctions between primordiality and modernity, between particularism and cosmopolitanism, to the end that reality is severely
misconstrued. For most of mankind these guiding forces are in
constant and complementary interaction, and are in a world-wide
process of mutual accommodation, each providing benefits and exact-
ing tolls unknown to the other. The problem of ethnically-based language maintenance in the United States (and in various other developed
or developing nations) is precisely the problem of readjusting an imbalance between these forces so as to permit all men to more freely
and more maturely benefit from each, rather than from only one or
the other.

        The problems of language maintenance in the United States
are here considered at the very time that our country is convulsed,
as never before, by the need to liberate millions of its citizens from
primordial restrictions of a particularly debilitating and shameful
kind. This co-occurrence heaps additional difficulty upon any attempt
to distinguish between primordial attachments and to strengthen some
while weakening others. Since native linguistic competence cannot be
preserved without preserving some form of para-linguistic difference,
a discussion of language maintenance at this time runs the risk of
eliciting charges of parochialism and ghettoization or worse. Actually,
two different kinds of ghettos must be overcome. One is the ghetto
of ethnic superiority which rejects change and egalitarian participation
in modern culture and in society at large. This type of ghetto is far

weaker in the United States than it has ever been, and is becoming
increasingly enfeebled. The other ghetto is that which considers
everything ethnic to be foreign or worthless. This type of ghetto,
regrettably, is still all too evident around us. The co-existence of
these two kinds of parochialism implies that there is no easy route
to language maintenance in the United States. Such maintenance is
faced by the task of consciously preserving certain carefully selected
cultural differences at the same time that we strain to attain other
carefully selected cultural similarities or equalities. Language maintenance must pursue both unity and diversity, both proximity and
distance. However, in this respect it is merely a reflection at the
national-cultural level of a problem that every mature individual
must solve within himself even when ethnic considerations are entirely absent.

The recommendations herewith presented derive from the
author's values and biases concerning not only the general worth-
whileness of safeguarding linguistic and cultural diversity in American life, but also from his biases concerning the spheres in which
such diversity is desirable and the intensiveness with which language
maintenance is to be pursued. Far different recommendations would
flow from a model of American society which aimed at securing cultural autonomy within an officially protected multi-language and
multi-culture political framework. Far different ones would be
offered on the basis of a desire to maintain major population groups
on a fully intact, separate, monolingual, non-English speaking basis.
No such verzuiling is desired (Moberg 1961); nor is it a sine qua non
for the successful pursuit of language maintenance. Every nation,
new or old, that engages in language maintenance efforts must define
the domains (if any) in which cultural and linguistic unity must receive
precedence over cultural and linguistic diversity. Every nation,
developing or developed, that pursues planned reinforcement of language maintenance must decide on the appropriateness of extensive
vs. intensive efforts toward that goal.

The present recommendations neither envision nor seek the
disestablishment of English as the common language of American
unity and as the basic language of American culture, government,
and education for all Americans. Rather, they have in mind the
planned reinforcement of non-English languages and their underlying
non-core cultures for those who desire them, for those who are willing

and able to expend considerable efforts and sums of their own to maintain institutions and organizations of their own on behalf of their languages and cultures, and for those who are willing to do so within a framework of mutual interaction with American core society and its democratically maintained and developed institutions and processes. Thus, not only is cultural pluralism rather than cultural separatism espoused, but cultural bilingualism rather than merely functional bilingualism is emphasized. Non-English languages and non-core cultures are considered to be maintainable and reinforceable primarily within the spheres of American-ethnic family life, of the self-defined American-ethnic community, the self-defined American-ethnic school and cultural organization, under the direction of the self-defined American-ethnic teacher, writer, artist, and cultural or communal leader. Both language maintenance and ethnicity have become and must remain entirely voluntaristic behaviors in the United States. Their ideological mainsprings must derive largely from an interpretation of Americanism, American culture, and American national well being. However, such behaviors and interpretations are particularly dependent on an encouraging and facilitating environment. It is to recommendations for maintaining such an environment that we now turn.

Establishing a Climate for Language Maintenance

For the foreseeable future there will continue to be non-English-speaking groups in the United States, regardless of either official or unofficial encouragement or discouragement. However, accidents of history and geography are insufficient to assure either the numerical adequacy of proficient speakers of standard and regional variants of most languages, or the required psychological predisposition.

Fundamentally, language maintenance efforts are justifiable and desirable because: either they serve the national interest (both in utilitarian and in an idealistic sense), and/or they promote various group interests that need not be in conflict with the national interest, and/or they contribute powerfully to the enrichment of individual functioning. The cultural and political unity of the United States seems to be sufficiently assured so that there need be no fear of "Balkanization" as a result of non-English language maintenance and "non-core" ethnic cultural diversity within subgroups of the American population. There is no longer any reasonable basis upon which to fear an entrenchment on our shores of the political and social cleavages which cultural and linguistic diversity have forced upon Belgium or Canada in the West, or upon India and Ceylon in the East. A common pattern of commitment to and participation in American political processes and social values has developed and become fully and naturally established among almost all subgroups within American society. Common patterns of food preference, of entertainment, of occupational aspiration, of dress, of education, and of language have become widely and deeply ingrained. However, the process of strengthening these unities and communalities has proceeded so far and so rapidly as to endanger the cultural and linguistic diversity that many subgroups desire and that our national welfare may well require. Our political and cultural foundations are weakened when large population groupings do not feel encouraged to express, to safeguard, and to develop behavioral patterns that are traditionally meaningful to them. Our national creativity and personal purposefulness are rendered more shallow when constructive channels of self-expression are blocked and when alienation from ethnic-cultural roots becomes the necessary price of self-respect and social advancement, regardless of the merits of the cultural components of these roots. For these groups and individuals that desire it there must be openly sanctioned and publicly encouraged avenues of linguistic and cultural distinctiveness which will provide both a general atmosphere and specific facilitation for diversity within the general framework of American unity.

All Americans, and speakers of non-English languages in particular, are aware of the value our society and its institutions place upon cultural and linguistic unity. The desirability of such unity is explicitly or implicitly conveyed by citizenship requirements, by voting requirements, by the common public school, by the many agencies whose task it is to "naturalize" and Americanize immigrants and our indigenous or semi-indigenous ethnic populations, by national holidays, and even by the very openness of American economic and political life which normally requires little else of ethnics than that they join with de-ethnicized Americans in advancing themselves by advancing the common good. There is a "message" which immigrants, other ethnics, and their children quickly get—that ethnicity is foreignness, that both have no value, that they are things to forget, to give up. The frequent and enduring contrast between war, disharmony, and poverty abroad, and relative peace, acceptance, and prosperity here clearly shouts this message. Governmental and private agency

conferences on Americanization and on cultural enrichment for
disadvantaged ethnic populations reinforce it. Social prejudice and
economic competition bring the message home in hundreds of ways,
both subtle and obvious, even though both are usually less intense
than in most other countries. Given a general climate which constantly reinforces unity—often by assuming it to be so obviously and
universally desirable that no public discussion of it is deemed necessary—it is essential that diversity, too, receive constant support at
underlying philosophical and operational levels.

        Positive statements by leading American personages concern-
ing the merits of cultural diversity and its benefits to American society have been relatively few and have hardly reached the "general
public." Sentiments to this effect are directed toward minority group
audiences from time to time, but are largely superfluous. A statement by the Governor or the President directed toward Spanish-
Americans or Italo-Americans on Columbus Day normally reaches
only those who are already aware of their ethnic heritages. It is
usually recognized for what it usually is—a politically self-serving
appeal or ritual time-filler of little general or genuine significance.
Such statements imply a relegation of ethnicity to a "one-day-a-year"
affair commemorating the long ago and the far away. They rarely
seek to foster a more accepting view of ethnicity among non-ethnics.
What is needed, therefore, rather than statements such as these, are
statements that will reach the general public with the message that
cultural differences—here and now, on an everyday as well as on a
"high culture" and festive level—are meaningful, desirable, and
worth strengthening. They should be made before non-ethnic audiences assembled to consider non-ethnic problems if they are to have
their greatest impact and if they are to be disseminated widely through
non-ethnic mass media.[3] If a "special day" for such statements
seems desirable, it might be far better to release them on the Fourth
of July than to reserve them for Polish-American Day, or German-
American Day, or other such isolated "heritage" days.

        But statements alone are too intermittent, too fleeting, and
too unreliable to bring about a major change of climate. Those of
the kind that would do the most good are rare, because few leading
figures in American life are concerned with the role of ethnicity and
diversity. Few have thought deeply about it and, under ordinary
circumstances, few can be expected to do so in the future. Many

consider ethnicity to be a far more ephemeral phenomenon than it really is. It is taken to be an issue that belongs to the 19th century, that will die of its own accord, that is petty and sectarian, and therefore one that does not deserve serious attention. This view is mistaken on psychological grounds alone. Although fragments of ethnicity's "little tradition," such as foods and dances, embarrass many second- and third-generation Americans when subjected to outside scrutiny, these same individuals frequently experience a private void which a fuller but selectively synthesized ethnicity might fill. While they have lost contact with the deeper and more meaningful ethnicity, they object to being publicly characterized in terms of the quaint but isolated fragments that they have maintained. Certainly, neither their their own foods and dances nor the silent-treatment on the part of "American" peers and leaders will enable them to find personal satisfaction, on the one hand, or to reinforce language maintenance, on the other. In order to accomplish either of these goals <u>cultural and linguistic diversity must become a serious topic of public interest</u>. A federal "Commission on Biculturism (or Bilingualism) in American Life" might help bring this to pass. Such a Commission composed of ethnic and non-ethnic leaders, social scientists, educators, and distinguished "cultural figures" would be in a position to focus interest on the meaningfulness, legitimacy, and potential creativity of cultural and linguistic diversity within American unity. Such a Commission—and the recurring national conferences and reports that it might sponsor—could raise language maintenance to the level of an avowed national concern.[4]

All in all, cultural and linguistic diversity must be publicly recognized, publicly discussed, and publicly supported if language maintenance is to be quickly, fully, and effectively reinforced. Appeals on behalf of such diversity can be supported by reference to American values, traditions, and history. As a possibly vital and creative force in American life, cultural diversity has all too long been ignored or given only apologetic and embarrassed glances. If language maintenance is to be seriously pursued in the future, public rehabilitation of this topic will be necessary. Bilingualism does not exist in a vacuum; it exists in the context of ethnic, religious, and cultural differences. It cannot be supported on a national scale without supporting biculturism. Biculturism requires awareness of one's heritage, identification with it (at least on a selective basis), and freedom to express this identification in a natural and uninhibited manner.

It can only be enriching for our country to discover that the languages which have recently been brought to our attention are inextricably related to diverse behavioral patterns and behavioral products which can be every bit as acceptable and as valuable as the languages themselves. The languages can only function in conjunction with meaningful patrimonies. Intimately meaningful patrimonies can only enrich America and the lives of its citizens.

How can such awareness be made tangible and real for ethnics and non-ethnics alike? One approach having general, climate-building value might be to establish ethnic "Williamsburgs" at appropriate points throughout the United States. Several cities and states could profitably establish "nationality committees" whose purpose would be to preserve ethnic neighborhoods and settlements that might otherwise be scheduled for demolition, abandonment, or oblivion. Much as Williamsburg, Virginia, manifests our continued esteem for the best of colonial architecture, dress, and life style, much as Den Fynske Landsby manifests current reverence for the Danish peasant community of Bygone days—so publicly supported museums, libraries, streets, neighborhoods, and settlements dedicated to preserving and honoring the cultural diversity of American life would lend dignity and status to the much maligned immigrant roots of American biculturism.[5] Of course, biculturism must not remain rigidly fixed and rooted in the past. It must not be preservative and nothing more. But it must have tangible—and, if need be, idealized—public access to its earliest American roots. The immigrant past must be as worth preserving as the colonial past, the "old south," and the frontier ghost-town. Each of these provides a point of departure, a point of reference, and a point of pride. Our Chinatowns, our Little Italys, our Little Warsaws could be turned into bastions of support and respect for cultural-linguistic diversity, if they were intelligently and sympathetically redeveloped with this goal in mind. Every national value needs a shrine to embody it. If cultural and linguistic diversities are to become genuine national values—discussed as such by our statesmen, treated as such by scholars, policy makers, and community leaders—then they too must have their palpable shrines, that can be visited by ordinary American citizens of all ages and all backgrounds. It would represent, in short, another effort to make cultural and linguistic diversity "normal," by treating it openly, making it visible, and declaring it valuable.

Specific Support for Language Maintenance

In addition to rehabilitating the mainsprings of language
maintenance so that it may have a favorable climate within which to
function, language maintenance itself must be reinforced so that it
can more successfully aid in attaining the goal of cultural bilingualism. Here too many old taboos must be discarded if language maintenance is to be seriously pursued.

One such taboo is that Americans of immigrant origin must
give up their contacts with the countries from which they emigrated.
Such contacts have far too frequently and automatically been viewed
as indicative of un-American sentiments. Thus, overly long residence in the foreign country of one's birth or overly frequent visits
to that country can jeopardize an immigrant's naturalization or lead
to the loss of his passport. [6] The implication behind such policies
is that America cannot fully trust its naturalized citizens; that it
views their relationships with their ethnic motherlands as a species
of bigamy; that the motherlands represent a fatal fascination from
which the United States must be protected. Even greater opprobrium
is attached to motherlands which seek to maintain active contacts with
former inhabitants who are now citizens of the United States. Currently, most countries seeking to sponsor clubs, courses, publications, and other means of active and continued contact with their
former citizens would be considered as engaging in suspicious activities, the more so the further these countries are from Anglo-Saxon
Europe. Such attitudes tend to defeat language maintenance and are
rooted in a bygone age. Naturalized citizens residing abroad are our
most effective ambassadors. To the extent that their trips abroad
renew and update their own language facility, and to the extent that
ethnic mother tongues become more attractive or more functional for
their children or grandchildren, further gains are effected for language maintenance. These latter consequences are much more likely
to come to reality than are any of the traitorous suspicions which
impart such an unsavory air to our current policies.

"Old Country" contacts with naturalized American citizens
and their children should be fostered under favorable international
circumstances. [7] Italian governmental efforts to keep Italian language,
literature, and customs alive among Italo-Americans may be thought

of as a form of reverse lend-lease and may very well be a form of debt-repayment. Such efforts help to keep Italian alive and closer to its standardized form among Italo-Americans. They help overcome the constant Anglification and petrification that obtains when a language of immigrants does not have all of the normal avenues for use, growth, and change. Among second and third generations it helps dispel the lingering association of ethnic mother tongues with poverty, insecurity, immigrant status, mixed speech, and cultural mummification. That this is not an unheard of approach to language maintenance may be seen from recent acts of the government of the Province of Quebec.[8] Surely there is sufficient ingenuity in American governmental circles to enable us to initiate, control, and (if need be) discontinue activities of this kind as international conditions dictate. For the sake of language maintenance it would seem to be worth our while to institute agreements concerning such activities, at least with a few "safe" countries, at the earliest opportunity.

There can be no doubt that the major force weakening language maintenance in the United States today is the restriction of immigration. Not only are the numbers of immigrants admitted far smaller than half a century ago, but the lion's share of the available quota is awarded to immigrants most likely to assimilate and least likely to perpetuate their non-English mother tongues. It is worth speculating what would occur if larger numbers of Eastern and Southern European immigrants, as well as larger numbers of Near Eastern, Far Eastern, and African immigrants, could enter the United States, primarily on the basis of sponsors willing to guarantee that such immigrants would not become public charges. All available evidence indicates that newer immigrants from parts of the globe not favored by current United States immigration policy differ quite markedly from immigrants of half a century ago. They are far less likely to be rural dwellers, far more likely to have received formal education, and far more likely to come with specialized skills suitable for modern technological employment. These characteristics have various implications for language maintenance. Some imply a more rapid assimilability, and some a greater language maintenance potential. Probably both of these directions would be pursued by different clusters of immigrants. A large proportion of newer immigrants of currently "unfavored origins" would become assimilated much more rapidly than did their pre-World War I predecessors. Nevertheless, a small proportion of them would certainly be inclined to oppose cultural and linguistic assimilation and would be more likely to do so successfully—at least for an initial generational period—than was the case for the average immigrant of half a century ago. Their formal training in their respective mother tongues, their greater historical, cultural, and linguistic sophistication, and their greater awareness of language needs in American affairs and of the value of language skills in personal professional advancement would certainly lead toward successful maintenance. Indeed, there is every possibility that both directions (acculturation and non-acculturation) might be integrated and pursued simultaneously by modern immigrants in a manner quite beyond the ken of older immigrants arriving half a century or more ago.

Newer immigrants are far more inclined toward and capable of adopting a pattern somewhat similar to that devised by third-generation Americans of older immigrant stock, namely, a pattern of selective maintenance within the context of pervasive Americanization. They adopt general American speech, dress, food, recreational, educational, residential, and occupational patterns much more rapidly than did pre-World War I immigrants. On the other hand, if properly motivated, they can and do combine these general American patterns with selective culture maintenance patterns which safeguard many linguistic, religious, and representational elements derived from their countries of origin. Thus a consciously balanced cultural pluralism is much more attainable for immigrants today than it was for their forebears. Both the American and the Old World patterns and ingredients that are most meaningful to them may be characterized as urban, "high culture," and selective.

American immigration policy is in many ways still governed by a pre-World War I mentality. Not only is it uninfluenced by considerations of current national needs, it is also curiously innocent of any awareness of the extent to which the entire world has been "Americanized" in the last fifty years. Most immigrants reaching our shores today are much more like Americans than has been the case furing the last 100 years or more. While this fact should lay the ghost of separatism and irredentism (which still influences American immigration policy), it should as well facilitate non-conflicted, non-derogatory and non-exclusionary language and culture maintenance.

In addition, the advance of automated industry requires an infusion
of technical skills and high-level talents which bypass direct competition with unskilled and semi-skilled American labor—another classical source of opposition to immigration. After a hiatus of more
than a century, it can once more be said that we are in a period
when larger and more diversified immigration can simultaneously
contribute to national needs, self-maintenance processes, and har-
monious cultural pluralism. It is high time our immigration policy
were revised with these considerations in mind.

        Even under our current anachronistic policy, priorities
might be introduced that would tend to strengthen the language main-
tenenace potentials within the American population. Once language
maintenance efforts are recognized as being in the public interest,
it becomes simple to recognize that certain types of immigrants
are more likely to contribute to language maintenance than others.
Once the language loyalist is cleared of the suspicion of being an
"enemy of the people" it is but a logical next step to realize that
teachers, writers, artists, musicians, religious functionaries,
organizational leaders, and other intellectuals are more likely to
contribute consciously to the perpetuation of the language resources
of the United States than are other categories of immigrants. Actually, such individuals are in terribly short supply among most American ethnic groups, primarily because relatively few sought to come
to the United States during the pre-World War I immigration peak.
Once language maintenance becomes a national desideratum, it
would seem to be possible to select prospective immigrants so as to
maximize the likelihood of contributing to this goal. [9]

        As for assistance to those segments of American ethnic
groups that are already engaged in language maintenance efforts,
there are a host of steps that might be taken to strengthen these
efforts directly. Certainly dependence on immigration alone is
neither practical nor wise. Immigrants and non-immigrants alike
require an environment that is supportive of language maintenance
in the same way that other matters in the national interest are supported. In an era of unprecedented governmental assistance to American colleges and universities for the establishment and maintenance
of language and area study centers (under the National Defense Education Act), it would seem only logical to offer assistance to the
institutions of American ethnic groups whose activities are clearly

related to language maintenance. In addition to supporting instruction in Chinese, Hungarian, Russian, and dozens of other "neglected" languages now taught to Americans for whom these languages are truly "foreign," it would seem also to be highly desirable to support instructional and other languages maintenance efforts directed at those Americans for whom these languages are still not entirely "foreign." Government aid to ethnic group schools engaged in formal mother tongue instruction would involve only relatively minor innovations and reformulations in current policies. Any financial relief would encourage them to continue what often has seemed a most difficult task, and to improve and intensify their current efforts. In some cases the question of public support for religiously sponsored institutions would doubtless arise (Fishman 1959). But this can easily become a false issue. There are many effective schools to which the religious issue is not applicable at all. At any rate, support for language instruction can be kept quite separate from support for religious instruction. Certainly there is legal precedent for such a distinction and, given sufficient conviction that language maintenance is in the national interest, additional precedents can be established and maintained. Finally, the constitutional restrictions bearing upon the separation of Church and state need not hinder the great private foundations that have done so much to support and replenish the cultural and educational resources of American society. As yet, none has supported the language maintenance efforts of American ethnic groups—whether in the educational, literary, dramatic, musical, or scholarly spheres—and a change in this respect would simultaneously signify the rehabilitation of language maintenance and the social maturation of American foundations.

Untouched by religious complications are several colleges and universities[10] as well as hundreds of periodicals, radio broadcasts, and cultural or scholarly institutions of American ethnic groups. Whether by tax exemption, by direct support, or even by indirect facilitation and encouragement, means could be found for giving recognition and assistance to these vehicles of language maintenance. Not only has there been no studied attempt to do this but negative and exploitative steps have often been taken (or implied), of which language loyalists are painfully aware.[11] They frequently have long memories of hostile governmental attitudes dating back to their home countries. Under the best of circumstances they would tend to be suspicious of governmental "impartiality" since their own

is not an impartial posture. Having concluded that language maintenance is in the public good, they frequently interpret governmental
disinterest or neglect as thinly veiled opposition and, what is worse,
disdain. Why should their work be considered "beneath the dignity"
of attention by government, by foundations, and by the public at
large? Why does an unofficial conspiracy of silence and an implication of lunacy surround their efforts? Are they not working on behalf
of an intellectually, culturally, and politically valuable goal? Why
then have they been ignored and ruled out from Sputnik-inspired largesse available to others? If we, as well, grant that language maintenance is a desideratum, then there can be no argument that it is in
grave need of assistance and that it has received neither the support
nor the attention best calculated to foster its creative contribution to
American life. Given the current status of language maintenance in
most ethnic groups in our midst, nothing would seem better calculated
to strengthen it than the preparation of cadres of young and rigorously
educated bilingual-bicultural cultural leaders. Ethnic group schools
are in the best position to accomplish this—but are frequently unable
to do so without assistance. [12]

A final area of language maintenance support is to be found
in facilities that are or could be entirely under public auspices.
Chief among these are the public schools. While our schools are
certainly more language conscious than they have been in previous
years, they are not nearly as inventive or as concerned as they
might be and their official consciousness of language maintenance is
practically nil. FLES programs are woefully limited in terms of
their numbers and the languages involved, and distressingly ineffective in terms of teacher competence and pupil learning. Foreign
language programs at the high school level are only slightly less
remiss in each of these respects. Pitifully little is being done today
to effectively and widely introduce such major world languages as
Russian, Chinese, or Arabic into American public education at any
level. The few exceptional schools in which these languages are
taught to a few exceptional children received deserved publicity,
but their impact on the total picture is meager. The fearful bureau-
cratic complexity of American educational enterprises is such that
all the institutional characteristics tend to discourage rather than
encourage either greater variation or wider coverage in language
instruction. Thus, it is initially difficult to introduce additional
languages because teachers are not available to teach them. It is

difficult to locate suitable teachers because training programs are not available to train them. In most states even a completely bilingual individual with university training in both languages is not considered "trained" and eligible for certification as a public school teacher until he has taken a number of college courses in the field of "professional education." Furthermore, it is difficult to hire trained teachers because salaries are so low as to be non-competitive with other sources of income available to such individuals. And it is difficult also to recruit teachers willing to accept appointments at current salaries because too few children in any one school would elect to study, say, Russian, to provide a teacher with a full program. Difficulty is thus pyramided upon difficulty and the entire structure moves ahead at a snail's pace. The final irony is that methods and materials of instruction are all geared to teaching monolinguals, with the result that foreign language teachers are least successful when they work with students who possess competence in a second language based upon their out-of-school experiences (Brault 1964).

A number of innovations that might prove to be of some value have either not been tried at all or have been tried on too limited a scale. There have been a few NDEA-sponsored Language Institutes for the express purpose of preparing educators who are themselves of a particular ethnic background so that they might teach the standard version of their own ethnic mother tongue to pupils who are also of this background.[13] These institutes serve several purposes simultaneously: (i) they remove common ethnicity between teachers and pupils from the realm of taboo and place it in the realm of an explicitly acknowledged and functionally activated factor in language learning;[14] (ii) they recognize the particular language learning assets and problems of children with an ethnic mother tongue and they prepare teachers to cope with these constructively; (iii) they prepare special teaching and learning materials oriented toward raising the levels of mastery of, and overcoming the deviations from, standard speech among teachers and pupils; (iv) they explicitly involve the government, the teacher, and the pupil in a joint language maintenance venture. Certainly, such institutes should be increased in size, in number, and in the variety of languages covered. The preparation of teachers and of teaching-learning materials via such institutes will begin to ameliorate the problem of where to recruit appropriate personnel for public school languages programs, that might in the future be related to the ethnic composition of large

proportions of the student bodies in many urban centers. However,
this approach alone is far too limited to result in any early language
maintenance gains. Additional approaches are required and only
quite normal degrees of ingenuity and good will are needed to uncover
them.

The MLA Foreign Language Proficiency Tests (available
only for French, German, Italian, Russian, and Spanish) already
utilized by the State Education Departments of New York, Pennsylvania, Delaware, and West Virginia represent a potentially important facilitative device (Starr 1962). Individuals who have reached
necessary levels of language proficiency by informal means (home,
neighborhood, travel)—rather than by the "normal" route of accumu-
lating college credits—can attest to their proficiency through these
examinations and obtain state-approved teaching licenses or certificates. This approach to the certification of foreign language teachers
should be far more widely adopted. [15] If properly encouraged, it has
the potential of providing many localities with teachers of uncommon
languages. Such languages almost always have an ethnic base and
their availability under public auspices greatly encourages language
maintenance. Pupils studying these languages in the public schools
would most frequently be of the "appropriate" ethnic background.
Even if this were not the case, language maintenance would benefit
if only from publicizing that an ethnic mother tongue had "broken
through" the silence barrier and had received "public recognition." [16]

Another significant means of public school recognition might
well be the granting of formal credit to pupils for language skills
acquired outside of school auspices. Thousands of public school
pupils, at the elementary as well as the secondary level of instruction, attend one or another type of ethnic group school during after-
school hours. Our evidence indicates that mother tongue instruction
in these schools is at least as effective as—if not more so than—
foreign language instruction under public school auspices. The combination of student background factors, teacher dedication, and
appreciable exposure over a number of years results in language
skills that are by no means too rudimentary to deserve recognition
and encouragement by public schools authorities. Recognition might
take one or another of several forms: certificates of merit, advanced
placement in public high school language courses, credit toward

graduation, etc. In each case, an appropriate yet simple evaluation or review mechanism would need to be instituted. It is difficult to exaggerate the stimulus to mother tongue instruction in ethnic group schools that would result from any form of recognition by the public schools. Again and again teachers, principals, and activists affiliated with ethnic group schools offering mother tongue instruction mention the "double insult" of having their mother tongue "excluded" from the public school program while at the same time the public school refuses to recognize that their children are diligently studying another language and culture at their own expense and on their own time. "If our children were merely collecting stamps or building models, they would get some encouragement from school authorities; for studying Greek they get no recognition at all!"[17]

However, much more than "recognition" or other indirect motivators may be possible in those localities where truly substantial numbers of students enter the first grade with a home-and-neighborhood tongue other than English. Under these circumstances it would be highly desirable for a few public schools to experiment with programs that provide a major part of their instruction in non-English mother tongues, until students have acquired, at the very least, adequate literacy in these languages. In such cases the mother tongue might well remain both a medium and a subject of instruction throughout the elementary school years, with the gradual and appropriate introduction of English beginning on a small scale in the first grade and increasing in each successive year of study.[18] An experimental return to the bilingual public school that functioned in several American cities during the late 19th and the early 20th century would appear to be particularly justified in the case of Mexican-American population concentrations in the Southwest. Such attempts should be labeled frankly as experimental and as intensive language maintenance efforts so as to avoid any implications of social or cultural segregation. Where such attempts are not feasible it might still be possible to group bilingual children separately for early, intensive and specially devised instruction in their mother tongue, under the guidance of teachers who are themselves fully literate and educated in it. There is recent evidence that even the high school level is not too late for effective and lasting reinforcement of language skills and attitudes among bilingual youngsters (Nance 1963).[19]

There are still other possible approaches to bolstering
foreign language programs in our public schools in such a way as to
directly or indirectly foster language maintenance. Approximately
a thousand exchange teachers from abroad are annually appointed to
public elementary and secondary schools throughout the United States.
Ordinarily, a condition of such appointments is that exchange teachers
possess sufficient mastery of English to teach in that language throughout the school day. Rarely has it occurred to American school
authorities that these same foreign teachers might well be utilized
to teach their own mother tongues—either during the regular school
day or in after-school classes.[20] Indeed, rarely has it occurred to
spokesmen and functionaries of foreign language instruction in American school to utilize even the best local representatives of the few
languages taught in our schools. Utilization of native speakers would
have more than mere pedagogic value; it would also imply the respectability of ethnicity, the mentionability of language maintenance, the
"Americanness," as it were, of speaking and safeguarding languages
other than English. Indeed, native speakers could well serve as
"cultural representatives" beyond the confines of the school's few
language courses. They could and should serve as consultants and
participants in various courses dealing with the several cultures that
have contributed to ours, and in which the range of creative human
diversity is educatively illustrated. Such an enterprise could seek
a genuinely comparative approach to the understanding of human institutions and the variability of cultures, showing they need not be
"foreign" however much they are "different." This is much more
than the antiseptic study of immigrant roots and the songs, dances,
and games that pertain to them. It is an acknowledgment that the
roots of Amĕrican life are still capable of legitimate fruits of a
"high tradition" to this very day.

All in all, the public school's approach to non-English languages and to non-core cultures in the United States has been that of
all official levels of American life, namely, that ethnicity in America
and its cultural and linguistic components deservé neither disciplined
nor dignified recognition. Thus it would seem that as long as these
languages and cultures are truly "foreign" our schools are comfortable with them. But as soon as they are found in our own backyards,
the schools deny them. However, by denying them we not only deny
a part of ourselves (a dangerous act in any democracy) but we limit
the extent to which public school instruction in languages and cultures

is live, real, and meaningful. Ethnicity is still so uncomfortable
and guiltladen an area for the essentially middle-class public school
teacher, principal, superintendent, and curriculum expert that it is
less objectionable to cut pupils off from deep understanding and appreciation than to give ethnically-based linguistic and cultural materials
their due recognition.

While the public school can certainly become a much more
valuable vehicle of language maintenance, and of language instruction,
than it currently is, it does have other and more central goals to
pursue. The curricular demands placed upon it and the administrative and social pressures to which it is exposed effectively preclude
it from becoming primarily or even significantly concerned with language maintenance. Indeed, there is no public institution in American
life whose avowed primary purpose is language maintenance. No
other national resource is so unprotected and "unassigned." A Language Maintenance section in the Department of Health, Education,
and Welfare is urgently needed so that language maintenance becomes
someone's full-time responsibility and concern.[21] A network of language camps for selected children and youth could be sponsored for
language maintenance purposes—not unlike the 4-H clubs that are
sponsored to encourage farm children to become proud and skilled
farmers. Guide books and text books could be prepared for parents
and teachers.[22] Consultation services could be made available to
schools and to cultural institutions. Necessary demonstration projects and research efforts could be assisted or conducted.[23] Financial aid could be channeled. The coordination of FLES programs
with the remaining non-English language islands could be attempted.
Above all, the veil of embarrassed silence could be pierced and removed. This latter goal must come before all else and must be
continually pursued together with all else. Its importance goes
beyond language maintenance per se. Intelligent, creative, unembarrassed, unharassed, evolving ethnicity will certainly contribute
to language maintenance but it will also contribute to the enrichment
of millions of lives and to the authenticity of American civilization.

Conclusion

It is odd indeed that a nation which prides itself on "know
how," resourcefulness, and ingenuity should be so helpless with

respect to deepening and strengthening its own inner life. We laugh
at the taboos of "backward" peoples and pride ourselves on our own
rational procedures. Yet, in the entire area of ethnicity and language
maintenance we are constrained by a taboo in some ways stronger
than those which govern our sexual or racial mores. Sex problems
and race issues are discussed in the press, debated in Congress,
studied in schools and accorded consideration by foundations. In the
area of ethnicity, however, wise men react as children—with denial,
with rejection, with repression. If language loyalty and ethnicity had
truly ceased to function in major segments of American intellectual
and cultural life, if they really evoked no pained or puzzled feelings
of responsibilities unmet and sensitivities undeveloped, these topics
would receive far more open, more dispassionate, and more imagina-
tive consideration.

Nevertheless, on the basis of data obtained by the Language
Resources Project and on the basis of impressions gained in the pursuit and analysis of these data, it seems there are still good prospects
of maintaining or attaining cultural bilingualism among many different,
carefully selected ethnic subgroups in the United States. These
groups can be so selected—over and above their self-selection—and
so instructed that the advantage of having an ethnic mother tongue
would be considerable in developing and maintaining bilingual facility.
In many ways human talents are like other resources; they must be
discovered and preserved if they are to be available. However, in
other ways, human talents are quite unique; they can be prompted,
augmented, and created by appropriate recognition, training, and
reward. Within every language group studied there are subgroups
consciously ready, willing, and able to benefit from a more favorable
"language policy" in the United States. The adoption of such a policy
would itself create additional subgroups of similar capacity, above
and beyond those currently discernible.

In her fascinating volume <u>New Lives for Old</u>, Margaret
Mead (1956) points out that Western interest in preserving the "quaint"
customs and cultures of primitive peoples has often been no more
than a thinly disguised means of excluding these peoples from independent regulation of their own affairs and from reaping the fruits of
their own personal and natural resources. Certainly, every people
must have the right to reject its past, to break sharply with its

heritage, and to adopt a new way of life. However, just as "guided traditionalism" may be a subterfuge for exploitation and the prolongation of backwardness, so "guided acculturation" may be a subterfuge serving exactly the same ulterior purposes. Either approach can be used for the self-aggrandizement of the "powers that be." Neither approach is calculated to develop freedom of choice or creative cultural evolution.

Language maintenance in America does not require, nor would it benefit from, the forced ghettoization of linguistic groups. But neither will it benefit from the non-productive sentimentality of ethnicity for one day a year, from the instrumentalism of "anti-communist letters to the homeland" to influence elections, or from the pollyanna-like pageantry in which little children sing and dance bedecked in partly mythical and wholly archaic folk costumes. Language maintenance will benefit only from explicit and substantial public recognition of its value and its legitimacy, and from public support for those willing and able to engage in it. The same must be said for ethnicity, with the additional emphasis that without greater recognition accorded to meaningful, evolving ethnicity, there can be no enduring language maintenance in the United States. Ethnicity in America is not an all-or-none affair. Nor is it a logical affair. It is not at all understandable or describable in Old World terms alone. For some it is composed of half-forgotten memories, unexplored longings, and intermittent preferences; for others, it is active, structured, elaborated and constant. For some it is exclusionary and isolating; for others it is an avenue toward more secure and more authentic participation in general American affairs. For some it is hidden and has negative or conflicted overtones; for others it is open, positive, and stimulating. For some it is archaic, unchanging and unalterable; for others it is evolving and creative. For some it is a badge of shame to ignore, forget, and eradicate; for others it is a source of pride, a focus of initial loyalties and integrations from which broader loyalties and wider integrations can proceed. For some it is interpenetrated by religion and formal organization; for others it is entirely secular and associational. Not all modes of ethnicity contribute to language maintenance, but many do. All in all, the variations and variabilities of ethnicity in America today are largely unknown. This ignorance represents a stumbling block to the American sociologist or applied linguist, whose approaches to ethnicity are usually

far too simple and far too condescending. It represents a major
gap in our ability to understand or facilitate language maintenance.
But above all else, the absence of such knowledge represents an area
of self-ignorance for all Americans—philosophers, scientists, and
laymen alike. It is certainly high time that we began to know ourselves,
accept ourselves, and shape ourselves in this area just as realistically
and as determinedly as we have tried to do in many other areas in
recent years.

> The point about the melting pot is that it did not happen. . . .
> The fact is that in every generation, throughout the his-
> tory of the American republic, the merging of the vary-
> ing streams of population differentiated from one another
> by origin, religion, outlook has seemed to lie just ahead—
> a generation, perhaps, in the future. This continual
> deferral of the final smelting of the different ingredients. . .
> suggests that we must search for some systematic and
> general cause for this American pattern of subnationali-
> ties. . . which structures people, whether those coming
> in afresh or the descendants of those who have been here
> for generations, into groups of different status and char-
> acter. (Glazer and Moynihan 1963)

The conclusions quoted above require only minor extension from the
point of view of this presentation, namely, that precisely because
they are true, after two centuries of pretense to the contrary, it is
time that the diversity of American linguistic and cultural existence
be recognized and channeled more conscientiously into a creative
force, rather than be left at worst as something shameful and to be
denied, or at best something mysterious to be patronized. If we can
rethink in this light our unwritten language policy and our unproclaimed
ethnic philosophy, the recommendations presented here on behalf of
language maintenance—or others of far greater practical and positive
application—may yet be implemented.

NOTES

[1] An interesting exception to this tendency, and one of particular relevance to our topic, is the "Appeal of a Meeting of Professors
in Scandinavian Countries on Behalf of Ethnic Groups and of Languages

in Danger of Becoming Extinct" published in <u>Revue de Psychologie des Peuples</u>, 17 (1962), 350-56.

[2] The governmental agency which supported the Language Resources Project for three years requested, entirely on its own initiative, that a section devoted to suggestions for planned reinforcement of non-English language resources in the United States be included in the Project's final report. It was never quite clear to me how certain or how extensive such future reinforcement might be. Thus I struggled with the suspicion that the Project itself, which was not supposed to help concretely in language maintenance efforts, was indirectly doing so, while at the same time I suspected that my direct recommendations for future assistance to language maintenance might actually remain a strange and pious document and little more. To complicate the role-problem even further, I was aware of the fact that the Language Resources Project was being viewed as a harbinger of governmental-blessings-yet-to-come by language loyalists throughout the nation. As the director of the Project I was considered, at times, to be an actual or potential savior. In seeking cooperation or information from innumerable individuals, organizations, and groups unaccustomed to social research, I frequently felt that some reference to the possibility of governmental assistance in the future would open many doors for the Project. Nevertheless, I was not at all sure whether there really would be any such assistance, and if there was, for what purposes. As a result, I requested cooperation or information primarily on a research basis.

[3] <u>The New York Times</u> reported on May 2, 1963, that Dr. Calvin E. Gross, Superintendent of Schools, made the following statement to "850 teachers and supervisors attending the [New York City School] system's annual curriculum conference. Many in the audience appeared shocked. . . . Dr. Gross. . . urged that Puerto Rican children and other new arrivals to the city be enabled to develop biculturally and bilinguistically. Dr. Gross said that instead of trying to remake Puerto Rican children and telling them to forget their language, these children should be told: 'You are Puerto Rican and you have something to be proud of. Keep your culture—we'll help you develop it—but we also give you something else.' He deplored the 'melting pot' approach in which new arrivals are 'made over in our image.'" Although limited to a specialized audience this statement may be expected to have had greater impact in view of its presentation <u>in the context of general American educational goals</u> than a similar

statement presented in the context of education for children of foreign backgrounds. Thus, the San Jose (California) Mercury News of July 14, 1963, reports a state-wide conference of educators on "Teaching English as a Second Language" under the headline "Schools Fear Enrollment Hike as a Result of Bracero Cutback." At this conference, Helen Hefferman, Chief of the Bureau of Elementary Education of the California State Department of Education, declared that "children of Mexican descent are to be encouraged to retain their first language and become more skillfull in its use [as they learn English]."

[4] Other countries too have long traditions of royal or national commissions for focusing attention on and seeking solutions to important social issues. The new Canadian "Commission on Biculturism" (with representatives of the English, French, and "New" Canadians) might serve as a particularly appropriate example, although fortunately the U.S.A. does not have the vexing problems which have led to the establishment of that body.

[5] The entertainability of this recommendation, as well as the greater respectability of American Indian as contrasted with immigrant ethnicity, is indicated by the Department of the Interior's endorsement of the "restoration of Indian culture on the Seneca Reservation in western New York State. It left up to Congress a decision on whether an effort should be made to construct something like the restoration of colonial Virginia at Williamsburg" (New York Times, August 13, 1963, p. 33). Amana, Iowa and Solvang, California perform this function for the German and Danish cultures respectively, but are much too isolated and too modest for purposes of major impact.

[6] A U.S. Supreme Court decision, rendered May 18, 1964, declared this practice to be unconstitutional.

[7] Note, e.g., Bill 18, Loi instituant le ministère des affaires culturelles, sanctionnée le 24 mars 1961, Assemblée Legislative de Quebec. This bill establishes not only "l'Office de la Langue Française" but also "le Département du Canada Française d'outre-Frontières."

[8] LeDevoir of Montreal reported on May 9, 1963, that M. Georges-Émile Lapalme "le ministre des affaires culturelles a lancé un appel à la France la suppliant d'apporter une aide concrète à l'essor de la culture française en Amérique du Nord." The week before the Minister was present at the first such act of financial assistance provided by France and announced that additional assistance was expected

in the future. He stressed that it was the presence of the government
in these matters rather than funds advanced that French-speaking
minorities are in need of throughout the continent.

[9] After the initial formulation of this chapter (Spring 1963)
President John F. Kennedy submitted a draft bill to Congress calling
for increased immigration without regard to country of origin and
giving "first priority to persons of useful skills and attainments...
with the greatest ability to add to the national welfare... [such as]
engineers, doctors, teachers and scientists" (New York Times, July
23, 1963, pp. 1, 12-13). In response to a copy of the first draft of
this chapter Myer Feldman, Deputy Special Counsel to the President,
indicated that "Language has always been a major force for cohesion
between nations, a valuable resource at all times, and a useful aid
to those seeking to improve their own skills in the articulation of
ideas. Your discussion of the immigration legislation is consistent
with the basis for the legislation submitted by the President" (letter,
July 29, 1963). Political commentators quickly observed that "con-
gressional approval of these [proposed] changes, most of them controversial, is not believed likely this year and promises to be difficult
at any time in the House of Representatives" (New York Times, op.
cit.). Immigration and population experts have long been calling for
similar revisions in American immigration policy. E.g., Frank
Lorimer, "Issues in Population Policy," in The Population Dilemma,
Philip M. Hauser, ed. (Englewood Cliffs, N.J., Prentice-Hall, 1963).

[10] Given sufficient support and recognition many ethnically
founded and maintained institutions of higher education could train
language maintenance leaders in specific "unusual" languages. Among
these are: Alliance College (Cambridge Springs, Penn.), St. Mary's
College (Orchard Lake, Mich.) and Villa Maria College (Buffalo,
N.Y.), in Polish; Suomi College (Hancock, Mich.), in Finnish; Mari-
anapolis College (Thompson, Conn.), in Lithuanian; St. Basil's
College (Stamford, Conn.), in Ukrainian; St. Procopius College
(Lisle, Ill.), in Czech; Luther College (Decorah, Iowa), in Norwegian;
Yeshiva University (New York, N.Y.) and Brandeis University (Wal-
tham, Mass.), in Hebrew and Yiddish. Higher education itself could
contribute significantly to language maintenance by the establishment
of many more chairs for ethnically infused languages and their cultures, particularly where these enjoy considerable local support.
Social research on language maintenance might contribute to this
goal by telling the story of the introduction of ethnically based

languages into a number of "general" American high schools and
colleges much more exhaustively than we have attempted to do in
these pages.

[11] One example is FCC ruling 58-734-61564 referred to on
p. 89, above. My attention was directed to this entire episode by
language loyalists who had concluded that the decision of the Com-
mision that a number of factors must be considered "in determining
the suitability of foreign language programming" was evidence of
"intercover" federal policy to discontinue such programming whenever
possible.

[12] An alternative to the support of ethnic group schools—
particularly where such support is rendered difficult as a result of
Church-state problems—is the establishment of non-ethnic schools
conducted entirely in critical non-English languages. A few private
schools of this kind already exist, but these are primarily in French,
limited to the "early childhood education" level, non-ethnic (or anti-
ethnic) in pupil-teacher composition, and expensive. The possibility
of such schools at the college level is demonstrated by the University
of Pacific's "Spanish College," in which "all subjects (except English)
are taught in Spanish as a novel step toward better Latin American
relations and as a recognition of California's Spanish heritage" (Palo
Alto Times, Sept. 19, 1963, p. 8).

[13] The major undertaking of this kind is the Franco-American
Institute at Bowdoin College (Brunswick, Maine) conducted by Professor Gerard J. Brault of the University of Pennsylvania, during the
summers of 1961, 1962 and 1963, In several instances, other NDEA
Language Institutes not explicitly intended for teachers of particular
ethnic backgrounds have, nevertheless, been largely composed of
such teachers.

[14] Since teachers of religiously-affiliated ethnic group ("private") schools have been admitted to these institutes on the usual
tuition-free basis (although without the weekly stipend normally offered
to students at NDEA institutes), one more precedent has been established for language maintenance aid to ethnic groups schools under
religious sponsorship. As a result, it might be possible to organize
such institutes for teachers employed by ethnic group schools and to
offer instruction in Polish, Hungarian, Ukrainian, Greek, Yiddish,
and other languages rarely available in public school settings but still
amply represented in the American population.

[15] For a report of early successes with the proficiency examination approach in the foreign languages area see "Modern Foreign Language Proficiency Tests for Teacher Certification; Report of Results in 1963 Administrations." Albany, New York State Education Department, 1964.

[16] A first step in the direction of such "recognition" has, on several occasions, been the organization of after-school language clubs for students interested in various languages that are still "uncommon" to the public school curriculum. When a sufficient number of pupils have joined such a club the transition to a regularly scheduled course during the normal school day can be made more easily.

[17] The New York Post, May 13, 1962, p. 22, reports a precedent of possible importance in this connection: "School districts in the state are giving credits to students for outside-of-school religious instruction with the approval of the State Education Department.... High school students have been granted a fourth of a unit toward their Regents credits for each year of religious instruction.... Such credits fall into the same category as dancing or music instruction given outside the school." Language instruction may also be credited in this fashion. Similar opportunities exist in a few other states but are seldom known or utilized. Certainly, institutions of higher education should pose no difficulty in recognizing language proficiency—however attained—for purposes of admission and placement.

[18] For several alternative suggestions concerning such programs see the section on "Basic Plans for Bilingual [Public] Schools," in Bruce A. Gaarder's "Teaching the Bilingual Child: Research, Development and Policy," Proceedings of the Conference on Teaching the Bilingual Child (Austin, Texas State Education Agency, 1964).

[19] For a review of recent public school efforts to conduct special Spanish programs for children of Mexican-American origin, see the Texas Foreign Language Association Bulletin, 5 (1963), number 3. Also note the experimental bilingual public school as well as the system-wide bilingual language arts program in Dade County, Florida, briefly described in Modern Language Journal, 48 (1964), p. 239.

[20] During the 1962-63 school year, a group of exchange teachers from Puerto Rico appointed to teach in New York City Schools set up after school classes in Spanish in a number of schools with substantial Puerto Rican enrollments. This activity was part of a larger program known as "Operation Understanding" which also sent

666

6666666666666666666

exchange teachers from New York to Puerto Rico, so that they could become more familiar with the home language and culture of Puerto Rican students in New York schools.

[21]What is proposed here is similar to the special recognition given to "educational media" by the separate establishment of Title VII under the National Defense Education Act of 1958. Educational media research and development might have been included under another title, e.g., with the Cooperative Research Program. However, as a result of their separate legal and budgetary status much more attention has been directed toward them than would otherwise have been the case. Although no separate Title for language maintenance is being advocated here, a separate section with its own staff, budget, and program is recommended. Unfortunately, language maintenance does not have nearly as strong a lobby as that which the educational-media-industries (including gadgetry, electronics, radio, and T.V.) were able to marshal on behalf of Title VII.

[22]While our increased sensitivities and needs have prompted the preparation (under NDEA Title VI auspices) of dictionaries, texts, grammars, and records in many exotic languages during the last few years, an anthology of non-English American literature for elementary or secondary school use still does not exist. There is also a great dearth of teaching materials and pedagogic tools for teachers working with children of particular ethnic backgrounds. The recent appearance of Gerard J. Brault's "Cours de Langue Française Destiné aux Jeunes Franco-Americains" (Philadelphia, University of Pennsylvania, 1963) may serve as a model of what is needed in scores of other languages as well, stressing as it does both language maintenance and greater fidelity to standard French and to the "high tradition" of French culture.

[23]Although further studies are indeed needed, it must be more fully understood that what is sought is more than an analysis of the current situation; it is a search for ways of transcending the present in the future. In view of the greater possibility of cultural bilingualism as compared to daily functional bilingualism, it would seem particularly desirable to initiate studies of ethnic group schools engaged in language maintenance efforts. Since the school is a meeting ground for several generations, since it represents an extended and conscious enculturating effort, and since it deals with both ethnically and ideologically elaborated language maintenance, it would seem to be an important and potentially fruitful arena for immediate inquiry.

REFERENCES

Brault, G. J. Some misconceptions about teaching American ethnic children their mother tongue. Modern Language Journal, 48 (1964), 67–71.

Dobzhansky, T. The Biological Basis of Human Freedom (New York, Columbia University Press, 1956).

Fishman, J. A. Publicly subsidized pluralism: the European and the American contexts; also The American dilemmas of publicly subsidized pluralism. School and Society, 87 (1959), 246–48 and 264–67.

Glazer, N., and Moynhan, D. P. Beyond the Melting Pot (Cambridge, M.I.T. and Harvard University Press, 1963).

Mead, Margaret. New Lives for Old (New York, Morrow, 1956).

Moberg, D. O. Social differentiation in the Netherlands. Social Forces, 39 (1961), 333–37.

Nance, Mrs. Afton D. Spanish for Spanish-Speaking Pupils (Sacramento, State of California Department of Education, 1963) (Mimeographed).

Starr, W. H. MLA foreign language proficiency tests for teachers and advanced students. PMLA, 77 (1962), no. 4, part 2, 1–12.

3 | Language Maintenance in a Supra-Ethnic Age

The Current Status of Non-English Language
Resources in the United States

In 1960 the non-English language resources of the United
States were undoubtedly smaller than they had been a decade or two
previously. Nevertheless, they were still huge, both in absolute
terms and relative to their 20th century high-water marks in the
1920's and 1930's.

Approximately 19 million individuals (11 per cent of the entire American population) possessed a non-English mother tongue in
1960. These mother tongues represent a very high proportion of
those that have evolved to the point of becoming standard literary
languages as well as many that have not yet reached this stage of
development. Relative to 1940, the quantitative position of the colonial languages—Spanish, French, and German—has remained superior
to that of all but the most recently reinforced immigrant languages.
However, even in the case of most of the immigrant languages that
did not benefit from post-war immigration and that suffered most from
internal attrition and external apathy, some subgroups still retain
sufficient cultural-linguistic intactness to maintain functional bilingualism and to provide good prospects of marked gain (in either functional or cultural bilingualism) with well designed and vigorous reinforcement efforts.

The non-English press boasted over 500 periodic publications
in 1960 and continued to have a circulation of approximately five and
one-half millions, as well as a "pass-along" readership estimated
to be equally large. Although non-English dailies and weeklies have

regularly lost circulation since 1930, monthlies have experienced circulation gains in recent decades. Non-English broadcasting also seemed to be in a far better state of health in 1960 than was usually expected to be the case—with over 1600 "stations" broadcasting more than 6,000 hours of non-English language programs every week in the continental United States. However, this picture largely reflects the continued strength of Spanish broadcasting, which alone accounts for two-thirds of all non-English broadcasting in the United States. Both the non-English press and non-English broadcasting (with the exception of Spanish broadcasting) are largely dependent upon and oriented toward a first-generation clientele. The latter, in turn, represent slightly less than half the claimants of almost all non-English mother tongues in the United States. Thus, although immigrant status itself is not predictive of either language maintenance or language loyalty, both of these phenomena are heavily dependent upon immigrant status— with the colonial languages marking the only noteworthy exceptions to this generalization.

In 1960 there were at least 1800 (and probably a good many more) ethnic "cultural" organizations in the United States. Many, including the largest among them, serve first-, second-, and third-generation members. Nearly three-quarters of all ethnic cultural organizations favor maintenance of their non-English ethnic mother tongue. However, the very fact that ethnic organizations have been more successful than either the non-English press or non-English broadcasting in attracting second and third generation interest has also led most of them to exceedingly marginal and passive approaches to ethnicity and to language maintenance. The organizations represent bulwarks of structural more than of behavioral-functional pluralism.

The most active language maintenance institution in the majority of ethnic communities in the United States is the ethnic group school. Over 2,000 such schools currently function in the United States, of which more than half offer mother tongue instruction even when there are many "non-ethnics" and "other-ethnics" among their pupils. On the whole, they succeed in reinforcing or developing moderate comprehension, reading, and speaking facility in their pupils. They are far less successful in implanting retentivist language attitudes which might serve to maintain language facility after their students' programs of study have been completed, approximately at the

age of fourteen. Although the languages learned by pupils in ethnic
group schools are "ethnic mother tongues," rather than true mother
tongues, the levels of facility attained usually are sufficient to provide a foundation for cultural bilingualism. This foundation, however,
is rarely reinforced after the completion of study in the ethnic group
school.

Mother tongue teachers in ethnic group schools rarely view
themselves as powerful factors in determining language maintenance
outcomes. They feel that their pupils do not accomplish much with
respect to the more active domains of language maintenance. They
typically report that their pupils become increasingly less interested
in mother tongue instruction as they advance through the grades and
attribute this (and other instructional difficulties) to parental apathy
or opposition to the mother tongue. They tend to view the mother
tongues they teach as not being among the most prestigeful in the
United States (an honor reserved for French and Spanish almost exclusively). However, the determinants of language prestige (unlike
the determinants of instructional difficulties) are attributed to "American" rather than to ethnic factors. When group maintenance is seen
as being in conflict with language maintenance, the former is frequently preferred, except in the case of mother tongue teachers associated with very recent immigrant groups, most of whom reject the
possibility of any such conflict.

The relationship between ethnicity, language, and religion
remains strong, although the latter tends to withdraw from the tri-
partite association. Religion is organizationally "successful" in the
United States, and therefore its less successful companions, ethnicity
and language, lean upon it heavily for support. But the more "successful" religion becomes, the more de-ethnicized it becomes, the more
amenable to mergers with other de-ethnicized churches, and the
more disinterested in language maintenance. Language maintenance
in historically ethnic churches is continued on a habitual (rather than
an ideological-purposive) basis, on ethnic (rather than on religious)
grounds, and in conjunction with adult (rather than youth) activities.
The triple melting pot—leading toward de-ethnicized Catholicism,
Protestantism, and Judaism-- and the mere passage of time represent
the two most prevalent religious solutions to the "embarrassment"
of language maintenance. Traditional ritual protection of non-English

vernaculars (such as exists in the Greek Catholic and Eastern Orthodox Churches) functions more as a significant delaying factor than as
a crucial outcome factor in this connection.

Ethnic cultural-organizational leaders and rank-and-file
ethnics display essentially similar patterns with respect to language
maintenance efforts and processes. In both instances, immigrants
are more retentive—within the family and outside it—than are second-
generation individuals. Older children are more linguistically retentive than younger children, first children more so than last children,
children more so than grandchildren, organizationally affiliated children more so than unaffiliated children. Whereas first-generation
leaders consist of both cultural and organizational activists, second-
generation leaders are almost exclusively organizational activists.
Although they favor language maintenance, they do so with essentially
non-ethnic rationales and their support for language maintenance is
attitudinal rather than overt. Philosophies or rationales of biculturism and bi-lingualism are weak or non-existent.

There are two large worlds of non-English languages in the
United States. One is the officially recognized and supported world
of "foreign language" instruction in non-ethnic high schools and colleges. The other is the largely unrecognized and unsupported world
of ethnic language maintenance efforts. These two worlds meet in
the persons of foreign language teachers, over half of whom are of an
immediate ethnic background appropriate to one of the languages they
teach. Teachers of ethnically more infused, less prestigeful languages (e.g., German and Italian, as contrasted with French and
Spanish)—particularly those at the college and university level—are
most likely to have been ethnically exposed and to be in favor of language maintenance efforts. However, these same teachers are also
under the greatest strain toward professionalization and are, therefore, least inclined to utilize the resources of minority cultural-
linguistic groups (native speakers, publications, broadcasts, choral-
dramatic presentations) for instructional purposes (Fishman and
Hayden 1964).

Detailed integrative case studies of six separate cultural-
linguistic groups provide much independent support for the above
generalizations. In general, language maintenance and language shift

have proceeded along quite similar lines in the three high prestige colonial languages (French, Spanish, German) and the three low prestige immigrant languages (Yiddish, Hungarian, Ukrainian). Although differing widely with respect to period of settlement, numerical size, balance between low-culture and high-culture language retentivism, religious protection of the vernacular, and social mobility of their speakers, the drift has been consistently toward Anglification and has become accelerated in recent years. Differences between the six language groups seem to be great only in connection with the race of change toward Anglification.

Among the Spanish and Ukrainian speakers sizable contingents of young and youthful bilinguals are still available. In the Ukrainian case this is primarily due to recent large immigration. In the Spanish case it is due to the absence of economic mobility. Symbolically elaborated ethnicity, language loyalty, and religious protection of the vernacular are absent in the Spanish case and present in the Ukrainian. All in all, certain pervasive characteristics of American nationalism (mobility on a non-ethnic, ideological, mass-culture base) and of most immigrant heritages (non-ideological ethnicity, cultural and economic "backwardness") seem to have been much more effective in jointly producing essentially similar outcomes than have the various uniquenesses of ethnic heritages or of immigrational-settlement patterns in safeguarding cultural and linguistic differences.

The modal characteristics of language maintenance efforts among southern and eastern European immigrants arriving during the period of mass immigration are roughly summarizable as follows:

a. Language is rarely a consciously identified or valued component of daily, traditional, ethnicity. Ethnicity itself is minimally ideologized or organized in terms of conscious nationalistic or symbolic considerations.

b. Rapid immersion in the American metropolis and acceptance of American national values results in the fragmentation of traditional ways. Those fragments of ethnicity that are retained in a disjointed and altered fashion are usually insufficient for the maintenance of functional bilingualism beyond the first generation.

c. Ethnicity and language maintenance become increasingly
and overly dependent on that major organizational institution previously available in the "old country" setting and most successfully
transplanted to the United States: the Church. However, the Church
has increasingly withdrawn from ethnicity and from language maintenance in order to pursue its own organizational goals.

d. Attempts to utilize the formal organizational mechanisms
of high culture and of industrialized metropolitan and modern national
life on behalf of language and culture maintenance proceed without
benefit of a popular ideological base that might either compete with
or be joined to American nationalism.

e. As a result, neither traditional intactness nor ideological
mobilization is available to the second generation. "Revolts" are common when maximal claims are advanced by the first generation and
become uncommon when such claims are no longer pressed.

f. Those of the second generation "outgrow" the fragmented
ethnicity of the first but frequently retain an attachment to more marginal expressions of ethnicity via the Church, other organizations,
and familial remnants of traditional ethnicity. While these have been
insufficient for functional language maintenance, they have often preserved a positive attitude toward the ethnic language and culture.
This positiveness becomes more evident as the second generation
advances through adulthood.

g. The third generation approaches ethnicity with even
greater selectivity, frequently viewing the ethnic mother tongue as a
cultural or instrumental desideratum and viewing ethnicity as an
area of appreciation or a field of study. De-ethnicized language
maintenance elicits interest in the third generation although facility
is rare.

Of all the foregoing, what can be considered new or striking
in the light of previous studies or common knowledge ? Certainly the
availability of systematic empirical data—rather than anecdotal impressions—is new for many of the domains under discussion. The
vastness of language maintenance efforts, even after generations of
attrition, is certainly striking, but so is the fact that these efforts

are so largely habitual and unfocused even within the very operation
of organizations, schools, churches, and the mass media. The conscious, ideologically based and rationally directed efforts of language
loyalists normally reach and influence only a small fraction of even
the first generation of speakers of non-English languages. The uniformly changed role of religion with respect to language maintenance—
from initially wholehearted support to implacable opposition or un-
movable apathy—is also striking and hitherto largely unappreciated.
Similarly notable is the fact that opposition to language maintenance
in the second and third generations of immigrant stock is now most
commonly on a low key and unideologized. The days of bitter language
disputes seem to be over, even between the age groups formerly
involved in such disputes. The continuation of favorable language
maintenance sentiments much beyond the time of functional language
maintenance is also striking, particularly in that it goes hand in hand
with a continued acceptance of ethnicity and even a search for ethnicity of an appropriately selective and marginal nature. While language
maintenance becomes a progressively weaker and smaller component
of such ethnicity, organizational (including religious) involvement,
cultural interests, and modified-disjointed festive acts become relatively more prominent and are maintained much longer. Thus it is
that the most striking fact of all comes into focus—that a vast amount
of marginal ethnicity can exist side by side with the gradual disap-
pearance of language maintenance, with the two phenomena interacting and contributing to each other.

      In summary, language maintenance in the United States is
currently strongest among those immigrants who have maintained
greatest psychological, social, and cultural distance from the institutions, processes, and values of American core society. Ideological
protection of non-English mother tongues without concomitant with-
drawal from interaction with American society (i. e. , the pattern
adopted by urban religionists and by secular-cultural nationalists in
the United States) has been a somewhat less effective bulwark of language maintenance than has ethnic-religious separatism based upon
intact rural "little traditions. " Where neither ideological nor ethno-
religious protection has obtained language shift has proceeded in
proportion to mobility within the larger sphere of American society,
as reflected by indices of education, occupation, or income. Either
type of protection has been exceedingly rare. As a result, between-

group differences in language maintenance have come to reflect immi-
grational recency, settlement concentration, numerical size, and
social mobility much more than differences in post-immigrational
maintenance efforts. Within-group differences in language maintenance
have also come to depend primarily on the same set of factors, together with rurality, and to a smaller but nevertheless noticeable
degree upon conscious maintenance efforts.

Our current information concerning behaviors directed
toward ethnic mother tongues on the part of their erstwhile and sometime speakers must be viewed in the perspective of the transitions
that these tongues have most commonly experienced in the United
States. From their original status as vernaculars of entire religio-
ethnic communities they are now the vernaculars only of very recent
or otherwise·atypical sub-populations. Instead of their earlier use
in all the domains of life related to the particular socio-cultural patterns of their speakers, they are now predominantly employed in
fewer and particularly in symbolic or restricted domains. Nevertheless, concomitant with accelerated de-ethnization and social mobility,
and concomitant with their relegation to fewer and narrower domains,
non-English mother tongues have frequently experienced increases in
general esteem during the past 15-20 years. They are more frequently
viewed positively and nostalgically by older first- and second-
generation individuals who had characterized them as ugly, corrupted,
and grammarless in pre-World War II days. The third generations
view them (almost always via translations) with less emotion but with
even greater respect. Thus, instead of a "third generation return"
(Hansen 1940) there has been an "attitudinal halo-ization" within
large segments of all generations, albeit unaccompanied by increased
use. Such a negative relationship between use rates and attitudinal
positiveness over time was not foreseen by most earlier studies of
language maintenance or language shift in immigrant contact settings.
In the United States this development is an aspect of the continued and
growing affective functioning of increasingly marginal ethnicity. In
the absence of basic economic, geographic, cultural, or psychological
separation between most ethnics and American core society, ethnic
mother tongues survive longest at two extremes: the highly formal
(the ritual-symbolic) and the highly intimate (the expressive-emotive).
At these extremes they remain available to successive generations
as reminders of ethnicity, and when needed, as reaffirmers of ethnicity.

At the level of overt behavioral implementation of maintenance or shift, most language reinforcement efforts—though much
weakened by ideological and numerical attrition—continue along the
traditional lines of information programs, religio-ethnic schools,
periodic publications, broadcasts, cultural activities, etc. However,
even in connection with language reinforcement efforts the transition
to more marginal ethnicity and to more restricted language maintenance is evident. Thus, taking the field of ethnic periodic publications as an example, we note concomitant and continued shifts from
more frequent to less frequent publications as well as shifts from
all-mother-tongue, to mixed, to all-English publications. The process of de-ethnization has also brought with it a few novel avenues of
reinforcement. As even the more "exotic" ethnic mother tongues
(i. e. , mother tongues not usually considered among the major carriers
of European civilization and, therefore, most frequently associated
with foreign ethnicity in the minds of average Americans) have ceased
to be primarily associated with immigrant disadvantages or with full-
blown religio-ethnic distinctiveness, these have been increasingly
introduced as languages of study and research at the university, college, and public high school levels. Although bilingual public schools
such as those that existed before the First World War have hardly ever
been reintroduced, and although the bilingual college (or monolingual
non-English college) which passed from the American scene at about
the same time has also hardly ever been reintroduced, both are increasingly viewed as "experimental" possibilities on the part of non-
ethnic (rather than ethnic) authorities. Seemingly, massive displacement has greater inhibitory impact on language planning efforts than
it does on language reinforcement efforts. The latter are essentially
conservative and seem to require less in the way of highly specialized
leadership. The former are essentially modificatory and dependent
upon expert linguistic advice in concert with compliance producing
or persuasive authority. Thus archaic or rustic orthographic, lexical,
and structural features continue to characterize most non-English
mother tongues spoken in the United States and interference proceeds
apace, both because planning and enforcing authorities are lacking and
because the old find it more difficult to adopt conscious and systematic
innovations.

Vocal advocates of language shift have practically disappeared,
although institutional support for shift still exists along quiet but

pervasive lines. Religious bodies have been particularly persistent
in de-ethnicizing parishes and Anglifying church activities as they
have gained in institutional autonomy and centralization. The Roman
Catholic Church has been most active along these lines whereas
Churches in which non-English languages are ritually protected (e. g.,
the Byzantine Rite Catholic and Eastern Orthodox Churches) have, by
comparison, remained relatively conservative. In general, religion
has more quickly and more successfully disassociated itself from
ethnicity and arrived at independent legitimization in the United States
than has the use of non-English mother tongues.

     As for the cognitive aspects of language response, the mar-
ginalization of ethnicity has resulted in greater cognitive dissociation
between ethnic identification and language maintenance. Far from
being viewed as components of groupness (whether in the sense of
resultant or contributing factors), non-English mother tongues are
increasingly viewed in terms of non-ethnic cultural or non-ethnic
practical considerations. At the same time, knowledge of language
history, literature, and synchronic variants has remained rare.

     The foregoing must not, however, be hastily accepted as
constituting paradigms for the progress of language maintenance or
language shift in all possible immigrant-based contact settings. It
may be applicable only to those settings characterized by sharply
unequal power configurations, by incorporation as the type of control,
by marked plurality and recent immigration as the plurality pattern,
by intermediate stratification and substantial mobility within the
social structure, and by widespread mutual legitimization of acculturation and de-ethnization as accompaniments of urbanization, industrialization, mass culture, and ever-widening social participation (Schermerhorn 1963). In general, we know (or suspect) much more about
the dynamics of language maintenance and language shift in the American immigrant contact situation than we do about these processes in
settings involving indigenous populations utilizing more equally "official" languages (e. g., Riksmaal-Landsmaal, Spanish-Guarani,
Schwyzertütsch-Romansh, etc.). This imbalance has resulted in a
skewing of conclusions and concepts among students of language maintenance and language shift.

     If these findings have general significance it is primarily in
their revealing that language shift may be accompanied by a heightening

of certain attitudinal, cognitive, and overt implementational responses
to languages that are being displaced. In general, ethnicity and culture maintenance appear to be much more stable phenomena than
language maintenance. On the one hand, most immigrants become
bilingual (i. e., English displaces the hitherto exclusive use of their
mother tongue in certain kinds of interactions) much before they em-
bark on de-ethnization or seriously contemplate the possibility of biculturism. On the other hand, marginal but yet functional ethnicity
lingers on (and is transmitted via English) long after the ethnic mother
tongue becomes substantially dormant or is completely lost. Curiously
enough, the lingering of marginal ethnicity prompts and supports
respect, interest, and nostalgia for the ethnic mother tongue, causing
language loyalists to entertain renewed hopes for revitalization even
though displacement is far advanced. Thus the very resultants of
deep-reaching socio-cultural change carry with them seeds of further
change and of reversal.

Questions and Interpretations

        The foregoing findings invite comments and interpretations.
Why has this state of affairs come into being? How is it to be understood, both in terms of American life and in terms of even wider
relevance? Certainly it is not enough to say that too few have cared
or that many have cared too little, since that too needs to be explained
and since history records numerous instances of decisive impact of
the few upon the many—in the domain of language, no less than in
others.

        In the planning stage of this study, the investigators were
impressed with the tremendous spread of "input variance" relevant
to the question uppermost in our minds. The socio-cultural worlds
of carriers of non-English languages in the United States reveal many
and important differences: old immigrants and new immigrants,
prestige languages and non-prestige languages, peasants and intellectuals, rurality and urbanness, religious reinforcement and nationalistic reinforcement, traditional ethnic roots and modern high culture
roots, social mobility and its absence. It seemed only logical that
the status of language maintenance efforts in the United States would
vary significantly from one language to another, and that this variation,

considered as a dependent or consequent variable, could be related to the tremendous variation in the cultural-linguistic carriers of language maintenance, considered as an independent or antecedent variable. Although this approach has revealed some moderately important and consistent relationships, these have been fewer than expected, and directionally uniform. Thus, upon concluding our study, we must be more impressed with the paucity of "output variance," particularly in long-range terms, and with the tremendous power of the intervening contextual variable to which all non-English-speaking cultural-linguistic groups in the United States have been exposed: American nationalism.

The American Dream and the American Experience. The alchemists of old sought a universal solvent, an elixir, that could transmute all manner of baser metals into a single desired one. American nationalism may be viewed as such a solvent, although whether the cultural ingredients upon which it has acted were in any sense baser than the product that it has produced will always be open to question. Indeed, the solvent has not really been entirely effective as a solvent. Nevertheless, it has been a catalyst, and it has dissolved the basic ingredients of functional bilingualism: the desire and ability to maintain an intact and different way of life. It is this realization which has prompted us to suggest that the preservation and revitalization of America's non-English language resources (even for the purpose of cultural bilingualism) requires, first and foremost, several planned modifications in the goals and processes of American society.

American nationalism has been described as an extreme form of western European nationalism in that it is particularly non-ethnic and essentially ideological in nature (Kohn 1961 [a]). Even the ethnicity of the early English-speaking settlers, who imparted to American nationalism ingredients of content and of direction that it has nevor lost, was strongly colored by the growing de-ethnization and ideologization of British life in the 17th and 18th centuries. There were, as there are today, Englishmen, Scotsmen, Welshmen, and Irishmen—and several regional varieties of each—but there was also (and, for many, primarily) Great Britain,[1] a supra-ethnic entity which increasingly involved all of the foregoing in supra-ethnic problems and processes (Kohn 1940). The supra-ethnic political struggles and the supra-ethnic religious struggles that had convulsed the

British Isles for generations before the colonization of New England
not only led to this colonization but also stamped it with a view of
ethnicity as an aspect of social structure which was different from
that of New France, New Spain, or New Amsterdam. The problems
of religious diversity and of political participation were so much
greater that the importance of purely ethnic manifestations in society
paled by comparison. The ancient links between ethnicity and religion
that existed in most other parts of Europe had already been weakened
to the point that these were never fully re-established by British settlers in the New World. The relationships between man and God, between man and state, and between man and environment were formulated increasingly in non-ethnic terms. Even the term "Englishman"
had political and ideological rather than ethnic connotations. Thus,
a supra-ethnic outlook was transplanted, usually at a purely subcon-
scious level. Later, as rivalries developed with colonists of non-
British origin, with other colonial powers, with the mother country,
and with the Old World itself, supra-ethnicity became a conscious
value and a rallying cry. By then it had already become a fact of life,
even though not fully a way of life.

From the early supra-ethnic beginnings of American nationalism, the American Dream contained two recognizable components:
those of process and those of promise. The components of process
guaranteed personal freedom (and, therefore, political democracy
and the separation of Church and State) as well as the determining use
of reason (rather than ascribed status) in guiding public affairs. The
components of promise held forth vistas of happiness in human affairs,
limitless individual and collective advancement, and social inclusiveness in community affairs. In a very basic sense, each of these ingredients is supra-ethnic if not anti-ethnic. America offered initially
and officially that which many today, all over the world, take to be
the goals of all social evolution: freedom of physical, intellectual,
and emotional movement in constantly expanding social, economic,
and cultural spheres. American nationalism came to stand for all
that was modern, good, reasonable, inclusive, and participationist
in human relations. America has made good the promise of its nationalism for many millions and with dramatic rapidity.

The American Dream is crucial to language maintenance outcomes not only because of the importance of primum mobile. It is

also crucial because, on the one hand, it has failed to answer certain questions of a substantive nature, and, on the other, most of our non-English-speaking immigrants lacked any substantial counter-dream. In implying that freedom, equality, capacity, participation, and reason were sufficient guides to human behavior, it did not provide the substantive cultural ingredients of national life that both ethnicity and religion provide. In merely requiring an affirmation of its processes and promises it more quickly disarmed non-English speakers whose ethnicity had been transmuted and elaborated in consciously creative directions. In offering so much and seeming to ask so little in return, it overpowered the masses of immigrants whose primordial ethnicity was still largely intact and, therefore, still largely innocent of ideology. The overpowering nature of American nationalism is also an indication that it can be as uncompromising and as conformity-producing as the nationalisms known elsewhere throughout the world.

It is frequently claimed that Americanism processes and promises require cultural pluralism for their maturation and protection. Be this as it may, it is doubtless true that cultural pluralism was never explicitly "covered" by the formulators of the American Dream, nor has it been consciously and fully desired by the millions who subsequently subscribed to the Dream. Indeed, the prime factor leading most immigrants to our shores was the American Dream itself and its implicity contract and not any dream of cultural pluralism (Bruner 1956; Lerner 1958; Mead 1956). Not only was cultural pluralism a highly unlikely dream for most immigrants prior to their immigration, it was a rarely articulated or accepted dream after arrival. In most cases, ethnicity and language maintenance lived in America as they had in Europe: on a primarily traditional and non-ideological plane. Even when they crumbled or changed, they most commonly did so on a non-ideological basis. By and large, their carriers were conscious only of the American Dream, which is supra-ethnic in content. It is a Dream in which the Queen's English is no more than a "vehicle of communication" for the pursuit of perfection in human affairs, constant individual and collective advancement, and social inclusiveness in community processes. It is a vision which has spread round the world and excited envy, admiration, or both in distant places. Like most visions, it implies more than it specifies. The fact that it has emasculated both levels of functional ethnicity (upon one or another of which language maintenance has always relied), without at the same time providing for structural assimilation in more primary relationships (Gordon 1964), cannot clearly be used to its discredit—since it neither promised to maintain the former nor to attain the latter. That primordial ethnicity could not fully maintain itself under the impact of this Dream, and that ethnicity cannot fully and quickly disappear in a new world animated by this Dream alone, are as much due to the nature of ethnicity as to the Dream itself.

   Ethnicity and Language Maintenance. Ethnicity designates a constellation of primordial awarenesses, sentiments, and attachments by means of which man has traditionally recognized the discriminanda that relate him to some other men while distinguising him from others. Blood ties, geographic proximity, common customs and beliefs—these constitute primitive principles of human organization that are still very much in evidence throughout the world. So basic are they in socialization and in subsequent experience that they frequently appear as "givens" in nature. Even when man progresses to more complex and more abstract bases of social grouping (religion, ideology, the nation, the profession, even "mankind"), the earlier principles of interaction remain recognizable in his behavior and from time to time proclaim their dominance. Both levels of human organization seem to be required for meeting different personal and societal needs in the modern world. However, the kind and proportion of behavior actually guided by primordial considerations and the kind and proportion guided by considerations of a larger scale vary from country to country, from group to group, from person to person, and from occasion to occasion. Language may affect human behavior either through its more primitive, primordial or through its more modern, larger-scale involvements.

   The folk-urban continuum (Redfield 1947, 1953) has been referred to in several of the foregoing chapters not because it is presumed that villages, cities and states are totally different environments, but because it casts light upon continuity and discontinuity in primordial behaviors when these are introduced into more modern political and social contexts (Geertz 1963). The fact that there are more nuances than clear-cut polarities in the rural-urban continuum (particularly when the continuum is viewed in historical and cross-cultural perspective [Benet 1963]) does not make the transition from predominantly rural to predominantly urban settings any smoother

for those whose lot it is to quickly go from one to another. Under
these circumstances, even without extirpation and transplantation,
ethnicity and its various primordial components change in content,
in saliency, and in relevance to daily life (Bruner 1961; Lewis 1952).
There is no doubt that the mass of immigrants of the 1880-1920 period
(upon whom language maintenance in the United States still largely
depends in almost every case except Spanish and, perhaps, Ukrainian)
hailed from far more rural, more homogeneous, more traditional,
more ethnic contexts than those that they entered in the United States.
There is no doubt that their language behavior was usually imbedded
in ethnicity rather than in ideology. Finally, there is no doubt that
language maintenance required (and usually did not find) a new foundation when its potential carriers came to feel at home in the American
environment.

In its encounter with a non-traditional, secular world in which
social interaction and social grouping are rationalized by forces em-
anating from progress and efficiency, justice and equality, nation and
world, the ethnicity of underdeveloped and undermobilized populations
has responded in two quite different ways. In many instances it has
been symbolically elaborated and elevated to a higher order principle
with claims for competitive legitimacy in the modern world of ideas
and conscious loyalties. In other instances it has merely regrouped
or restructured itself, changing in content, saliency, and part-whole
articulation, but remaining far closer to the little tradition level from
which it stems than to any modern Weltanschauung. While both of
these transformations of old world ethnicity were attempted by immigrants to the United States, various circumstances conspired to make
the latter approach much more common and much more acceptable
than the former.

The relatively few intellectuals and political activists who
sought to raise the ethnicity of rank-and-file immigrants to the level
of religion, ideology, and nationalism by no means dismally failed.
Indeed, given the difficulties they faced they were remarkably successful. They frequently united hitherto separated, particularistic ethnic
populations into groups conscious of common nationality. They provided the energy and directing force that led many of the major formal
organizations and undertakings of immigrants on American shores.
They both pointed out and helped create Great Traditions in literature,

history, and ideology which at least temporarily lifted their followers
out of complete reliance on primordial ethnicity, provided them with
pride in their heritage, and helped counteract feelings of insecurity
vis-à-vis the accomplishments of American civilization. However,
in the main and in the long run, they were unsuccessful and their fate
may best be described as an alienation of the dedicated. They succeeded far better in foisting an identity between ethnicity and nationalism on the general, de-ethnicized American public (which reacted
in typical early second-generation horror)[2] than they did in gaining
acceptance of this same identity among their own co-ethnics. Their
symbolic transmutations of everyday ethnic life probably led as many
co-ethnics and their children to even more universalized, less ethnically delimited or rationalized interests in language, literature,
and justice than to the kind of cultural-national self-definitions that
these elites originally had in mind. In the last analysis they failed
to permanently mobilize a sufficiently large proportion of their more
primordially oriented co-ethnics, who were orientated in much more
mundane directions. As a result, very little of language maintenance
in the United States currently remains (or ever has been) under nationalistic ideological auspices.

        Most immigrants to the United States, until comparatively
recent times, may best be viewed as underdeveloped ethnic populations
whose mobilization into modern life occurred under the aegis of the
American Dream, the American city, and the American state (Steward
1951). They accepted the ideal norms of the new society round about
them with relative and accelerating ease. In contrast to the relative
disadvantage and lack of mobility that they had known in their own
homelands they perceived and experienced rapid and marked improve-
ments in their new homes (Shuval 1963). They eagerly accepted
those values and norms that were required to maximize the benefits
for which they had come. However, it is important for us to realize
that their little traditions, though severely dislocated and weakened,
showed an amazing capacity to regroup and even to innovate under
these circumstances.

        Although the ethnicity of immigrants to the United States did
not become as ideologized or modernized as ethnic elites had hoped,
it did move in that direction in the form of conscious organizational-
associational activity. Indeed, as the ethnicity of daily life increasingly

weakened its organized associational transmutations appeared in bold and abnormal relief (Anderson and Anderson 1959/60). The churches, the organizations, the schools grew pari passu with the retreat of primordial ethnicity in the home and the neighborhood. The new expressions of ethnicity were well suited for urban, modern existence but they were also entities in themselves and had goals and needs of their own. They carried language maintenance as best they could and for as long as it served their own purposes. If the result has been markedly negative insofar as attaining or retaining functional bilingualism is concerned, it has been somewhat more positive with respect to other aspects of primordial ethnicity. Above all, the new instrumentalities preserve a new kind of ethnicity, simultaneously more conscious and more marginal than the old, but seemingly more capable of endurance in the American environment (or in other modern contexts). It is in this sense that ethnicity in the United States is not merely a vestigial remains but also a new creation on behalf of a kind of group solidarity and consciousness not provided for in the American Dream. In America, as elsewhere in today's world, circumstances bring about a modernization of ethnicity rather than its complete displacement. Whereas the majority of human interactions are governed by involvement, participation, and creativity on a larger scale of human organization, earlier, more primordial levels are still needed and still exist. It is not only non-Western intellectuals who currently vacillate between tradition and modernity (Shils 1961); it is not only non-Western peoples who currently alternate between emulation and solidarity in search of a more adequate great tradition (Orans 1959); most modern Americans and most modern Europeans do so as well. There are limits to the ability of larger-scale and more modern bonds and principles to solve the longings of mankind. The primordial and the modern show a capacity to co-exist side by side, to adjust to each other, and to stimulate each other.

The supra-ethnicity of the American Dream could not have found a better instrument for the enfeeblement of primordial ethnic particularities (including the displacement of ethnic languages) than the frenetic and polyglot American metropolis and the American "ways of life" which developed in it (Benet 1963; Bruner 1961). In these inauspicious surroundings the maintenance of ethnic languages became more conscious than it had ever been before, but without either a great tradition or a little tradition to maintain it. That it drew more

strength from the latter than from the former seems quite natural
under the circumstances of its carriers. Only in the case of two
colonial languages—French and German—was a somewhat de-ethnicized
and prestigeful great tradition available to buttress language maintenance among both intellectuals and common folk.[3] In connection with
other languages, there was rarely any awareness or conviction that
anything outstanding had been achieved nor the sophistication or experience needed to differentiate between assertive transmutations of
ethnicity and more purely creative transmutations on firmer ethnic
foundations. The latter were rediscovered—selectively to be sure—
by second and third generations. However, this came to pass only
after the second generation had revolted against the irrationally all-
encompassing claims of atomized ethnicity and after the remnants of
primordial ethnicity were too feeble to seriously address similar
claims to the third.[4]

      Under the impact of American ideology and American mass
culture, language maintenance turned for support first to the one and
then to the other. The ideology closest to it was the religion with
which it had been intimately associated on its home grounds. Indeed,
as a result of centuries of co-existence, primordial ethnicity and
religion had completely interpenetrated each other. At times each
had come to the other's rescue (Jakobson 1945). Each had formed
the other; each had changed the other. What better ally, then, for
language maintenance in America than religion? Immigrant religions
both courted and supported language maintenance, and religion was
protected in American nationalism. Indeed, what other real ally was
there?

      Religion and Language Maintenance. Ethnic romanticists
seem to view ethnicity in much the same way as religious mystics
view religion: something pure, direct, unaltered, and unanalyzable.
On the other hand, folk-immigrants, prior to arrival in the United
States, may be said to have behaved as if their ethnicity were their
religion. Each daily act, no matter how mundane, was within the pale
of sanctity and colored by its hue. Subsequently, after varying exposure to modern American life, many immigrants came to behave
as if their religion were their ethnicity. Religion came to be substi-
tuted for ethnicity and to preserve those remnants of primordial ethnicity that were amenable to it. Such preservation was rarely sufficient for the purposes of functional language maintenance.

As religiously-committed American historians look back
upon the language issues that convulsed their Churches at one time
or another, it strikes many of them that the linguistic particularism
under which their predecessors labored were particularly misguided.
How could anything as universal, as timeless, and as ultimate as
religious truth ever have appeared to be inextricably dependent upon
a particular vernacular (or even upon a particular sacred tongue)?
The fact that religions have rendered various languages holy or have
declared them to be particularly appropriate for the expression and
preservation of religious attachments is conveniently overlooked when
the advancement of religion—which may be distinguished from the
advancement of religiosity—dictates that the bonds with particular
languages need to be sundered. The Lord giveth and the Lord taketh
away, in languages as in all else, and in sacred languages almost as
much as in vernaculars.

Not only are the historical bonds between language and religions frequently overlooked in examining the particular bonds that
existed during earlier stages of immigration to the United States, but
the specific benefits to the Churches accruing from these bonds are
generally ignored. Frequently, no effort is made to indicate the light
in which the maintenance of particular vernaculars was viewed in
former days, namely as a form of ethnic traditionalism firmly associated with religious traditionalism and, therefore, conducive to religious loyalty. Rather than a factor which strengthened immigrant
Churches as organizations and institutions at a time when they were
particularly weak, language maintenance is now preferably viewed as
a temporary device of an established Church seeking to safeguard the
faith of childish and unruly immigrants susceptible to the wickedness
of the great city and to the blandishments of competing creeds. It is
in this vein that a recent study recognizes "the immigrant phase" of
the Catholic Church as one in "which the primary challenge was to
guard the faith of Catholics and to defend the Church against calum-
nies" (Deedy 1963):

> Looking back now, one of the curiosities of those years
> is the absence from the Catholic press of any strong
> notion of solidarity in faith or in patriotism. Catholic
> readers were first Irish or German or Slovak, then
> Catholic. . . . Catholic publications played party to this

> folly by catering to the nostalgias, culture, and nation-
> alism of the particular immigrant group served.... There
> was frequently cause to wonder whether a given publica-
> tion was first Catholic or first Irish, German, French,
> and so on.

Obviously, language maintenance presented a very special problem
to the Roman Catholic Church. In contrast to the national Protestant
Churches which dealt with immigrants of a single ethnic origin, and
unlike the Greek Catholic and Eastern Orthodox Churches that had
long ago become decentralized along separate national lines, the
Roman Catholic Church in America was simultaneously Irish, Angli-
fied, "Americanist," and centralized. Whereas the other immigrant
Churches lacked de-ethnicized, English-speaking American roots,
the Roman Catholic Church as a result of over a century of effort had
already developed such roots by the time masses of non-English-
speaking Catholics arrived. Horrified by the "regressive" centrifugal
prospects of re-ethnization, the Catholic hierarchy in America may
well have become (and remained) the second major organized de-
ethnicizing and Anglifying force in the United States, next to the American public school system. What appeared to be at issue was not
merely the hard-won beachhead of American respectability (for a
Church that had been recurringly exposed to anti-papism and know-
nothingism), not only the loyalty of younger, English-speaking parish-
oners, but the very structural unity and authority of the Church itself,
as various ethnic groups sought the kinds of parish government, the
kinds of parish organizations, the kinds of religious services, the
kinds of religiously sanctioned and sanctified ethnic practices that
were in keeping with their particular Catholic traditions. No wonder,
then, that a policy of strenuous resistance was developed in connection with language mainenance and other manifestations of ethnic particularism. Mass immigration was still in high gear when this policy
of resistance culminated in Pope Leo XIII's encyclical of January 22,
1899, Testem Benevolentiae, "which praised the spirit and the progress of the Church in America, but which deplored the 'contentions
which have arisen... to the no slight detriment of peace'" (Deedy
1963). The promulgation of this encyclical is correctly taken as
ushering in the "post-immigration period" (even though mass·immi-
gration continued for another generation) in that ethnic parishes, like
the ethnic press, "came tightly within the orbit of church authority."

The apostolic letter "had the effect of dropping a blanket of silence" and of producing "a speedy metamorphosis," such that the 20th century was entered in a spirit "subdued and reserved, if not completely docile," a spirit conducive to a "truly American church, indeed" (Deedy 1963). Several of our studies reveal the lengths to which various Catholic and non-Catholic ethnic groups went in their lack of docility on behalf of ethnic and linguistic continuity. Nevertheless, from that day to our own, language maintenance in the United States has not been able to look upon organized religion as a dependable source of support.

Basically, the retreat of American religious bodies from the arena of language maintenance is due to much more pervasive factors than a papal encyclical which influenced only Roman rite Catholics at best. By the same token, recent actions of the Ecumenical Council permitting the use of vernaculars in the mass and in other Roman Catholic religious rituals can hardly be expected to materially strengthen language maintenance. The separation of religion from life as a result of secularization, ritualization, and organizational primacy is what is most fundamentally involved in this retreat. Indeed, the forces leading to the de-ethnization of formerly ethnic religions in the United States are quite similar to those that have affected ethnic organizations, ethnic schools, and "Ethnic ideologies." All continue to retain remnants of ethnicity, and these remnants function as bulwarks of ethnicity, and of language maintenance for the first generation which can fill them out and join them together via memories and sentiments, if not via overt behaviors. However, they cannot function as such for subsequent generations, in whose case they serve rather to smooth the path to further de-ethnization and to successively more selective, and more marginal, and reformed ethnicity.

Mass Culture and Language Maintenance. As ethnicity has become increasingly unable to support language maintenance, and as religion has grown increasingly unwilling to do so, the needs, values, and institutions of American society have been pointed out and appealed to on its behalf. Is it not good to know several languages? Is it not important? Does it not contribute to success in life? Does it not contribute to the national welfare? Should it not be publicly supported? These appeals all involve the utilitarianization of behavior and, as a

result, they are, themselves, atraditional and supra-ethnic. That
knowledge must be useful is an American bias of long standing. If
bilingualism can be proved to be both good and useful, then we shall
obviously "do something about it." If language maintenance can be
made out to be concretely useful to the country and to the man in the
street, it may yet be accorded a place of honor within American mass
culture. However, there is a basic antithesis between ethnicity and
mass culture.

        Mass culture produces (or induces) both conformity and
fluidity. On the one hand, it manufactures, popularizes, and dis-
tributes products—including cultural products—for a mass market.
In this sense it is dependent upon standardization of products and
homogenization of tastes and is, therefore, diametrically opposed to
both particularism and traditionalism. However, once having replaced
the old with the new, it establishes a cycle of replacement, both as a
psychological principle and as a factor of the economy. Thus, tastes
and behaviors are not merely widely homogenized. They are also
rendered more fluid, more responsive to fashionability and obsoles-
cence, and therefore more widely homogeneous even with a constantly
changing repertoire or inventory. While social differentiations based
on nativity, religion, age, sex, and class do not disappear—indeed,
they become the best predictors of life style variables (Wilensky
1964)—behavior becomes more widely uniform and more widely
changeable within and across these lines of differentiation, particularly as rich societies become richer and as the impact of abundance
becomes more visible. Thus it is that the conformity-producing and
the change-producing aspects of American mass culture are related
to each other, and are in concerted opposition to the rooted particularism of primordial ethnicity. Mass culture has effectively reduced
the hold of either behavioral or structural ethnicity, in the United
States and elsewhere, as the two have come into greater contact.
This has usually led to the further erosion of ethnically-based language
maintenance among those for whom no other firm basis for language
maintenance has existed. Incongruities between structure and culture
in American life are undeniable. Nevertheless, they may well represent a transitional stage on the road to a more congruent alignment
via mass culture and affluence. Both structural lag and growing accommodation are evident today.

The inroads of mass culture on ethnicity become clear to us, first of all, in connection with our consideration of the transmittal of language maintenance within the family. They become additionally apparent in connection with participationism in the American dream and in metropolitan life. The adolescent period appears to be the juncture at which the impact of mass culture on ethnically-based language maintenance is most clearly felt. In traditional society the problem of adolescent transition is significantly attenuated. There is far greater continuity and identity between the values, behaviors, and skills of the family and those of the larger society. Indeed, there is frequently no marked transition from the one to the other. Youth movements arose in modern Europe primarily as a result of the problems of middle-class youth faced by the barriers of social and economic dislocation in entering an increasingly non-familial type of society. In their case the values, behaviors, and skills required by society seemed particularly unclear or non-continuous with those of the family. This has been much less so for either lower-class or upper-class youth. Until comparatively recently there was little mass culture in Europe which could provide a transitional buffer between the experienced ethnic patterns of the family and the uncertain patterns of adult life outside the family. As a result, adolescent youth movements arose and middle-class adolescence was quite properly viewed as a sociological and political phenomenon rather than a psychological one, as it has long appeared to be in the United States. Here, an adolescent culture has developed, relying completely on mass culture as a non-institutional transition between family patterns of values, behaviors, and skills and those of middle-class society or the oncoming family of procreation. The adolescent of ethnic origin was particularly caught up by American mass culture, for in his case the discontinuity between family and society was most marked.

Indeed, the facts of life were such that in the United States ethnic society itself (to the extent that it existed) became decidedly and increasingly discontinuous with the ethnic family. To whatever extent it could, given the impact of metropolitan life, the family most frequently attempted to cling to ethnic traditions in a primordial, holistic manner. However, ethnic society (the ethnic Church, the ethnic organization, the ethnic school) tended increasingly toward organizational structure, toward ritualized ideology and pragmatic ethnicity, i.e., toward discrete, useful, and organizationally-

dominated expressions of marginal ethnicity. The family's store of
daily, holistic ethnicity actually became largely unnecessary for entry
into ethnic society. At the same time, ethnicity traditionally made no
provision for age homogeneous groups, whether adolescent or other.
Thus the ethnic adolescent came to view his family's values, behaviors,
and skills as doubly malfunctional: malfunctional for a role in ethnic
society and malfunctional for a role in general society. Faced by
conflicting total claims, the usual result was revolt on the one hand
and a headlong pursuit of mass culture on the other. [5]

However, as was true with respect to American urbanization
and American nationalism, mass culture need not be viewed entirely
as a debilitating factor in language maintenance. It also contains
shreds of reinforcement. Adolescents grow up and mass culture becomes less exclusively dominant the more they find a place for themselves in adult society. The ethnic ex-adolescent comes to derive
certain stabilizing satisfactions from marginal ethnicity, particularly
in a society built upon the shifting sands of mass culture. Just as
over-acceptance of ethnicity in childhood led to its over-rejection in
adolescence, so over-rejection, in turn, is frequently followed by
re-evaluation and by ideological and behavioral selectivity. Thus
de-ethnization and re-ethnization follow upon each other, perhaps in
cycles of decreasing intensity, while the ubiquity of mass culture
tends to render both processes meaningful. Of course, the re-
ethnization of the adult second generation (which may actually be more
responsible for that of the third than has usually been appreciated)
is manifestly insufficient for language maintenance on an ethnic base.
Indeed, de-ethnicized language maintenance must, of necessity, be
far different from that which we have emphasized here. It must
derive its impetus from the American Dream and from American
mass culture, instead of directly or indirectly from ethnicity. If
this were to be accomplished, language maintenance not only would
be much changed (and therefore possibly much more attractive to
ethnics), but it might contribute to the reformulation of its new-found
protectors as well.

NOTES

[1] The terms "Britain" and "British" were originally derived
from regionally delimited ethnic and linguistic entities in northern

France and southern England. Their successive semantic metamor-
phoses, culminating in "Great Britain," are themselves products of
centuries of de-ethnization and ideologization.

[2] Only rarely and comparatively lately have there been glim-
mers of recognition that behavioral ethnicity is essentially non-
ideological and, therefore, that it poses no ideological threat to
American nationalism. For this very reason ethnicity has always
been far less of a danger to unity and loyalty in the United States
(whether to American substantive ideology or to American procedural
ideology) than the openly divisive and organizationally active ideologized forces that the United States has always recognized as legitimate:
organized self-interest in economic, religious, and political pursuits.

[3] This is generally overlooked in discussions of the maintenance of the major colonial languages in the United States. These
have benefited not only from priority, numerical resources, concentration of settlement, prestige, and homeland reinforcements, but
from the fact that Americans did not continually identify the great
traditions of these languages with foreign nationalism.

[4] Generational designations are still employed too sweepingly
and generational processes described too grossly in most discussions
of American immigrant phenomena. Each generation passes through
childhood, adolescence, maturity, and old age. It is unlikely that its
ethnic attitudes and behaviors or its relationships with its "older generation" remain invariant during its life-span. Furthermore, the
second generation whose adolescence occurred during the 1920's and
1930's was probably quite different from the second generation whose
adolescence corresponded with the 1950's and 1960's, if only because
their American environments, their ethnic communities, and their
respective "older generations" were much different at these two points
in time. Indeed, whereas native-born children of mixed parentage
classically have been grouped together with the second generation in
census studies (as well as in others), it may now be more appropriate
to group them with the third, in view of the accelerated pace of acculturation. All of these matters remain to be studied.

[5] The less frequent revolt among recent second-generation
adolescents might, therefore, well be attributable to a three-way
lessening of distance between the ethnic family and general society,
between the ethnic family and ethnic society, and between ethnic society and general society.

REFERENCES

Anderson, R. T. , and Anderson, G. Voluntary associations and ur-
    banization: a diachronic analysis. American Journal of
    Sociology, 65 (1959/60), 265-73.
Banks, A. S. , and Textor, R. B. A Cross-Polity Survey (Cambridge,
    M.I.T. Press, 1963).
Benet, F. Sociology uncertain: the ideology of the rural-urban
    continuum. Comparative Studies in Society and History,
    6 (1963), 1-23.
Brault, G. J. Some misconceptions about teaching American ethnic
    children their mother tongue. Modern Language Journal,
    48 (1964), 67-71 (in press).
Bruner, E. M. Primary group experience and the process of accul-
    turation. American Anthropologist, 58 (1956), 605-23.
_____ Urbanization and ethnic identity in North Sumatra. Amer-
    ican Anthropologist, 63 (1961), 508-21.
Deedy, J. G. , Jr. The Catholic press: the why and wherefore, in
    Martin E. Marty, et al. , The Religious Press in America
    (New York, Holt, Rinehart and Winston, 1963).
Fishman, J. A. , and Hayden, R. G. The impact of exposure to ethnic
    mother tongues on foreign language teachers in American
    high schools and colleges, in J. A. Fishman, et al. , Lan-
    guage Loyalty in the United States (New York, Yeshiva Uni-
    versity, 1964), Chapter 13. (Mimeo.) Also in Modern Lan-
    guage Journal, 48 (1964), 262-74.
Geertz, C. The integrative revolution: primordial and civil politics
    in the new states, in his Old Societies and New States (New
    York, Free Press, 1963), pp. 106-57.
Gordon, M. Assimilation in American Life (New York, Oxford Uni-
    versity Press, 1964).
Hansen, M. The Immigrant in American History (Cambridge, Mass. ,
    Harvard University Press, 1946).
Hughes, E. C. Race relations and the sociological imagination.
    American Sociological Review, 28 (1963), 879-90.
Jakobson, R. The beginnings of national self-determination in Europe.
    Review of Politics, 7 (1945), 29-42.
Kohn, H. Genesis of English nationalism. Journal of the History of
    Ideas, 1 (1940), 69-94.
_____ American Nationalism (New York, Collier, 1961) (a).

Kohn, H. The Idea of Nationalism: A Study in Its Origin and Back-
    ground (New York, Macmillan, 1961) (b).
Lerner, D. The Passing of Traditional Society (Glencoe, Ill. , Free
    Press, 1958).
Lewis, O. Urbanization without breakdown: a case study. Scientific
    Monthly, 75 (1952), 31-41.
Mead, Margaret. New Lives for Old (New York, Morrow, 1956).
Orans, M. A tribe in search of a great tradition; the emulation-
    solidarity conflict. Man in India, 39 (1959), 108-14.
Redfield, R. The folk society. American Journal of Sociology, 42
    (1947), 293-308.
_____ The natural history of the folk society. Social Forces,
    31 (1953), 224-28.
Schermerhorn, R. A. Toward a general theory of minority groups.
    Paper presented at the 58th Annual Meeting of the American
    Sociological Association. Los Angeles, August 28, 1963.
Shils, E. The Intellectual between Tradition and Modernity: The
    Indian Situation (= Comparative Studies in Society and His-
    tory, 1961, Supplement I).
Shuval, Judith T. Immigrants on the Threshold (New York, Atherton,
    1963).
Steward, J. H. Levels of socio-cultural integration: an operational
    concept. Southwestern Journal of Anghropology, 7 (1951),
    374-90.
Useem, J. Notes on the sociological study of language. SSRC Items,
    17 (1963), 29-31.
Wilensky, H. L. Mass society and mass culture. American Socio-
    logical Review, 29 (1964), 173-97.

4 | Language Maintenance and Language Shift as a Field of Inquiry: Revisited

The study of language maintenance and language shift is concerned with the relationship between change (or stability) in language usage patterns, on the one hand, and ongoing psychological, cultural or cultural processes, on the other hand, in populations that utilize more than one speech variety for intra-group or for inter-group purposes. That languages (or language varieties) sometimes displace each other, among some speakers, particularly in certain interpersonal or system-wide interactions, has long aroused curiosity and comment.[1] However, it is only in quite recent years that this topic has been recognized as a field of systematic inquiry among professional students of language behavior.[2] It is suggested here that the three major topical subdivisions of this field are: (a) habitual language use at more than one point in time or space; (b) antecedent, concurrent or consequent psychological, social and cultural processes and their relationship to stability or change in habitual language use; and (c) behavior toward language, including directed maintenance or shift efforts. It is the purpose of this paper to discuss each of these three topical subdivisions briefly, to indicate their current stage of development, and to offer suggestions for their further development.

1.0 Habitual Language Use at More Than One Point in Time

The basic datum of the study of language maintenance and language shift is that some demonstrable change has occurred in the pattern of habitual language use.[3] The consequences that are of PRIMARY concern to the student of language maintenance and language shift are NOT interference phenomena per se[4] but, rather, degrees of maintenance or displacement in conjunction with several sources and

domains of variance in language behavior. Thus, the very first re-
quirement of inquiry in this field is a conceptualization of variance in
language behavior whereby language maintenance and language displacement can be accurately and appropriately ascertained. In the
course of their labors linguists, psychologists, anthropologists, and
other specialists have developed a large number of quantitative and
qualitative characterizations of variance in language behavior. By
choosing from among them and adding to them judiciously, it may be
possible to arrive at provocative insights into more sociolinguistic
concerns as well. Whether those aspects of variance in language behavior that have, in the past, been conceived of as qualitative, can
be rendered ultimately commensurable with those that have more
frequently been considered quantitative is a topic to which we will
return, after first considering the two aspects separately.

1.1 Degree of bilingualism

For the student of language maintenance and language shift
the QUANTIFICATION of habitual language use is related to the much
older question of ascertaining DEGREE OF BILINGUALISM. This
question, in turn, has been tackled by a great number of investigators
from different disciplines, each being concerned with a somewhat
different nuance. Linguists have been most concerned with the analysis of bilingualism from the point of view of SWITCHING OR
INTERFERENCE. The measures that they have proposed from
their disciplinary point of departure distinguish between phonetic,
lexical and grammatical proficiency and intactness.[5] At the other
extreme stand educators who are concerned with bilingualism in terms
of TOTAL PERFORMANCE CONTRASTS in very complex contexts
(the school, even the society).[6] Psychologists have usually studied
degrees of bilingualism in terms of speed, automaticity, or habit
strength.[7] Sociologists have relied upon relative frequencies of use
in different settings.[8] Thus, since a great number of different bilingualism scores or quotients are already available, the student of language maintenance and language shift must decide which, if any, are
appropriate to his own concerns. Since the study of this topic cannot
be reduced to or equated with the concerns of any particular discipline
it seems highly likely that a combination or organization of approaches

to the measurement and description of bilingualism will uniquely
characterize the study of language maintenance and language shift.

1.11 The need for a combination of interrelated measures

It would seem that the linguist's interest in itemizing examples of interference and switching introduces an outside criterion into
the study of language maintenance and language shift which may not
at all correspond to that utilized by the speech communities or speech
networks under study. The linguist's distinction between what is
English and what is French and the distinction made by English-
French bilinguals may differ so widely that the linguist's conclusions
about the drift of shift, based upon interference and switch data, may
be seriously in error.

However, even where a linguist is obviously interested only
in a carefully delimited question about the relative frequency of a
particular instance or class of interferences or shifts, it is clear
that it may be far easier to answer this question in some cases than
in others (e.g., it may be easier to answer in connection with encoding than in connection with inner speech; it may be easier to answer
in connection with writing than in connection with speaking; it may be
easier to answer in connection with formal and technical communication than in connection with intimate communication), for the "density,"
stability and clarity of interference and switching varies for the same
individual from occasion to occasion and from situation to situation.
Although interference and switching are lawful behaviors, there are
advanced cases of language shift in which even linguists will be hard
pressed to determine the answer to "which language is being used?"
particularly if a single supra-level answer is required.

Similarly, concern with relative proficiency, relative ease
or automaticity, and relative frequency of language use in a contact
setting are also not necessarily indicative of overall language maintenance or shift. Conclusions based on such measures may be particularly wide of the mark in bilingualism-plus-diglossia settings[9]
in which most speakers use both languages equally well (correctly),
effortlessly and frequently but differ primarily in connection with the
topics, persons, and places (or, more generally, the situations and

situation types or domains) in which these languages are used. Thus, in conclusion, the contribution that the student of language maintenance and language shift can make to the measurement of bilingualism, is precisely his awareness (a) that VARIOUS measures are needed if the social realities of multilingual settings are to be reflected and (b) that these measures CAN BE ORGANIZED in terms of relatively GENERAL VARIANCE CONSIDERATIONS. Of the many approaches to variance in language use that are possible the following have greatest appeal to the present writer:

a. MEDIA VARIANCE: WRITTEN, READ and SPOKEN language. Degree of maintenance and shift may be quite different in these very different media. [10] Where literacy has been attained prior to interaction with an "other tongue," reading or writing in the mother tongue may resist shift longer than speaking. Where literacy is attained subsequent to (or as a result of) such interaction the reverse may hold true (23). More generally, the linguist's disinclination to be concerned too with the written language is a luxury that cannot be afforded in the study of language maintenance and language shift, where the contrasts involved are so frequently between languages that vary greatly in the extent to which they have literary or other "higher" functions for the speech networks under study.

b. OVERTNESS VARIANCE: Degree of maintenance and shift may be quite different in connection with INNER SPEECH (in which ego is both source and target), COMPREHENSION (decoding, in which ego is the target), and PRODUCTION (encoding, in which ego is the source). Where language shift is unconscious or resisted, inner speech may be most resistant to interference, switching and disuse of the mother tongue. Where language shift is conscious and desired, this may less frequently be the case (24).

c. DOMAIN VARIANCE, which will be discussed separately in section 1.2, immediately below.

1.2 Location of bilingualism: The domains of language behavior

The QUALITATIVE aspects of bilingualism are most easily illustrated in connection with the LOCATION of language maintenance

and language shift in terms of DOMAINS of language behavior.[11]
What is of concern to us here is the most parsimonious and fruitful
designation of the societally or institutionally clusterable occasions
in which one language (variant, dialect, style, etc.) is habitually employed rather than (or in addition to) another. Thus far this topic
has been of systematic concern only to a very few linguists, anthropologists and sociologists. Their interest has not yet led to the
construction of data collection and organization procedures of wide
applicability in the study of multilingual speech networks that appear
to be very different one from another. One of the major difficulties
in this connection is that there is little consensus concerning the
definition and classification of the domains of language behavior in
bilingual communities.[12]

   a. More than thirty years ago Schmidt-Rohr differentiated
nine domains of language (31), namely: the family, the playground
and the street, the school (subdivided into language of instruction,
subject of instruction, and language of recess and entertainment),
the church, literature, the press, the military, the courts, and the
governmental bureaucracy ("Verwaltung").[13] Schmidt-Rohr also
deserves recognition in connection with his claim that each domain
had to be studied separately and a total inter-domain configuration
presented if various "types" of bilingualism were to be differentiated
and understood. Some subsequent students of language maintenance
and language shift have required a more differentiated set of domains
(17). Others have been satisfied with a much more abbreviated set.[14]
Still others have required greater differentiation within particular domains. Domains such as these, regardless of their particular designation or number are oriented toward institutional contexts or toward
socioecological co-occurrences. They attempt to designate the major
clusters of interaction situations that occur in particular multilingual
settings. Domains such as these help us understand that language
choice (41) and topic (16b), appropriate though they may be for analyses of individual language behavior at the level of face-to-face encounters, are themselves related to widespread socio-cultural regularities.
Language choices, cumulated over many individuals and many choice
instances, become transformed into the processes of language maintenance or language shift. If many individuals (or sub-groups) tend to
handle topic x in language X, this may well be because this topic pertains to a domain in which that language is "dominant" for their society

or for their sub-group. Certainly it is a far different social interaction when topic x is discussed in language Y <u>although it pertains to a domain in which language X is dominant</u>, than when the same topic is discussed by the same interlocutors in the language most commonly employed in that domain. By recognizing the existence of domains it becomes possible to contrast the language of topics for particular sub-populations with the language of domains for larger populations.

b. The appropriate designation and definition of domains of language behavior obviously calls for considerable insight into the socio-cultural dynamics of particular multilingual settings at particular periods in their history. Schmidt-Rohr's domains reflect multilingual settings in which a large number of socio-ecological co-occurrences, even those that pertain to governmental functions, are theoretically permissible to all of the languages present, or, at least, to multilingual settings in which such permissiveness is sought by a sizable number of interested parties. Quite different domains might be appropriate if one were to study habitual language use among children in these very same settings. Certainly, immigrant-host contexts, in which only the language of the host society is recognized for governmental functions, would require other and perhaps fewer domains, particularly if younger generations constantly leave the immigrant society and enter the host society. Finally, the domains of language behavior may differ from setting to setting not only in terms of number and designation but also in terms of level.[15] One approach to the interrelationship between domains of language behavior defined at a societal-institutional level and domains defined at a socio-psychological level (the latter being similar to the situational analyses discussed earlier) will be presented in our discussion of the <u>dominance configuration</u>, below.

c. The "governmental administration" domain is a social nexus which brings people together primarily for a certain <u>cluster of purposes</u>. Furthermore, it brings them together <u>primarily</u> within a certain set of status, role and enviornment co-occurrences. Although it is possible for them to communicate about many things, given these purposes and surroundings, the topical variety is actually quite small in certain media (e.g., written communication) and at certain formality levels (e.g., formal communication), and is noticeably skewed in the direction of <u>domain purpose</u> in almost all domains. Thus, a

domain is a socio-cultural construct abstracted from topics of communication, relationships and interactions between communicators
and locales of communication in accord with the institutions of a society and the spheres of activity of a culture in such a way that individual behavior and social patterns can be distinguished from each
other and yet related to each other.[16] The domain is a higher order
of abstraction or summarization which arrives out of a consideration
of the socio-cultural patterning which surrounds language choices
that transpire at the intra-psychic and socio-psychological levels.
Of the many factors contributing to and subsumed under the domain
concept some are more important and more accessible to careful
measurement than others. One of these, topic, will only be referred
to in passing in this paper (however, see 25). Another, role-relations,
will be discussed in some detail.

       d. In many studies of multilingual behavior the family domain
has proved to be a very crucial one. Multilingualism often begins in
the family and depends upon it for encouragement if not for protection.
In other cases, multilingualism withdraws into the family domain after
it has been displaced from other domains in which it was previously
encountered. Little wonder then that many investigators, beginning
with Braunshausen several years ago (6), have differentiated within
the family domain in terms of "speakers." However, two different
approaches have been followed in connection with such differentiation.
Braunshausen (and, much more recently, Mackey, 66) have merely
specified separate family "members": father, mother, children,
domestic, governess and tutor, etc. Gross, on the other hand, has
specified dyads within the family (31): grandfather to grandmother,
grandmother to grandfather, grandfather to father, grandmother to
father, grandfather to mother, grandmother to mother, grandfather
to child, grandmother to child, father to mother, mother to father,
etc. The difference between these two approaches is quite considerable. Not only does the second approach recognize that interacting
members of a family (as well as the participants in most other domains
of language behavior) are listeners as well as speakers (i.e., that
there may be a distinction between multilingual comprehension and
multilingual production), but it also recognizes that their language
behavior may be more than merely a matter of individual preference
or facility but also a matter of role-relations.[17] In certain societies
particular behaviors (including language behaviors) are expected (if
not required) of particular individuals vis-à-vis each other. Whether

role-relations are fully reducible to situational styles for the purpose
of describing habitual language choice in particular multilingual settings is a matter for future empirical determination.

     The family domain is hardly unique with respect to its dif-
ferentiability into role-relations. Each domain can be differentiated
into role-relations that are specifically crucial or typical of it in particular societies at particular times. The religious domain (in those
societies where religion can be differentiated from folkways more
generally) may reveal such role-relations as cleric-cleric, cleric-
parishioner, parishioner-cleric, and parishioner-parishioner. Similarly, pupil-teacher, buyer-seller, employer-employee, judge-
petitioner, all refer to specific role-relations in other domains. It
would certainly seem desirable to describe and analyze language use
or language choice in a particular multilingual setting in terms of the
crucial role-relations within the specific domains considered to be
most revealing for that setting. The distinction between own-group-
interlocutor and other-group-interlocutor may also be provided for
in this way.[18] Language usage variance <u>within</u> role-relations, in
turn, may then be further analyzed in conjunction with specific topics
or locales, as implied earlier. Thus, the domain level of analysis
exists within a hierarchy of analytic levels, each of which provides
partial information concerning the societally patterned diversification
or specialization of language varieties that exist within the repertoire
of a speech community.

     As an example of the empirical fruitfulness of the domain
concept we may briefly examine the findings of a study of 34 children
of Puerto Rican background who lived in the "downtown" area of Jersey
City, an area in which Puerto Rican bilingualism has been intensively
studied.[19] The children, whose ages ranged from 6 to 12 and who
were evenly divided by sex, attended a parochial school within the
neighborhood. All children had been born on the mainland. The children were interviewed individually for data collection purposes and
their production tape recorded. The pupils were presented with a
modified version of a word naming task developed by Cooper[20] for
use with adults. In the modified word naming task, subjects were
asked to name, within 45-second periods, as many objects as could
be found in each of the four settings: kitchen, school, church, and
neighborhood, to represent the domains of family, education, religion,
and neighborhood, respectively. The children named objects for all

four domains in one language and then named objects for all four
domains in other language. Half the children first named the objects
in English and the other half first named them in Spanish.

An analysis of variance of the children's word naming scores
indicated significant effects for age, domain, language, and for the
interactions of language with domain, and of age with domain. The
significant effect encountered for age indicates that word naming
fluency (the number of words produced when both languages are combined) was related to the age of the respondents, the older children
producing more words. This suggests a developmental trend of increasing proficiency (in terms of productivity).

The main effect for domain, on the other hand, indicates
that when words given in both languages are combined, a greater number of words were produced in some domains than in others. The
mean scores for domains were subjected to a Newman-Keuls test of
significance. The results showed overall language fluency for the
domains of education, family and neighborhood to be the same and
superior to that for the domain of religion. Thus, the first three contexts appeared to be equally salient for children as stimuli for the
production of discrete lexical items, whereas the religious domain
proved to be a less salient stimulus.

The significant effect for language indicates that, on the
average, more words were produced in one language than in the other
when all domains are combined, with the greater number of words
being produced in English. However, the significant language by
domain interaction indicates that relative proficiency varied as a
function of domain. This variation can be seen in Table 1, which
presents the average number of words named in each language and
domain. It can be observed that English was favored over Spanish
for the domains of neighborhood, religion, and education. However,
with respect to the domain of family, no difference between the English and Spanish averages was observed. (The significant age by
domain interaction is due to the fact that the older children are more
superior to the younger ones in the education domain than in any of
the others.)

The validity of these findings was attested to both by participant observation, self report and other (as well as less structured)

Table 1.   Mean Number of Words Named
by Language and Domain

Domain

Language	Education	Religion	Neighborhood	Family
English	10.5**	7.7**	9.6**	9.0
Spanish	7.8	6.5	8.0	9.0

**p < .01 for difference between pairs of English and Spanish means.

speech production data. Obviously, were the trends here revealed
to continue one would expect the increased displacement of Spanish
from all but the home domain, and, therefore, from all but the role-
relationships, topics and locales must intimately relate to that domain. Comparisons with similar data obtained from the parents of
these children would reveal whether the generations are shifting in
the same direction and at the same rate. Phonological and semantic
analyses of the actual word-naming data produced by subjects might
well be of interest to linguists[21] and to psychologists[22] pursuing other
aspects of the entire constellation of language maintenance and language shift.

The above considerations are sufficient to indicate that the
student of language maintenance and language shift obviously requires
a highly complex sort of evidence on habitual language use. Indeed,
we can barely begin to approximate data collection and analysis in
accord with all possible interactions between the several parameters
and dimensions of language use mentioned thus far. However, only
when our data will correspond more closely to complex models of
language use will it become possible for students of language maintenance and language shift to derive valid and refined dominance con
figurations capable of representing the direction or drift of changes
in bilingual usage over time.

1.21 The domains of language behavior and the compound-
coordinate distinction

If the concept of domains of language behavior proves to be
a fruitful and manageable one (given future empirical attempts to

render it more rigorously useful) it may also yield beneficial results in connection with other areas of research on bilingualism, e. g. , in connection with the distinction between COORDINATE and COMPOUND bilingualism (16, p. 140). The latter distinction arose out of an awareness (mentioned by several investigators over the years) that there are "at least two major types of bilingual functioning, " [23] one (the compound type) being "characteristic of bilingualism acquired by a child who grows up in a home where two languages are spoken more or less interchangeably by the same people and in the same situations" and the other (the coordinate) being "typical of the 'true' bilingual, who has learned to speak one language with his parents, for example, and the other language in school and at work. The total situations, both external and emotional, and the total behaviors occurring when one language is being used will differ from those occurring with the other." [24] From our previous discussion of domains of language behavior it is clear that these two types of bilingual functioning[25] have been distinguished on the bases of some awareness, however rudimentary, that BILINGUALS VARY WITH RESPECT TO THE NUMBER AND OVERLAP OF DOMAINS IN WHICH THEY HABITUALLY EMPLOY EACH OF THEIR LANGUAGES. However, this is true not only initially, in the acquisition of bilingualism (with which the compound-coordinate distinction is primarily concerned) but also subsequently, THROUGHOUT life. Initially coordinate bilinguals may become exposed to widespread bilingualism in which both languages are used rather freely over a larger set of overlapping domains (Figure 1). Similarly, compound bilinguals may become exposed to a more restrictive or dichotomized enviornment in which each language is assigned to very specific and non-overlapping domains.

Going one step further it appears that the domain concept may facilitate a number of worthwhile contributions to the understanding of the compound-coordinate distinction in conjunction with language maintenance and language shift per se. Thus, domain analysis may help organize and clarify the previously unstructured awareness that language maintenance and language shift proceed quite unevenly across the several sources and domains of variance in habitual language use. Certain domains may well appear to be more maintenance-prone than others (e. g. , the family domain in comparison to the occupational domain) across all multilingual settings characterized by urbanization and economic development, regardless of whether

Figure 1. Initial Type of Bilingual Acquisition
and Subsequent Domain Overlap Type

BILINGUAL ACQUISITION TYPE	DOMAIN OVERLAP TYPE	
	Overlapping Domains	Non-Overlapping Domains
Compound ("Interdependent" or fused)	Transitional bilingualism: the older second generation. The "high school French" tourist who remains abroad somewhat longer than he expected to.	"Cultural bilingualism": the bilingualism of the "indirect method" classroom whereby one language is learned through another but retained in separate domains.
Coordinate ("Independent")	Widespread bilingualism without social cleavage: the purported goal of "responsible" French-Canadians. The "direct method" classroom.	One sided bilingualism or marked and stable social distinctions, such that only one group in a contact situation is bilingual or such that only particular domains are open or appropriate to particular languages.

Figure 2.   Type of Bilingual Functioning and Domain Overlap
During Successive Stages of Immigrant Acculturation

BILINGUAL FUNCTIONING TYPE	DOMAIN OVERLAP TYPE	
	Overlapping Domains	Non-Overlapping Domains
Compound ("Interdependent" or fused)	2. Second Stage: More immigrants know more English and therefore can speak to each other either in mother tongue or in English (still mediated by the mother tongue) in several domains of behavior. Increased interference.	1. Initial Stage: The immigrant learns English via his mother tongue. English is used only in those few domains (work sphere, governmental sphere) in which mother tongue cannot be used. Minimal interference. Only a few immigrants know a little English.
Coordinate ("Independent")	3. Third Stage: The languages function independently of each other. The number of bilinguals is at its maximum. Domain overlap is at its maximum. The second generation during childhood. Stabilized interference.	4. Fourth Stage: English has displaced the mother tongue from all but the most private or restricted domains. Interference declines. In most cases both languages function independently; in others the mother tongue is mediated by English (reverse direction of Stage 1, but same type).

immigrant-host or co-indigenous populations are involved. Under
the impact of these same socio-cultural processes other domains
(e. g. , religion) may be found to be strongly maintenance oriented
during the early stages of interaction and strongly shift oriented once
an authoritative decision is reached that their organizational base
can be better secured via shift. Certain interactions between domains
and other sources of variance may remain protective of contextually
"disadvantaged" languages (e. g. , family domain: internal speech,
husband-wife role relations), even when language shift has advanced
so far that a given domain as such has been engulfed. On the other
hand, if a strict domain separation becomes institutionalized such
that each language is associated with a number of important but distinct domains, bilingualism may well become both universal and stabilized even though an entire population consists of bilinguals interacting with other bilinguals. Finally, in conjunction with language
maintenance and language shift among American immigrant groups,
the interaction between domain analysis and the compound-coordinate
distinction may prove to be particularly edifying. Thus, as suggested
by Figure 2, most late 19th and early 20th century immigrants to
America from Eastern and Southern Europe began as compound bilinguals, with English assigned to quite specific and restricted domains.
With the passage of time (involving increased interaction with English-
speaking Americans, social mobility, and acculturation with respect
to other-than-language behaviors as well) their bilingualism became
characterized, first, by far greater domain overlap (and by far greater
interference) and then by progressively greater coordinate functioning.
Finally, language displacement advanced so far that the mother tongue
remained only in a few restricted and non-overlapping domains. Indeed, in some cases, compound bilingualism once more became the
rule, except that the ethnic mother tongue came to be utilized via
English rather than vice-versa, as was the case in early immigrant
days. Thus the domain concept may help place the compound-
coordinate distinction in sociocultural perspective, in much the same
way as it may well serve the entire area of language maintenance and
language shift. [26]

1.3 The dominance configuration

Sections 1.1 and 1.2, above, clearly indicate the need for
basic tools of a complex and sophisticated sort. Precise measurement

of DEGREE OF MAINTENANCE OR DISPLACEMENT will be possible
only when more diversified measures of degree of bilingualism (including attention to media and overtness variance) are at hand. Precise
measurement of DOMAINS OF MAINTENANCE OR DISPLACEMENT
will be possible only after concerted attention is given to the construction of instruments that are based upon a careful consideration of the
various domains of language behavior (and the role-relations, topics
and locales—these being the three components of situational variation[27])
mentioned in a scattered international literature. The availability of
such instruments will also facilitate work in several related fields of
study, such as the success of intensive second-language learning programs, accurate current language facility censuses, applied "language
reinforcement" efforts, etc. Given such instruments, the inter-
correlations between the several components of variance in degree
of bilingualism will become amenable to study, as will the variation
of such inter-correlations with age or with varying degrees of language ability, opportunity and motivation. The relationship between
maintenance or displacement in the various domains of language will
also become subject to scrutiny.[28] Speculation concerning the relationship between shifts in degree and direction of bilingualism and
shifts in the domains of bilingualism will finally become subject to
investigation.[29] Finally, out of all of the foregoing, it will become
possible to speak much more meaningfully about the DOMINANCE
CONFIGURATIONS of bilinguals and of changes in these configurations
in language maintenance-language shift contexts.[30]

1.31 Earlier use of the concept

Weinreich reintroduced the concept of DOMINANCE CONFIG-
URATION as a result of his well founded dissatisfaction with the current practice of "tagging two languages in contact as respectively
'upper' and 'lower' at any cost" (88, p. 98). He correctly observes
that "the difficulty of ranking two mother-tongue groups in hierarchi-
cal order is aggravated by the need to rank functions of the languages
as well," but adds, in conclusion, that "it is therefore expedient,
perhaps, to restrict the term DOMINANT to languages in contact situations where the difference in mother-tongues is coupled with a significant difference in social status" (88, p. 98). For the purposes of
studying language maintenance or language shift, this last recommendation would seem to be questionable on two counts. On the one hand

it jumps from the INDIVIDUAL to the GROUP OR SOCIETAL level of
analysis, whereas both the study of bilingualism and of language
maintenance or language shift frequently require a determination of
language dominance in the individual per se. On the other hand, it
jumps from LANGUAGE to NON-LANGUAGE criteria, whereas both
of the aforementioned levels of inquiry usually require a determination of language dominance (or of change in dominance) based on language use alone.[31]

      For our purposes the domainance configuration constitutes
an attempt to represent the direction or status of language maintenance or language shift in such a way as to integrate a multiplicity of
considerations that are usually considered separately. "The dominance of a language for a bilingual individual can only be interpreted
as a specific configuration or syndrome of characteristics on which
the language is rated" (88, p. 79). Weinreich proposes seven characteristics on the basis of which dominance configurations may be
constituted (in conjunction with the study of language interference):
(a) relative proficiency, (b) mode of use,[32] (c) order of learning,
(d) emotional involvement, (e) usefulness in communication, (f) function in social advance, and (g) literary-cultural values.[33] From the
point of view of coordinated investigation into language maintenance
or language shift several of these characteristics would seem to be
of uncertain value. Thus, item (a) above would seem to be further
analyzable into several components, as has already been suggested
in sections 1.1 and 1.2. Characteristic (b) certainly appears to be
important and has already been referred to in section 1.1. Item (c)
as well as items (e) through (g) appear to be antecedents, concurrents
or consequences of language contact situations rather than aspects of
degree or direction of bilingualism per se. As such they deserve to
be considered in the second and third topical subdivisions of the study
of language maintenance or language shift (see sections 2 and 3, below) rather than entered into the dominance configuration per se.
Characteristic (d) is also of this latter variety and may properly be
conceived of as the resultant of many experiences and values including
those pertaining to characteristics (e) through (g) above. Thus, although global determinations of "the linguistic dominance of bilinguals," such as Lambert's (59), may well be both premature and insufficiently revealing from the point of view of the study of language
maintenance and language shift, the particular configuration pattern suggested by Weinreich also would seem to require substantial revision.

1.32 Some preliminary suggestions

Tables 2a and 2b are primarily intended to serve as possible
presentation formats for dominance configurations based upon several
DOMAINS and SOURCES OF VARIANCE in language behavior mentioned earlier in this discussion. The types of language use data
favored by linguists, psychologists and educators have been set aside
temporarily in favor of grosser "frequency of use" data. However,
of primary interest at this time are the suggested parameters rather
than the rough data presented. An inspection of this Table reveals
several general characteristics of the dominance configurations:
(a) the dominance configuration summarizes multilingual language
use data for a particular population studied at two points in time or
space; (b) a complete cross-tabulation of all theoretically possible
sources and domains of variance in language behavior does not actually obtain. In some instances, logical difficulties arise. In others,
occurrences are logically possible but either necessarily rare or rare
for the particular populations under study; (c) each cell in the dominance configuration summarizes detailed process data pertaining to
the particular role-relations (parent-child, teacher-pupil, etc.) pertinent to it and the situations, network types (open and closed) and/or
transaction types (interactional and personal) encountered;[34] (d) some
of the domains utilized do not correspond to those listed in section
1.2, above, nor are all of the domains previously listed utilized here.
This should sensitize us further to the probability that no invariant set
of domains can prove to be maximally revealing, notwithstanding the
efforts expended in pursuit of such a set (14, 51, 66, 80); (e) an exhaustive analysis of the data of dominance configurations may well
require sophisticated pattern analysis or other mathematical techniques which do not necessarily assume equal weight and simple addi-
tivity for each entry in each cell; (f) a much more refined presentation of language maintenance or language shift becomes possible than
that which is provided by means of mother tongue census statistics
(54, 72).[35] Word naming scores, self-ratings of frequency of usage,
observed occurrences of various phonological, lexical, or grammatical realizations, all of these and many other types of scores or indices can be utilized for dominance configuration analysis of speech
communities or networks. The need to summarize and group language
usage data necessarily leads to some loss of refinement when proceeding from specific instances of actual speech in face to face interaction

Table 2a

Intra-group Yiddish-English Maintenance and Shift in the United States: 1940-70
Summary Comparisons for Immigrant Generation "Secularists" Arriving
Prior to World War I ("Dummy Table" for Dominance Configuration)

Sources of Variance		Family role-rels.			Neighb. role-rels.		Work role-rels.			Jew Rel. / Cult. role-rels.	
Media	Overtness	1	2	3	1	2	1	2	3	1	2
Speaking	Production Comprehension Inner										
Reading	Production Comprehension										
Writing	Production Comprehension										

Table 2b
Part of "Dummy Table" in Greater Detail

Media	Overtness	Domains	Role-Relations	Summary Ratings 1940	Summary Ratings 1970
Speaking	Production	Family	Husband-Wife	Y	Y
			Parent-Child	Y	E
			Grandparent-Grandchild	-	E
			Other: same generation	Y	Y
			Other: younger generation	E	E
		Neighborhood	Friends	Y	E
			Acquaintances	Y	E
		Work	Employer-Employer	E	E
			Employer-Employee	E	E
			Employee-Employee	E	E
		Jewish Rel. / Cult.	Supporter-Writer, Teacher, etc.	Y	Y
			Supporter-Supporter	Y	Y

to grouped or categorized data. However, such summarization or simplification is an inevitable aspect of the scientific process of discovering meaning in continuous multivariate data by attending to differential relationships, central tendencies, relative variabilities and other similar characterizations. Moreover, the ultimate "summary" nature of the dominance configuration and the further possibilities of collapsing domains according to higher order psychological or sociological similarities (e.g., "public" vs. "private" language use) obviates the proliferation of atomized findings.[36]

All in all, the dominance configuration represents a great and difficult challenge to students of bilingualism and of language maintenance or language shift. It is possible that once this challenge is recognized, serious problems of configurational analysis will also arise, as they have in other substantive areas requiring attention to patterns of quantitative or qualitative measures.[37] However, it is unnecessary to prejudge this matter. It does seem fitting to conclude that the dominance configuration—if it is to have maximal analytic value—might best be limited to those aspects of DEGREE OF BILINGUALISM and of LOCATION OF BILINGUALISM which further inquiry may reveal to be of greatest relative IMPORTANCE and INDEPENDENCE. Initial attention to the study of spoken production (as suggested by Table 2b) has already demonstrated the rich yield that a self-imposed limitation of this kind can produce in appropriately selected speech communities.[38]

2.0 Psychological, Social and Cultural Processes Related to Stability or Change in Habitual Language Use

The second major topical subdivision of the study of language maintenance and language shift deals with the psychological, social and cultural processes associated with habitual language use. Under certain conditions of interaction the relative incidence and configuration of bilingualism stabilizes and remains fairly constant over time within various bilingual-diglossic speech communities. However, under other circumstances one variety or another may continue to gain speakers to the end that bilingualism initially increases and then decreases as the variety in question becomes the predominant language of the old and the mother tongue of the young. The second

subdivision of the study of language maintenance and language shift
seeks to determine the processes that distinguish between such obviously different conditions of interaction as well as the processes
whereby the one condition is transformed into the other. The processes pertaining to this topical subdivision may be conceived of either
as antecedent, concurrent (contextual), or consequent variables, depending on the design of particular studies. Their major common
characteristic is that they are primarily OUTSIDE of language per se.

      Although it is currently impossible to specify in advance an
invariant list of psychological, social and cultural processes or variables that might be of universal importance for an understanding of
language maintenance or language shift, it may nevertheless be instructive to note those that have been mentioned by scholars who have
devoted greatest attention to this topic thus far. Weinreich discusses
the following ten "socio-cultural divisions" in some detail: geographic
obstacles or facilitations,[39] indigenousness, cultural or ethnic group
membership, religion, race, sex, age, social status, occupation,
and rural vs. urban residence (88, pp. 89-97). Haugen also lists
many of these same categories and, in addition, family, neighborhood, political affiliation (including nationality and citizenship) and
education (38, p. 91). Mackey's list of external functions specifies
several "variables" that may presumably modify language use: dura-
tion of contact, frequency of contact and "pressures" of contact
derived from "economic, administrative, cultural, political, military,
historical, religious or demographic" sources (66, pp. 61-63).

      Underlying (or overlying) psychological, social and cultural
PROCESSES are less fully listed or discussed by any of the above
scholars than are demographic GROUPINGS or instiutional CATEGO-
RIES per se. The result of such reliance on disjointed categories has
been that no broadly applicable or dynamic theories, concepts or findings have been derived from most earlier studies. Indeed, the study
of language maintenance and language shift currently lacks either a
close relationship to theories of sociocultural change more generally
or to theories of intergroup relations more specifically. Just as an
understanding of social-behavior-through-language must depend upon
a general theory of society so the understanding of language maintenance or language shift must depend on a theory of socioculture contact and sociocultural change.

2.1 The paucity of cross-cultural and diachronic regularities

It would seem that since we are concerned with the possibility of stability or change in language behavior on the one hand, we
must be equally concerned with all of the forces contributing to stability or to change in societal behavior more generally, on the other.
Thus the selection of psychological, social and cultural variables for
the study of language maintenance and language shift may well be
guided not only by impressions of what seem to be the most relevant
processes in a particular contact situation but also by more general
theories of personal, social, and cultural change. This is not to
imply that all forces leading to CHANGE in other-than-language behaviors NECESSARILY also lead to language SHIFT. Indeed, whether
or not this is the case (or, put more precisely, a determination of
the circumstances under which language and non-language behaviors
change concurrently, consecutively or independently) constitutes one
of the major intellectual challenges currently facing this field of inquiry. If this challenge is to be met, it will be necessary for the
study of language maintenance and language shift to be conducted
within the context of studies of intergroup contacts that attend to
important other-than-language processes as well: urbanization (rural-
ization), industrialization (or its abandonment), nationalism (or de-
ethnization), nativism (or cosmopolitanization), religious revitalization (or secularization), etc.

Our current state of generalizeable knowledge in the area of
language maintenance and language shift is insufficient for the positing of relationships of cross-cultural or diachronic validity. Indeed,
many of the most popularly cited factors purportedly influencing maintenance and shift have actually been found to "cut both ways" in different contexts or to have no general significance when viewed in broader
perspective. Thus, Kloss illustrates that no uniform consequences
for language maintenance or language shift are derivable from (a) absence or presence of higher education in the mother tongue,[40]
(b) larger or smaller numbers of speakers, (c) greater or lesser
between-group similarity, and (d) positive or hostile attitudes of the
majority toward the minority (55, pp. 9-13). The presence of so
many ambivalent factors is a clear indication that complex interactions between partially contributory factors (rather than a single
overpowering factor) must frequently be involved and that a typology

of CONTACT SITUATIONS (as well as a theory of sociocultural
change) may be required before greater regularity among such factors can be recognized.

Although debunking represents a rather primitive level of
scientific development it may be a necessary stage on the path to
greater maturity. Although we cannot currently formulate universally applicable regularities in our area of inquiry we can indicate
that several earlier attempts along these lines fall somewhat short
of their mark.

2.11 A few questionable generalizations

a. LANGUAGE MAINTENANCE IS A FUNCTION OF INTACT-
NESS OF GROUP MEMBERSHIP OR GROUP LOYALTY, PARTICU-
LARLY OF SUCH IDEOLOGIZED EXPRESSIONS OF GROUP LOYALTY
AS NATIONALISM. Among the evidence pointing to the need for refining or justifying this view is that which reveals that the Guayqueries
of Venezuela preserved their groupness by preserving their property
relations while giving up their language and religion (45); that lower
caste groups in India pursue Sanskritization (emulation) rather than
solidarity as a means of GROUP mobility (73); that "the Raetoromans,
like the Italian Swiss, cultivate the fullest possible loyalty to their
language without aspiring to such nationalistic goals as political independence" (88, p. 100); that the "Yiddishist" movement in Eastern
Europe before and after World War I similarly concentrated on a language program rather than on political organization (88, p. 100);
that second and third generation Americans frequently maintain "cultural (refinement) bilingualism" after ethnic group loyalty disappears
at any functional level and, vice versa, that vestiges of behavioral
ethnicity often remain generations after language facility has been
lost (20); that many auslands-deutsche maintained their self identification as Germans in the midst of Polish or Ukranian majorities, long
after completely giving up their German mother tongue (57); that
language loyalty is low in many newly developing and highly nationalistic African states (8, 85);[41] etc. Thus, it would seem, on the one
hand, that language maintenance has continued under various and
highly different forms of group membership, some of which have involved significant changes in traditional social relationships and in
pre-established role-relations. On the other hand, it appears that

group loyalty can be similarly (if not more) ubiquitous, continuing
both with and without language maintenance. The American readiness
to use language as an index of acculturation may, in itself, be quite
culture bound (78). Hymes' observation that "some languages do not
enjoy the status of a symbol crucial to group identity" (47, p. 30) and
Weinreich's observation that "the connection (between language maintenance and group maintenance) is thus at least flexible and cannot be
taken entirely for granted" (88, p. 100) really represent important intellectual challenges to the study of language maintenance and language
shift. We very much need a more refined understanding of the circumstances under which BEHAVIORS TOWARD LANGUAGE and BEHAVIORS
TOWARD THE GROUP are related to each other in PARTICULAR ways.
We can recognize today that the pre-World War II views of many German students of language maintenance and language shift (as to whether
language and language consciousness create—or are derived from—
race, peoplehood and consciousness of kind) were too simplified and
too colored by then current political considerations. However, the
fact remains that the relationship between language-saliency and
group-saliency is almost as speculative today as it was at that time,
although it seems clear that a language undergoing massive displacement may be retained most fully by increasingly atypical and self-
consciously mobilized populations as displacement progresses. Nevertheless, it is also clear that ideologies normally mobilize only a
relatively younger, more active and, perhaps, more alienated or dislocated segment of any large population. Language maintenance may
depend <u>most</u> on nationalist ideologies in populations whose lives have
otherwise been <u>greatly dislocated</u> and it may also depend <u>least</u> on
such ideologies in those populations that have best preserved their
total social context against the winds of change.[42]

b. URBAN DWELLERS ARE MORE INCLINED TO SHIFT;
RURAL DWELLERS (MORE CONSERVATIVE AND MORE ISOLATED)
ARE LESS INCLINED TO SHIFT. This is one of the most reasonable
and best documented generalizations in the study of language maintenance and language shift.[43] Nevertheless, it runs counter to the first
mentioned generalization, above, in that CONSCIOUSNESS of ethnicity
and the ESPOUSAL of nationalism have been primarily urban phenomena. Language revival movements, language loyalty movements,
and organized language maintenance efforts have commonly originated
and had their greatest impact in the cities. Intelligentsia and middle

class elements, both of which are almost exclusively urban, have
frequently been the prime movers of language maintenance in those
societies which possess both rural and urban populations, Indeed,
urban groups have been "prime movers," organizers or mobilizers
more generally, that is in connection with other than language matters
as well as in connection with language behavior and behavior toward
language. Thus, whereas small rural groups may have been more
successful in establishing relatively self-contained communities
which reveal language maintenance through the preservation of traditional interaction patterns and social structures, urban groups,
exposed to interaction in more fragmented and specialized networks,
may reveal more conscious, organized and novel attempts to preserve or revive or change their traditional language. The urban environment does facilitate change. However, the DIRECTION OF
SUCH CHANGE has not always favored language shift at the expense
of language maintenance. WHEN it has favored the one and WHEN
the other (and when urban-inspired language shift has actually signi-
fied a return to a languishing ancestral language), represents a
further challenge to this field of study.[44]

c. THE MORE PRESTIGEFUL LANGUAGE DISPLACES
THE LESS PRESTIGEFUL LANGUAGE. Our earlier discussions of
SOURCES OF VARIANCE and DOMAINS OF LANGUAGE BEHAVIOR
may have prepared us for the realization that language prestige is
not a unit trait or tag that can be associated with a given language
under all circumstances. Indeed, our earlier discussions were necessary precisely BECAUSE the prestige of languages can vary noticeably
from one context to another for the same interlocutors, as well as
from one speech network to another within the same speech community.
It is for this very reason that Weinreich recommends that "as a technical term...'prestige' had better be restricted to a language's value
in social advance," (88, p. 79). However, even this limitation does
not make the concept "prestige" any more useful for research purposes since social advance itself is relative to various reference
groups. Advance in family and neighborhood standing may require
a different language than advance in occupational or governmental
standing. The fact that an overall hierarchy of reference groups may
exist does not mean that the top-most reference group will be dominant in each face-to-face situation.[45]

It may be precisely because "prestige" obscures so many different considerations and has been used with so many different connotations[46] that the relationship between prestige data and language maintenance or language shift data has been rather more uneven than might otherwise be expected. Thus, whereas Hall claims that "It is hard to think of any modern instance in which an entire speech community is under pressure to learn a sub-standard variety of a second language" (34, p. 19), it is really not very hard to do so: A Low German dialect displaced Lithuanian in East Prussia before World War I, although many Lithuanians there were highly conversant with Standard German (28, p. 61). Unstandardized Schwyzertütsch is replacing Romansh, although several generations of Raetoromans have known Standard German as well (87, pp. 284-286). Standard German completely displaced Danish in a trilingual area of Schleswig, but it was itself then increasingly displaced by the local Low German dialect (83). Obviously, Schwyzertütsch maintains itself quite successfully in competition with Standard German, Landsmaal achieved considerable success (into the 1930's, at the very least) in competition with Dano-Norwegian; Yiddish won speakers and adherants among Russified, Polonized and Germanized Jewish elites in Eastern Europe before and after World War I; Castillian speaking workers settling in more industrialized Catalonia tend to shift to Catalan, etc. Indeed, the entire process whereby a few classical languages were displaced by "lowly" vernaculars and whereby some of the latter, in turn, were later displaced by still other and even "less prestigeful" vernaculars (13; the latter are still referred to as "dialects" in many popular— as well as in all too many sociolinguistically insensitive scholarly— publications, e.g., Yiddish, Ukrainian, Byelo-Russian, Flemish, Afrikaans, Macedonian, to mention only European derivatives) indicates that the prestige notion is easily discredited unless serious qualifications and contextual redefinitions are attempted. This too may be an appropriate task for the study of language maintenance and language shift.[47]

All in all we would be hard put to find a single conclusion in this field of study that would not be subject to question in the light of cross-cultural and diachronic study. This is not due to the fact that earlier conclusions are necessarily erroneous. It is simply due to the fact that they pertain to a limited set of parameters and circumstances and that neither the original investigators nor their subsequent

critics have been in a good position to state just what these were or
are. A partial rectification of this state of affairs might obtain if the
world wide literature on language maintenance and language shift
could be subjected to secondary analysis on the basis of an advanced
and uniform theoretical model. Under such circumstances, indeed,
parameter estimation rather than merely hypotheses testing alone
might finally become possible in this field of study.

2.2 Toward more general theory and a more inclusive comparative
     approach

     a. When bilingual speech networks are in touch with each
other on the one hand, as well as with monolingual speech networks
on the other, they are differentially involved in the crucial socio-
cultural processes that influence or regulate their interaction. These
processes serve to increase or decrease interaction between populations or sub-populations in question, to either detach them from or
to confirm them in their accustomed sources of authority, to either
lead them to influence others or to be particularly receptive to influence from others, to either emphasize or minimize their own groupness and its various manifestations, to either rise or fall in relative
power or control over their own and each other's welfare, to either
view with positiveness or negativeness the drift of the interaction
between them and to react toward this drift on the basis of such views.
We must look to these engulfing sociocultural processes and, particularly, to indices of individual and group involvement in them, in our
efforts to explain the direction or rate of language maintenance and
language shift.

     b. However, after having appropriately selected and speci-
fied one or more variables from among the endless subtleties that
make up the "process" of sociocultural change, it may still be found
that their cross-cultural and diachronic study reveals inconsistent
results. The "same" process (e.g., "urbanization," as measured
by constant indices such as those selected and cross-culturally applied
by Reissman, 76)[48] may result in language shift away from hitherto
traditional language in some cases, in language shift back to traditional languages in other cases, while revealing significantly unaltered
maintenance of the status quo in still others. Under such circumstances

a typology of contact situations might serve to control or regularize
a number of group or contextual characteristics, in the manner of
moderator variables, and, by so doing, reveal greater order in the
data.

We all have an intuitive impression that the "American immigrant case" (24) is different from the "Brazilian immigrant case"
(90); that the "Spanish conquest case" (7, 15) is different from the
"Anglo-American conquest case" (12, 32); that the "immigrant case,"
in general, is different from the "conquest case," in general; that
the "Yiddish speaking immigrant to America case" (23) is different
from "German speaking immigrant to America case" (55), etc. The
question remains how best to systematize these intuitive impressions,
i. e. , what variables or attributes to utilize in order that contract
situations might be classified in accord with the differences between
them that we sense to exist. In the terms of R. A. Schermerhorn's
recently formulated typology (80) the "American immigrant case"
immediately prior to World War I would be characterized as revealing
(i) sharply unequal POWER CONFIGURATIONS between non-English-
speaking immigrants and English-speaking "old-Americans"; (ii) incorporation (rather than extrusion or colonization) as the TYPE OF
CONTROL exercised by American core society over the immigrants;
(iii) marked plurality and recent immigration (rather than duality,
intermediate plurality without recent immigration, or any other of a
continuum of patterns) as the PLURALITY PATTERN; (iv) intermediate stratification and substantial mobility within the STRATIFICA-
TION PATTERN; (v) widespread mutual legitimization of acculturation and de-ethnization as the INTERPRETATION OF CONTACT in
philosophical or group image terms; and (vi) growing industrialization, mass culture and social participation as MAJOR SOCIAL
FORCES.[49]

Given the above typological framework it has proved possible
to summarize the current status of language maintenance and language
shift among pre-World War I immigrants in terms of a very few PRE-
CONTACT FACTORS, HOST FACTORS, and PRODUCT FACTORS
(24). Unfortunately, Schermerhorn's typology for intergroup contacts
is so recent that it has not yet been widely tested on either practical
or theoretical grounds, whether in conjunction with language
maintenance-language shift or in conjunction with other topics in the

area of intergroup relations. However, it may be expected that any
typology based upon six parameters, each with several subdivisions,
is likely to be somewhat unwieldy and require simplification.

At the opposite extreme of complexity from Schermerhorn's
typology is one which is derivable from an intensive review of the extensive literature on auslandsdeutschtum.[50] One of the major differentiations among the German settlers seems to have been the ORIGI-
NAL LEGITIMIZATION AND CONCENTRATION OF THEIR SETTLE-
MENTS. A three way break is recognizable here: STAMMSIEDLUN-
GEN (settlements founded as a result of official invitation and assistance from non-German governments), TOCHTERSIEDLUNGEN (settlements founded by those who left the earlier Stammsiedlungen and
who settled elsewhere as GROUPS, but without governmental invitation or assistance), and EINSIEDLUNGEN (the immigration of German
individuals or of small occupationally homogeneous groups into non-
German communities). Another related distinction is that between the
relative "cultural development" of the settlers and their hosts. During the decade before the Second World War the two most frequently
recognized co-occurrences were (a) EINSIEDLUNGEN of "culturally
more mature" Germans living in the midst of a "culturally less developed" population, as opposed to (b) STAMM- and TOCHTERSIEDLUN-
GEN of "culturally younger" Germans surrounded by a "more mature,
nation-oriented" population. Thus, although only two diagonal cells
of a theoretically complete two-by-two typology are extensively discussed it is possible to find examples of the remaining cells as well.
Even when limited to the two co-occurrences mentioned above very
interesting and consistent differences appear both in rate and in stages
of language shift and acculturation.[57] The implications of this rough
typology and of the regularities that it has suggested deserve consideration in connection with quite different intergroup contact settings.[52]

c. Although the study of language maintenance or language
shift need not be completely limited to the comparison of separate
cases it is nevertheless undeniably true that the comparative method
is quite central to inquiry within this topic area. Certainly the comparative method is indispensable in our pursuit of cross-cultural and
diachronic regularities. Assuming that a relatively uniform set of
appropriate sociocultural process-measures could be selected and

applied and assuming that a recognizably superior typology of contact situations were available it would then become possible to study:

(i) The same language group in two separate interaction contexts that are judged to be highly similar (with respect to primary sociocultural process(es) and contact type), e. g. , two separate German STAMMSIEDLUNGEN in rural Poland.

(ii) The same language group in two separate interaction contexts judged to be quite dissimilar (with respect to major sociocultural process(es) and contact type), e. g. , one German-Swiss community in contact with Swiss Raetoromans and another German-Swiss community in Cincinnati, Ohio.

(iii) Different language groups in two separate interaction contexts judged to be highly similar (with respect to major sociocultural process(es) and contact type), e. g. , a Polish-speaking and a Slovak-speaking community, both of rural origin, in Cincinnati, Ohio.

(iv) Different language groups in two separate interaction contexts judged to be quite dissimilar (with respect to major sociocultural process(es) and contact type), e. g. , a German STAMMSIEDLUNG in rural Poland and a Slovak community in Cincinnati, Ohio.

Thus, by judiciously contrasting groups, sociocultural processes and types of contact situations (not necessarily taken two at a time, if higher level interaction designs prove to be feasible) it should become possible to more meaningfully apportion the variance in language maintenance or language shift outcomes. Furthermore, the greater our insight with respect to sociocultural processes and the more appropriate our typology of intergroup contact situations, the more possible it becomes to meaningfully assemble and analyze language maintenance and language shift files. Such files would permit both cross-cultural and diachronic analysis, of primary as well as of secondary data, based upon comparable data, collected and organized in accord with uniform sets of sociocultural processes and contact categories. This state of affairs is still far off but it is the goal toward which we might attempt to move within this second topical subdivision of the study of language maintenance and language shift, once more basic methodological and conceptual questions reach a somewhat more advanced level of clarification.

3.0 Behavior Toward Language in the Contact Setting

The third (and final) major topical subdivision of the study
of language maintenance and language shift is concerned with BEHA-
VIOR TOWARD LANGUAGE (rather than with language behavior or
behavior through language), particularly, with more focused and conscious behaviors on behalf of either maintenance or shift per se.
Strictly speaking this subdivision may be properly considered a sub-
topic under 2.0, above. However, it is of such central significance
to this entire field of inquiry that it may appropriately receive separate recognition. Three major categories of behaviors toward language are discernible within this topical subdivision:

3.1 Attitudinal-affective behaviors

We know all too little about language oriented attitudes and
emotions (running the gamut from language loyalty—of which language
nationalism is only one expression—to language antipathy—of which
conscious language abandonment is only one expression) as distinguished from attitudes and emotions toward the "typical" speakers
of particular language variants. The features of language that are
considered attractive or unattractive, proper or improper, distinctive
or commonplace, have largely remained unstudied. However, in multilingual settings, particularly in those in which a variety of "social
types" are associated with each language that is in fairly widespread
use, languages per se (rather than merely the customs, values and
cultural contributions of their model speakers) are reacted to as
"beautiful" or "ugly," "musical" or "harsh," "rich" or "poor," etc.
Generally speaking, these are language stereotypes (17). However,
the absence or presence of a "kernel of truth" (or of verifiability
itself) is entirely unrelated to the mobilizing power of such views.

The manifold possible relationships between language attitudes and language use also remain largely unstudied at the present
time. Although Lambert reports a positive relationship between success in school-based second language learning and favorable attitudes
toward the second language and its speakers (60), this finding need
not be parallelled in all natural multilingual contact settings. Thus,
Ruth Johnston reports a very low correlation between subjective and

objective (external) assimilation in the language area (50). Many
older Polish immigrants in Australia identified strongly with English,
although they hardly spoke or understood it several years after their
resettlement. On the other hand, many young immigrants spoke English faultlessly and yet identified strongly with Polish, although they
spoke it very poorly (49). Similarly, in summarizing my findings
concerning current language maintenance among pre-World War I
arrivals in the United States coming from rural Eastern and Southern
European backgrounds, I reported a long-term distinction between
attitudes and use, namely, an increased esteem for non-English
mother tongues concomitant with the increased relegation of these
languages to fewer and narrower domains of language use (24). Thus,
the particular non-English mother tongues in question were now found
to be viewed positively and nostalgically by older first and second
generation individuals who had formerly characterized these tongues
as ugly, corrupted and grammarless in pre-World War II days.
Younger second and third generation individuals were found to view
these mother tongues (almost always via translations) with less emotion but with even more positive valence. Instead of a "third generation return" (35) there seemed to be an "attitudinal halo-ization" within
large segments of all generations, albeit unaccompanied by increased
usage. This development (a negative relationship over time between
USE RATES and ATTITUDINAL POSITIVENESS) was not predictable
from most earlier studies of language maintenance or language shift
in immigrant or non-immigrant settings. We are far from knowing
whether its explanation in American contextual terms (i. e., in terms
of the greater acceptability of marginal rather than either primordial
or ideologized ethnicity) would also apply to other settings in which
similar developments might obtain. [53]

3.2 Overt behavioral implementation of attitudes, feelings and beliefs

        Both language reinforcement ("language movements") and
language planning may be subsumed under this heading. Language
reinforcement may proceed along voluntary as well as along official
routes and encompasses organizational protection, statutory protection, agitation and creative production. As for language planning,
it has not always been recognized that much (if not most) of its activity (codification, regularization, simplification, purification,

elaboration, and the implementation and evaluation of all of the foregoing) occurs in the context of language maintenance or language shift
(21).

The possible relationships between language reinforcement
(or language planning), on the one hand, and the waxing or waning of
actual language use (or of other sociocultural processes) are largely
unknown at this time. Data from the American immigrant case imply
that a number of unexpected relationships may obtain in that novel
reinforcements may be introduced as actual language use diminishes.
Thus, as even some of the more "exotic" mother tongues (i.e.,
mother tongues not usually considered to be among the major carriers
of European civilization and, therefore, hitherto usually associated
only with foreign ethnicity in the minds of "average Americans" (40)
have ceased to be primarily associated with immigrant disadvantages
or with full-blown religio-ethnic distinctiveness among their own
sometime- and erstwhile-speakers, they have been increasingly introduced as languages of study at the university, college and public
high school levels (21).[54] At the same time, massive displacement
seems to have had greater inhibitory impact on language planning
efforts in the American immigrant case than it has had on language
reinforcement efforts. The latter are essentially conservative and
seem to require less in the way of highly specialized leadership. The
former are frequently innovative and dependent upon expert personnel
working in concert with compliance producing or persuasive authority.
To what extent this differential impact also holds true in other types
of language shift settings is currently unknown but worthy of study.

Advocates of languages that are undergoing displacement are
often much more exposed to (and identified with) the values and methods of their linguistic competitors than were their less exposed (and
less threatened) predecessors. As a result, they are more likely to
adopt organized protective and publicity measures from more "advan-
taged" co-territorial (other-tongue) models to serve language maintenance purposes. The introduction of a few ethnically infused languages into the curricula of American high schools, colleges and
universities represents just such a recent innovation on behalf of
mother-tongue maintenance—and an even more de-ethnicized[55] one
than was the innovative establishment of ethnic group schools, cultural organizations and camps prior to World War I. In contrast,

the normal processes of controlled language change and the more
aroused processes of conscious language planning may require more
than "last ditch" ingenuity. However, to what extent reinforcement
and planning are differently balanced given varying degrees of displacement or augmentation is currently unknown but worthy of study.[56]

3.3 Cognitive aspects of language response

Constantly flitting between the above two categories and
overlapping partially with the one, with the other, or with both are
such matters as: CONSCIOUSNESS of mother tongue (or "other
tongue") as an entity separate from folkways more generally; KNOWL-
EDGE of synchronic variants, language history and literature; and
PERCEPTIONS OF LANGUAGE AS A COMPONENT OF "GROUPNESS."
We have little systematic information concerning the circumstances
under which language consciousness, language knowledge and language-
related groupness-perceptions do or do not enter into reference group
behavior in contact situations. As a result, it is difficult to say at
this time whether or when language maintenance and language shift
are ideologically mediated as distinguished from their more obvious
situational and instrumental determinants discussed thus far. We
recognize very gross long-term contrasts in this connection, namely,
that there were periods and regions when language "was in no way
regarded as a political or cultural factor, still less as an object of
political or cultural struggle" (56, p. 6); that there were other periods and regions marked by a sharp increase in such regard, so that
language became a principle (in the name of which people... (rallied)
themselves and their fellow speakers consciously and explicitly to
resist changes in either the functions of their language (as a result
of a language shift) or in the structure or vocabulary (as a consequence of interference)" (88, p. 99),[57] and that there currently seems
to be less of this than previously, particularly if we compare African
with European nation building. However, gross differentiations such
as these are patently insufficient to enable us to clarify the conditions
under which language becomes a prominent component in PERCEP-
TIONS of "own-groupness" and "other groupness." This topic
(language-related groupness-perception) is, of course, closely related to one previously mentioned, namely, the role of language in
group membership and in group functioning (see section 2.11a, above).

In the American immigrant case we have seen a growing dissociation between self-perceived ethnic identification and language maintenance. Far from being viewed as necessary components of groupness (whether in the sense of resultants or contributors) non-English mother tongues appear to be viewed increasingly in terms of non-ethnic CULTURAL or non-ethnic PRACTICAL considerations (24, 71). At the same time, some form of ethnic self-identification is frequently still reported by many of those who no longer claim any facility at all in their ethnic mother tongues, implying that in the American immigrant case some kind of ethnicity usually appears to be a much more stable phenomenon than language maintenance (29). Most immigrants became bilingual much before they embarked on de-ethnization or seriously contemplated the possibility of biculturism. However, there were obviously exceptions to this process, both in the United States and in other contact settings. We certainly do not seem to be in a position to indicate the underlying regularities in this subtle area of inquiry at the present time, except to point out that the segments of the population among which language consciousness, language interest, and language-related groupness-perceptions are likely to be in evidence are normally quite small and elitist in nature.

We know very little about the interaction among the three components of behavior toward language or about the interaction between any of these components and the larger psychological, social and cultural processes discussed earlier. Rather than being a "natural," omnipresent condition, either in monolingual or in multilingual settings, heightened and integrated behaviors toward language may be related to somewhat rare and advanced symbolic and ideological extensions of primordial ethnicity. Such extensions may well require a particular level of sociocultural development and a particular group of custodians for their preservation and further elaboration. They almost certainly require a relatively advanced level of elitist concentration on intra-elitist concerns, often in advance of elitist concerns for communication within the masses. Nevertheless, none of these desiderata need have invariable consequences for behavior toward language. Even where heightened and integrated behaviors toward language are culturally present they will not be equally operative in all situations or among all population sub-groups. Furthermore, even where they are culturally present they need not be uniformally related to other symbolically elaborated forms of behavior. Thus, this area remains the most unsystematized topical sub-division of the study of language maintenance and language shift. Perhaps it can be clarified in the future as a result of concomitant clarification and constant interrelation in connection with the two other major sub-divisions within this field of inquiry.

3.4 Interference and switching

Within the topical sub-division of behavior toward language we once again meet the topic of interference and switching, first introduced in section 1.1, above. The absence or presence of interference and switching can have cognitive, affective and overt implementational implications for language maintenance and language shift. Certainly, both interference and switching are related to the domains and variance sources of bilingualism, on the one hand, and to socio-cultural processes and type of interaction, on the other hand. Moreover, within this topical sub-division it is appropriate to stress that where attitudes and awarenesses concerning purism obtain, interference is sometimes viewed as an imperfection—not in the speaker or in his productions but in the language itself.[58] At the opposite pole, there are multilingual contact situations in which conscious, purposive interference obtains. In these instances speakers attempt to incorporate into their language usage as many elements or features as possible from another language including (in very advanced cases) interference in stress patterns, intonation, and Denkformen.[59] In either case (i.e., when interference occurs although it is considered undesirable, or when interference occurs and is considered desirable) interference is not always considered to be all of one piece. Certain occurrences are considered to be more acceptable, excusable, permissible, necessary than others. In either case it can become a factor in hastening language shift, particularly since bilinguals tend to interpret interference in each of the languages known to them quite differently. Finally, at a point when language shift is appreciably advanced, certain sounds and forms of the language undergoing displacement may become so difficult for the average speaker (while errors in connection with them may become so stigmatized among purists) that this in itself may accelerate further shift. All in all, recognition of interference, attitudes toward interference, and the behavioral consequences of interference represent interesting and important topics within the field of language maintenance and language shift.

4.0 Summary and Conclusions

        Various language maintenance and language shift phenomena
have long been of interest to scholars and to laymen. Several sub-
topics within this area have undisputed relevance to the daily concerns
and joys of millions. Others, of more theoretical interest, are closely
related to topics of recognized concern to linguists, anthropologists,
sociologists, psychologists, political scientists, educators, etc. Culture contact and language contact will always be with us, and out of
these contacts will come modifications in habitual behavior as well
as attempts to restrain or channel such modifications. Whether (or
when) language habits change more or less quickly than others, whether
(or when) language loyalties are more or less powerful than others,
indeed, whether (or when) men can live in a supra-ethnic tomorrow
without strong links (linguistic or non-linguistic) to their ethnic yesterday and today—these are questions to which there are currently
no definitive answers. However, interest in social-psychological
aspects of language behavior is currently growing (whether under that
name or under the name of sociolinguistics, anthropological-linguistics,
ethnolinguistics, the ethnography of speaking, the ethnography of communication, the sociology of language, or some other designation).
In most instances, there is some recognition of BEHAVIOR TOWARD
LANGUAGE as a crucial topic within the field of social behavior
through language. This growing interest will undoubtedly contribute
answers to many of the currently unanswerable questions within the
field of language maintenance and language shift.

        Three major sub-divisions of the study of language mainte-
nance and language shift have been suggested. The first deals with
the precise establishment of habitual language use in a contact situation. This requires instruments just beginning to become available
for the measurement of DEGREE OF BILINGUALISM and of LOCATION
OF BILINGUALISM along sociologically relevant dimensions. Degree
of bilingualism, hitherto recognizable in terms of automaticity, proficiency, and code-intactness at the phonetic, lexical and grammatical
levels, must also be investigated with respect to media variance and
overtness variance. LOCATION OF BILINGUALISM requires investigation with respect to functional diversification in appropriately designated domains of language, each domain being abstracted from patterned role-relations, topics, locales and/or other lower order

phenomena. The complex relationships between the several components of degree of bilingualism and location of bilingualism may be
represented by a DOMINANCE CONFIGURATION which, in turn, may
or may not be reducible to a single index of direction of bilingualism.
The drift of language maintenance or language shift may be established
by diachronic measures pertaining to some or all of the above factors.

The second major topical sub-division of the study of language maintenance and language shift deals with psychological, social
and cultural processes that are associated with ascertained changes
in habitual language use. No conceptual systematization of these
processes is currently available although several preliminary typologies of "contact situations" exist and require further refinement in
cross-cultural perspective. The greatest encouragement in this
topical sub-division comes from the accelerating interdisciplinary
work on sociocultural and politico-operational change (including work
on development and modernization). To the extent that the study of
language maintenance and language shift will become increasingly
linked to ongoing theoretical and empirical refinements in the study
of psycho-socio-cultural stability and change more generally the more
rapidly will mutually rewarding progress occur.

The third (and final) major sub-division of the study of language maintenance and language shift pertains to behavior toward language, including (but not limited to) more focused and conscious behaviors on behalf of maintenance or shift. Three major sub-topics
within this topic are recognizable: attitudinal-affective behaviors
(loyalty, antipathy, etc.), overt behavioral implementation (control
or regulation of habitual language use via reinforcement, planning,
prohibition, etc.), and (overlapping partially with each of the two
foregoing sub-topics) cognitive behaviors (language consciousness,
language knowledge, language-related group-perceptions, etc.).

This topical area, too, is still in its infancy although even
here interesting work is now being begun.

The exhaustive study of language maintenance and language
shift ultimately involves the diachronic and synchronic interrelation
of the above three topical sub-divisions along conceptual lines. In
terms of systematic inquiry the field as such is still in its infancy.

Since the basic instruments required for the establishment of degree
and direction of language maintenance or language shift are now beginning to be available (certainly this is true relative to the situation
five years ago) it would now seem to be most crucial to devote increasing amounts of theoretical and empirical attention to the comparative
(cross-network, cross-speech community, cross-polity and cross-
cultural) study of the psycho-socio-cultural antecedents and concomitants of language maintenance and language shift. When the time will
come for another attempt to review recent work in this topical area
substantial progress along these very lines will doubtlessly be noted.

NOTES

A revised version of a paper which originally appeared in Linguistics,
1964, 9, 32-70 and as an appendix to my Language Loyalty in the United States. The original publication was prepared during 1963-64
when I was a Fellow of the Center for Advanced Study in the Behavioral
Sciences, Stanford, California. For their critical comments concerning the original I would like, once again, to acknowledge the stimulation received from John J. Gumperz, Einar Haugen, John E. Hofman,
Wallace E. Lambert, Vladimir C. Nahirny, Leonard Savitz, Thomas
A. Sebeok, M. Brewster Smith and the late Uriel Weinreich. For the
stimulation I have received from their work during the past five years,
I am primarily indebted to Charles A. Ferguson, John J. Gumperz
and Dell Hymes. Their concepts and insights are reflected in almost
every revision which distinguishes between this version and the original.
    [1]E.g., "Everything is Greek, when it is more shameful to
be ignorant of Latin" (Juvenal, Satires, Sat. VI, 1.187) and "...Jews
that had married wives of Ashdod, of Ammon and of Moab; And their
children spake half in the speech of Ashdod, and could not speak in
the Jews' language, but according to the language of each people"
(Nehemiah, 13:23-24), to mention only two classical Western references.
    [2]Anthropologists, historians, linguists, sociologists and
psychologists have recognized and studied many phenomena related
to language maintenance and language shift in their pursuit of other
topics such as culture change and acculturation, nationalism, language
interference, intergroup relations, second language learning and

bilingualism. However, only rarely and recently has such interest led to a definition and formulation of this field of study in its own right. Among earlier partial efforts to do so one must mention those to be found in the huge "auslandsdeutsche Volksforschung" and "sprachwissenschaftliche Minderheitenforschung" literatures which continued from the latter part of the 19th century into World War II days (see e. g. , 27, 53, 57, 63, 65, 75, 81), the 1953 Conference of Anthropologists and Linguists, and the work of Uriel Weinreich (87, 88) and Einar Haugen (36, 38). My indebtedness to the last two investigators is quite evident. Some of the earlier terms proposed for the phenomena here referred to have been Spracherhaltung (53), language persistence (72), language replacement (62), language shift (62), language retention (36), and language displacement (38). The terminology here employed (language maintenance and language shift) is derived from my recently completed study of the non-English language resources of American immigrant groups (18). Although somewhat more cumbersome than previously proposed terms, "language maintenance and language shift" may have the advantage of more clearly indicating that a continuum of processes and outcomes exist.

[3] Changes in habitual language use may be recognized in conjunction with any one (or more) of several kinds of language varieties, e. g. , between varieties that are considered to be different languages (English and German in the American Midwest, or French and Netherlandish in Belgium), between varieties that are considered to be different regional variants of the same language ("southern" and "non-Southern" in Washington, D. C.), between varieties that are considered to be different social-class variants of the same regional variant ("middle class" and "lower class" in New York City), etc. Only the first kind of habitual language behavior, that involving changes in use patterns with respect to different languages, will be focused upon in this paper, although most of the topics considered should also be applicable to changes in language behavior with respect to other kinds of varieties as well.

[4] Weinreich makes this point very strongly: "Whereas interference, even in its sociocultural setting, is a problem in which considerations of linguistic structure enter, the matter of language shifts is entirely extra-structural" (88, pp. 106-107). My own position is represented by the word PRIMARY above, and is discussed briefly in sections 1. 1 and 3. 4. It does seem to me that certain interference phenomena may well be of concern to us in connection with several aspects of the study of language maintenance and language shift.

[5] Thus, Haugen suggests, "distinct tests... on each of the levels of phonemics, grammar, and basic lexicon" (38, p. 76), with several further differentiations within these levels, some of which are indicated in this paper. Mackey goes even further and suggests that separate measures are also required at the semantic and stylistic levels (66).

[6] Among the most recent measures are those of Herschel T. Manuel which seek to enable "educators to compare the achievement of a student in one language with his achievement in another" (68). It is typical of educational concerns to be more interested in determining the overall extent of bilingualism than in describing it in terms of quantified componential analysis.

[7] For a recent critique of speed-related and socially uncontextualized psychological measures of bilingualism in particular, and of similarly unproductive biases in most linguistic and sociological measures of bilingualism, more generally, see my "Sociolinguistic perspective on the study of bilingualism," Linguistics, 1968, 39, 21-49.

[8] See, e.g., Hayden (39), John E. Hofman (43, 44), and Nahirny and Fishman (71). Perhaps the most influential examples of this approach are found in the work of Moses N. H. Hoffman (42) and Seth Arsenian (2).

[9] Bilingualism is an individual characteristic. Diglossia is a societal characteristic (see Charles A. Ferguson, "Diglossia," Word, 1959, 15, 325-340). These two kinds of characteristics need not necessarily co-vary. There may be monolingual individuals in a society which is essentially diglossic, and vice-versa. The study of language maintenance and language shift seeks to arrive at a determination of societal status (or, at least, of speech-network status) on the basis of aggregating data on individuals. For further discussion of this problem, see my "Bilingualism with and without diglossia; Diglossia with and without bilingualism," Journal of Social Issues, 1967, 23, no. 2, 29-38).

[10] Writing and reading are here differentiated as separate media primarily because each is capable of independent productive and receptive maintenance or shift. In general, the formal dimensions presented here make use of more distinctions than may be necessary in any one multilingual setting.

[11] Haugen, Weinreich, and Mackey all refer to "functions" of language rather than to "domains." However, in recent years,

Jakobson, Hymes, Sebeok, Weir, and other linguists and anthropologists have popularized the term "functions" in quite a different connection (see section 1.22). As a result, it seems preferable to revert to the term "domain" (probably first advanced by Schmidt-Rohr, 81, 1. 179) in an attempt to avoid confusion.

[12] The most extended recent discussion of the location of bilingualism in societal or institutional terms, rather than merely in terms of linguistic description, on the one hand, or in terms of immediate face-to-face speech context (interactional) processes, on the other hand, are those of Weinreich, Haugen, and Mackey. Weinreich concludes that "a general survey of language functions in the bilingual communities of the world is not yet available" (88, p. 87). Haugen concludes that it is "necessary to devise subtler measures... to draw a full profile of the speaker's activities and assign measures of language function and skill for both languages" (38, p. 95). Mackey's theoretical cross-classification of external "functions" according to a set of "contacts" and "variables" (66) is referred to at various points throughout this review. My own most extensive attempt to explain the concept of domain and to indicate its utility for the macrosocietal study of language maintenance and language shift was, initially, "Who speaks what language to whom and when" (25) and, subsequently, "The relationship between macro- and micro-sociolinguistics in the study of who speaks what language to whom and when," in Hymes, Dell and John J. Gumperz, Directions in Sociolinguistics (in press). Scores of empirical examples of the utility, reliability and validity of the domain level of analysis of societal bilingualism are presented in my Bilingualism in the Barrio (with R. L. Cooper and Roxana Ma, et al.), Indiana University Language Sciences Monographs, 1971. A few of these examples have been incorporated into the present revised review.

[13] Within a year of his original publication, Schmidt-Rohr felt it necessary to release a revised second edition. The major differences between the two are recognizable in the intense nazification and racialization of terms and interpretations as well as in the panegyric to National Socialism in the introduction and appendix to the second edition. A revised and somewhat improved statement of his domains appeared a few years later, together with a self-report questionnaire for use by Auslandsdeutsche (82).

[14] Mackey has recommended only five domains (66): home, community, school, mass media, and correspondence, thus combining a media aspect with four domains mentioned above. At this time

there is no empirical evidence concerning the adequacy of these domains. Both Barker (5) and Carroll Barber (3), in their studies of
acculturating populations (Spanish American or Yaqui Indian) in Arizona, restricted themselves to four domains: familial (intimate),
informal, formal and intergroup. In Barber's analysis the formal
domain is limited to religious-ceremonial activities, while the intergroup domain is limited to economic, legal, and recreational activities. A similar consolidation or restriction in domains and activities
is evident in J. W. Frey's analysis (26) of Amish "triple talk" where
three domains—home, school and church—suffice. It is quite obvious
that Barker and Barber have formulated their domains at a more psychological level, whereas Frey's, like Schmidt-Rohr's, are along
more ecological-institutional lines. The relationships between different domain levels such as these may enable us to investigate bilingualism and language maintenance or shift in newer and more stimulating ways (25).
     [15]We can safely reject the implication still encountered in
certain discussions of domains (14, 80) that there might be an invariant set of domains applicable to all multilingual settings. If language
behavior is related to sociocultural organization, as is now widely accepted, then different kinds of multilingual settings should benefit
from analyses in terms of different domains of language use, whether
defined intuitively, theoretically, or empirically. Obviously the work-
sphere domain, overlooked by Schmidt-Rohr, will be an appropriate
domain for the analysis of many multilingual settings. Although the
search for cross-culturally applicable/comparable "spheres of activity" is, certainly, a highly important concern of the student of language maintenance and language shift, it must be recognized that the
cross-cultural correspondence between domains may depend upon
rather different limits or boundary conditions, particularly when
widely different cultures are being compared.
     [16]In contrast to "domains of language behavior" the functions
of language (9, 47, 48) stand closer to socio-psychological analysis
for they abstract their constituents primarily in terms of purposive-
motivational considerations. The proposed functions have been advanced to help answer the questions "why did he speak and say it the
way he did when he did?" The proposed domains are oriented more
toward macro-societal normative regularities than toward individual
purposes, although these two levels should be commensurable with
each other. The list of "functions" varies widely from one author to
another. For example, Karl Buhler (9): Auslösung, Kundgabe, Dar-

stellung; Roman Jakobson (48): referential, emotive, conative, poetic, phatic, metalingual; Dell Hymes (47): expressive, directive, poetic, contact, metalingual, referential, contextual; Edward Sapir (70): communication, socialization, cultural transmittal and accumulation, individualization; George Barker (4): group-defining functions (coordinating group activity, symbolizing group membership, transmitting patterns of thought and behavior), group-relating functions (relating the individual to the group, relating one group to another). Additional functional categories particularly related to utterances have most recently been reviewed by Ervin-Tripp (16b). Other lists of functions have been proposed by Kenneth Burke, J. R. Firth, C. K. Ogden and I. A. Richards, Bruno Snell, and a host of others interested in language, literature or life. While a mere enumeration cannot pretend to do justice to the historical relationships between the several systems of functions listed here, it should be noted that all of the lists have in common "an interpretation of the factors of the speech event in terms of motive or purpose" (47, p. 30).

[17] Unfortunately, the term role is currently employed in several somewhat different ways, e.g., "role in society" (mayor, untouchable, bank president), "role relation" vis-à-vis particular others (husband-wife, father-child, teacher-pupil), "occasional role" (chairman, host, spokesman), and "momentary role" (initiator of a communication, respondent, listener). My own use of the term has increasingly narrowed down to that of "role-relations." For further detail on the concept of role, see Ward H. Goodenough, "Rethinking 'status' and 'role'; toward a general model of the cultural organization of social relationships," in Michael Banton (ed.), Relevance of Models for Social Anthropology, New York, Praeger, 1965.

[18] These remarks are not intended to imply that all role-relation differences are necessarily related to language-choice differences. This almost certainly is not the case. Just which role-relation differences are related to language-choice differences (and under what circumstances) is a matter for empirical determination within each multilingual setting as well as at different points in time within the same setting. This observation also applies to the variety of "social occasions" and "encounters" discussed by Goffman, only some of which may need to be retained (particularly for more traditional societies) once more general parameters such as those presented here have been studied adequately.

[19] Edelman, Martin; R. L. Cooper, and J. A. Fishman, The contextualization of schoolchildren's bilingualism, Irish Journal

of Education, 1968, ii, 2, 106-11; also: Modern Language Journal,
1969, 52, 179-82.
     [20] Cooper, Robert L. , Two contextualized measures of
degree of bilingualism, in Fishman, J. A. , R. L. Cooper and Roxana
Ma, et al. , Bilingualism in the Barrio, Bloomington, Indiana University Language Sciences Monographs, 1971.
     [21] Fishman, Joshua A. and Eleanor Herasimchuk, The mul-
tiple prediction of phonological variables in a bilingual speech community, American Anthropologist, 1969, 648-57.
     [22] Berney, Tomi D. , R. L. Cooper and J. A. Fishman,
Semantic independence and degree of bilingualism in two Puerto Rican
communities, Revista Interamericana de Psicologia, 1968, 2, 289-
94; also Modern Language Journal, 1969, 52, 182-85.
     [23] See Weinreich (88, pp. 9-10, 35 and 81-82) for several
early examples of the "two types of bilingualism" school of thought,
many of which are quite similar to the coordinate-compound distinction. Still other early examples are found in the work of Schmidt-
Rohr (81), Swadesh (86), and, most recently, in that of Vildomec
(86a).
     [24] There continues to be a culture-bound suspicion that the
latter type of bilingualism is not only "truer" but also inherently
"healthier. " See, e.g., Jakobson (62, p. 44) and Hymes (47, p. 43)
to the effect that if the contexts of language use are not kept distinct
"there may be personality difficulties" (47) and "even pathological
results" (62). Schmidt-Rohr, Geissler and others working under much
greater political-ethnocentric influence considered compound bilingualism to be the cause of racial degeneration and to lead to loss of depth,
clarity and uniqueness in the individual (27, 33, 64, 81).
     [25] It is generally recognized that the labels coordinate and
compound identify the extremes of a continuum of neurological organization and psychological functioning, although for the sake of simplicity they are usually treated as if they pertained to a dichotomy.
     [26] For an empirical example of reference to the compound-
coordinate distinction from the point of view of its sociolinguistic contextualization, see Berney, Tomi D. , R. L. Cooper and J. A. Fishman, Semantic independence and degree of bilingualism in two Puerto
Rican communities, Revista Interamericana de Psicologia, 1968, 2,
289-94.
     [27] "Situation" and "setting" have frequently been used inter-
changeably in sociolinguistic literature. In this paper "setting" is
intended to be the broader and more multi-faceted concept. An

exhaustive consideration of a multilingual "setting" would require attention to language choice data, sociocultural process data, data on attitudinal, emotional, cognitive, and overt behaviors toward language, etc. "Situation" is reserved for use in characterizing the intersection between particular role-relations, places and topics, e.g., pupil-teacher, classroom and school-work. For greater theoretical detail concerning "sociolinguistic situations," see Bock, Philip K., Social structure and language structure, Southwestern Journal of Anthropology, 1964, 20, 393-403. For an empirical example of the utility of this definition of "situation," in conjunction with various domains, for the study of normative language views of language "appropriateness" among bilinguals see Greenfield, Lawrence and Joshua A. Fishman, Situational measures of normative language views in relation to person, place and topic among Puerto Rican bilinguals, in Bilingualism in the Barrio (Fishman, J. A., R. L. Cooper, Roxana Ma, et al), Bloomington, Indiana University Language Sciences Monographs, 1971.

[28] Students of acculturation have asked whether there are "orders of structured activities which are 'pillars' of a culture in the sense that effects on contact in these orders ramify widely into other orders of the culture. (If so)... are they the same orders in different cultures or do they vary from culture to culture? Are there 'carrier' activities in the contact situation which though relatively unaffected by contact themselves, nevertheless set up indirect effects on other sets of structured activities?" (14, p. 37). These questions have very precise parallels in the study of language maintenance or language shift. Our ability to answer them will depend on our ability to specify the domains of language appropriately and to intercorrelate degrees of shift in the several domains.

[29] For a recent study conducted essentially along these lines, see that of Joan Rubin (77). The growth of bilingualism in Paraguay seems to be due to a clearcut domain difference such that each language controls several crucial domains. As a result monolinguals find it more and more necessary to learn the "other tongue," whether it be Spanish or Guarani. Rubin considers Paraguay to have "the highest degree of bilingualism in the world" due to the mutually exclusive domain pattern which has developed there.

[30] The question of dominance (or direction) of bilingualism arises less frequently today in the United States (or in other acculturated immigrant settings) where English (or another officially

established language) may be assumed to be dominant and uniformally "available" in various bilingual contexts so that degree and location considerations do not apply to it nearly as much as they do to the immigrant languages. This situation must not be assumed to be universally the case in multilingual settings.

[31] If one mixes language and non-language criteria the relations between them cannot be examined. As for individual and societal assessments of dominance, although both are clearly possible, it is not at all necessary for them to agree, particularly when small or atypical speech networks drawn from the larger speech community are examined for analysis. A strictly macro-societal assessment of language use by an individual or small speech network would very likely account for a small proportion of the total noted variance, since by concentrating largely on institutional (domain) and situational analysis it would continue to regard as error variance whatever metaphorical (i.e., non-situational, or contrastive) switching may obtain. Similarly wasteful would be any attempt to describe the macro-societal language status in terms of face-to-face interactions between dyads. Nevertheless, since there is an inherent commensurability between normative behavior at the individual and societal levels, there is no reason why the dominance configurations of individuals and groups cannot be contrasted or compared with each other with respect to situational or domain relevant behavior alone.

[32] Weinreich uses this term to refer to visual (writing, reading) exposure as contrasted with aural-vocal exposure. This is equivalent to my term "media variance" in section 1.1.

[33] In an earlier discussion (87) Weinreich presented a much different approach to the dominance configuration, more similar in many respects to that of Schmidt-Rohr, but with certain quantitative (rather than entirely qualitative) features.

[34] For further details concerning several of these parameters, see Blom, Jan-Peter and John J. Gumperz, Some social determinants of verbal behavior, in Hymes, Dell and J. J. Gumperz (eds.), Directions in Sociolinguistics, New York, Holt-Rhinehart, 1972. For a suggested model linking these parameters to each other, see Cooper, Robert L., How can we measure the roles which a bilingual's languages play in his everyday behavior? in Kelly, Louis G. (ed.), The Description and Measurement of Bilingualism: An International Seminar, Toronto, University of Toronto Press, 1969. In the same volume, see my discussion of "The description of societal bilingualism"

for a consideration of the dangers of fixation on micro-analysis alone
if our goal is to relate bilingual usage to other societal behavior and
to social structure as well.

[35] For a comparison of census data, dominance configuration
data, and detailed role-process data dealing with related phenomena,
see (24), in which the relationship between these several approaches
is examined.

[36] The patterns yielded by the dominance configuration should
enable us to either conform or significantly revise Kloss's intuitive
five-fold classification of patterns of language use in multilingual settings (54): (i) only the given language is used for all communication
purposes; (ii) the given language is used alongside another for all
purposes; (iii) the given language is used only in correspondence and
reading—alone or alongside another language also used for these same
purposes; (iv) the given language is used only for business purposes,
particularly with foreigners; (v) the given language is used only for
advanced educational or scientific pursuits. Similarly, Carman's ten-
stage analysis of language shift among immigrants settling in Kansas
(10) may benefit by the empirical comparisons made possible by dominance configuration analysis.

[37] Other problems of a technical measurement or recording
nature can be anticipated, although no attempt will be made to discuss
them at this time: the construction of individual as well as group
measurement devices; the need to disguise or insulate questions on
language use ("One can gain the confidence of a bilingual by getting
him to talk about the things he is interested in much more easily than
by asking him searching questions about his language, " 37, p. 21);
adjustments needed for the study of inter-group as well as intra-
group bilingualism; determining the utility of self-report data (such
as 49, 50), as contrasted with observed or demonstrated language
use data. Psychology and sociology have a long tradition of self-
report data (e. g. , in the measurement of attitudes or preferences),
although self-reports sometimes show little correlation with observed
or demonstrated behavior. Nevertheless self-report data continue to
be considered important in these disciplines, at least as a level of
behavior noteworthy in itself. The relationships between self-reports
of habitual language use in given domains or sources of variance and
the observations of field workers or the production of Ss themselves
have yet to be fully studied although it is much clearer today than it
was only a few years ago that the agreement can be very high but

depends on the kind of language behavior data that is being sought and
the kind of subjects whose usage is being focused upon. Global self-
report data from language conscious subjects appears to have very
high reliability and validity indeed. In this connection see Fishman,
Joshua A. and Robert L. Cooper, Alternative measures of bilingualism, Journal of Verbal Learning and Verbal Behavior, 1969, 8, 276-
82; Fishman, Joshua A. , A sociolinguistic census of a bilingual
neighborhood, American Journal of Sociology, 1969, 75, 323-39. ;
and Fishman, Joshua A. , Bilingual attitudes and behaviors, Language
Sciences, 1969, 5, 5-11.

[38] The primary attempt to empirically test the utility of the
dominance configuration approach and to compare it to the older,
uncontextualized dominant-balanced approach to the measurement
and description of bilingualism is that of Fishman, Joshua A. , Robert
L. Cooper, Roxana Ma, et al. , Bilingualism in the Barrio, Bloomington, Indiana University Language Sciences Monographs, 1971.

[39] Weinreich points out that geographic obstacles (mountains,
deserts, etc.) or facilitations (rivers, trade routes, etc.) in the path
of group contact have frequently influenced group interaction and,
therefore, language contact, including language maintenance or language shift.

[40] The realization that higher education (even when it is in
the mother tongue) can be a two-edged sword represents a recent
partial change in Kloss's thinking relative to his own earlier position
(53) and that of von Pritzvald (75), Kuhn (57), and many others impressed with auslands-deutsche phenomena in Slavic or other "underdeveloped" areas. On the other hand, Kloss continues to list "affiliation with denominations, fostering parochial school," among the six
factors favorable to language maintenance for "normal, non-insulated"
minority groups in the United States (55, pp. 6-7). Perhaps this
should be taken as a SEPARATION rather than as an EDUCATION
variable.

[41] The nationalism of several African and Asian developing
countries seems to be much more characterized by NATIONISM than
by the nationalistic elaboration of ethnicity per se. It is much more
concerned with the political and economic conditions of NATIONHOOD
than with the internal, substantive content of PEOPLEHOOD. The
political and administrative limits of many new nations are now usually defined in advance of their formation rather than in the process
of their formation. The new nations are less frequently formed as

the result of the "painful but glorious" unification of hitherto particu-
laristics who have groped to define the language, the history, the
customs, and the missions that unite them and set them apart from
others. They are formed along supra-ethnic lines that normally follow colonial demarcations which depended on the fortunes of conquest
and the skills of treaty-making. Political and economic self-
determination are much more prominent considerations in the new
nations than is cultural self-determination of the pre- and post-World
War I variety. Political leadership is much more evident than cultural leadership. The Western experience has typically been that
industrialization preceded urbanization and (particularly in Eastern
Europe) that nationalism preceded nationism and that the first set
of phenomena preceded the second. In the new nations, the reverse
sequences seem to be more common, and these may be among the
major sociocultural determinants de-emphasizing language issues in
connection with local or regional languages, on the one hand, and
which favor the continued use of supra-regional and colonial language,
on the other. Indeed, it may be that language concerns are most
noticeable today only where we find sociocultural distinctions remaining, even after the attainment of considerably more politico-operational
integration than has currently been attained in most new nations, particularly when hitherto backward, exploited or disadvantaged groups
begin to experience great and rapid economic and cultural development in their own areas of primary population concentrations (as,
e.g., the French-Canadians, Flemings, Jura-regionists, etc.). I
have elaborated further on the distinction between nationalism and
nationism, and on the implications of each for language behavior and
behavior toward language, in Nationality-nationalism and nation-
nationism, in Fishman, Joshua A., C. A. Ferguson and J. Das Gupta
(eds.), Language Problems of Developing Nations, New York, Wiley,
1968, pp. 39-52. I have related this distinction to other differences
between new nations and the solutions they adopt to their language
problems in National languages and languages of wider communication in the developing nations, Anthropological Linguistics, 1969, 11,
111-35.
        [42] I have explored the relationship between nationalism and
language behavior (as well as behavior toward language) in detail in
my "Nationalism, language, and language planning," a book-length
manuscript; for a summary statement see The impact of nationalism
on language planning, in Joan Rubin and Bjorn Jernudd (eds.), Can

Language Be Planned? Honolulu, University of Hawaii Press, 1972,
pp. 3-20. Other evidence of the great maintenance capacity of relatively unideologized populations, as well as of unideologized speech
varieties, is reported by A. Tabouret-Keller, Sociological factors of
language maintenance and language shift: a methodological approach
based on European and African examples, in Fishman, J. A., C. A.
Ferguson and J. Das Gupta (eds.), Language Problems of Developing
Nations, New York, Wiley, 1968, pp. 107-18, as well as by Verdoot,
Albert, Zweisprachige Nachbarn, Wein, Wilhelm Braumüller, 1968.
The superficiality of ideological penetration is repeatedly demonstrated
in my Yiddish in America, Bloomington, Research Center in Anthro-
pology, Folklore and Linguistics, Indiana University, 1965, and
Hungarian Language Maintenance in the United States, Bloomington,
Uralic and Altaic Series, Indiana University, 1966.

[43] See, e.g., the reports of the American Council of Learned
Societies (1), Carman (10), Geissler (27), Gerrullis (28), Haugen (36),
Hofman (44), Kloss (55), Kuhn (57), Pihlblad (74), Smith (84), Willems
(90), etc. However, note Fishman's and Hofman's distinction between
the importance of the rural-urban factor in connection with between-
group as contrasted with within-group language maintenance differentials (19).

[44] The related over-generalization that the upper and middle
classes are more inclined to shift than are the lower classes requires
no separate extended considerations here in view of the above remarks.
(See, e.g., H. A. Miller's claim than "when languages have given
way... it has been the intellectual class that has yielded while the
simple, uneducated class has clung to its language" (6, p. 60). Like
both of the previously mentioned over-generalizations this one is
derived from over-reliance on data from a particular kind (or kinds)
of language contact setting(s). Even within the "immigrant case"
differences are encountered in this connection. Thus while Willems
reports that among German speakers in Brazil the middle and upper
classes were more retentive (90), I have concluded from several
studies of immigrants in the United States that the lower classes have
been more retentive (22). It is obvious that these two immigrant contexts differ in many respects, particularly in connection with status
differentials between the immigrant and indigenous populations.
Rather than conclude that rural-urban or class differences must
always work in a particular maintenance or shift direction it is far
wiser to examine the social processes in which these populations are
involved in order to determine their language behavior consequences.

On a world-wide polity level language maintenance seems basically
to be neither a population density (rural-urban) nor an economic factor, but, rather, an intactness of regionalism factor. The latter, of
course, is itself subject to population density and economic changes.
For the empirical evidence as well as an extended discussion of this
relationship see my Some contrasts between linguistically homogeneous and linguistically heterogeneous polities, in Fishman, Joshua
A., and C. A. Ferguson, J. Das Gupta (eds.), Language Problems
of Developing Nations, New York, Wiley, 1968, pp. 53-68.
          [45]Herman makes this quite clear in his discussion of (a) con-
ditions under which "background factors" will or will not dominate
over "immediate situation factors" with respect to language choice,
and of (b) conditions in which "immediate situation factors" will or
will not dominate over "personal factors" (41). His paper is definitely
among the more stimulating attempts to provide social-psychological
theory for this area of study.
          [46]For example, usefulness in communication, literary-
cultural merit, emotional significance, overall respect, overall popularity, etc., in addition to practical utility in social advance.
          [47]In general, the phenomenological validity of the "prestige"
concept is so general (i.e., speakers so commonly regard their language as appropriately prestigeful for their purposes) and the objective determination of the concept so difficult that the former level may
be a better one to investigate than the latter. The fact that Hasidim
in Williamsburg regard Yiddish as more appropriate for most of their
purposes than either English, Hebrew or Hungarian, needs to be
examined from the point of view of their values, goals and social
organization rather than from any "more objective" point of view.
Dominance configuration data (revealing "who speaks what language
to whom, when and about what") plus language attitude and language
interpretation data ("what difference does it make, in social meaning,
if message m_1 is said in l_1 or in l_2?") when taken together, constitute the empirical bases for determining the significance of variety
switching to those that utilize or recognize them. Probably the best
known approach to determining the global social meaning of language
varieties to their speakers (or hearers) is that devised by Lambert,
W. E., A social psychology of bilingualism, Journal of Social Issues,
1967, 23, no. 2, 91-109. For a sociolinguistically more detailed
approach, see Kimple, James, Jr., R. L. Cooper and J. A. Fishman,
Language switching and the interpretation of conversations, Lingua,
1969, 23, 127-34. More intuitive but, nonetheless, highly suggestive

differentiation of the dimensions along which speakers perceive language "prestige" to be operative are reported in Ferguson, Charles A., Myths about Arabic, Monograph Series on Language and Linguistics (Georgetown University), 1960, 12, 75-82, and in Nader, Laura, A note on attitudes and the use of language, Anthropological Linguistics, 1962, 4, no. 6, 24-29. The importance of language attitudes for the mastery of standard American English is discussed at a similarly intuitive level in my The breadth and depth of English in the United States, in Marckwardt, Albert H. (ed.), Language and Language Learning, Champaign, Illinois, National Council of Teachers of English, 1968, pp. 43-53.

[48] Another variable which has recently been much studied is "modernization." Whether one prefers to emphasize the cross-culturally comparable aspects of modernization (see, e.g., Smith, David H. and Alex Inkeles, The O-M scale: a comparative socio-psychological measure of individual modernity, Sociometry, 1966, 29, 353-77), the socioculturally unique aspects of modernization in a particular context (see, e.g., Stephenson, John B., Is everyone going modern? A critique and a suggestion for measuring modernism, American Journal of Sociology, 1968, 74, 265-75), or a combination of the two (see Jocob, Philip E., Henry Teune and Thomas Watts, Values, leadership and development: a four-nation study, Social Science Information, 1968, 7, 50-92), the need for further specification and categorization of the contexts of language maintenance and language shift will probably remain. Specification of the ongoing sociocultural and politico-operational processes in one setting—and their relation to dominance configuration data—may be advisable before inter-setting comparisons are attempted.

[49] The inclusion of "major social forces" in Schermerhorn's typology carries one step beyond my own convictions that sociocultural processes should be treated as variables rather than as classificatory attributes. Nevertheless Schermerhorn's approach does not preclude the study of degrees of any particular major social force, taken as an independent variable, in conjunction with his overall typological approach.

[50] Kuhn (57a) seems to have developed the typology of German Sprachinseln further than did any of his contemporaries. He provides typologies according to (i) origin and colonization type, (ii) surroundings, and (iii) period of settlement and age. In all, he discusses 15 characteristics of German Sprachinseln, most of which are applicable to all types.

[51] In the case of EINSIEDLUNGEN of "culturally more mature" Germans the following progression of rough stages appears: (i) "other tongue" for communication with non-Germans, (ii) "other tongue" for communication with other German immigrants, (iii) "other tongue" for family communication, (iv) "other tongue" for internal speech, (v) national de-identification, (vi) ethnic-religious de-identification, (vii) intermarriage. In the case of STAMM- and TOCHTERSIEDLUN-GEN of "culturally younger" Germans the following stages are most frequently differentiated: (i) national de-identification, (ii) ethnic de-identification, (iii) "other tongue" for communication with non-Germans and for internal speech, (iv) "other tongue" for communication and intermarriage. An overarching Protestant-Catholic difference (Catholics being more likely to experience rapid umvolkung) is also repeatedly stressed (30, 57, 65).

[52] Yet another typology of contact settings may be derived from Weinreich's paper on bilingualism in India (89) in which exposure to contact, group size, functional importance of languages, and linguistic diversity are the major classificatory topics.

[53] That language attitudes are distinct from language commitments, and that language commitments are related to overt behaviors whereas language attitudes are not necessarily so related at all, is demonstrated in my Bilingual attitudes and behaviors, Language Sciences, 1969, no. 5.

[54] Similar phenomena also occurred some fifty or more years ago in connection with the de-ethnization of the mother tongues of German and Scandinavian immigrants to the United States (36, 55).

[55] For two examinations of inter-generational differences in behavioral and ideological ethnicity and their relationship to varieties of language behavior see my Varieties of ethnicity and language consciousness, Monograph Series on Languages and Linguistics (Georgetown University), 1965, 18, 69-79, and American immigrant groups: ethnic identification and the problem of generations, Sociological Review, 1965, 13, 311-26.

[56] The relationship between language maintenance or shift and the acceptance of language planning innovations is one of the major foci of a four-country study currently being conducted by the present author, Charles A. Ferguson, Jyotirindra Das Gupta, Joan Rubin and Bjorn Jernudd.

[57] The implication of this quotation is that language loyalty is necessarily or primarily defensive in nature; however, perceived threat (or advantage) may be reacted to aggressively as well. Thus,

language loyalty may seek to expand the permissible or required domains of one's language, i.e., to INSIST ON CHANGES rather than
merely to resist them.

    [58]Negative attitudes toward mother tongues viewed by their
speakers as suffering from excessive interference are revealed by
such designations as gemixste pickles and die schonste lengvitch (in
referring to American-German); Yankee-Dutch (Netherlandish);
Yankee-Yiddish and Yinglish (Yiddish); Minnesota Norwegian (Norwegian); Finglish (Finnish); Spanglish (Spanish); to mention instances
only from the American immigrant scene. A common international
designation is "jargon," this term (or an equivalent) sometimes being
accepted as the official name of vernaculars (rather than being restricted to makeshift languages alone). It may very well be that languages or styles revealing considerable stable intermixture at both
the lexical and grammatical levels are particularly likely to develop
when more substantial language shift is inhibited through ascriptive
limitations in the inter-group role-relations available to members
of certain speech communities at the same time that their intra-
group role relates are greatly dislocated, particularly with respect
to those that hitherto required language usage of the most careful
(formal) variety. Further comments concerning the social circumstances that seem to me to lead to pidginization are found in my Sociolinguistics, Rowley (Mass.), Newbury House, 1970.

    [59]There have been many proposed "language reforms" along
such lines; see, e.g., the proposal of Elias Molee (70) in connection
with American English with respect to the planned "Germanification"
of American English.

                              REFERENCES

1. American Council of Learned Societies, Conference on Non-
         English Speech in the United States, Bulletin, 1942, no. 34.
2. Arsenian, Seth, Bilingualism and mental development (New York,
         Teachers College, Columbia University, 1937).
3. Barber, Carroll, Trilingualism in Pascua; social functions of
         language in an Arizona Yaqui village. M.A. Thesis, Univer-
         sity of Arizona, 1952.
4. Barker, George C., The social functions of language, Etc.,
         1945, 2, 228-34.

5. Barker, George C., Social functions of language in a Mexican-American Community, Acta Americana, 1947, 5, 185-202.
6. Braunshausen, Nicolas. Le bilinguisme et la famille, in Le Billinguisme et l'Education, Geneva-Luxemburg, Bureau International d'Education, 1928.
7. Bright, William, Elements of acculturation in the California Indian languages, University of California Publications in Linguistics, 1960, 4, no. 4, 215-46.
8. Broshnahan, L. F., Some aspects of the linguistic situation in tropical Africa, Lingua, 1963, 12, 54-65.
9. Buhler, Karl, Sprachtheorie (Jena, Gustav Fischer, 1934).
10. Carman, J. Neale, Foreign-Language Units of Kansas; Historical Atlas and Statistics (Lawrence, University of Kansas Press, 1962).
11. Chambers, W. W., Language and nationality in German pre-Romantic and Romantic thought, Modern Language Review, 1946, 41, 382-92.
12. Cook, S. F., The conflict between the California Indian and white civilization, Ibero-Americana, 1943, 21, 1-194; 22, 1-55; 23, 1-115; 24, 1-29.
13. Deutsch, Karl W., The trend of European nationalism—the language aspect, American Political Science Review, 1942, 36, 533-41.
14. Dohrenwend, Bruce P., and Robert J. Smith, Toward a theory of acculturation, Southwestern Journal of Anthropology, 1962, 18, 30-39.
15. Dozier, Edward P., Resistance to acculturation and assimilation in an Indian pueblo, American Anthropologist, 1951, 53, 56-66.
16a. Ervin, Susan M., and Charles E. Osgood, Second language learning and bilingualism, Journal of Abnormal and Social Psychology, 1954, 49, Supplement, 139-46.
16b. Ervin-Tripp, Susan M., An analysis of the interaction of language, topic and listener, American Anthropologist, 1964, 66, part 2, 86-102.
17. Fishman, Joshua A., The process and function of social stereotyping, Journal of Social Psychology, 1956, 43, 27-64.
18. Fishman, Joshua A., et al., Language Loyalty in the United States (New York, Yeshiva University, 1964). (A mimeographed report in three volumes to the Language Research Section, U.S. Office of Education.) (For a one-volume

abridgement, see <u>Language Loyalty in the United States</u>,
The Hague, Mouton, 1966.)

19. Fishman, Joshua A., and John E. Hofman, Mother tongue and
     nativity in the American population, in Fishman, J. A., et
     al., <u>Language Loyalty in the United States</u>, Chapter 2.

20. Fishman, Joshua A., and Vladimir C. Nahirny, The ethnic group
     school in the United States, in Fishman, J. A., et al.,
     Language Loyalty in the United States, Chapter 6. (Also,
     <u>Sociology of Education</u>, 1964, 37, 306-17.)

21. Fishman, Joshua A., Planned reinforcement of language main-
     tenance in the United States; suggestions for the conserva-
     tion of a neglected national resource, in Fishman, J. A.,
     et al., <u>Language Loyalty in the United States</u>, Chapter 21.

22. Fishman, Joshua A., Language maintenance in a supra-ethnic
     age; summary and conclusions, in Fishman, J. A., et al.,
     <u>Language Loyalty in the United States</u>, Chapter 22.

23. Fishman, Joshua A. Language maintenance and language shift
     in certain urban immigrant environments: the case of Yid-
     dish in the United States, <u>Europa Ethnica</u>, 1965, 22, 146-58.

24. Fishman, Joshua A., Language maintenance and language shift:
     the American immigrant case, <u>Sociology</u>, 1965, 16, 19-39.

25. Fishman, Joshua A., Who speaks what language to whom and
     when, <u>Linguistique</u>, 1965, 2, 67-88.

26. Frey, J. William, Amish "triple talk," <u>American Speech</u>, 1945,
     20, 85-98.

27. Geissler, Heinrich, <u>Zweisprachigkeit deutscher Kinder im Aus-
     land</u> (Stuttgart, Kohlhammer, 1938).

28. Gerullis, Georg, Muttersprache und Zweisprachigkeit in einem
     preussischlitauischen Dorf, <u>Studi Baltici</u>, 1932, 2, 59-67.

29. Glazer, Nathan, and Moynihan, Daniel P., <u>Beyond the Melting
     Pot</u> (Cambridge, M.I.T. and Harvard University Press,
     1963).

30. Grentrup, Theodor, ·<u>Religion und Muttersprache</u> (Munster,
     Aschendorffsche Verlagsbuchhandlung, 1932).

31. Gross, Feliks, Language and value changes among the Arapho,
     <u>International Journal of American Linguistics</u>, 1951, 17, 10-
     17.

32. Gulick, John, Language and passive resistance among the eastern
     Cherokees, <u>Ethnohistory</u>, 1958, 5, 60-81.

33. Güntert, Hermann, Neue Zeit—Neues Ziel, <u>Wörter und Sachen</u>,
     1938, 19 (n.s. 1), 1-11.

34. Hall, Robert A., Jr., Bilingualism and applied linguistics, Zeitschrift für Phonetik und allgemeine Sprachwissenschaft, 1952, 6, 13-30.

35. Hansen, Marcus L., The Immigrant in American History (Arthur M. Schlesinger, ed.), Cambridge, Harvard University Press, 1940).

36. Haugen, Einar, The Norwegian Language in America, 2 vols. (Philadelphia, University of Pennsylvania Press, 1953).

37. Haugen, Einar, Some pleasures and problems of bilingual research, International Journal of American Linguistics, 1954, 20, 116-22.

38. Haugen, Einar, Bilingualism in the Americas: A Bibliography and Research Guide (Publication No. 26 of the American Dialect Society) (Alabama, University of Alabama Press, 1956).

39. Hayden, Robert G., Some community dynamics of language maintenance, in Fishman, J. A., et al., Language Loyalty in the United States, Chapter 12.

40. Hayden, Robert G., and Fishman, Joshua A., The impact of exposure to ethnic mother tongues on foreign language teachers in American high schools and colleges, in Fishman, J. A., et al., Language Loyalty in the United States, Chapter 13.

41. Herman, Simon N., Explorations in the social-psychology of language choice, Human Relations, 1961, 14, 149-64.

42. Hoffman, Moses N. H., The Measurement of Bilingual Background (New York, Teachers College, Columbia University, 1934).

43. Hofman, John E., Mother tongue retentiveness in ethnic parishes, in Fishman, J. A., et al., Language Loyalty in the United States, Chapter 9.

44. Hofman, John E., The language transition in some Lutheran denominations, in Fishman, J. A., et al., Language Loyalty in the United States, Chapter 10.

45. Hohenthal, W. D., and Thomas McCorkle, The problem of aboriginal persistance, Southwestern Journal of Anthropology, 1955, 11, 288-300.

46. Homeyer, Helen, Some observations on bilingualism and language shift in Italy from the sixth to the third century B. C., Word, 1957, 13, 415-40.

47. Hymes, Dell H. , The ethnography of speaking, in Gladwin, T. ,
    and W. C. Sturtevant (eds.), Anthropology and Human
    Behavior (Washington, D. C. , Anthropology Society of Wash-
    ington, 1962), pp. 13-53.
48. Jakobson, Roman, Closing statement: linguistics and poetics,
    in Sebeok, T. A. (ed.), Style in Language (Cambridge,
    M. I. T. Press, 1960), pp. 350-77.
49. Johnston, Ruth, Factors in the Assimilation of Selected Groups
    of Polish Post-War Immigrants in Western Australia, Un-
    published Ph.D. Dissertation, University of Western Aus-
    tralia (Perth), 1963.
50. Johnston, Ruth. A new approach to the meaning of assimilation,
    Human Relations, 1963, 16, 295-98.
51. Jones, Frank E. , and Wallace E. Lambert, Attitudes toward
    immigrants in a Canadian community, Public Opinion Quar-
    terly, 1959, 23, 538-46.
52. Joos, Martin, The isolation of styles, Monograph Series on
    Languages and Linguistics, Institute of Languages and Lin-
    guistics, Georgetown University, 1959, 12, 107-13.
53. Kloss, Heinz, Spracherhaltung, Archiv für Politik und Geschichte,
    1927, 8, 456-62.
54. Kloss, Heinz, Sprachtabellen als Grundlage für Sprachstatistik,
    Sprachenkarten und für eine allgemeine Sociologie der
    Sprachgemeinschaften, Vierteljahrsschrift für Politik und
    Geschichte, 1929, 1 (7), 103-17.
55. Kloss, Heinz, German-American language maintenance efforts,
    in Fishman, J. A. , et al., Language Loyalty in the United
    States, Chapter 15.
56. Kohn, Hans, The Idea of Nationalism: A Study of Its Origin and
    Background (New York, MacMillan, 1945).
57. Kuhn, Walter, Die jungen deutschen Sprachinseln in Galizien;
    ein Beitrag zur Method der Sprachinselforschung (Münster,
    Aschendorffsche Verlagsbuchhandlung, 1930).
57a. Kuhn, Walter, Deutsche Sprachinsel-Forschung (Plauen,
    Gunther Wolff, 1934).
58. Labov, William, Phonological correlates of stratification,
    American Anthropologist, 1964, 66, part 2, 164-74.
59. Lambert, Wallace E. , Measurement of the linguistic dominance
    of bilinguals, Journal of Abnormal and Social Psychology,
    1955, 50, 197-200.
60. Lambert, Wallace E. , R. C. Gardner, H. C. Barick, and K.

Tunstall, Attitudinal and cognitive aspects of intensive study of a second language, Journal of Abnormal and Social Psychology, 1963, 66, 358-68.

61. Lambert, Wallace E., Psychological approaches to the study of language, Part II: On second-language learning and bilingualism, Modern Language Journal, 1963, 47, 114-21.

62. Lévi-Strauss, Claude, Roman Jakobson, C. F. Voegelin, and Thomas A. Sebeok, Results of the conference of anthropologists and linguists (= Memoirs, Supplement to International Journal of American Linguistics, 1953, 19, no. 2).

63. Loesch, Karl C. von, Eingedeutschte, Entdeutschte und Renegaten, in Karl C. von Loesch (ed.), Volk unter Vökern, Bücher des Deutschtums, Band I (Breslau, Ferdinand Hirt, 1925).

64. Loesch, Karl C. von, Volkstümer und Sprachwechsel, Wörter und Sachen, 1936, 17, 153-63.

65. Mackensen, Lutz, Heimat, Kolonie, Umvolk, Folk, 1937, 1, 24-55.

66. Mackey, William F., The description of bilingualism, Canadian Journal of Linguistics, 1962, 7, 51-85.

67. Mak, Wilhelm, Zweisprackigkeit und Mischmundart in Oberschlesien, Schlesisches Jahrbuch für deutsche Kulturarbeit, 1935, 7, 41-52.

68. Manuel, Herschel T., The Preparation and Evaluation of Interlanguage Testing Materials (Austin, University of Texas, 1963). (Mimeographed)

69. Miller, Herbert A., Races, Nations and Classes (Chicago, Lippincott, 1924).

70. Molee, Elias., Plea for an American Language or Germanic-English (Chicago, Anderson, 1888).

71. Nahirny, Vladimir C., and Joshua A. Fishman, Language maintenance among intellectual and organizational leaders of four American ethnic groups, in Fishman, J. A., et al., Language Loyalty in the United States, Chapter 11.

72. Nelson, Lowry, Speaking of tongues, American Journal of Sociology, 1947, 54, 202-10.

73. Orans, Martin, A tribe in search of a great tradition: the emulation-solidarity conflict, Man in India, 39, 2, 108-14.

74. Pihlblad, C. Terence, The Kansas Swedes, Southwestern Social Science Quarterly, 1932, 13, 34-47.

75. Pritzwald, Kurt Stegmann von, Sprachwissenschaftliche Minder-

heitenforschung, Wörter und Sachen, 1938, 19 (n. s. 1) 52-
72.

76. Reissman, Leonard, The Urban Process: Cities in Industrial
Societies (New York, Free Press, 1964).

77. Rubin, Joan, Bilingual usage in Paraguay, in J. A. Fishman
(ed.), Readings in Sociolinguistics (The Hague, Mouton,
1968), pp. 512-30.

78. Samora, Julian, and William N. Deane, Language usage as a
possible index of acculturation, Sociology and Social Research,
1956, 40, 307-11.

79. Sapir, Edward, Language, Encyclopedia of the Social Sciences,
1933, 9, 155-69.

80. Schermerhorn, Richard A., Toward a general theory of minority
groups, Phylon, 1964, 25, 238-46.

81. Schmidt-Rohr, Georg, Mutter Sprache (Jena, Eugen Diederichs
Veriag, 1933). (Title of first edition: Die Sprache als
Bildnerin der Volker, Munich, 1932.)

82. Schmidt-Rohr, Georg, Zur Frage der Zweisprachigkeit,
Deutsche Arbeit, 1936, 36, 408-11 and 443-44.

83. Selk, Paul, Die sprachlichen Verhältnisse im deutsch-dänischen
Sprachgebiet südlid der Grenze (Flensburg, Veriag Heimat
und Erbe, 1937). (Ergänzungsband, 1940.)

84. Smith, Christina A., Mental Testing of Hebridean Children in
Gaelic and English (London, 1948).

85. Spencer, John (ed.), Language in Africa (Cambridge, Cambridge
University Press, 1963).

86a. Swadesh, Morris, Observations of pattern impact on the phonetics of bilinguals, in Spier, Leslie, A. Irving Hallowell,
and Stanley S. Newman (eds.), Language, Culture and Personality, Essays in Memory of Edward Sapir (Menasha,
Sapir Memorial Publication Fund, 1941).

86b. Vildomee, Verboj, Multilingualism (Leiden, Sijthoff, 1963).

87. Weinreich, Uriel, Research Problems in Bilingualism, with
Special Reference to Switzerland, unpublished Ph.D. Dissertation, Columbia University, 1951.

88. Weinreich, Uriel, Languages in Contact (New York, Linguistic
Circle of New York, 1953).

89. Weinreich, Uriel, Functional aspects of Indian bilingualism,
Word, 1953, 13, 203-33.

90. Willems, Emilio, Linguistic changes in German-Brazilian communities, Acta Americana, 1943, 1, 448-63.

Part III. Societal Bilingualism

5 | Societal Bilingualism: Stable and Transitional

Societal bilingualism is such a frequently used term that it is time that we paused to consider it in its own right rather than as a means of illustrating more general sociolinguistic phenomena. The psychological literature on bilingualism is so much more extensive than its sociological counterpart that workers in the first field have often failed to establish contact with those in the other. In this essay my purpose is to relate these two research traditions to each other by tracing the interaction between their two major constructs: bilingualism (the term employed by psychologists and psycholinguists) and diglossia (the term used by sociologists and sociolinguists).

Diglossia

Since Ferguson first advanced it in 1959 the term diglossia has not only become widely accepted by sociolinguists and sociologists of language, but has been further extended and refined. Initially it was used only in connection with a society that recognized two or more languages for intra-societal communication. The use within a single society of several separate codes (and their stable maintenance rather than the displacement of one by the other with the passage of time) was found to depend on each code's serving functions distinct from those considered appropriate for the other code. One set of behaviors, attitudes, and values supported, and was expressed in one language; another set of behaviors, attitudes, and values, supported and was expressed by the other. Both sets of behaviors, attitudes and values were fully accepted as culturally legitimate and complementary, that is to say, non-conflicting. Indeed, little if any conflict between them was possible in view of their functional

separation. This separation most frequently took the form of a High
(H) language, used in conjunction with religion, education and other
aspects of High Culture, and a Low (L) language, used in everyday
household pursuits and in the lower work sphere. Ferguson called
High and Low "superposed languages."

To Ferguson's original construct, others have made several
significant additions. Gumperz (1961, 1962, 1964a, 1964b, 1966) is
primarily responsible for our greater awareness that diglossia exists
not only in multilingual societies which officially recognize several
"languages," and not only in societies that utilize highly divergent
and even genetically different vernacular and classical varieties, but
also in societies which employ separate dialects, registers, or functionally differentiated language varieties of whatever kind. Gumperz
has also provided most of the conceptual apparatus by which investigators of multilingual speech communities try to discern the societal
patterns governing the use of one variety rather than another, particularly at the level of small group interaction. My own contribution
(Fishman 1964, 1965a, 1965c, 1965d, 1965e, 1966a, 1968a), on the
other hand, is focused on trying to trace both the maintenance and the
disruption of diglossia at the national or societal level. In addition I
have attempted to relate diglossia to psychologically pertinent considerations such as compound and coordinate bilingualism (1965b). In
this chapter I am trying to extend and to integrate these several
previous attempts and to do so, wherever possible, in connection
with entire polities or other large and complex speech communities.

Speech communities characterized by both diglossia and bilingualism

For purposes of simplicity it seems best to represent the
possible relationships between bilingualism and diglossia by means
of a four-fold table such as that shown in Figure 1.

The first quadrant of Figure 1 refers to those speech communities in which both diglossia and bilingualism are widespread.
At times such communities may comprise an entire nation, but since
widespread, if not all-pervasive, bilingualism would be required, few
nations are fully bilingual and diglossic. An approximation to such
a nation is Paraguay, where more than half of the population speaks

Fig. 1:   The Relationships between Bilingualism and Diglossia

DIGLOSSIA

BILINGUALISM   +   -

+	1. Both diglossia and bilingualism	2. Bilingualism without diglossia
-	3. Diglossia without bilingualism	4. Neither diglossia nor bilingualism

both Spanish and Guarani (Rubin 1962, 1968). A substantial portion
of the formerly monolingual rural population (although generally still
using Guarani when expressing social distance or stressing status
within the rural sphere) has added Spanish to its linguistic repertoire
in matters of education, religion, government and High Culture. For
their part the vast majority of city dwellers, having come relatively
lately from country regions, maintain Guarani for matters of intimacy
and group solidarity, even in the midst of their recently acquired
Spanish urbanity (see Figure 2). It should be noted that Guarani is
not an "official" language in Paraguay, recognized and utilized for
purposes of government, formal education, the courts, and so on,
although it was finally recognized as a "national language" at the 1967
constitutional convention. In diglossic settings, it is not uncommon
for the H variety alone to be recognized as "official" without this fact
threatening the acceptance or the stability of the L variety within the
speech community. Accordingly, the existence of a single "official"
language should not divert the investigator from recognizing the fact
of widespread and stable multilingualism at the levels of societal and
interpersonal functioning. (See Table 1)

Below the level of nationwide functioning there are many
more instances of stable diglossia co-occurring with widespread bilingualism, for example, the Swiss-German cantons in which the
entire population of school age and older alternates between High
German (H) and Swiss German (L), each with its own firmly established and highly valued functions (Ferguson 1959; Weinreich, U.
1951, 1953). Traditional (pre-World War I) Eastern European Jewish males communicated in Hebrew (H) and Yiddish (L). Many of

Fig. 2: <u>National Bilingualism in Paraguay</u>

Ordered dimensions in the choice of language in a diglossic society
(Rubin 1968)

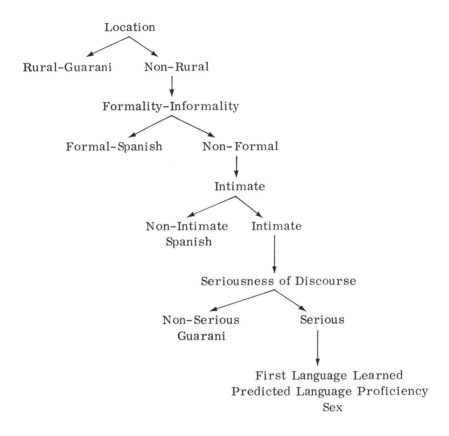

their descendents have continued to do so in various countries of
resettlement, even while adding to their repertoire a Western language, notably English in certain domains of <u>intragroup</u> communication, as well as for broader <u>intergroup</u> contacts (Fishman 1965a,
1965e; Weinreich, U. 1953; Weinreich, M. 1953). This development
is significantly different from the traditional Eastern European Jewish pattern in which males whose occupational activities brought
them into regular contact with various strata of the non-Jewish

TABLE 1
Linguistic Unity and Diversity, by World Region

(Rustow 1967)

	No. of Countries by Percent of Population Speaking Main Language									
Region	90-100	80-89	70-79	60-69	50-59	40-49	30-39	20-29	10-19	Total 10-100%
Europe	17	4	2	2	2	---	---	---	---	27
East and South Asia	5	3	4	3	1	4	---	1	---	21
Oceania[a]	2	---	---	---	---	---	---	---	---	2
Middle East and Northern Africa	8	6	2	3	1	2	---	---	---	22
Tropical and South- ern Africa	3	---	---	2	5	8	7	5	3	33
The Amer- icas	15	6	---	---	2	2	1	---	---	26
World Total	50	19	8	10	11	16	8	6	3	131

[a] Not including New Guinea, for which no breakdown by individual language was available

co-territorial population utilized one or more co-territorial languages (which involved H and L varieties of their own, such as Russian, German or Polish, on the one hand, and Ukrainian, Byelorus-
sian or "Baltic" varieties, on the other), but did so for intergroup
commercial, scientific or technological communication just as do
many minorities in various parts of the world to this very day.
(Blanc 1964; Ferguson 1959; Nader 1962).

All of the foregoing examples have in common the existence
of a fairly large and complex speech community such that both a
range of compartmentalized roles, and ready access to these roles
are available to its members. If the role repertoires of these speech
communities were more limited, their linguistic repertoires would
also be or become more restricted in range, with the result that one
or more separate languages or varieties would become superfluous.
Furthermore, if the roles were not kept separate (compartmentalized)
by the power of their association with quite separate though complementary values, domains of activity and everyday situations, one
language or variety would displace the other as role and value distinctions became blurred or merged. Finally, unless access to the
range of compartmentalized roles, languages or varieties were widely
available the bilingual population would be not a broadly based population segment, but a small privileged caste or class (e.g., as was and
still is the case with respect to H in most of traditional India or China).

We must conclude from the foregoing that if we view their
several registers as separate varieties or languages (in the same
sense as the examples given), many modern speech communities
commonly thought of as monolingual are, instead, marked by both
diglossia and bilingualism. Diglossia and bilingualism may be said
to exist wherever speech communities exist in which speakers
(a) engage in a considerable range of roles (as all but the extreme
upper and lower levels of complex societies are coming to do);
(b) wherever access to several roles is encouraged or facilitated by
powerful social institutions and processes; and (c) wherever the roles
are clearly differentiated as to when, where, and with whom they are
felt to be appropriate.

Such an approach to the subject provides a single theoretical
framework for viewing both bilingual speech communities and speech

communtities in which linguistic diversity is realized through varieties not (or not as yet) recognized as constituting separate "languages."
It follows that rather than becoming fewer in modern times, the number of speech communities characterized by diglossia and the widespread command of diversified linguistic repertoire has greatly
increased in consequence of modernization and growing social complexity (Fishman 1966b). In such communities each generation
begins anew with a monolingual or restricted repertoire base of
hearth and home, and must be rendered bilingual or provided with a
fuller repertoire by the formal institutions of education, religion,
government or the work sphere. In diglossic-bilingual speech communities children do not attain their full repertoires at home or in
their neighborhood playgroups. Indeed, those who most commonly
remain at home or in the home neighborhood (the pre-school young
and the post-work old) are most likely to be functionally monolingual
(as Lieberson's tables on French-English bilingualism in Montreal
amply reveal, see Table 2).

Diglossia without bilingualism

From the co-occurrence of bilingualism and diglossia we
turn to polities in which diglossia obtains, but bilingualism is generally absent (quadrant 3). Here we find two or more speech communities united politically, religiously, and/or economically into a
single functioning unit notwithstanding the socio-cultural cleavages
that separate them on other counts. At the level of this larger, but
not always voluntary, unity, two or more languages or varieties must
be recognized as obtaining. However at least one of the speech communities involved will be marked by relatively impassable group
boundaries and such an emphasis upon ascribed rather than achieved
status, that both role and linguistic access is severely restricted for
"outsiders"—frequently meaning all those not born into the speech
community. At the same time linguistic repertoires in one or both
groups are limited in consequence of role specialization.

Examples of such situations are not hard to find (cf. the
many instances listed by Kloss 1966). Pre-World War I European
elites often stood in this relationship with their countrymen, by speaking for their intragroup purpose either French, or some other

TABLE 2

Percentage Bilingual, by Age and Sex, Montreal Area, 1931-61

(Lieberson 1965)

	Males					Females				
	Montreal-Verdun		Montreal-Outremont-Verdun			Montreal-Verdun		Montreal-Outremont-Verdun		
Age	1931	1941	1941	1951	1961	1931	1941	1941	1951	1961
	(1)	(2)	(3)	(4)	(5)	(6)	(7)	(8)	(9)	(10)
0-4	4.1	5.7	5.7	3.3	2.5	4.0	5.6	5.7	3.4	2.5
5-9	18.2	11.3	11.5	9.7	9.9	18.0	11.5	11.8	9.7	9.6
10-14	43.4	22.2	22.6	20.5	22.4	41.4	21.9	22.3	20.1	21.9
15-19	62.4	51.4	51.7	50.6	49.6	54.7	43.1	43.5	44.5	46.7
20-24	67.2	67.1	67.2	64.9	59.4	53.3	51.5	51.7	48.2	44.4
25-34	61.9	68.8	68.8	68.8	59.7	49.0	47.8	48.1	47.8	41.1
35-44	62.2	63.6	63.7	68.1	65.3	44.5	40.9	41.2	45.2	45.5
45-54	59.3	60.3	60.3	62.7	63.6	41.6	35.6	36.0	37.4	42.6
55-64	57.4	53.7	53.8	57.3	57.2	37.1	31.2	31.6	30.8	34.5
65-69	56.4	49.4	49.6	49.7	52.0	34.3	28.0	28.5	26.5	28.5
70+	51.2	42.9	43.3	42.2	44.0	31.2	24.4	24.7	23.5	24.5

fashionable H tongue (cf. for instance, elites at various times and in various places used Danish, Salish, Provencal, or Russian etc.), with the masses speaking another, not necessarily linguistically related, language for their intra-group purposes. Since the majority of elites and the majority of the masses never interacted with one another they never formed a single speech community (i. e. , their linguistic repertoires were discontinuous and their inter-communications were by means of translators or interpreters (a certain sign of intra-group monolingualism). Since the majority of the members of both the elites and the masses led lives characterized by extremely narrow role repertoires, their linguistic repertoires also were too narrow to permit widespread societal bilingualism to develop. Nevertheless, the body politic in all of its economic and national manifestations tied these two groups together into a "unity," although closer inspection revealed an upper and a lower class, each with a language appropriate to its own restricted concerns. Some have suggested that the modicum of direct interaction that takes place between servants and masters of differing mother tongue brings into being the marginal languages (pidgins) characteristic of such settings.

Thus, the existence of national diglossia does not imply widespread bilingualism amongst rural or recently urbanized African groups, as distinguished from somewhat more Westernized populations in those settings; nor amongst most lower caste Hindus, as distinguished from their more fortunate Brahmin compatriots; nor amongst most lower class rural French-Canadians, as distinguished from their upper and upper middle class city cousins, and so on. In general, this pattern is characteristic of polities that are largely economically underdeveloped and unmobilized, combining groups that are locked into opposite extremes of the social spectrum, and, therefore, conducive to groups that operate within extremely restricted and discontinuous linguistic repertoires (Friedrich 1966). Obviously, such politics are bound to experience language problems as their social patterns alter in the direction of industrialization, widespread literacy and education, democratization, and modernization in general. Since few polities which exhibit diglossia without bilingualism initially developed out of prior socio-cultural consensus or unity, rapid education, political or economic development experienced by their lower classes is likely to lead to secessionism or to demands that their submerged language or languages be given official recognition. The

TABLE 3

Frequency of Mother Tongue Use in Conversations by Oldest and Youngest Children of Four Ethnic Backgrounds*

(Fishman 1966c)

In conversation with:	Almost Always		Frequently		Almost Never		Almost Always		Frequently		Almost Never		Almost Always		Frequently		Almost Never		Almost Always		Frequently		Almost Never	
	N	%	N	%	N	%	N	%	N	%	N	%	N	%	N	%	N	%	N	%	N	%	N	%
Grandparents	6	26.1	6	26.1	11	47.8	6	20.0	9	30.0	15	50.0	15	57.6	5	19.2	6	23.2	26	96.3	--	----	1	3.7
Father	7	18.4	10	26.4	21	55.2	5	15.0	23	34.3	34	50.7	22	38.3	17	26.7	21	35.0	42	84.0	6	12.0	2	4.0
Mother	5	16.1	4	12.9	22	71.0	5	9.8	19	37.4	27	52.9	16	29.1	14	25.4	25	45.5	41	89.1	5	10.9	--	----
Brothers and sisters	--	----	2	8.7	19	82.6	--	----	7	18.9	30	81.1	7	19.4	5	13.8	24	66.7	20	50.0	18	45.0	2	5.0
Friends	3	10.0	7	23.3	20	66.7	--	----	10	22.7	34	77.3	4	9.8	9	21.9	28	68.3	15	27.3	20	36.4	20	36.4
Husband and wife	2	11.1	1	5.6	15	83.3	--	----	1	4.5	21	95.5	3	15.0	--	----	17	85.0	4	36.4	3	27.3	4	36.4
Own child	1	5.6	3	16.7	14	77.8	--	----	1	5.3	18	94.7	3	20.0	--	----	12	80.0	4	50.0	3	37.5	1	12.5

*Data reported by parents. The German and Polish parents studied were primarily second generation individuals. The Jewish and Ukrainian parents studied were primarily first generation individuals. All parents were ethnic cultural or organizational "leaders."

language problems of Eastern Europe and of India, as well as those
of Wales, Canada, and Belgium, stem from origins such as these.
It is this pattern of development that may yet convulse modern West
African nations if their de-ethnicized Westernized elites do nothing
to foster widespread and stable bilingual speech communities, i. e.
communities which incorporate the masses and which recognize
both the official language of wider communication and at least the
more numerous languages.

Bilingualism without diglossia

We turn next to those situations in which bilingualism obtains
but diglossia is generally absent (quadrant 2). Here we see even
more clearly that bilingualism is essentially a characterization of
individual linguistic versatility while diglossia is a characterization
of the societal allocation of functions to different languages or varieties. Under what circumstances do bilinguals function without benefit
of a well-developed and widely accepted social consensus as to which
language to use between which interlocutors, for communication concerning what topics, or for what purpose? Under what circumstances
do the speech varieties or languages involved lack clearly defined or
protected separate functions? To answer briefly, such circumstances
are those of rapid social change, of great social unrest, of widespread
abandonment of earlier norms before the consolidation of new ones.
In such circumstances, children typically become bilingual at a very
early age, while still largely confined to home and neighborhood,
since their elders (children of school age and adults alike) carry into
the domains of intimacy a language learned outside its confines. Formal institutions tend to make individuals increasingly monolingual in
a language other than that of home and ultimately, to replace the latter entirely (see Tables 3 and 4).

Many studies of bilingualism and intelligence or of bilingualism and school achievement have been conducted within the context
of bilingualism without diglossia (for a review see Macnamara 1966).
Often investigators have not sufficiently understood that there were
several other possible contexts for the study of bilingualism. As a
result, many of the purported "disadvantages" of bilingualism have
been falsely generalized to the phenomenon at large, instead of being

TABLE 4
1940-1960 Totals for 23 Non-English
Mother Tongues in the USA

(Fishman 1966c)

Language	1940 Total	1960 Total	Total Change n	%
Norwegian	658,220	321,774	-336,446	-51.1%
Swedish	830,900	415,597	-415,303	-50.0%
Danish	226,740	147,619	- 79,121	-65.1%
Dutch/				
Flemish	289,580	321,613	+ 32,033	+11.1%
French	1,412,060	1,043,220	-368,840	-26.1%
German	4,949,780	3,145,772	-1,804,008	-36.4%
Polish	2,416,320	2,184,936	-231,384	- 9.6%
Czech	520,440	217,771	-302,669	-58.2%
Slovak	484,360	260,000	-224,360	-46.3%
Hungarian	453,000	404,114	- 48,886	-10.8%
Serbo-				
Croatian	153,080	184,094	+ 31,014	+20.3%
Slovenian	178,640	67,108	-111,532	-62.4%
Russian	585,080	460,834	-124,246	-21.2%
Ukrainian	83,600	252,974	+169,374	+202.6%
Lithuanian	272,680	206,043	- 66,637	-24.4%
Finnish	230,420	110,168	-120,252	-52.2%
Rumanian	65,520	58,019	- 7,501	-11.4%
Yiddish	1,751,100	964,605	-786,495	-44.9%
Greek	273,520	292,031	+ 18,511	+ 6.8%
Italian	3,766,820	3,673,141	- 93,679	- 2.5%
Spanish	1,861,400	3,335,961	+1,474,561	+79.2%
Portuguese	251,660	181,109	- 34,551	-16.0%
Arabic	107,420	103,908	- 3,512	- 3.3%
Total	21,786,540	18,352,351	-3,434,189	-15.8%

TABLE 4 cont'd

In 1940 the numerically strongest mother tongues in the United States were German, Italian, Polish, Spanish, Yiddish, and French, in that order. Each of these languages was claimed by approximately a million and a half or more individuals. In 1960 these same languages remained the "big six" although their order had changed to Italian, Spanish, German, Polish, French, and Yiddish. Among them, only Spanish registered gains (and substantial gains at that) in this 20-year interval. The losses among the "big six" varied from a low of 2.5% for Italian to a high of 44.9% for Yiddish. The only other languages to gain in overall number of claimants during this period (disregarding the generational distribution of such gains) were Ukrainian, Serbo-Croatian, "Dutch"/Flemish, and Greek. The greatest gain of all was that of Ukrainian (202.6%!). Most mother tongues, including five of the "big six," suffered substantial losses during this period, the sharpest being that of Danish (65.1%). All in all, the 23 non-English mother tongues for which a 1940-1960 comparison is possible lost approximately one-sixth of their claimants during this interval. Yet the total number of claimants of non-English mother tongues in the United States is still quite substantial, encompassing nearly 11% of the total 1960 population (and an appreciably higher proportion of the white population).* For a discussion of 1970 figures for several larger immigrant languages in the United States, see my paper in Goldene Keyf, 1972, no. 74.

---

* The 1940 and 1960 totals shown in Table 4 must not be taken as the totals for all non-English mother tongue claimants in those years. Figures for Armenian were reported in 1940 but not in 1960. Figures for Chinese and Japanese were reported in 1960 but not in 1940. Total figures for "All other" languages were reported in both years. None of these inconsistent or non-specific listings are included in Table 4. Adding in these figures, as well as the necessary generational estimates based upon them, the two totals would become 1940: 22,036,240; 1960: 19,381,786.

related to the absence or presence of social patterns which reach
substantially beyond bilingualism (Fishman 1965b, 1966a).

The history of industrialization in the Western world (as
well as in those parts of Africa and Asia which have experienced industrialization under Western auspices) is such that the means of
production (capital, plant, organization) have often been controlled
by one speech community while the productive manpower was drawn
from another (Deutsch 1966). Initially, both speech communities
may have maintained their separate diglossia-with-bilingualism patterns or, alternatively, an overarching diglossia without bilingualism.
In either case, both the needs and the consequences of rapid and massive industrialization and urbanization frequently impelled members
of the speech community providing productive manpower to abandon
in haste their traditional socio-cultural patterns, and to learn (or at
least be taught) some variety of the language associated with the
means of production, long before such workers were absorbed into
the socio-cultural patterns and privileges to which that language and,
most particularly, its H variety pertained. In response to this imbalance one group reaction further stresses the advantages of the
newly gained language of education and industry, while others,
attempt to replace the new language by an elaborated version of their
own largely pre-industrial, pre-urban, pre-mobilization tongue.

Under circumstances such as these in many speech communities of the lower and lower middle classes, there is no well established, socially protected and recognized functional differentiation of
languages. Dislocated immigrants and their children (for whom a
separate "political solution" is seldom possible) are particularly inclined to use their mother tongue and other tongue for intra-group
communication in seemingly random fashion (Fishman, Cooper and
Ma et al., 1968; Nahirny and Fishman 1965; Herman 1961). Since
the formerly separate roles of the home domain, the school domain
and the work domain are all disturbed by the massive dislocation of
values and norms resulting from simultaneous immigration and industrialization, the language of work (and of the school) comes to be
used at home. As role compartmentalization and value complemen-
tarity decrease under the impact of foreign models and massive
change the linguistic repertoire also becomes less compartmentalized.
Languages and varieties formerly kept apart come to influence each

other phonetically, lexically, semantically, and even grammatically much more than before. Instead of two or more carefully separated languages each under the eyes of caretaker groups of teachers, preachers and writers, several intervening varieties differing in degree of interpenetration may obtain. The standard varieties of the languages of immigrants are given no language maintenance support under these circumstances, yet at the same time the varieties they use may come to be ridiculed as "debased" or "broken."

Bilingualism without diglossia thus tends to be transitional both in the linguistic repertoires of speech communities and in the speech varieties involved per se. Without separate though complementary norms and values to establish and maintain functional separation of the speech varieties, that language or variety which is fortunate enough to be associated with the predominant drift of social forces tends to displace the others. Furthermore, pidginization (the crystalization of new fusion languages or varieties) is likely to set in when members of the work force a) are too dislocated to maintain or develop significantly compartmentalized, limited access roles in which they might be able to safeguard a stable mother tongue variety; and b) when social change stops short of permitting them to interact sufficiently with members of the "power class" who might serve as standard other-tongue models.

Neither diglossia nor bilingualism

Only very small, isolated, and undifferentiated speech communities may be said to reveal neither diglossia nor bilingualism (Gumperz 1962; Fishman 1965c). Given little role differentiation or compartmentalization and frequent face-to-face interaction between all members of the speech community, no fully differentiated registers or varieties may establish themselves. Given self-sufficiency, no regular or significant contacts with other speech communities may be maintained. Nevertheless, such groups—whether bands or clans—are easier to hypothesize than to find (Owens 1965; Sorenson 1967). All speech communities seem to have certain ceremonies or pursuits to which access is limited, if only on the basis of age. Thus, all linguistic repertoires contain certain terms that are unknown to cer-

tain members of the speech community, and certain terms that are
used differently by different sub-sets of speakers. In addition, metaphorical switching for purposes of emphasis, humor, satire, or
criticism must be available in some form even in relatively undifferentiated communities. Finally, such factors as exogamy, warfare,
expansion of population, economic growth and contact with others all
lead to internal diversification and, consequently, to repertoire diversification. Such diversification is the beginning of bilingualism; its
becoming a societal norm is the very hallmark of diglossia. Quadrant
four tends to be self-liquidating.

Conclusions

Many efforts are now underway to achieve a rapprochment
between psychological, linguistic and sociological work on bilingualism. The student of bilingualism, most particularly the student of
bilingualism in the context of social issues and social change, should
benefit from an awareness of the various possible relationships between individual bilingualism and societal diglossia illustrated here.
One of the fruits of such awareness will be that problems of transition and dislocation will not be mistaken for the entire gamut of societal bilingualism.

NOTE

A revision of "Bilingualism with and without diglossia; diglossia with
and without bilingualism," Journal of Social Issues, 1967, 23, no. 2,
29-38. Also included in my Sociolinguistics, Rowley, Mass.,
Newbury House, 1970.

REFERENCES

Blanc, Haim. Communal Dialects in Baghdad. Cambridge, Harvard
        University Press, 1964.
Deutsch, Karl W. Nationalism and Social Communication. Cam-
        bridge, MIT Press, 1966 (2nd edition).
Ferguson, Charles A. Diglossia. Word, 1959, 15, 325-40.

Fishman, Joshua A. Language maintenance and language shift as
        fields of inquiry. Linguistics, 1964, 9, 32-70.
_____ Yiddish in America. Bloomington (Indiana), Indiana
        University Research Center in Anthropology, Folklore and
        Linguistics, Publication 36, 1965a.
_____ Bilingualism, intelligence and language learning. Modern
        Language Journal, 1965b, 49, 227-37.
_____ Varieties of ethnicity and language consciousness. Mon-
        ograph Series on Language and Linguistics (Georgetown Uni-
        versity), 1965c, 18, 69-79.
_____ Who speaks what language to whom and when? Linguis-
        tique, 1965d, no. 2, 67-88.
_____ Language maintenance and language shift; the American
        immigrant case within a general theoretical perspective.
        Sociologus, 1965e, 16, 19-38.
_____ Bilingual sequences at the societal level. On Teaching
        English to Speakers of Other Languages, 1966a, 2, 139-44.
_____ Some contrasts between linguistically homogeneous and
        linguistically heterogeneous polities. Sociological Inquiry,
        1966b, 36, 146-58. (Revised and expanded in Fishman,
        J. A., C. A. Ferguson, and J. Das Gupta (eds.), Language
        Problems of the Developing Nations. New York, Wiley,
        1968, in press.)
_____ Language Loyalty in the United States. The Hague,
        Mouton, 1966c.
_____ Sociolinguistics and the language problems of developing
        nations. International Social Science Journal, 1968a, 20,
        211-25.
_____ Readings in the Sociology of Language. The Hague,
        Mouton, 1968b.
_____ Robert L. Cooper and Roxana Ma, et al. Bilingualism in
        the Barrio. Final Report on Contract No. OEC-1-7-062817-
        0297 to DHEW. New York, Yeshiva University, 1968.
Friedrich, Paul. The linguistic reflex of social change: from Tsarist
        to Soviet Russian kinship. Sociological Inquiry, 1966, 36,
        159-85.
Gumperz, John J. Speech variation and the study of Indian civiliza-
        tion. American Anthropologist, 1961, 63, 976-88.
_____ Types of linguistic communities. Anthropological Lin-
        guistics, 1962, 4, no. 1, 28-40. (Also in Fishman, J. A.,
        ed., Readings, pp. 460-72.)

Gumperz, John J. Linguistic and social interaction in two communities. American Anthropologist, 1964a, 66, no. 2, 37-53.

_____ Hindi-Punjabi code switching in Delhi, in Halle, Morris (ed.), Proceedings of the International Congress of Linguists. The Hague, Mouton, 1964b.

_____ On the ethnology of linguistic change, in Bright, William (ed.), Sociolinguistics. The Hague, Mouton, 1966, pp. 27-38.

Kloss, Heinz. Types of multilingual communities: a discussion of ten variables. Sociological Inquiry, 1966, 36, 135-45.

Lieberson, Stanley. Bilingualism in Montreal: a demographic analysis. American Journal of Sociology, 1965, 71, 10-25.

Macnamara, John. Bilingualism in Primary Education. Edinburgh, Edinburgh University Press, 1966.

Nader, Laura. A note on attitudes and the use of language. Anthropological Linguistics, 1962, 4, no. 6, 25-29.

Owens, Roger C. The patrilocal band: a linguistically and culturally hybrid social unit. American Anthropologist, 1965, 67, 675-90.

Rubin, Joan. Bilingualism in Paraguay. Anthropological Linguistics, 1962, 4, no. 1, 52-58.

_____ Language and education in Paraguay, in Fishman, J. A., C. A. Ferguson, and J. Das Gupta (eds.), Language Problems of the Developing Nations. New York, Wiley, 1968, in press.

Rustow, Danknart A. A World of Nations: Problems of Political Modernization. Washington, Brookings Institution, 1967.

Sorensen, Arthur P., Jr. Multilingualism in the Northwest Amazon. American Anthropologist, 1967, 69, 670-84.

Weinreich, Max. Yidishkayt and Yiddish: on the impact of religion on language in Ashkenazic Jewry, in Mordecai M. Kaplan Jubilee Volume. New York, Jewish Theological Seminary of America, 1953. (Also in Fishman, J. A., ed., Readings, pp. 382-413.)

Weinreich, Uriel. Research problems in bilingualism, with special reference to Switzerland. Unpublished Ph.D. Dissertation. Columbia University, 1951.

_____ Languages in Contact. New York, Linguistic Circle of New York, 1953.

6 | The Description of Societal Bilingualism

1. Thesis

Current advanced thinking concerning societal bilingualism—
such as that which marked our discussions on this topic during the
Moncton Seminar*—clearly represents a break with traditional models. Those models viewed societal bilingualism as an inter-group
phenomenon resulting from the contact between essentially separate
monolingual groups. Given this thesis the basic sociological task
was to contrast bilingual "middlemen" with their respective monolingual compatriots to determine when and why the "other tongue" (L_2)
was employed and to predict the rate of shift to a monlingual status,
the latter being considered their only natural and stable basis of social
interaction. Psychological and linguistic research were also held
captive by this thesis. Psychologists concentrated on measures of
how well L_2 was mastered (i.e., how quickly, how correctly, how
complicatedly). Because they viewed bilingualism as basically "un-
natural" they had to discover some "price," some toll had to be revealed in comparison with monolingual normality. Linguists joined in
the hunt and found evidence of "interference" at every level: phonetic,
lexical, grammatical, and semantic. The natural state of languages
was supposedly one of pristine purity and separation. Bilinguals
forced languages into unfortunate intercourse and it was unlikely,
indeed, to find that no "damage" had been done to either or both.

It seems clear to me that the thesis which consciously or
unconsciously guided so much past research on bilingualism in general, and on societal bilingualism in particular, was, in large part,
a result of erroneous generalization from limited Western experi-

ence. Bilingualism was confused with some of its atypical concomitants: large scale immigration and other social or personal dislocations related to disharmonious intergroup contacts. The acculturating
immigrant or his offspring, the Westernizing "native," the struggling
"foreign language" student, the downtrodden but dedicated "minority
group" patriot, these were the bilingual subjects on whom bilingual
research and bilingual theory were based. The notion of widespread,
stable, intra-group bilingualism (such as exists even today in over
half of the world) was unrepresented in the work on societal bilingualism, and as a result that work was simultaneously sterile and less
than accurate.

2. Antithesis

Our discussions concerning societal bilingualism at Moncton
showed how far the pendulum has swung from the initial (conscious or
unconscious) theses of bygone years. Instead of being viewed as the
temporary or transitional consequence of separate, monolingual
societies "in (unfortunate) contact," societal bilingualism is now
viewed as a (possibly) stable and widespread phenomenon in its own
right. Instead of searching for the differences between bilingual
"middlemen" (be they students, elites, traders, assimilators, etc.)
and their "more normal" monolingual compatriots modern sociolinguistic research on bilingualism seeks to determine which members
of a bi- (or multi-) lingual society employ which variety (from among
a whole repertoire available in the bilingual community), in which
functional context. Membership in a bilingual society is viewed as no
different from membership in any tongue, in that it results in norm-
regulated communicative interaction such that certain usage is considered appropriate (and is, therefore, effective) in certain contexts.
Indeed, it is because of this basic similarity between societies marked
by widespread and stable bilingualism, on the one hand, and monolingual societies on the other, that it is felt that the study of societal
(intra-group) bilingualism should be of interest to all students of
societal interaction. Because the markers of differentiable varieties
(the relative frequencies with which given linguistic variables are
realized in particular ways) are somewhat more easily recognizable
in bilingual than in monolingual societies the differentiable contexts

of social interaction (intersections between specifiable role-
relationships, locales, topics and purposes) may also become more
recognizable. Thus, those scholars concerned with social process
analysis per se, or with the functional demarcation of structural
groupings (age groups, occupational groups, educational groups,
ethnic groups, religious groups, etc.) may well be attracted to the
study of societal bilingualism as an arena which offers easier access
to theoretical and methodological clarifications of all-pervading significance.

A very similar counterpart position describes the antithesis
linguistic view of bilingualism. Instead of witch-hunting for bilingual
interference, modern sociolinguistics recognizes the linguistic repertoires of bilingual speech communities as an instance of the repertoires that characterize all functionally diversified speech communities. Indeed, it is because of this basic similarity that the differentiation of the linguistic repertoires of bilingual speech communities
should be of interest to all students of modern descriptive linguistics.
Sociolinguistic differentiation may be more recognizable in most bilingual than in most monolingual repertoires, and, as a result, the
study of bilingual repertoires may contribute to the solution of basic
theoretical and methodological problems facing modern linguistics
as a whole.

How the worm has turned! However, as with all intellectual
revolutions (and modern sociolinguistics is such a revolution for both
of the parent disciplines involved) the antithesis view of societal
bilingualism is marked by certain excesses. These are accidents of
intellectual history which derive—as did the thesis model—from the
societal and disciplinary problems which happened to co-occur with
the rise of modern sociolinguistics itself.

3. Critique

In correcting or counteracting the biases and limitations of
the classical ("thesis") approaches to societal bilingualism the modern sociolinguistic "antithesis" reveals a number of unjustifiable (and
unnecessary) biases of its own.

a. At one level, no particular attention is merited by the objection to the reality of groups ("Groups do not behave; individuals behave. Groups are frequently no more than constructs of the social scientist"). Social psychology and sociology were forced to demonstrate the reality of groups quite early in their development and this demonstration continues to be performed successfully whenever the consequences of human grouping are revealed. The "antithesis" discovery that some groups are structural or analytic devices of the scientist's own making whereas others are functionally real "out there" ("real communities are aggregates whose members exchange messages frequently and who share norms for the interpretation of messages") is truly touching but sadly anticlimactic for anyone who is aware of the intellectual history of sociology, social psychology or political science. The differences between structuralism and functionalism cannot be fruitfully examined on the grounds of "reality," but rather on the grounds of their contrastive contributions to particular problems to be investigated and answered.

Thus, the only reason why the "antithesis" objection to the reality of groups needs to be taken seriously at all is that in its iconoclastic blindness, it may make it impossible for sociolinguistics to do that which it is best fitted to do: describe and measure societal bilingualism. To define groups out of existence, to fail to describe functional groups merely because of theoretical bias with respect to structural groups, to fail to seek out the web between process and structure and thereby constantly improve the formulation of structural grouping is to resign from a responsibility rather than to face it responsibly.

b. The reluctance to struggle with structural grouping, and, indeed, the reluctance to consider that functional groups represent the same level of reality as individual functioning, is related to another atomistic excess of "antithesis" sociolinguistics in relation to bilingualism (as well as in relation to other sociolinguistic concerns). "Antithesis" sociolinguistics is faced by the Heisenberg-like dilemma of seeking to describe synchronic systems so accurately that all else is lost sight of: first and foremost, a parsimonious approach to the notion of linguistic repertoire.

Initially the construct of "language" was successfully revealed to be an "abstraction" covering a repertoire of varieties, each
with contextually appropriate social meanings. Subsequently the construct "variety" has been attacked for being merely an "abstraction"
covering a constantly varying range and frequency of realizations of
particular phonetic and syntactic "variables." As a result, it is no
longer deemed sufficiently refined or accurate to designate the languages or varieties employed in a bilingual setting, since any such
designation represents an inevitable grouping or lumping in contrast
to the ultimate descriptive finesse currently attainable in describing
differential realizations of "variables" considered one at a time.

A similar reluctance characterized the approach of "antithesis" sociolinguistics to the question of when particular varieties are
employed in bilingual societies. The opposition to structural categories leads to a basic reliance on purported interpersonal meanings.
Changed frequencies and ranges of variable-realizations are related
to phenomenologically experienced changes in situations or to phenomenologically experienced changes in metaphors (humor, contrast,
emphasis, etc.). Just as there is reluctance to take the risks inherent in grouping when designating populations and codes, so is
there a hypersensitivity towards designating the kinds of contexts
(situational environments that have societal relevance) in which designated kinds of societal members utilize designated varieties.

The "antithesis" sociolinguistic approach to societal bilingualism is oriented to micro-process with such a vengeance that it
not only is unable to cope parsimoniously with nomothetic formulations and macro-structure problems, but it also defines these formulations and problems as unreal and non-existent. As a result, it
often fails to objectify its findings by reporting frequencies of occurrence or non-occurrence of whatever it is that is being studied ("dependent variable") in precisely defined kinds of individuals, situations
or codes. Some high-priests of antithesis sociolinguistics have re-
signed from the replicability goals of social science in pursuit of a
fuller understanding of momentary interpersonal subtlety. Clinical
sociolinguistics is at hand!

c. A final excess of sociolinguistic antithesis thinking as it
applies to the measurement and description of societal bilingualism

is its lack of interest (if not active opposition) with respect to attitudinal factors. This opposition has a long prior history in linguistics
proper where what an informant <u>actually</u> says rather than what he
<u>thinks</u> he says (or what he thinks <u>about</u> what he says, or what he thinks
he <u>should</u> say) is the only matter of interest. The antithesis opposition to recognizing cognitive-affective <u>self-regulation</u> of usage also
has prior social anthropological origins from the fact that the dominant style of research in that field is one of participant and non-
directive observation in small communities of very ordinary, unmobilized, "unspoiled" membership. Most directly, however, the
reluctance to recognize self-regulation (and self-monitoring or self-
report), or to study those social networks in whose bilingualism such
factors are most marked, is derived from the prominence of these
very factors and these very populations in the earlier work on intergroup bilingualism against which much of sociolinguistics has revolted.

As with the other excesses with which the sociolinguistic
revolution has confronted the study of societal bilingualism the reluctance to engage in attitudinal, ideological and self-report inquiry
strikes at a worthwhile point. Much earlier work on societal bilingualism (indeed, much of the earlier work in which I myself have
engaged) is probably too far removed from the primary data of actual
speech because of its well nigh exclusive preoccupation with self-
report. However, if such work failed to examine the relationship between language attitudes, ideologies and actual language behavior
and, furthermore, if such work dealt almost exclusively with sub-
populations selected because of their particular suitability with respect
to the one-sided methodology employed, these very same charges are
now equally (though oppositely) true of the antithesis approach to the
study of societal bilingualism.

As a result of its insistence on <u>deriving</u> the speech norms of
a bilingual society and its reluctance to study those individuals (teachers, writers, politicians, students and other sophisticates) who can
<u>verbalize</u> these norms and possibly consciously <u>guide</u> their own lan-
guage behavior (and that of others), the antithesis approach to societal bilingualism cuts itself off from studying important segments of
many bilingual societies. It is false to suppose that only intergroup
bilinguals or "cultural bilinguals" show little switching (due to their

more frequent "middleman" role vis-à-vis monolinguals). It is false to suppose that language ideologies and movements arise only as a result of the encounters between conflicting monolingual populations. Indeed, no valid societal description can be attained without studying the ideologically more mobilized segments of bilingual societies where such obtain (and they are not necessarily seeking to disturb the existing functional allocation or variation of codes), and without contrasting their bilingual attitudes with their bilingual behaviors in a whole host of contexts.

It is as harmful for the study of societal bilingualism to ignore attitudes and ideologies as to overemphasize them. As with opposition to societal-grouping and opposition to code-grouping, the antithesis approach to the role of attitudes and self-report in societal bilingualism has gone too far and has, in the end, thrown out the baby with the bath water.

4. Synthesis

Both microsociology and macrosociology represent long-standing and fruitful modes of inquiry; it would be a pity if the study of societal bilingualism were not to develop so as to benefit from both, or at the very least, so as to benefit from whichever of the two happened to be more appropriate to the variety of problems clamoring for attention. The "antithesis" approach that was so fully examined during our deliberations at Moncton is related in its origins and predilections to the current rejuvenation of microsociology under the general label of ethnomethodology. Ethnomethodology seeks to discover the rules by which members of a social order carry out their practical, everyday activities. The members of a social order have knowledge of these rules but, for most of them, it is knowledge-in-use rather than knowledge that is ideologically or otherwise consciously organized and available for accurate and coherent self-report. One of the tasks of ethnomethodology is to discover (and then to formally describe) the rules that organize "talk" in society. As a result of its basic concern with the everyday rounds of societal behavior in general and its interest in "talk" or conversations in particular (and the relationships between "talk" and other common social behaviors) ethnomethodology obviously contributes not only a welcome but a necessary approach to the study of societal bilingualism.

The past decade has also witnessed a revival of interest in
macrosociology with its emphases on the structure of total societies
as well as on their contrasts or similarities to each other. In macrosociology the processes of social interaction continue to remain of
paramount interest but they can no longer be analyzed or compre-
hended without recourse to social structure. Since its task is (frequently) the characterization of entire nations (rather than only of
particular face-to-face interaction networks) macrosociology faces
a very complex task and one admittedly surrounded by methodological
problems. In struggling with its problems macrosociology frequently
makes use of comparative data and draws upon a greater variety of
data than is necessary for ethnomethodological work. At its best,
when it is most penetrating and stimulating, macrosociological research draws upon historical records (including law-codes), qualitative impressions, demographic data, attitude and opinion data, behavioral surveys purposely located in terms of a stratified sampling
plan, etc. Rather than being at loggerheads with microsociology
(including, but not limited to ethnomethodology) macrosociology must
constantly pursue sure roots at lower-order levels of analysis, otherwise its structural and stratificational categories will be erroneously
derived and its findings unenlightening or misleading. Because sociology also needs to be able to comprehend and compare societies and
nations as "wholes," because some attributes of societies (and of
modern societies in particular) manifest themselves at no other level
as clearly as at the national level (e.g., national mobilization and
integration), it would be a pity, indeed, if the study of societal bilingualism (or of other sociolinguistic concerns) were so constrained as
not be able to proceed along macro-sociological lines even when it
was germane to a problem at hand to do so.

The study of societal bilingualism is currently an exciting,
vigorous area of inquiry for investigators in various countries working in various intellectual traditions. This being the case, I am sure
that the next decade will witness many investigations of the kinds
that were underrepresented in our deliberations at Moncton. We
need studies of societal bilingualism that do not get so lost in the
minutia of description (in terms of any current equilibrium model)
that they are unable to <u>demonstrate</u> changes in the bilingual pattern
as a result of social change. (I underscore <u>demonstrate</u> to emphasize
that I do not mean "anecdotal commentary," initially provocative

though that may be.) We definitely need studies that contrast intellectual and ideologized groups with more ordinary members of national
societies at various stages of modernization. There must certainly
be studies of societal bilingualism under stress. There must also be
studies that seek a rapprochement with the older tradition of research
on intergroup bilingualism since societal bilingualism is not always
(and, perhaps, not even usually) entirely of one kind or the other.
Degree of mastery is frequently of importance in bilingual societies,
particularly when language maintenance or language shift are high-
lighted in the process of internal political, economic, and cultural
conflict.

        The study of societal bilingualism is now both too vital and
too mature to be long delayed and misled by sectarian biases. It will
doubtlessly select what is best from all theoretical and methodological
traditions and, in this process, contribute to their enrichment as
well.

7 | The Multiple Prediction of Phonological Variables in a Bilingual Speech Community

In Collaboration with Eleanor Herasimchuk

Thus far the sociolinguistic description of phonological variables has been limited substantively to the speech of monolinguals
and limited methodologically to the level of simple cross-tabulation
(Labov 1964, 1966, 1968). Our report attempts to go beyond both
of these restrictions. It deals with selected phonological variables
in the speech of Spanish-English bilinguals in the Greater New York
City Area and it attempts to relate the occurrence or non-occurrence
of particular variants of these variables to a larger set of sociolinguistic and demographic factors.

Data Collection

The data analyzed for our purposes was obtained as part of
the bilingualism project in a Puerto Rican neighborhood in New York
City, described in earlier chapters of this Volume.* To repeat
briefly, the neighborhood studied by a team of linguists, psychologists and sociologists included 431 Puerto Ricans (or individuals of
Puerto Rican parentage) living in 90 households. All of these individuals were covered in a language census which obtained the demographic data we have used for the purpose of this report. Our
linguistic data was obtained in the course of two to four hour psycholinguistic interviews and testing sessions with a random stratified
sample of those Puerto Ricans over the age of thirteen who lived in
the study neighborhood.

---

*Bilingualism in the Barrio, by J. A. Fishman, R. L.
Cooper, Roxana Ma, et al. Bloomington, Indiana University Language
Sciences Monographs, 1971.

Speech contexts

The psycholinguistic interviews and testing sessions were designed to elicit speech data in five different contexts which form a continuum from most formal or careful to most informal or casual as follows:

Context D: List reading. Subjects were asked to read two different lists of separate words, one in English and one in Spanish. The speech obtained in this fashion was considered to be representative of the most careful pronunciation available to the subjects.

Context C: Text reading. Subjects were asked to read four different paragraphs, two in English and two in Spanish. The speech obtained in this fashion was considered to be representative of careful pronunciation.

Context WN: List recitation (word naming). Subjects were asked to "name as many words as come to mind that have to do with (domain)." This task was performed separately in English and in Spanish for each of the following domains: family, neighborhood, education, work, religion. The speech data obtained in this fashion was considered to be representative of intermediate pronunciation (neither markedly careful nor casual).

Context B: Careful speech. Subjects were asked factual questions concerning five taped "playlets" to which they had just listened. Ideally, half of the questions were asked and answered in Spanish and half were asked and answered in English. The speech data obtained in this fashion was considered to be representative of somewhat, though not completely, casual pronunciation.

Context A: Casual speech. Subjects were asked their personal opinions and preferences regarding the problems that figured in the "playlets" to which they had just listened. The speech data obtained in this fashion was considered to be representative of the most informal pronunciation that could be elicited by an interviewer.

In view of the restricted corpuses obtained in the reading contexts in
the study population, only the last three contexts (WN, B, A) will be
examined in the discussion that follows.

Linguistic Variables

The taped speech samples obtained for the above mentioned
five contexts were independently scored by two linguists on seven
Spanish and ten English phonological variables. The reliability of
scoring varied only slightly and irregularly from context to context
and from one language to the other, the reliability coefficients obtained ranging from .73 to .94 with a median of .90.[1] The present
report deals only with selected values on one Spanish and one English
variable in order to illustrate a method of analysis hitherto not
utilized in sociolinguistic research. The particular linguistic values
selected for presentation in this study are further explained in the
section on Results, below.

Demographic Variables

Four demographic factors (sex, age, education, and birthplace) are included in the analyses we report upon.[2] The reliability
coefficients for the various items of obtained demographic information are all .90 or higher.

Sex has consistently proved to be a non-significant demographic variable in accounting for phonological variation in Puerto
Rican Spanish; however, it was included in the present study merely
in order to provide a comparison with prior studies.

Age was categorized in two separate ways. As a three-
category variable the categories employed were: <25, 25-34, >34.
As a two-category variable, categories utilized were: <25 and 25
and over. We categorized age in two different ways in order to learn
whether one categorization is more related to linguistic variation
than the other, and also to summate both age categorizations into one
age variable.

Education was categorized in three different ways. As a four-category variable, the categories employed were: <7 years, all in Puerto Rico; 7 or more years, all in Puerto Rico; partially in Puerto Rico and partially in continental USA; all in continental USA. As a two-category variable education was categorized in two different ways: first, all in Puerto Rico vs. all or part in continental USA, and, second, all USA vs. all or part in Puerto Rico. Once again, our analytic technique enabled us to summate these three different ways of categorizing education as well as to tell whether there is any difference between them in explaining linguistic variation.

Birthplace was categorized in two different ways. As a four-category variable the categories used were: Highland Puerto Rico, Coastal Puerto Rico other than San Juan and suburbs, San Juan and suburbs, and continental USA. As a two-category variable the categories utilized were Highland Puerto Rico vs. all other birthplaces. As previously explained, the multiple categorization of demographic variables made it possible to compare the effectiveness of these two categorizations of birthplace in explaining linguistic variation, as well as to summate them into one birthplace variable.

Statistical Analysis

The statistical technique utilized in this report is that of analysis of variance via multiple regression analysis. Analysis of variance being a technique designed to answer questions concerning the separate (as well as the interactional) significance of several simultaneous effects, such analyses could be utilized to tell us whether speech context, sex, age, education, or birthplace are each separately significant in explaining variation in the production of a particular linguistic variant, or whether the interaction between any two of them (e. g. , between context and birthplace) has explanatory significance. [3] In the present study multiple regression analysis could tell us whether or not certain explanatory parameters (e. g. , context plus age) are already so powerful in explaining variation in the production of a particular linguistic variant that it is unnecessary or non-productive to add other explanatory parameters, however significantly related in themselves to such variation.

Hypotheses

Spanish variables

Our general hypothesis was that linguistic variation in Puerto Rican Spanish (PRS) in the speech community under study consists of contextual variation primarily and demographic variation only secondarily. We hypothesized thus because we consider our subjects as constituting a single speech community except for regionally related differences between speakers of highland origin and speakers of coastal origin. They all learned the norms of Spanish communicative competence pretty much in the same way and at the same developmental period of their lives. However, these norms incorporate contextual variation. Too few of our *S*s had had sufficient exposure to formal, educated Spanish to constitute an educated network which might develop speech norms of its own that might significantly alter the contextual variation norms which exist for the speech community as a whole.

More significantly, we hypothesized that except for a highland-coastal difference on a few variables no other significant demographic factors would be encountered to explain any linguistic variation in Puerto Rican Spanish beyond contextual variation. The test of this hypothesis against one illustrative Spanish variant (where a variant is described as one of the realizations that a variable can assume) is detailed below.

English variables

Our general hypothesis concerning linguistic variation in Puerto Rican English in the same speech community was that it would consist primarily of demographic variation, and of contextual variation only secondarily (if at all). Our subjects did not seem to us to constitute a unitary English speech community, with its own contextual norms of communicative competence in that language. In general, the English speaking horizons and experiences of most of our subjects had remained too limited for contextual varieties of English to have developed (or to have been adopted) and to have been stabilized. However, within the speech community there are persons whose English has been significantly modified by substantial influences such as those that derive from American education in particular, and from longer residence in the continental United States in general. We would expect the English of such individuals to be different from the English of those with other demographic characteristics, and who do not share these experiences. We expected such differences in the use of English between demographic groups to be pervasive, rather than contextualized along a casualness-carefulness dimension for intragroup purposes. The test of this hypothesis against one illustrative English variant is given below.

Results

Spanish variant SpC-Ø

SpC-Ø refers to the dropping of the plural marker s where the following word begins with a consonant. An example of this realization would be (los) muchacho comen, as opposed to the standard realization (los) muchachos comen (SpC-1) or the common PRS variation (los) muchachoh comen (SpC-2). This variable (SpC) had a very high number of occurrences and the realization in question showed considerable contextual variation, accounting for just 17% of the cases in the most formal speech context but 62% in the least formal context.* S in this morphophonemic environment was realized quite differently from s in other environments. For instance, s before a consonant within a word showed zero realization only 11% of the time in the least formal context. Similarly, s marking a plural article preceding a word beginning with a consonant was realized as zero only 23% of the time in the least formal speech context. In these environments S-2 or [h] was the preferred realization 81% and 70% of all times respectively in style A. Thus SpC is definitely a favorable environment for zero realization of s, with the further advantage, for our present purposes, that there was substantial variation in the realization of SpC-Ø across contexts. Under these circumstances, then, we decided to ask whether other parameters of a directly demographic nature might also be significantly related to differential production of SpC-Ø.

----

*See Table 3, Chapter 15, Bilingualism in the Barrio, 1968.

If we examine the first column (labelled r) in Table 1 we note that only Context, in each of its aspects, correlates significantly with differential use of SpC-∅. The second aspect of Context (that which differentiates between Word Naming, on the one hand, and B + A, on the other hand) correlates with SpC-∅ almost as well (-.423) as do both aspects taken together (column 3, R = .424).

The fact that only the two aspects of Context correlate significantly with SpC-∅ is corroborated in column 8 where only the two aspects of context yield significant F ratios. Thus we can safely conclude that in the speech community under study demographic differences per se are not significantly related to differential use of SpC-∅ whereas contextual differences per se are so related. However, if we are to stop our prediction of SpC-∅ with context alone we will have accounted for only 18.0% of the causal variance (see column 6). If we add sex of speaker to the prediction of SpC-∅ we can account for 24.4% of the causal variance. This increase is due to a slight tendency (column 1: r = -.240) for males to use SpC-∅ more frequently than females.

If we continue to add successive demographic variables our multiple prediction of SpC-∅ continues to rise (see column 5) and finally reaches the appreciable figure of .602. A multiple correlation of this magnitude accounts for 36.2% of the causal variance in SpC-∅, a substantial increase beyond that accounted for by context alone.

Although no demographic variable is in itself significantly related to differential use of SpC-∅, sex of speaker approaches such significance; but this results from the fact that in our speech community more women are of Highland origin in Puerto Rico. The Context by Birthplace interaction therefore also approaches significance, indicating that some birthplace groups show more contextual variation than do others.

Subsidiary Table 1a reveals the mean number of occurrences of SpC-∅ in the three different contexts for our sample as a whole and for two different birthplace sub-samples. This table confirms that the effective contextual difference comes between WN and the two conversational styles. Table 1a also confirms the greater contextual sensitivity of Highland born Ss for whom we find greater average contextual differences than those found for other Ss.

English variant EH-2

EH-2 represents the standard American English sound [æ], as in <u>cat</u>, <u>bad</u>, <u>ham</u>. Two other variants of this EH variable were recognized: EH-1, as in New York City [kɛᵊnt, bɛᵊd, hɛᵊm]; and EH-3, as in accented English <u>cahn't</u>, <u>bahd</u>, <u>hahm</u>. EH-2 serves fairly effectively to differentiate accented from native English speakers, as the sound is not available in Spanish phonology. Mastery of this phone seems to imply mastery of a number of other typically English sounds not available in Spanish.

Use of the three variants of EH changed only slightly and irregularly with context,* supporting the hypothesis of more or less fixed usage of one sound by any given speaker. EH-2 showed an overall higher incidence of occurrence, and, for this reason, was chosen over EH-1 for testing. It is also less ambiguously American, for EH-1 can be approximated by the Spanish [ɛ] or [e], so that a score of EH-1 does not clearly isolate the sound as English, but marks some form of dialect realization. For reasons both of numerical frequency and of phonological exclusiveness EH-2 is a very good variant for the statistical testing of relationships between differential use of sounds and the characteristics of their users.

Table 2 gives quite a different picture from that previously shown in Table 1. The values in column 1 indicate that neither of the two aspects of Context are significantly related to differential use of EH-2. Indeed, even when both aspects of Context are taken together, Context is still the least important multiple predictor of EH-2, except for Sex of Speaker (column 4). If we utilize Context alone we are able to account for only 3.6% of the casual variance pertaining to differential use of EH-2 (column 6). If we add Sex of Speaker to Context our prediction rises only to 5.8%. However, as soon as we consider such demographic variables as Age, Education, and Birthplace, a radical change occurs.

---

*See Figure 15, Chapter 15, <u>Bilingualism in the Barrio</u>, 1968.

Table 1. Analysis of Variance via Multiple Regression Analysis of
Puerto Rican Spanish SpC-ø (n = 34)

Source	(1) r	(2) r²	(3) R	(4) ·R²	(5) Cum R	(6) Cum R²	(7) ΔR²	(8) F_{r^2}	(9) F_{R^2}	(10) F ΔR²
1. Context: WN vs. B vs. A	.380*	.144						5.4*		
2. Context: WN vs. all other	-.423*	.180	.424	.180	.424	.180	.180	7.0*	3.0	2.5
3. Sex	-.240	.058	.240	.058	.494	.244	.064	2.0	2.0	2.5
4. Age: <25 vs. 25-34 vs. >34	-.055	.003						<1		
5. Age: <25 vs. all other	-.021	.000	.156	.024	.509	.259	.015	<1	<1	<1
6. Educ: <7 yrs. PR vs. 7 or + yrs. PR vs. PR and US vs. US only	-.116	.013						<1		
7. Educ: all PR vs. other	.111	.012						<1		
8. Educ: all USA vs. other	-.022	.001	.193	.037	.535	.286	.037	<1	<1	<1
9. Birthplace: Highland vs. Coastal vs. San Juan vs. USA	.063	.004						<1		
10. Birthplace: Highland vs. all other	-.163	.027	.216	.047	.585	.342	.056	<1	<1	<1
11. Context x Birthplace	.239	.057	.239		.602	.362	.020	2.0	2.0	<1

*Significant at .05 level

Table 1a. Contextual Differences in Mean Number of Occurrences
of SpC-0, for Total Sample and for Birthplace Groups

Birthplace Groups	WN	B	Contexts A	Total
Highland	27.13	57.27	66.58	49.17
Other	30.38	53.29	57.05	56.09
Total	29.13	54.17	59.87	54.39

Of the three major demographic variables related to differential use of EH-2 the most important per se is clearly Education
(column 1). If we combine all three aspects of Education we obtain
a multiple correlation of .753 (column 3) which itself accounts for
56.7% of the casual variance (column 4).

Those of our Ss who were partly or entirely educated in the
United States are more likely to utilize EH-2 than those entirely educated in Puerto Rico (notice the minus correlations in column 1).
This relationship between differential use of EH-2 and education is
further clarified in subsidiary Table 2a which shows it to be consistent for each speech context.

If Education is now combined with the variables that precede
it in Table 2 (Context, Sex of Speaker, and Age) then the resulting
cumulative multiple correlation with EH-2 rises to .785 (column 5)
and we have accounted for 61.6% of the causal variance in differential
use of EH-2 (column 6).

Although neigher Age nor Birthplace are as strongly related
to EH-2 as is Education, their independent correlations with EH-2
are clearly significant (columns 1 and 8). When all three of them are
added to Context and Sex of Speaker we arrive at a cumulative correlation of .810 (column 5) which indicates that we have accounted for
65.6% of the causal variance in differential use of EH-2 (column 6).

While Context itself is not significantly related to differential
use of EH-2 the interaction between Context and Birthplace is significantly related to such use. This implies that certain birthplace groups
show more contextual variation than do others. Although our sample
as a whole increasingly uses EH-2 as it proceeds from WN (35.79)

Table 2. Analysis of Variance via Multiple Regression Analysis of
Puerto Rican English EH-2 (n = 26)

Source	(1) r	(2) r^2	(3) R	(4) R^2	(5) Cum R	(6) Cum R^2	(7) ΔR^2	(8) F_{r^2}	(9) F_{R^2}	(10) $F_{\Delta R^2}$
1. Context: WN vs. B vs. A	.174	.030						<1		
2. Context: WN vs. all other	-.112	.013	.189	.036	.189	.036		<1		
3. Sex	-.136	.018	.136	.018	.241	.058	.022	<1		<1
4. Age: <25 vs. 25-34 vs. >34	-.524	.275						9.1**		
5. Age: <25 vs. all other	.555	.308	.556	.309	.582	.338	.280	10.7**	5.17*	4.2*
6. Educ: <7 yrs. PR vs. 7 or + yrs. PR vs. PR and US vs. US only	.717	.514						25.2**		
7. Educ: all PR vs. other	-.722	.521						26.1**		
8. Educ: all USA vs. other	-.589	.347	.753	.567	.785	.616	.278	12.8**	9.45**	4.1*
9. Birthplace: Highland vs. Coastal vs. San Juan vs. USA	.446	.199						6.0*		
10. Birthplace: Highland vs. all other	-.309	.095	.491	.241	.810	.656	.040	2.5	3.67	<1
11. Context x Birthplace	.428	.183	.428	.183	.815	.664	.008	5.4*	5.4*	<1

*Significant at .05 level
**Significant at .01 level

Table 2a. Contextual Differences in Mean Number of Occurrences
of EH-2 for Total Sample and for Educational Groups

Educational

Groups	WN	B	A	Total
Educated entirely in Puerto Rico	15.75	16.43	19.40	16.46
Educated partially or entirely in USA	60.71	64.43	65.17	63.35
Total	35.79	38.57	51.71	40.20

Table 2b. Adding Another Linguistic Variable in the Analysis of Variance
via Multiple Regression Analysis of English EH-2 (n = 26)

Source	(1) r	(2) r^2	(3) R	(4) R^2	(5) Cum R	(6) Cum R^2	(7) ΔR^2	(8) F_r^2	(9) F_{R^2}	(10) $F \Delta R^2$
12. UH-3 (frequency of use)	-.703**	.494	.703	.494	.891	.794	.130	23.52**	23.52**	8.13*

*Significant at the .05 level
**Significant at the .01 level

to B (38.57) to A (51.71) this variation occurs primarily between B
and A for our Highland born subjects and between WN and B for other
subjects, who use EH-2 more frequently in all contexts.

Incremental prediction of EH-2

In accounting for differential use of EH-2 Age and Education
are not only significant variables in themselves, they are also incrementally significant in this respect. Column 10 of Table 2 shows that
it pays to add Age as a predictor of differential use of EH-2 when one
has previously used only Context and Sex of Speaker in this connection.
Or to put it differently, .338 (column 6), the cumulative prediction of
EH-2 based on three variables (Context, Sex of Speaker and Age) is
significantly better than the cumulative prediction based on only the
first two of these three (.058). Similarly, Table 2 indicates that it
pays to add Education to our prediction of differential use of EH-2,
even after Context, Sex of Speaker and Age have been used cumulatively in this connection. The cumulative prediction of EH-2 based
upon these four variables (.616) is significantly greater than that
based only on the first three (.338). About Birthplace or the interaction between Birthplace and Context the same cannot be said. While
it is true that their cumulative addition to the prediction of differential
use of EH-2 (after Context, Sex of Speaker, Age and Education have
all been cumulatively utilized for this purpose) does increase the multiple prediction of EH-2 from .616 to .656 to .664, these increases,
though welcome, are not statistically significant. Thus, if Birthplace
were an embarrassing or difficult measure to obtain, we would be justified in deciding to forego it since it does not produce a significant
increment in our efforts to account for differential use of EH-2.

Using one linguistic value to predict another

While the attained cumulative prediction of differential use
of EH-2, primarily on the basis of demographic variables, is high
indeed, the question inevitably arises as to whether it can be further
improved. Although there may be some possiblity of improvement
by using additional demographic variables it seems far wiser to look
elsewhere for some more distinctive variance. Additional demographic variables would inevitably be highly correlated with those

already utilized, and consequently could hardly disclose any different
or really new components of the differential use of EH-2.   Since at
this point relatively little of the differential use of EH-2 remains un-
explained we need a predictor that is both maximally <u>unrelated</u> to the
prior predictors and <u>maximally</u> related to EH-2.   Because another
linguistic value might possess exactly those characteristics, we examined the utility of UH-3 in furthering the cumulative prediction of
EH-2 with results given below.

<u>English variant UH-3</u>

        UH-3 represents the sound most used by Spanish speakers
unable to make the medial English [ʌ].   Use of UH-3, then, is saying
<u>cot</u> for <u>cut</u>, <u>com</u> for <u>come</u>, with the vowel being somewhat higher and
more tense than in the actual examples given.   Phonetically the sound
is represented as [ɔ, ɔ , or ŋ].   The other accented variant for UH,
[a] as <u>cahm</u> for <u>come</u>, did not prove to be as productive in the speech
community under study.   As in the case of EH-2, UH-2 or [ʌ], the
standard sound, is not available to a speaker whose phonology is
mainly Spanish.   On the other hand, a speaker who is able to produce
UH-2 with any facility almost never resorts to the interference variant UH-3; or at least such was the case given the data collecting techniques used in our study in which no interviewer used accented English
speech.   If a speaker could say [æ] we believed he could also say [ʌ].
Therefore, the American variant for one variable was tested against
the interference variant for another in the belief that a strong negative
relationship was likely to obtain between them.   If we were correct in
our belief then differential non-use of the one could be used to predict
differential use of the other and vice versa.

        As subsidiary Table 2b reveals we were quite right in turning
to the use of UH-3 in our effort to further improve the cumulative prediction of differential use of EH-2.   The correlation between these
two (column 1) is substantial enough for EH-2 to be a significant predictor of UN-3 (or vice versa) (columns 1 and 8).   However, in addition, UH-3 is also an incrementally significant predictor of EH-2.
Even when it is added after 11 prior predictors have been cumulated it
raises the multiple prediction of EH-2 by a significant amount (column
10), from .815 (column 5, line 11, Table 2) to .891 (column 5, Table
2b).   With the addition of UH-3 we have accounted for 79.4% of the

causal variance in the differential use of EH-2. This constitutes a
magnitude of explained variance rarely attained in the social science
literature.

Summary and Conclusions

An analytic method has been illustrated which has not hitherto
been applied in sociolinguistic description and prediction. By employ-
ing the analysis of variance via regression analysis, the investigator
is able to go far beyond the interaction between linguistic context and
a single demographic variable (the level of prior sociolinguistic description and prediction of variable phonological behavior). Not only
can a large and varied array of additional sociological, psychological
or linguistic predictor variables be utilized, but each additional predictor can be assessed with respect both to its own contribution and to
its incremental contribution to the overall prediction of differential
use of any phonological value.

In the illustrative material selected for presentation in this
report, differential use of a variant in Puerto Rican Spanish (SpC-∅)
was predicted best, as hypothesized, on the basis of speech context.
However, the addition of several demographic variables plus the
interaction between a particular demographic variable and speech
context, significantly boosted our ability to account for causal variance in the differential use of SpC-∅. Our final cumulative prediction was R = .602 which is equivalent to 36.2% of the causal variance
that needs to be explained.

Our efforts to explain and predict differential use of a value
in Puerto Rican English (EH-2) benefited most (as hypothesized) from
the separate and from the cumulative use of several demographic variables. However, after such variables had been utilized to the point
where their incremental contributions were no longer significant the
addition of another linguistic variable (UH-3) raised our final cumulative prediction of EH-2 to R = .891 which is equivalent to 79.4% of the
causal variance that needs to be explained.

The major reason for our being so much more successful in
predicting EH-2 than SpC-∅ was the fact that in their use of Spanish,
our bilingual subjects represented a single speech community with

little variation from one person to the next. However, interpersonal
variation was much greater in the community's use of English. There
was great variance in their contacts with English language institutions,
such as the school, the work sphere, and other out-of-neighborhood
speech networks. The use of demographic variables which were
probably related to differential contacts with such English speech networks markedly improved the prediction of differential use of English
linguistic values.

We were so much more successful in predicting EH-2 than
SpC-∅ because the speech community studied exhibited greater homo-
geneity of usage on Spanish variables than on English ones. Apart
from the range provided by differing regional styles and repertoire
ranges in Spanish, none of the variables used represented a cut-off
point separating two sets of speech networks or of phonological repertoires. In other words, everyone in the community mastered
basic Spanish phonology, even though some respondents could barely
converse in Spanish. English proficiency was more varied; some
respondents spoke English fluently, and others spoke almost no
English, with the range of ability between these extremes corresponding to a graduated mastery of English phonology. Thus a phonological
cut-off point could be established to determine English fluency,
whereas fluency per se in Spanish could not be determined solely by
phonological markers.

For similar reasons the use of a given English sound could
be used to predict the use or non-use of a given interference sound.
For Spanish we could primarily make intra-personal predictions
because, overall, most speakers tended to vary contextually in producing certain sounds. For English, we were primarily able to make
inter-personal predictions because those who were able to make certain sounds belonging to English phonology never or rarely used the
interference alternatives in use by others in the community.

NOTES

[1] A full report on the contextual variation encountered for
each variable, as well as on the factorial relationship between all
variables, is available in Chapter 15 of <u>Bilingualism in the Barrio</u>,

J. A. Fishman, R. L. Cooper, Roxana Ma, et al. Bloomington,
Indiana University Language Sciences Monographs, 1971.

[2]Social class, a variable frequently utilized in other sociolinguistic research on phonological variables, was not utilized in the
present research because of the severe restriction in range of our
overwhelmingly lower class Puerto Rican subjects. See Chapter 7
in Bilingualism in the Barrio, 1971.

[3]Multiple regression analysis is a technique designed to answer questions concerning the value of utilizing additional explanatory
parameters beyond those already used at any given stage in the explanatory process (Bottenberg and Ward 1963, Cohen 1965, 1968 a,
1968 b). See also Chapter 7 in Bilingualism in the Barrio, 1971.

REFERENCES

Bottenberg, R. A. and J. H. Ward, Jr. 1963. Applied Multiple
        Linear Regression. Lackland, Texas: Lackland A. F. N.
        PRL-TDR-63-6.
Cohen, J. 1965. "Some statistical issues in psychological research."
        In Handbook of Clinical Psychology, pp. 95-121. B. B.
        Wolmand (ed.). New York: McGraw-Hill.
_____. 1968a. "Prognostic factors in functional psychosis:
        a study in multivariate methodology." Address to New York
        Academy of Sciences, March 18, 1968 (mimeographed).
_____. 1968b. "Multiple regression as a general data-analytic
        system." Psychological Bulletin 70:426-43.
Fishman, J. A., R. L. Cooper and R. Ma, et al. 1968. Bilingual-
        ism in the Barrio. Two Volumes, Final Report. Yeshiva
        University, 1968.
Labov, W. 1964. "Phonological correlates of social stratification."
        American Anthropologist 66(2): 164-76
_____. 1966. The Social Stratification of English in New York
        City. Washington, D.C.: Center for Applied Linguistics.
_____. 1968. "The reflection of social processes in linguistic
        structures." In Readings in the Sociology of Language.
        J. A. Fishman (ed.). The Hague: Mouton.

Part IV. Language Planning

8 | Varieties of Ethnicity and Varieties of Language Consciousness

It is one of the puzzles of human behavior that much of what is close at hand, and even basic to one's own intellective concerns, is sometimes no better known than that which is more distant and peripheral. This puzzle—which philosophers of science and students of behavior have commented upon at length—was strongly underscored at the SSRC's 1964 Research Seminar on Sociolinguistics (held at Indiana University) when the linguists among us experienced considerable embarrassment in defining <u>languages</u> (as distinct from dialects, registers, patois, parlances, argots, etc.) while the sociologists among us experienced equally great difficulty in defining <u>ethnicity</u> (as distinct from nationality, race, religion, etc.). At the end of one heated discussion a distinguished linguist suggested that "ethnicity" be discarded as an unnecessary and confusing term. This met with the countersuggestion from a sociologist that the concept "a language" be discarded since it was not possible to define it in such a way as to help us answer such a simple question as "how many languages are spoken in area X?" Fortunately, this double suicide pact was never ratified and I for one came away from the summer's experience convinced that both terms were worthwhile but that both required considerable within-family scrubbing before they would be really fit for presentation before mixed company.

Ethnicity refers most basically to a primordial wholistic guide to human behavior. Its primary referent is to unmobilized man, to man living in a limited human and geographic environment uncomplicated by broader causes, loyalties, slogans or ideologies. For mankind under such limited social conditions we find it inappropriate to distinguish between those daily rounds that pertain to or derive from religion, nationality, or social class. As far as we can tell,

peasant and tribal societies themselves make no such distinctions
"from the inside" and their social structure, as viewed by us "from
the outside," reveals no fully differentiated roles corresponding to
those of pastor, politician, union leader, etc. Instead, we find a
fully integrated set of beliefs, views and behaviors, a "way of life"
that is "traditional" in that it invokes timeless custom as the directive guide to all the processes, problems and perspectives of life.
This then is the initial and primary meaning of ethnicity: an all-
embracing constellation, limited in its contacts with the outside world,
limited in its consciousness of self, limited in the internal differentiation or specialization that it recognizes or permits; a "given" that
is viewed as no more subject to change than one's kin and one's birthplace; a "given" that operates quite literally with these two differentiations (kinship and birthplace) uppermost in mind; a "given" in which
kinship and birthplace completely regulate friendship, worship, and
workmanship.

Language, as such, is usually not a conscious factor in the
primordial world—except, on occasion, as a boundary-maintaining
device—by which I mean to say that it is usually not something separately recognized, valued, loved, protected, cultivated and ideologized. Language norms exist, of course, as do minor variations in
code, register or style consonant with the relatively minor distinctions in role relations and in social situations recognized in that
world. But these norms of usage are symbolically unencumbered.
They are transmitted as are other norms—those of planting and sow-
ing, of dressing and eating—by example and by socialization within
the fold, and they change slowly over time, usually without the help
or hindrance of special caretakers such as language teachers, grammarians or professional bards. Ethnicity represents the primary
guide to behavior in the "classical" folk society[1] and in even more
limited tribal societies.

Many societies today exist at or close to this very level of
primordial ethnicity and 50 to 100 years ago there were many more
such. The bulk of the peasantry of Western Europe, including the
peasantries of Britain and France, was not at all far from this level
of social organization just a few centuries ago, at the very same time
that their rulers and their city-cousins were living on a far different
(though related) level of social organization, one that involved a

transformation of unconscious primordial ethnicity in the direction of conscious nationality. The bulk of the peasantry of Eastern and Southern Europe was still close to the level of primordial ethnicity half a century ago when mass immigration to the United States from those regions was fully underway. Is it any wonder then that when Polish and Ukranian peasants were approached by census takers toward the end of the 19th century and asked to designate their "nationality" and "religion" they answered that they were "Kaiser's people" or that they were "local (indigenous) people"? Is it any wonder then that many late 19th and early 20th century immigrants to the United States gave very strange, unreliable (and necessarily incorrect) replies to similar questions put to them by American immigration officers?[2] Is it any wonder that a Hungarian language census of the latter part of the 19th century (conducted and published in Hungarian) reported several thousand claimants of "Ungarisch" mother tongue? Is it any wonder that U.S. mother tongue census data for 1910 and 1920 reports thousands of claimants of "Slavish" and other non-existent or at least inappropriately labeled tongues? Is it any wonder that language statistics for India, Africa, New Guinea and other parts of the world today are confounded by the unawareness of the local populations (and by the ignorance of supposedly sophisticated census takers) as to just what to call the local vernaculars and populaces? It is a fact of primordial ethnicity that not only is there little language consciousness but that the languages employed may have no special designation or no better ones than "mother tongue," "our language," "simple language," "daily language," "high language," "book language," etc., i.e. terms with no group or societal name attached to them.

Let us briefly compare this state of affairs with another which evolved after many centuries in Western Europe but which was subsequently brought into being much more rapidly in other parts of the world as a result of much more rapid and externally pressured social change. Here we find a consciousness of national history, with its heroes and martyrs and national missions, national grievances, national ideals. Here we find a distinction between religion and nationality, even when everyone (or almost everyone) is of the same religion (or irreligion). Here we find pride in national literature with its poets and novelists and with its literary schools, periods and styles. Here we find a consciousness of national language, with its avowed beauty, subtlety and precision. Language (like the missions, the heroes, the ideals and the other national treasures to which it is explicitly related) becomes something to love, to fight for, to live for, to die for; something to safeguard, to develop, to enrich, to bring to others who are less fortunate. What has happened to (indeed, where is) primordial ethnicity under these circumstances?

Much has happened—much more than can be spelled out here—to the economy, to the political organization, to the social structure, to the communication possibilities, etc. As a result, there is both a broadening and a fractionization of concern. Instead of the local tribe or the local village, integrated on the basis of kinship and common, direct experience, there is the nation or the national group held together by symbols, instrumental organizations and ideological commitments. The formerly fully overlapping networks of kinship, friendship, worship and workmanship no longer fully overlap. In particular, there is a substantial distance between kinship-friendship networks on the one hand and broader economic and political networks (and allegiances) on the other hand. Not only are there farmers and shoemakers and carpenters and tailors (simple craftsmen—but, even so, far more specialized than the "do it yourself" inhabitants of primordial ethnic communities) but there are newspapers and movements and schools and unions and clubs. All of these provide the new, non-ethnic unity and the new non-ethnic diversity of modern "mobilized" society. As a result, both unity and diversity are organized and institutionalized at a symbolic level substantially beyond the reach of the family and the immediate community. It may still be there, but it is no more meaningful to ask the man in the street in Warsaw, Paris or Rome today to designate his ethnicity than it was to ask his peasant grandfather or great-grandfather to designate his nationality.

Primordial ethnicity is a construct that pertains to an all-encompassing web. This web comes apart and becomes segmentized, bit by bit, during successive periods of socio-cultural change. Its segments become separately transformed, symbolically elaborated and integrated via organizations, ideologies and political institutions. Nationalism—including language loyalty—is made up of the stuff of primordial ethnicity; indeed, it is transformed ethnicity with all of the accoutrements for functioning at a larger scale of political, social and intellectual activity. However, below the level of conscious

symbolic behavior, bits and pieces of primordial ethnicity may still
show through. Birthdays in France are not completely governed by
the Great Culture of de Gaulle. Wedding ceremonies in Germany are
not spelled out in detail by the values or mainsprings of German Kul-
tur. Funerals of common folk in Quebec are French-Canadian in
addition to being Catholic and they are somewhat different than Catholic funerals in Madrid, Warsaw, Rome and Mexico City. Even in the
United States, after all of the de-ethnization that has marked our
development as a nation, ethnicity is the substratum that continues
to mark the food preferences, the family occasions, the pastimes,
the residential patterns, the religious holidays, and a number of the
most significant biological transitions in millions of 100% (and even
of 150%) Americans.[3] These daily life patterns are ethnic at base,
precisely because they are relatively untransformed, unideological,
and unconscious. They provide us—and hundreds of millions of other
so-called "enlightened" people throughout the world—with much of
the color, the distinctiveness, the comfort, the folksiness, and the
continuity in those aspects of daily life that are relatively untouched
by national symbols and that are below the level of abstraction, organization and inclusiveness of the phenomena (and at the level of
analysis) that most anthropologists refer to by the term "culture."

There is a particularly American (including American social
science and American intellectual) discomfort and misperception with
respect to ethnicity. The discomfort stems from our own de-ethnicized
national history relative to the national development of the more traditional nations of the world. The latter developed out of long centuries of transforming ethnicity, both as a result of internal unification and as a result of external demarcation and liberation. We have
developed out of more recent, more heterogeneous, and more overtly
and initially ideologized roots. Our common traditions are very
largely symbolic and procedural rather than substantive in terms of
detailed traditions and interactions of daily life. Our position as a
"new nation" (in the sense that Lipset[4] uses this term) and our striv-
ing toward the "great society" (as this term and concept has recently
become popularized) are both necessarily derived from non-ethnic
roots and experiences. As a result, "ethnicity" is not a phenomenon
with which most American intellectuals are really familiar (since they
insist on confusing it with "American style" ethnic groups), it is not
one in which they are really interested, (for isn't ethnicity "something

old fashioned and unenlightened") and it is not one toward which they
are sympathetic (since they themselves are "liberated from that kind
of thing").

In addition, ethnicity has suffered in American social science
circles because, on the one hand, we feel uncomfortable about the
terms "race" and "nationality," and, on the other hand, real "ethnicity" per se, is not something that can be simply asked for on a questionnaire. In sociolinguistic studies we frequently want to determine
the background of our subjects in terms of the languages their parents
speak or spoke and in terms of the traditions of their current as well
as of their childhood homes and neighborhoods. Such information is
needed to help us locate and describe particular speech communities,
i.e. subjects with particular phonetic, lexical or syntactic features
in their verbal repertoires and with particular language skills, attitudes and behaviors more generally. In the early years of this century it was not uncommon to attempt to secure such identifying background information by simply asking for "race." Replies such as
"Norwegian," "Mexican," "Jewish (Polish)" etc., were not at all
viewed as inappropriate to this query. Subsequently this term came
under well-deserved scientific and popular opprobrium. The term
"nationality" or "national origin" then came into vogue during the
twenties and thirties, but it too ran into problems because by now the
phenomenon referred to had become modified and attenuated. What
was a third generation American of Norwegian or German ancestry
to reply to a question concerning national origin? He was American
born and so were his parents. Replies undoubtedly varied, some
respondents claiming American "nationality" (including some respondents who had themselves arrived here from abroad as children),
others claiming a "foreign" national origin (even when they were
third generation). As a result neither of these claims, in and of
themselves, were sufficiently predictive of language behavior, let
alone being predictive of other less structured behaviors.

Finally, today, we find many investigators referring to
"ethnic group membership." Unfortunately, on the one hand, this
term is not a bit clearer to the man in the street than its predecessors. On the other hand, we are so surrounded by egalitarian convictions and pressures that we feel too embarrassed to talk of "race"
(even when Negroes are involved) or to ask about "religion" (even

when Catholics are involved) even though these terms are somewhat clearer. We often try to cover an entirely heterogeneous set of phenomena by referring to "ethnic groups," or to "ethnic backgrounds" other than entering upon the difficult path of measuring and describing "ethnicity."[5]

        We must not misinterpret the fact that ethnicity cannot be discovered via a single item on a form or questionnaire, or the fact that it is not a term that the man in the street (our informant) understands (or uniformly misunderstands), or the fact that ethnicity has become a marginal aspect of modern American (and, more generally, of modern, urban, industrial, national) life, or the fact that ethnicity varies in the degree of its integration and in its relationship with religion and language (to mention only two of its initial primordial constituents) in its various transformations beyond the stage of primordial ethnicity, or the fact that it may therefore, be more or less predictive of other behaviors—we must not misinterpret all of the foregoing in such ways as to come to disregard the concept itself or the indisputable fact that certain stages of ethnicity have revealed very lawful relationships with certain kinds of language behaviors.

        Perhaps it would be helpful to conclude what has thus far been a theoretical discussion with some empirical examples of how the concept of ethnicity has been utilized and has proved helpful in my own recent research.

        Table 1 indicates how five "ethnic communities" in the United States (defined roughly in accord with Gumperz's "speech community") differed with respect to claimed routes and claimed success in transmitting their non-English mother tongues to their young in 1962.[6] A community of Mexican-Americans in San Antonio (Mex) and a community of Puerto Ricans in New York (PR) were the only ones of the five studied that claimed that home use and daily family life were still the major vehicles in this connection. A community of post-World War II Ukrainian immigrants in Newark (UK₁) were extremely sensitive to the falling off of language proficiency in their children. They had already begun to rely primarily upon non-religious language schools supported by their "ethnic community" for the transmission of their ethnic mother tongue (EMT), in view of the fact that "home use" had already become ineffective or unreliable

Table 1. Mother Tongue Maintenance in Five "Ethnic
Communities:" Approaches and Accomplishments

(How) Do the Young Learn the EMT?	Community				
	Mex	PR	UK$_2$	UK$_1$	FR$_2$
Home Use	48%	62%	0%	0%	0%
Lang. Schools	6	3	17	26	0
Parochial Schools	0	0	45	3	76
Do Not Learn	46	35	38	71	24

after only 15 years of post-war American metropolitan life (this being
a much more rapid rate of language shift than had obtained among
pre-World War I immigrants to the USA). A community of second
generation Ukrainian Americans living in a small Pennsylvania mining
town (UK$_2$) and a community of second generation Franco-Americans
in Fall River, Massachusetts (FR$_2$) had withdrawn one step further
from direct control over language maintenance in that they had come
to depend primarily on the services of an institution not even entirely
within their ethnic community or under its control, namely, the Eastern Orthodox and the Roman Catholic churches respectively. My
collaborators and I interpreted this Table (and several other related
Tables not shown here) as indicating that our Mexican-American and
Puerto Rican samples were still achieving an appreciable degree of
language maintenance and, furthermore, that they were doing so primarily by operating within the traditional pale of ethnicity. On the
other hand, we considered the second generation Franco-American
and Ukrainian samples as being both least successful and most de-
ethnicized in their approach. First generation Ukrainian Americans
still occupied a middle ground between these two extremes. Their
ethnicity (and their language maintenance) was no longer something
merely and primarily to be lived but, rather, something to be organized, studied, valued, and appreciated. Other urbanized minorities
who have embarked upon this route have found that it permits (indeed
it often facilitates) mobility within the host society and, therefore,
facilitates even more marginal ethnicity and language maintenance.

The degree to which ethnicity and language maintenance are
related is also illustrated in Table II. Here we see that those parishes
in the United States that still cling to ethnic mother tongues tend to

Table 2. Reasons Why Ethnic Mother Tongue Is Used in
Church Sermons and Taught in Parish Schools

Reasons	Sermons	Schools
Ethnic (native language, traditional language)	77%	29%
Other (beautiful language, practical language, cultural language)	23%	71%

do so for one set of reasons in connection with sermons and for another
set of reasons in connection with their schools for children. [7] Non-
English sermons are most often "justified" in very matter of fact
terms. It is enough to say that sermons are in the language that the
parishioners know best, in the language they speak most often at
home and on the street, in the language that they and their parents
and grandparents have always spoken, etc. These answers imply that
for many adults in these parishes (and it is for the adults that the
sermons are intended) language and religion and daily ethnicity are
still intimately linked, at least at the level of adult-adult interaction.
However, at the parent-child and at the child-child interaction levels
this is most frequently no longer the case. Most parent-child and
child-child interactions have drifted far away from the primordial
ethnic context. As a result, children are taught the ethnic mother
tongue not "simply" because it is theirs but rather because it is
beautiful, cultural, practical, required by higher authorities, etc.
Thus we see how language maintenance is differently rationalized
(and differently actualized or realized) for generations that differ appreciably in their proximity to or infusion with primordial ethnicity.
This difference between first and second generation rationales for
language maintenance came up again and again in my study of language maintenance among American immigrants groups—whether
rank and file members or intellectual-organizational leaders were
at the focus of inquiry. [8]

    I have chosen these two examples primarily because they
illustrate my conviction that ethnicity is a matter of degree far more
basically and far more provocatively than it is an all-or-none matter
of kind. Linguists, in borrowing sociological concepts, have all too
frequently asked which ethnic groups exist in a particular area (or

what is the ethnic background of informant X) rather than inquire of
the extent to which ethnicity is apparent in the behaviors of their subjects. The latter, admittedly, is a much harder question to go about
answering. It involves a knowledge of the traditional rounds of daily
life (as well as a knowledge of the conscious ideological elaborations
and symbols that have been derived from as well as grafted upon simple ethnicity); a knowledge of actual observances, actual beliefs,
actual friendship patterns, actual communication channels, etc.
Ethnicity is a dynamic (I think you are accustomed to saying "a contrastive") phenomenon. It depends upon (interacts with) a larger setting to determine its exact nature at any particular time. It is not a
pigeon-hole to which data can be assigned on the basis of superficial
or "nominal" criteria.

        You cannot be sure whether a certain phonetic range consti-
tutes a phoneme in standard French (or whether "phoneme" is a useful construct) simply by asking an informant to answer "yes" or "no"
on a questionnaire. You do not scrap the concept of "phoneme"
merely because there are allophones. You do not become disgusted
with phonemes simply because they are sometimes morphologically
conditioned. You do not ridicule a particular phonemic contrast,
let alone the analytic-descriptive construct of phonemes, merely because sound shifts occur. Nor do you expect all phonemic distinctions
in language X to be present in the speech of all regional groups, all
social classes, or on all social occasions entered into by the speakers of language X. Nor, finally, do you surrender your interest in
phonemic description simply because sociologists do not understand
it (as must be obvious to you from some of the above samples) or
because it cannot be explained to them in one or even in a few brief
lectures.

        I do not know what lies ahead for the concept "ethnicity" as
social scientists and linguists gain more experience in working together on socially imbedded language behavior in various parts of
the world. On the other hand, I do not know what will happen to the
concept "a language" either under those circumstances. However,
I am more than willing to come back to Georgetown University 100
years from now (if you will have me) in order to find out.

NOTES

I consider this paper as being a minor supplement to John J. Gumperz's stimulating article "Types of linguistic communities," Anthropological Linguistics, 1962, 4, no. 1, 28-40, which I have reprinted
in my Readings in the Sociology of Language, The Hague, Mouton,
1968. That paper, like the present one, is concerned with parallelism
between social complexity and complexity of linguistic situations.
However, while Gumperz spells out this parallelism in some detail,
I merely treat the extremes of the continuum which Gumperz presents
in order to utilize the obvious contrasts between socio-cultural settings for the purpose of examining the concept of ethnicity.

[1] The validity and utility of this category ("folk society") and
the rural-urban continuum from which it is derived have been substantially discussed in the anthropological and sociological literature.
For recent critical discussions see: F. Benet, "Sociology uncertain:
the ideology of the rural-urban continuum," Comparative Studies in
Sociology and History, 1963, 6, 1-23; also C. Geertz, "The integrative
revolution: primordial and civil politics in the new states," in his
Old Societies and New States, New York, Free Press, 1963, 106-59.

[2] Further details and discussion of all of these examples may
be found in "Ukranian language maintenance efforts" which constitutes
chapter 12 of my Language Loyalty in the United States, The Hague,
Mouton, 1965.

[3] For recent discussions of the surprising stability of residual ethnicity in American life see Nathan Glazer and Daniel P. Moyna-
han, Beyond the Melting Pot, Cambridge, M.I.T. and Harvard University Press, 1963; also Milton M. Gordon, Assimilation in American Life, New York, Oxford University Press, 1964.

[4] See Seymour M. Lipset, The First New Nation, New York,
Basic Books, 1963.

[5] I have taken care to speak of "ethnicity" rather than of
"ethnic groups" both because "ethnicity" is the more basic (and for
Americans the more novel) concept and because "ethnic group" poses
definitional and operational problems of its own. Ostensibly, ethnic
groups are merely groups marked off from others by differences in
ethnicity. However, the question immediately arises as to when a
group is a group, i.e. how much "groupness" (and by whose standards) is required? Does an ethnic group become and remain an
ethnic group when (and as long as) its own members consider it to be
a separate group or when (and as long as) outsiders consider it to be

such a group ? Do individuals belong to an ethnic group when they
themselves acknowledge such membership or when others attribute
such membership to them ? How is one to treat an aggregate of individuals who acknowledge no ties to each other, who practice few if
any folkway that differ from those of their neighbors, but whose
grandparents were clearly of the same ethnic background and who are
viewed by their neighbors as constituting a group apart, even though
they themselves have no such self-concept or self-aspiration ?

The above issues represent genuine concerns in sociology
and in social psychology for they obviously correspond to different
social realities. Groups whose members acknowledge membership
and groupness have different kinds and degrees of impact upon the
behaviors of these members than do groups whose existence is externally rather than internally defined and determined. The consequences of different kinds and intensities of groupness are constantly
being studied, particularly where acculturation, social disorganization and other processes of social change make it impossible to expect
similar values and behaviors from most individuals to whom some
common group-membership label is attached.

However, ethnic groups are of interest to linguists (and to
many sociologists as well), not because of any concern with how
groups are formed, dissolved and reformed, or with their varying
impact upon their members, but because of an analytic need for categories by means of which subjects of predictably different values and
behaviors can be easily located. My point is that such a "nominal"
(categorical) approach to human groups is likely to be productive
only in traditional settings where the groupness of groups is likely to
be as real internally as it is recognizable externally. In other settings,
particularly in modern and in modernizing societies, ethnic groups
may not function in this fashion at all. They may have little impact
on verbal behavior precisely because they do not correspond to real
speech-and-behavior communities. As a result it becomes doubly
appropriate to select and group subjects in accord with indices of
ethnicity rather than in accord with attributed (and—from a functional
point of view—often erroneously attributed) group membership.

[6] For further details see chapter 8 of Language Loyalty in the
United States ("Some community dynamics of language maintenance").

[7] For further details see chapter 6 of Language Loyalty in
the United States ("Mother tongue retentiveness in ethnic parishes").

[8] For further details see chapter 7 of Language Loyalty in
the United States ("Organizational interest in language maintenance").

9 | National Languages and Languages of Wider Communication in the Developing Nations

The past quarter century has brought into the constantly fluctuating family of nations several score new members, formerly colonies of the Western capitalist democracies, referred to variously as new or developing nations. [1] However, not only is their political independence recent but their search for sociocultural integration, [2] on the one hand, and for operational self-management (i.e., for effectiveness in the realms of public order and public service, as well as industrially, commercially, educationally, diplomatically and militarily), [3] on the other hand, are often of even more recent vintage and of greater uncertainty than is their political independence per se. These nations have been subjected to a huge amount of social science attention—and, in very recent years, also to sociolinguistic scrutiny— so that the contours of their similarities and dissimilarities (with respect to the paths that they have adopted in coping with the problems of socio-cultural and political-operational integration) are now beginning to be recognized.

As in all new areas of scientific inquiry the study of the new nations is faced by two overriding problems: first, that of finding the most fruitful dimensions for analysis and, second that of finding the most revealing units of measurement or description in connection with the afore-mentioned dimensions. In the comments that follow I would like to review six factors or dimensions that I believe to be heuristically useful in differentiating between the language policies and accompanying developments that tend to obtain where three different directions or clusters of cumulative decisions have been reached. For the moment I would like to refer to these types of decisions and directions merely as being of Type A, Type B and Type C, so that I can devote greater attention to the differentiating

Table 1. National Languages and Languages of Wider
Communication in the Developing Nations

Factors	I. Type A Decisions	II. Type B Decisions	III. Type C Decisions
1. Perceived socio-cultural integration	a. No integrating Great Tradition at the national level	a. One Great Tradition at the national level	a. Several Great Traditions seeking separate socio-political recognition
2. Selection of National language	b. Governed by considerations of political integra-tion: nationism	b. Governed by considerations of authenticity: nationalism	b. Governed by need to compromise be-tween political inte-gration and separate authenticities
3. Adoption of Lan-guage of Wider Communication (LWC)	c. Yes, as per-manent, national symbol	c. Often transi-tionally: for modern functions	c. Yes, as unifying compromise (working language: W)
4. Language Planning Concerns	d. Minor: exonor-mative standardiza-tion of LWC	d. Modernization of traditional lan-guage: H or L?	d. Modernization of several traditional languages
5. Bilingualism Goals	e. Local, regional; transitional to LWC	e. National; transitional to indigenous mono-lingual	e. Regional bilingual (H & L, W & N) & national bilingual (W & N)
6. Biculturism Goals	f. Transitional to modernity or new integration	f. Traditional plus modern spheres	f. Traditional plus modern spheres
Types	I. A-modal Nations	II. Uni-modal Nations	III. Multi-modal Nations

circumstances under which they are reached and implemented (in the hope that these are revealing also in their application to many countries) rather than attend to particular countries and their somewhat unique and even contradictory local circumstances at particular times.

1. Type A decisions are those which come about as a result of consensus (at least in leading circles) that there is neither an overarching sociocultural past (i.e., no pervasive feeling of unity of history, customs, values or missions traceable into the reasonably distant past) nor a usable political past (i.e., no pervasive tradition of independence, self-government, hallowed boundaries) that can currently serve integrative functions at the nationwide level. It is felt by elites in decision making capacities that there is as yet no indigenous Great Tradition (no widely accepted and visibly implemented belief-and-behavior system of indigenously validated greatness) that all or most of the inhabitants can immediately draw upon to make them one people and their country one nation.[4]

Both of these recognized lacks—i.e., the lack of perceived sociocultural integration at the nationwide level and the lack of felt political-operational integration at the nationwide level—lead to the early and relatively unconflicted arrival at Type A decisions, i.e., the selection of a Language of Wider Communication as the national or official language.[5] With remarkably few exceptions those nations in which views such as those just mentioned are widespread in leading governmental and intellectual circles have selected the language of their pre-independence Western rulers for all nationwide purposes. Similarly, a Western trained and modernly oriented elite has usually been continued and favored in positions of authority in all basic governmental services as well as in industry, commerce, education and culture. Both of these decisions—the selection of a (usually Western) Language of Wider Communication and the continuation of a Western trained elite—are similarly justified by the basic need to obtain and retain as much tangible aid, as much trained personnel and as much influence abroad as possible in order to meet the immediate operational demands of nationhood. Under these circumstances I would say that in nations in which Type A decisions prevail language selection serves nationism (i.e., the very operational integrity of the nation).

Nationism—as distinguished from nationalism—is primarily concerned not with ethnic authenticity but with operational efficiency. When Type A decisions prevail considerations of operational efficiency have often led to the adoption of local and regional languages for immediate operational purposes only, i. e. , the predominant elites of such nations have tended to view local and regional languages as serving merely transitional purposes vis-à-vis the viability of the nation as a whole. Only the Language of Wider Communication is seen as fulfilling nationwide purposes on a permanent basis, or as being linked to the developing national goals, national symbols, national rituals, national holidays and national identifications that such nations—just as do all nations—need and create.

In view of their wholehearted reliance on a (usually Western) Language of Wider Communication, nations in which Type A decisions are preferred need engage in only limited language planning activities.[6] As long as the metropolitan country's norms are also considered to be acceptable locally no indigenous attempts at language elaboration (i. e. , the addition of technical vocabulary) or codification (i. e. , standardization of grammar, orthography, lexicon or phonology) are needed. The metropolitan country's lead in these matters can be fully accepted with only relatively minor local adjustments. However, two other kinds of language planning are often engaged in by nations making Type A decisions. In order to promote the acquisition and mastery of the selected Language of Wider Communication a modicum of study of local languages may be fostered in order to facilitate the preparation of more effective (contrastively based) teaching and learning materials. These materials are often inexpensively available, both for younger and older learners, the latter often being reached via radio or other media that do not depend on the printed page. Nations making Type A decisions also may engage in a modicum of terminal literacy work in some of the local mother tongues among older adults that require literacy (e. g. , to attain agricultural modernization) but that can no longer be expected to master the adopted Language of Wider Communication. For them too, then, some special learning materials and teaching methods are devised.

Since the adopted Language of Wider Communication is the mother tongue of very few indigenous inhabitants the very process of teaching it to the point of functional mastery itself engenders a certain amount of bilingualism when and where Type A decisions are pre-

ferred. More widespread in nations opting for Type A decisions is
the traditional bi- (actually multi-) lingualism found in small but
interacting societies throughout the world. However, bilingualism
is viewed as having no nationwide function by the elites tending toward
Type A decisions. It is not a characteristic of their ideal citizen of
the future. Bilingualism, widespread though it is, is viewed as having only a transitional role and even that primarily for two populations:
the very young and the very old. The former manifest what we might
call "reading readiness bilingualism." They have not yet fully encountered the institutions of nationhood: the school, the government,
the military, the higher culture. After this encounter occurs it is
expected that their bilingualism will decrease. The old, on the other
hand, are viewed as having already passed beyond major interaction
with the institutions of nationhood. In both instances what is expected
is bilingualism en route to monolingualism. The young are expected
to give up their local tongues in exchange for the nationwide (and increasingly national) language which is also usually a worldwide Language of Wider Communication.[7] The old are expected to lose whatever smattering of the Language of Wider Communication they may
have acquired and to revert increasingly to their various local tongues.
Ultimately (i.e., given sufficiently many successive younger generations that have given up their local languages) the former process is
expected to win out over the latter.

Biculturism is also viewed as merely transitional by leading
circles favoring Type A decisions. The path that most elites and
intellectuals ideologize is one that leads from tradition (with its so-
called tribalism, localism or particularism) in one or another new
direction. One such new direction is modernity with its identifications
on a larger and proportedly more rationally influenced scale.[8] Some
elites that move nations toward Type A decisions are among the most
modern and pan-Western in the world insofar as tastes, sentiments
and behaviors are concerned. They have struggled to leave behind
their ethnicities—which they consider as merely childish, sentimental
or archaic vis-à-vis their current national roles—and they tend to
seek a thoroughly new socio-cultural order of national life rather than
merely the modernization of an old indigenous order. Their image
of the national future tends to be monocultural rather than bicultural.
Such elites most often seek a predominantly Western life-style (urban,
avowedly rational, technological), usually expressed via a Western
Language of Wider Communication, to provide the modern sociocul-

tural and the stable political-operational integration toward which
(they hope) their countries are moving.

Such views have been reported for elites of several developing nations but three examples must suffice at this time. In his paper
on Cameroonese elitist families Alexandre comments:

> The country is one of the more heterogeneous in
> West Africa with a variety of language groups belonging
> to several families.... There is no nationwide lingua
> franca.... The official languages are English (W. Cam-
> eroon) and French (E. Cameroon) on an equal footing
> at the federal level (but with de facto predominance of
> French). The school system continues, on the whole,
> the French colonial tradition with an European language
> used as a medium from the start. There are a few lit-
> eracy classes in some of the vernaculars organized by
> the Christian missions without any official recognition.
> Since independence there have been heated discussions
> among the intelligentsia between cultural nationalists,
> who favor a wider use of the vernaculars, and unifica-
> tionists, who fear that this would consolidate tribal con-
> sciousness and be detrimental to nation building. The
> federal government—and its French technical advisors—
> support the latter view. (Alexandre: Seminar on the
> Social Implications of Multilingualism in Eastern Africa,
> University College, Dar es Salaam, Tanzania, December
> 15-20, 1968.)

That such reliance on the language of former colonial rule
may yet come to be looked down upon by other or future elites in
these same locales, just as they are already derided today in a number of developing countries that have already attained greater indigenous integration, is evidenced by the following observation recently
published in a Dar es Salaam daily.

> There are leaders and bureaucrats who still look upon
> the English way of life as a superior culture, and, there-
> fore English as the language of "culture." They seize
> every opportunity to speak English and flaunt their knowl-
> edge of English before peasants and workers in the fields
> and offices. Some of them will even proudly assert that

> they can only think in English!! This is one manifesta-
> tion of cultural bankruptcy...[Others] who know little
> English nevertheless speak English after the manner of
> expatriate Englishmen. They do so because they subcon-
> sciously wish they were Englishmen. (The Nationalist,
> December 20, 1968)

Considerations such as these frequently lead to the displacement of elites and to attempts to rationalize other types of decisions
with respect to language policy and language planning.

Actually, the significant fact about elites forced to make and
to confirm Type A decisions is not that they invariably stress Westernization but that they are in search of new and effective ideological and
behavioral systems that promise rapid integrative returns on a large
scale. Acceptance of the West, rejection of the West, region-wide
and continent-wide integrative philosophies, all of these tend to be
present and to displace each other with ambivalent rapidity. The
same leaders who castigate their own indigenous ethnicity and predict
that

> In three or four years, no one will remember the
> tribal, ethnic and religious differences which have caused
> so much difficulty to the country and the people in the
> recent past. (p. 58)

may well also criticize their own strongest links with Western culture:

> The education that was given to us was designed to
> assimilate us, to depersonalize us, to Westernize us—
> to present our civilization, our culture, our own socio-
> logical and philosophical conceptions, even our human-
> ism as the expression of a savage and almost conscious
> primitivism—in order to create a number of complexes
> in us which would drive us to become more French than
> the French themselves. (Sékou Touré: La Lutte du
> Parti Démocratique de Guinée pour l'Emancipation Afri-
> caine, Conakry, Imprimerie Nationale, 1959, p. 156)

While the erratic pursuit of new integrative principles continues the demands of nationism per se require continual reinforcement of the Type A decisions taken initially.

2. The contrasts between Type A decisions and Type B decisions are many and noticeable. To begin with, the nations in which Type B decisions predominate tend to be based upon long-established sociocultural unities, and, not infrequently, upon rather well established political boundaries as well. There is widespread consensus—not limited only to elites but most consciously and ideologically elaborated by them—that a single Great Tradition is available to provide the indigenized and symbolically elaborated laws, beliefs, customs, literature, heroes, mission and identity appropriate for nationwide identification. Of course, not all inhabitants may care to be identified with the nation but insofar as such identification is desired and is expressed, there is only one hallowed Great Tradition that is felt to be available and appropriate for such recognized nationwide purposes.

The clearly preponderant Great Tradition available to nations in which Type B decisions prevail points to the selection of a single indigenous (or indigenized) language to serve as national language.[9] The Great Tradition and an indigenous (or indigenized) language have been associated with each other for so long a time that they are by now considered inseparable from the point of view of sociocultural integration at the national level. Both are considered to be interdependent and undeniable dimensions of national authenticity. Both undeniably contribute to and benefit from nationalism, i.e., the ideology of authenticity or identity based upon broader kinship, broader custom and broader cause. Whereas most nations making Type A decisions must first preserve the polity as an operational entity and then seek to develop national identity and identification over time, the elites of new nations making Type B decisions tend to believe that they already possess a strong national identity but must seek to render it more functional for the purposes of national well-being in the modern world.[10]

The Dar es Salaam newspaper cited earlier expresses these views forcefully and in the very combination proposed by our conceptual scheme:

> A common indigenous language in the modern nation
> states is a powerful factor for unity. Cutting across
> tribal and ethnic lines, it promotes a feeling of single
> community. Additionally it makes possible the expres-

sion and development of social ideals, economic targets
and cultural identity easily perceived by citizens. It is,
in a word, a powerful factor for mobilization of people
and resources for nationhood.

In Tanzania we have been blessed with such a language—Swahili. Whatever the existing variation of dialect and diction, and local mutilation of meanings of
given words notwithstanding, Swahili is spoken and understood throughout the length and breadth of the land.
Indeed there is a noticeable trend towards designating
Africans as Swahilis—though the historical Swahilis
are a distinct ethnic and sociological grouping.

Quite obviously this common language is a precious
heritage and asset. It can serve a double purpose.
Firstly it can reveal the wealth of political, economic
and social ideas and values of our past. In so doing, it
can reveal part of the historical foundation of Tanzania
as a nation. Secondly, it can be the medium of formulat-
ing the political, economic and social principles, plans
and goals of our nation in this day and age. In so doing
it will serve as the other linchpin in the foundation of
our identity.

Unfortunately, as Mr. Kawawa hinted when opening
the linguistics conference at the University College two
days ago, the colonial era made a great many Tanzanians
forsake their language and look upon English as a ven-
erable substitute. Now this mistake has got to be cor-
rected. Swahili must be accorded its legitimate place
as the language of Tanzanians in political and economic
communication, in social life, in administration, in education. At the same time it must be developed so that
it answers to the complex features of life in this age. It
is to be hoped that educationists, administrators, social
workers and the public at large will take up this challenge. (The Nationalist, December 20, 1968)

Because of the well-established gravitational pull of authen-
ticity-loyalties, when and where Type B decisions are preferred,

any world-wide Language of Wider Communication tends to be allocated only transitional goals in connection with operational efficiency considerations. There may well be an admitted immediate need for a Language of Wider Communication for modern higher education (particularly in the areas of technology and science) but, ultimately, this is rationalized on the grounds of pure expediency. Inevitably, there is a tendency to ideologize a future time when the nation will be strong enough and adequately self-sufficient (in terms of trained personnel and in terms of training and production facilities) so that any Language of Wider Communication that may currently be needed will no longer have a national role to fulfill and will become a mere foreign language.

However, in order to hasten that earnestly desired time the indigenous (or indigenized)[11] national language must usually first be modernized so that it can cope with modern technological, scientific, governmental and high cultural discourse. Such modernization of the national language is frequently complicated in two ways in nations in which Type B decisions are preferred. First of all a choice must often be made between a highly stylized, classical variety of the language (called H in the sociolinguistic literature) and one or another vernacular variety which has usually heretofore been considered unworthy of serious attention for serious purposes (called L in the sociolinguistic literature). Secondly, the chosen variety (H or L) must be subjected to the trials and tribulations of modernization per se, which process can take any one of several directions.

H and L may have parted company centuries ago and have gone widely separate ways in the interim, to such an extent that they are no longer mutually comprehensible. In some cases H and L have always been quite separate languages. In either case (whether separate languages or separate varieties) they have both been long accepted for separate intra-group purposes in those nations that reach Type B decisions and a choice must now be made between them with respect to modernization for national purposes. Because H is the language or variety that alone has been deemed appropriate for serious purposes it is also normally the variety that is selected for modernization. This choice is a troublesome one since the bulk of the population usually does not master H and since H has its traditional (i.e., its pre-modern) caretakers (scribes, teachers, grammarians,

poets, etc.) that resist its modernization and that often attempt to
constrain it along very classical or puristic lines that are maximally
distant from either vernacular or international sources.

Language planning in the context of Type B decisions is
largely concerned with tasks furthering (1) immediate instruction in
the Language of Wider Communication which is ("temporarily") needed
in the spheres of science, technology, higher education and modern
high culture, and (2) the modernization of that variety of the national
language which is ("ultimately") to displace the Language of Wider
Communication from all public national functions. For the purpose
of advancing both kinds of language planning institutes, centers,
academies, committees and/or commissions tend to be established,
governmentally and extra-governmentally, some of which may well
engage in considerable contrastive, historical and dialectological
work in the pursuit of their goals.

Most elitist and other population segments preferring Type
B decisions tend to arrive at a rather different view of bilingualism
than do their counterparts where Type A decisions are reached. That
bilingualism which involves the indigenous national language and the
(usually Western) Language of Wider Communication is seen as having current functional significance but only transitional ideal significance at the national level, with the latter (the LWC) rather than the
former (the indigenous language) destined to go. Stable and widespread societal bilingualism (referred to as diglossia in the sociolinguistic literature) is foreseen and ideologized only in terms of H and
L. H has always been viewed as appropriate to traditional high culture: traditional religion, law and scholarship. It is increasingly
viewed as appropriate for serious modern purposes as well, when
realized in its more modernized guise. L has always been viewed
as appropriate for everyday pursuits, for intimacy, humor and emphasis, even among the fortunate few who have mastered H, and it is
anticipated that it will continue to have these functions in the future.
In short, many planners and policy makers (when and where Type B
decisions are in the ascendency) look forward to a somewhat modernized emendation of the traditional intra-group bilingualism (diglossia)
that has always characterized their societies.

The above expectation is strengthened by the bicultural
image of the ideal citizen of the future in nations reaching Type B

decisions. On the one hand it is widely hoped he will command the
old indigenous wisdom which corresponds to the national Great Tradition. On the other hand, it is hoped he will master the new foreign
skills which are needed for modern nationhood. Both the new skills
and the old wisdoms are valued in their appropriate domains. They
may each be associated with quite separate customs, diets and behaviors but, if this is so, these merely reinforce the widespread and
stable diglossia by means of which they are controlled and combined. [12]
Examples of such views and designs are ample among elites in those
developing nations in which Islam, Hinduism and other ethnic religious
systems permeate all aspects of life. An example from China of several decades ago sums up the usual position quite strikingly:

> The old and the new must both be taught; by the old
> is meant the four Books, the five Classics, history,
> government and geography of China; by the new, Western
> government, science and history. Both are imperative,
> but we repeat that the old is to form the basis and the
> new is for practical purposes. (Chang Chih-Tung, Learn,
> translated by S. I. Woodridge, as quoted by David Nelson
> Rowe, Modern China: A Brief History, Princeton,
> Princeton University Press, 1959, p. 121)

Statements from elites of other regions are equally revealing, e.g.:

> In his [Gokälp's] opinion the Turks should accept
> from Western civilization only...its material achieve-
> ments and scientific methods and from Islam its religious
> beliefs without its political, legal and social traditions.
> All other elements of culture, and particularly all the
> emotional and moral values, except the religious ones,
> should be drawn from the Turkish heritage per se. (Uriel
> Heyd, Foundations of Turkish Nationalism: The Life and
> Teachings of Ziya Gokälp, London, Luzae and Harvill,
> 1950, pp. 150-151)

Finally a summary statement by a scholar who is well aware
of older traditions may be read as pertaining to language matters as
well as to other aspects of national development.

The nationalist movement, especially in those underdeveloped countries which have older traditions, must
willy-nilly make a new synthesis. The real problem of
these societies is that of finding the terms on which they
can coexist honorably with the technology and civilization
of the West. There is no question of rejecting the latter;
at the same time, however, it is not possible for these
societies to accept the West completely, to forget their
own past. (D. R. Gadgil, Economic Policy and Development, Poona, Sangam Press, 1955)

3. If Type A decisions are characterized by the perceived
absence of a clearly overriding indigenous Great Tradition that is
considered currently adequate to serve the purposes of socio-cultural
integration at the national level, and if Type B decisions are characterized by the felt presence of a single predominant indigenous Great
Tradition that serves these very purposes, then Type C decisions are
characterized by a conflicting or competing multiplicity of such Great
Traditions. Since each of these Great Traditions is numerically,
economically and ideologically strong enough to support separate and
large scale socio-cultural and political-operational integration their
co-occurrence within a single polity makes for rather constant internal tension and for nationalistic disunity, particularly in the absence
of superordinate threat. Indeed, in nations characterized by Type C
decisions the nation itself must stand for a supra-nationalistic goal
or purpose since nationalism per se is a rather well developed but
traditionally regional (i.e., sub-national) phenomenon. This fact has
long been recognized by elites in several nations, whether facing problems of religious, political or economic integration. Thus

Tilak faced the problem of identifying, indeed of in-
venting, an Indian nation. For such an identification he
needed a glorious past in which Indians could take pride.
The problem here was not that India lacked a glorious
past, but that she had too many of them, and each was
involved with communal animosities in the present. (K.
R. Minogue, Nationalism, New York, Basic Books, 1967,
p. 98)

At the regional level, language selection in nations making
Type C decisions is no more problematic than it was in nations

characterized by Type B decisions since, once again, regional Great Traditions inevitably have their language counterparts. It is at the broader national level, however, that language selection problems occur in nations characterized by Type C decisions, since any indigenous candidate for the role of national language would yield an unfair advantage to its native speakers, to its native region, and to its native Great Tradition in the management of supra-regional, i.e. national, affairs. In order to avoid giving any party an advantage—and in order to avoid constant rivalry for greater national prominence among the various contenders—a foreign Language of Wider Communication is frequently selected de jure or utilized de facto as (co-) official or as working language (W) at the national level (sometimes in conjunction with an indigenous national language which may actually be little employed by those who are ostensibly its guardians).

As in the great empires of antiquity a Language of Wider Communication is needed in nations characterized by Type C decisions primarily for purposes of political-operational integration and primarily at the level of written and formal interaction.[13] Whether established officially or not and whether established permanently or not the Language of Wider Communication comes to be particularly related to nationwide activities such as central (i.e. federal) governmental functioning, interregional communication, and, ultimately, to those personal interactions for which supra-regional stature is implied.

However, in opting for Type C decisions (in contrast to decisions of Type A or B) the regional level of socio-cultural and political-operational integration remains extremely lively and important. As a result, each regionally recognized official language requires modernization for its own regional governmental, educational, technological and modern cultural realizations. This means that the alternatives that we noted in our discussion of language planning in nations characterized by Type B decisions (namely, that a choice must often first be made between H and L varieties and that possibly divergent points of view must then be overcome with respect to classicization or vernacularization as guiding principles in modernization) are again present to complicate life in nations characterized by Type C decisions, but this time they are also present in each of several regional entities rather than at the national level alone. This is not to say that no language planning is conducted at the national level in nations characterized by Type C decisions for that is not necessarily the case.[14] The national authroities are frequently left with the delicate responsibility of planning for the wider acquisition of both the some-times co-official Language of Wider Communication and the indigenous national language, each of which is likely to have opponents in one region or another.

Nations characterized by Type C decisions also present greater complexity when we come to consider their bilingualism goals. From an intra-regional point of view traditional diglossia involving H and L languages or varieties is normally justified on a permanent basis. The model regional citizen of the future is viewed as bilingual at the very least. From a national perspective too bilingualism is frequently considered the natural and desired state of affairs involv-ing the indigenous national as well as the Western (or working) Lan-guage of Wider Communication. Once again, then, the model citizen is viewed as multilingual with each language having its well defined and rather exclusive functions.

Both the old wisdoms and the new skills are considered de-sirable on a long-term basis with respect to the images of the future that are encountered in nations characterized by Type C decisions. Here again different patterns of dress, of diet, of recreation and of education may co-exist within one and the same speech community as its members (or as certain networks of its members) go back and forth between traditional and modern behaviors during their daily rounds. These separate life styles emphasize and protect the sep-arate validity of each of the intra-regional and inter-regional lan-guages which are so plentifully evident in nations where Type C deci-sions prevail.

4. The major consideration that seems to govern subsequent language policy and language planning decisions in the new nations seems to be the interpretation locally made (and unmade) with respect to the absence of presence of socioculturally integrating Great Tradi-tions (and their integrative counterparts in economic, ethnic and attitudinal-behavioral terms) that correspond, at least roughly and at any given time, to the new boundaries of political-operational integra-tion. Elites making Type A decisions perceive their countrymen as

amodal in this respect. Type B perceive their context as unimodal
in this respect. Elites opting for Type C decisions view reality as
multimodal in this respect.[16]

Where new nations are self-defined as amodal (or where the
modes that exist are considered less important than certain supra-
national goals) the leadership tends to quickly select a (usually Western) Language of Wider Communication as the nationwide language in
order to maximize political-operational integration (nationism). At
least initially this language reveals exonormative standardization
(i. e., it follows the norms of the metropolitan country). Bilingualism
is viewed as having only local and transitional significance. The
model citizen of the future is viewed as a monolingual speaker of the
Language of Wider Communication (which has been adopted as the
official or national language) and as living as much in accord with a
thoroughly modern (urban, technological) or other newly integrative
life style as possible.

Where new nations are perceived by their decision makers
as unimodal their most influential interaction networks tend increasingly to stress that indigenous (or indigenized) language most intimately associated with an existing or developing dominant Great
Tradition. Considerations of more inclusive sociocultural authenticity (i. e. nationalism) tend increasingly to limit the role of the pre-
independence Language of Wider Communication to transitional roles
in the spheres of technology, government, higher education and modern High Culture. As the major indigenous language is modernized
(the H variety normally being chosen for such treatment) it is expected
to displace the (Western) Language of Wider Communication from the
spheres in which it has only of necessity been retained. Even then
bilingualism is often viewed as being desirable on a rather permanent
footing involving the H and L varieties of the indigenous national language, each predominant in different spheres of an avowedly bicultural national life style that incorporates everyday informal rounds
(L), traditional formality (H, classical), and modern skills (H, modernized).

Finally, those new nations that are self-defined as multimodal with respect to Great Tradition-based sociocultural integration gravitate toward recognizing regional languages for regional

authenticity and a Language of Wider Communication (which may or
may not be paired with an indigenous national language) as a working
language for the purposes of national political-operational integration.
The several recognized regional languages are each modernized
(once again, the H varieties usually being selected for modernization).
Bilingualism and biculturism are viewed as stable and desirable
phenomena, both at the regional and at the national levels. Regional
and sociocultural integration proceeds primarily on the basis of the
regional L and H varieties. National political-operational integration
depends on relatively widespread mastery of one or another of the
working language(s). Both the new skills and the old wisdoms are
retained in the image of the model citizen of the future.

Languages of Wider Communication seem likely to retain
long term significance under all three types of decisions. Under
amodal perceptions it is hoped that they will increasingly displace
local and regional languages. Under multimodal perceptions they
are depended upon to function as unifying working languages for
political-operational integration at the national level. Under uni-
mordal perceptions they continue to serve as vital languages in certain
higher and more modern domains although it may be hoped that they
can ultimately and ideally be dislodged. [16]

Indigenous national languages are in need of modernization
(elaboration, codification and, not infrequently, simplification) in
order to render their H varieties suitable for modern national purposes, at the same time that their more traditional H and L varieties
are retained for more traditional H and L functions in nations making
Types B and C decisions. We have now entered a new phase of geo-
graphically widespread planning of indigenous languages that must be
assisted in discharging new and complicated national functions. The
processes of language planning are currently little known and it is high
time that sociolinguists turned their disciplined attention from an
enumeration of new words to discovering what these planning processes
really are and which of them differentiate between cases of successful and unsuccessful planning. National languages and Languages of
Wider Communication constantly come and go on the world scene.
We neither can nor should forsee the time of being able to get along
without both. Our need, therefore, both for practical and for academic purposes, is to know the processes and the circumstances

through which human decisions influence their adoption, cultivation, displacement and replacement.

NOTES

The body of this paper was prepared for delivery as the keynote address at the Regional Conference on Language and Linguistics, Dar es Salaam, Tanzania, December 18, 1968. The entire paper, including footnotes, was prepared as a contribution to the Seminar on the Social Implications of Multilingualism in Eastern Africa, University College, Dar es Salaam, Tanzania, December 15-20, 1968; the paper has appeared in the volume of papers from the Seminar (Language Use and Social Change, ed. by W. H. Whiteley, London, Oxford University Press, 1971). Preparation of this paper was facilitated by the Institute of Advanced Projects, East-West Center, University of Hawaii, where the author spent the 1968-69 academic year as a Senior Specialist.

[1] There is some slight inaccuracy about each of these designations. The designation "new" is in conflict with the fact that several of the nations that are of interest to us enjoyed political independence within frontiers not markedly dissimilar from those obtaining today long before the period of Western colonization. The designation "developing" poses other difficulties since it is not at all clear how the line should be drawn between rapidly developing, slowly developing, negligibly developing and negatively developing nations. However, these designations are probably adequate to serve as primitives for discussions that have as their goal not the refinement of these terms per se but, rather, the discussion of differing language planning processes and their concomitant societal contexts in the nations of Africa and Asia that attained political independence, either again or for the first time, subsequent to the conclusion of the Second World War. Such discussion should help us compare the prevalence of certain societal and language planning processes in various kinds of new or developing nations, or to compare their prevalence in certain other nations that obtained political independence during other periods in history and that have had somewhat different experiences in connection with political consolidation, sociocultural integration, industrialization, urbanization, etc. As a result, even those studies that do not aim at refining the concept of national development per se

contribute directly to such refinement as a by-product of the contrasts or similarities that they disclose, between nations characterized by different developmental trends or indices.

Social science theory and data in connection with national development are currently undergoing both rapid expansion and refinement. For a brief review of the factors most frequently studied in connection with national developmental sequences see Terence K. Hopkins and Immanuel Wallerstein, The Comparative Study of National Societies, Social Science Information 6, No. 5, 25-58 (1967). The foregoing also constitutes an excellent review of the study designs employed in the comparative study of nations. An example of recent theoretical advances in the study of developing nations new and old, is Johan Galtung's Sociological Theory and Social Development (particularly Part II: Socio-economic development), NKanga, No. 2, Transition Books Limited, Kampala, Uganda. A helpful introduction to current issues and reformulations in this field is S. N. Eisenstadt's review article Some new looks at the problem of relations between traditional societies and modernization, Economic Development and Cultural Change 16, 436-450 (1968). Eisenstadt concludes that recent research "points out the need to examine the characteristics of those processes which may help in the transition to modernity as against those which may hinder it, and those which lead to the development and continuity of modern frameworks as against those types which impede the viability of such frameworks once they are established."

Because the concepts of national development and modernization essentially relate to multivariate continua, much of what is said in this paper should pertain to nations outside of Africa and Asia as well. Certainly most of the nations of Central and Eastern Europe experienced problems of development and modernization during the first half of this century that were very similar in many ways to those currently being studied in the new nations. (Non-Western models of development have thus far been little discussed. The need for such models is pointed out by Inayatullah, Toward a non-Western model of development, in Lerner, Daniel and Wilbur Schram, Communication and Change in the Developing Countries, Honolulu, East-West Center Press, 1967.) Indeed, we need go back only a bit further in Western European social and political development in order to find there, as well, changes, problems and processes quite similar in many ways to those evident in many parts of Africa and Asia today. Thus, while

no unilinear or irreversible theory of development is being posited it
is hoped that the present paper can provide some historical perspective as well as conceptual parsimony for those seeking preliminary
order in the welter of detailed information produced by language
policy, language planning and other sociolinguistic research in Africa
and Asia today.

As do all theoretical formulations this paper is intended to
summarize and systematize the data, literature and experience that
is currently known to the author and, then, to function as a point of
departure for subsequent empirical and theoretical efforts, many of
which will undoubtedly necessitate the revision, refinement or abandonment of the parameters here suggested.

[2] This term will be discussed and illustrated extensively below. In general, it refers to the never fully completed process of
shaping and reshaping broader cognitive-emotional identifications
and broader behavioral expressions of communality than are expressed
via the narrow kinship, neighborhood and ethnic traditions that individuals recognize as a result of their early socialization experiences
among family and friends.

[3] I use the term political integration or consolidation to cover
all of these operational processes that are to such a large extent
governmentally influenced or controlled and technological rather than
ethnic in nature. Of course, political consolidation and sociocultural
integration are closely interrelated phenomena, although they may be
studied separately. Education and transportation are not merely government services or operations without ethnic content or substantive
ethnic consequence. They both can facilitate wider sociocultural ties
and the dissemination of integrative sociocultural ideologies, loyalties and behavioral realizations. Similarly the adoption of wider
ethnic loyalties and perceived similarities can serve to facilitate industrial and commercial operations. For further discussion of the
interdependency between political and sociocultural integration, as
well as for indications of various stages of reintegration or reconsol-
idation, see my Nationality-nationalism and nation-nationism in
Fishman, Joshua A., Charles A. Ferguson and Jyotirindra Das Gupta
(eds.), Language Problems of Developing Nations, New York, John
Wiley, 1968. The interaction between various integrative factors
is well presented by Joseph J Spengler in his Theory, ideology, non-
economic values and politico-economic development, in Braibanti,
Ralph and J. J. Spengler (eds.), Tradition, Values and Socio-Economic

Development, Durham, Duke University Press, 1961 (Chapter 1).
        The concept of integration at the national level has recently
come to be of increasing interest to empirical social scientists. See,
e.g. DeLamater, John, Commitment to the political system in a
multi-state nation, unpublished ms., University of Michigan, 1967;
DeLamater, John, Daniel Katz and Herbert C. Kelman, On the nature
of national involvement: an empirical study, unpublished ms., University of Michigan, 1967; Deutsch, Karl W., P. E. Jacob, H. Teune,
J. V. Toscano, and W. L. C. Wheaton, The Integration of Political
Communities, Philadelphia, Lippincott, 1964; Jahoda, Gustav, The
development of children's ideas about country and nationality: Part
I, National symbols and themes; Part II, British Journal of Educational Psychology 33, 47-60; 33, 143-153 (1963); Katz, Daniel,
Herbert C. Kelman, and R. Flacks, The national role: some hypotheses about the relation of individuals to nation in America today,
Peace Research Society Papers (I) 1, 113-127 (1963); Kelman, Herbert C., Patterns of personal involvement in the national system: a
social-psychological analysis of political legitimacy, invited address
presented at the Eleventh Inter-American Congress of Psychology,
Mexico City, December 1967; Lawson, E. D., Development of pa-
triotism in children—a second look, Journal of Psychology 55, 279-
286 (1963); Morse, Stanley J. and Stanton Pearlman, Nationalism,
political protest and the concept of national role, unpublished ms.,
University of Michigan, 1968.
        I do not refer here to the substantial literature on national-
ism per se nor to the rapidly growing body of theory and data on
cross-polity comparisons. The former is largely historical in nature
(except for the still provocative volume by Karl W. Deutsch, Nationalism and Social Communication, Cambridge, M.I.T. Press, 1953;
second edition, 1966) and the latter, of necessity, deals only with
nationwide indices (see, e.g. Merritt, Richard L. and Stein Rokkan,
Comparing Nations: The Use of Quantitative Data in Cross-National
Research, New Haven, Yale University Press, 1966). Nevertheless,
both of these research traditions can yield valuable hypotheses for
those interested (as I am in my empirical work) in social behavioral
data pertaining to national integration.
        The legitimacy of the nation as a context for the comparative
study of social process data is particularly strong in connection with
language policy considerations, in view of the fact that such policies
are so typically nationwide. To the well known ideographic protest

that "you cannot add these units together, they cannot be compared,"
Galtung (p. 18, op. cit., footnote 1, above) replies: "People saying
this should never...count the members of their own family, for in
a strict sense no individuals are identical. However, counting has
never presupposed identity, only some kind of similarity used to define a set.... For the definition of a set all one wants is...at least
one element that serves as the criterion for membership in the set—
and then all kinds of comparisons can be carried out. But some people seem to feel that one can only compare identical elements, as if
identity were the only relation in the world. Moreover, if the elements
were really identical, what would be the use of comparing them?"

    In a similar vein Moore comments "...for every generaliza-
tion about structural relationships in social systems there is an exception, known best to the objector, in a suitably obscure corner of
the world. Yet it is the point of view adopted here that it is possible
and appropriate to deal with the major functional areas observable
in any continuing society (e.g. biological reproduction, socialization
of the young, economic production, maintenance of order) and to
analyze the general or typological relations that pertain among the
specific structures that fulfill these universal functions. Generalization also, however, involves a difficulty of an intrinsic sort. Theory
construction is a process of abstraction, the counterpart of which is
loss of information. No theory will yield a specific prediction, or
yield a specific guide to policy (given an end to be achieved) except by
reversing the process and adding information to the general proposi-
tion" (Wilbert E. Moore, The social framework of economic development, in Ralph Braibanti and Joseph J Spengler, eds., Tradition,
Values and Socio-Economic Development, Durham, Duke University
Press, 1961, p. 58).

    My own research goal in a forthcoming cross-national study
of language planning processes will be to determine how particular
population segments (e.g. teachers, university students) behave with
respect to announced language policies, i.e., what they do, what they
know and what they think in connection with the language planning
policies and products that are ostensibly directed toward them. Possible types of countries, as a context for such behavior, are an important element in the design of such research.

    [4] I have purposely stressed the phenomenological aspect of
sociocultural integration and political consolidation (i.e., what people
believe and say, particularly what elites believe and say to each other,

to specific audiences and to the population at large) rather than proportedly more objective indices of these two phenomena. Once again,
these two dimensions (the external or objective and the phenomenological or subjective) are often highly related and mutually determining.
If I tend to separate them here it is because of two considerations.
First of all, such a separation enables one to study the absence or
presence of interdependency between objective factors and surrounding belief systems—in a variety of contexts—rather than assume
that this is always and everywhere the same. In addition, the separation of the two and the stress on the phenomenological dimension
is necessary in order to recognize that we are dealing with a dynamic
system in which there are always elements of tension, pressure for
change and redefinition on behalf of alternative decisions.

   The same objective circumstances are differently viewed
and defined, because of differing goals and values. So is it also with
sociocultural integration. Whereas some elites interpret the status
quo in one way (e.g., that there is no usable past to unite the whole
country and, therefore, that only a superordinate future goal can
serve this unifying purpose) others will interpret it differently (e.g.,
that local or regional sociocultural unity is sufficient reason to set
aside wider national unity as unattainable or undesirable and to opt
for local autonomy instead). In the text of the present paper I have
avoided most references to such internal differences and tensions
only for the sake of the simplicity inherent in ideal models. Instead,
I have dealt with three different coherent rationales concerning socio-
cultural integration. By keeping in mind that ideal models are intended
to clarify the diversity of intermediate and shifting resolutions that
actually obtain (treating them as error variance above and beyond
which certain main effects are recognizable), it will more readily be
understood that rarely does any of these ideal rationales command
undisputed allegiance in any country at any time. Thus, it is always
important to examine which elites (and other population segments)
hold which views and, in addition, to determine the circumstances
under which their views (and behaviors) with respect to national integration and language policy tend to change.

   For a detailed discussion of how elites decide such matters
as "what shall be our history?" "are we many or are we one?" etc.
see Bell, Wendell and I. Oxaal, Decisions of Nationhood, Denver,
Social Science Foundation, University of Denver, 1964. Bell, Oxaal
and their associates in several studies that have appeared since 1964

(e.g. Moskos, Charles C., Jr., <u>The Sociology of Political Indepen-</u>
<u>dence</u>; Oxaal Ivar, <u>Black Intellectuals Come to Power: The Rise of</u>
<u>Creole Nationalism in Trinidad and Tobago</u>; Mau, James, Social
<u>Change and Images of the Future</u> (all three volumes: Cambridge,
Schenkman, 1967-1968) have admirably demonstrated how the views
of elites can be exhaustively studied and insightfully related to their
background characteristics (age, education, income, ethnicity, religion, poltical affiliation, etc.). However, what remains to be done in
sociolinguistic extensions of such studies of elites is not only to trace
the interest basis of their own views, but, in addition, to trace the
interest basis of the spread of these views to non-elite populations
previously unaware of them or uncommitted to them. This can be
accomplished via recurring studies which combine brief surveys of
large populations with intensive studies of specially selected naturally
occurring groups or interaction networks.

 Those familiar with the above-mentioned publications will
realize that my concept of Great Tradition is not identical with Redfield's in that it is for me primarily a phenomenological reality rather
than either an objectively great or traditional system. The myths that
integrate societies and polities are real enough as long as people
strive for or against them, value or deprecate them, counteract or
reinforce them. As a result of the power of these traditions, exoglos-
sic societies throughout history have come to believe that their languages were genuinely their own, truly a reflection of their particular
genius, and authentically related to their peculiar experiences. Thus,
Type A decisions are often merely a beginning point from which subsequently indigenized language and behavior systems not only may
but frequently do arise. Both France and Romania are equally proud
today to be the bearers and perfectors of Roman civilization, disregarding the fact that neither of them is ethnically of Romance origin.
Such unifying themes, dreams and bonds are continually planned, discovered, revealed and refurbished and their status as Great Traditions is measurable only by their effectiveness rather than by any
objective criteria of verifiability.

 [5]There is so much variation, from country to country, in
the use of terms such as "national" language and "official" language
that it is no longer possible to use them without some ambiguity as
to just what they imply. A distinction is sometimes made between
them such that more languages are recognized for official use (in
courts, government agencies, schools, mass media, etc.) than are

accorded the honorific status of being national. Thus, while the
designation national tends to stand for past, present or hoped for
sociocultural authenticity in the ethnic realm (nationality being a
broader level of integration growing out of coalescenses between
earlier and more localized ethnicities) the designation official tends
to be associated primarily with current political-operational needs.
If the languages designated by the two terms are not identical this is
indicative of the need to recognize political-operational demands that
are (temporarily?) more pressing than the demands of sociocultural
authenticity.

The term national language is used in this paper to designate
that language (or those languages) whose use is viewed as furthering
sociocultural integration at the nationwide (hence "national") level.

[6] The approach to studying language planning referred to in
this paper is that developed by Charles A. Ferguson, Joshua A. Fishman, Jyotirindra Das Gupta, Joan Rubin and Bjorn Jernudd in their
outline of a model cross-national study of language planning processes
(unpublished ms., Stanford University, 1968). This approach identifies several stages of language planning (policy formulation, elaboration and codification, implementation, evaluation and feedback, including cost/benefit analysis) as well as a host of interlocking questions
and methodologies to be followed in conjunction with studies of each
stage.

[7] The expectation that local mother tongues will be totally
displaced is probably unrealistic, particularly for sedentary populations that do not migrate from the villages of their birth to the capital
or to other more urban places. In their case A. Tabouret-Keller has
demonstrated that a diglossia pattern arises (primarily mother tongue
at home or with intimates and primarily a wider language at work or
with non-intimates) which is very similar to that which still exists
even among sedentary populations in Western Europe with respect to
use of local varieties and national standard languages. For further
details see her study, Sociological factors of language maintenance
and language shift: a methodological approach based on European
and African examples, in Fishman, Ferguson and Das Gupta, op. cit.,
footnote 3, above. Nevertheless, just as Provencal or Alsatian have
absolutely no national significance in France, notwithstanding the
diglossia patterns into which they enter vis-à-vis standard French,
no national significance is attributed to or desired for the multitude
of local vernaculars by elites favoring decisions of Type A.

[8] The traditionalism-modernity terminological dichotomy is
widely recognized as pertaining to a behavioral-attitudinal-valuational
continuum. This continuum has long been of interest to both empirical
and theoretical students of society. In recent years the number of
instruments and studies in this connection has increased many fold.
For an excellent summary and evaluation of social science data and
theory in this connection see the special issue of the Journal of Social
Issues devoted to modernity and tradition (Joseph Gusfield, Issue Editor), 1968 XXIV, No. 4, particularly the introductory paper by Gusfield, Tradition and modernity, conflict and congruence, pp. 1-8.
For other relevant studies, see Dawson, J. L. M., Traditional versus Western attitudes in West Africa: the construction, validation
and application of a measuring device, British Journal of Social and
Clinical Psychology 6, Part 2, 81-96 (1967); Inkeles, Alex, The modernization of man, Conspectus, India International Center, New Delhi,
1965, Vol. 1, No. 4 (reprinted in Weiner, Myron (ed.), Modernization: The Dynamics of Growth, New York, Basic Books, 1966);
Jahoda, Gustav, Aspects of Westernization: a study of adult-class
students in Ghana, British Journal of Sociology 12, 375-386 (1961)
and 13, 43-56 (1962); Kahl, Joseph A., The Measurement of Modern-
ism, Austin, University of Texas Press (Institute of Latin American
Studies, Latin American Monographs, No. 12), 1968; Levine, Donald
N., Wax and Gold, Chicago, University of Chicago Press, 1965;
Little, Kenneth, West African Urbanization: A Study of Voluntary
Associations in Social Change, New York, Cambridge University
Press, 1965; Mayer, Philip, Townsmen or Tribesmen, Capetown,
Oxford University Press, 1963; Smith, David H. and Alex Inkeles,
The OM scale: a comparative socio-psychological measure of individual modernity, Sociometry 29, 353-377 (1966). This last mentioned
paper not only presents a cross-nationally validated instrument for
the measurement of overall modernity but also provides a valuable
bibliography of other attempts to measure and describe individual and
societal modernity. For a critique of generalized measures of modernization and a plea for locally validated measures of modernism
see John B. Stephenson, Is everyone going modern? A critique and
a suggestion for measuring modernism, American Journal of Sociology
74, 256-264 (1968).

While I do not use the terms "development" or "modernization" to imply inevitable imitation or duplication of Western precedents
I have also not attempted to avoid the designation "Western" when

referring to certain languages and countries, on the one hand, or to
certain sociocultural and politico-economic developments, on the
other. Regardless of how ethnocentric the former references may
be, since east and west, north and south are certainly no more than
relative rather than absolute designations, their usage is firmly established and quite unambiguous. As for the latter reference (e.g.,
Western life styles, Western outlooks, etc.) I obviously do not intend
them in any invidious manner but merely as indications that, wherever they are encountered, they stem from social, political and economic processes that were initially set in motion and that have been
most continuously developed in those nations classically referred to
as Western. While "modernization" is assumed to imply Westernization in the latter sense, the concept of "development" makes no such
assumption.

[9] It is reasonable to ask whether the link between Great Traditions and their uniquely related languages is merely a by-product
of literacy, i.e., of a written Great Tradition. Although this is
probably usually the case (i.e., most Great Traditions are written
and, as a result, they intensify both their unifying functions as well
as their language links) it is not necessarily so. The Algonquin and
Iroquois Great Traditions were unwritten as was the pre-Islamic
Arabic standard developed by court-poets at a purely oral level.
Other oral Great Traditions have existed (and continue to exist today)
in other unified traditional societies. It, therefore, seems preferable to speak of unifying Great Traditions than of their probable but
not absolutely necessary by-products: written texts and standard
language varieties.

[10] The inapplicability of the foregoing paragraph to certain
new nations that have adopted or developed inter-regional lingua
francas as their national languages is intentional. Such nations are
intermediate between Type A and Type B. Like nations in which Type
A decisions have been reached they lack any overwhelming indigenous
center of gravity that clearly points to a single locus of sociocultural
integration at the national level. However, neither can all of the
locally available tongues and traditions be considered equally inap-
plicable for wider roles, particularly those of a political-operational
nature (such as commerce and communications between the provinces
and the capital). Thus, an indigenous language (usually one that has
already served as a lingua franca and therefore lost some of its
originally regional or local connotations) may be selected as national

or official at the same time as a Western Language of Wider Communication is utilized for higher education and High Culture pursuits. Obviously, the indigenous language so selected in such countries initially serves as an internal language of wider political-operational integration rather than as a language of sociocultural integration. Similarly, the Western Language of Wider Communication serves elitist and international communication purposes.

These intermediate cases may more rapidly develop into nations making Type B decisions, i. e. , they may more quickly succeed in developing national loyalties, customs, missions and symbols (anthems, costumes, celebrations, etc.) in what was initially only an internal language for political-operational viability than may be the case with nations that arrived at more classical Type A decisions involving a Western Language of Wider Communication alone for nationwide purposes. Type A decisions, if they succeed in providing political-operational stability, are, by definition, ultimately self-liquidating. Under such circumstances an indigenized Great Tradition ultimately is fashioned which provides sociocultural integration as well and which leads to self-perceptions and decisions of Type B. This transition between A and B, it might be hypothesized, is accomplished more quickly if an indigenous (rather than Western) Language of Wider Communication is employed. There is even some reason to believe that language policy per se is more successfully implemented when the latter is the case, e. g. ,

> The adoption of bahasa Indonesia as the first language of the new state met no resistance, largely because the language so established was not the language of the majority ethnic group—the Javanese. The imposition of an Indonesian language was not symbolic of the imposition of a majority—and this largely removed the whole question from the role of politics. (Joseph Fischer, Indonesia, in James S. Coleman (ed.), Education and Political Development, Princeton, Princeton University Press, 1965, p. 116)

Certainly, sustained failure to attain economic growth in nations making Type A decisions may lead to attempts to reach Type C decisions, or failing that, to subdivide into a number of separate units each of which may attempt A, B or C decisions depending on their own integrative perceptions and capacities. Similarly prolonged functional failures following upon Type B decisions may make new elites more sympathetic to Type C decisions than were their predecessors. Thus the conceptual approach advanced in this paper does not assign permanent slots to elites nor to the types of decisions reached by them. Developmental changes in society, polity and economy lead to changed language decisions and such changes can be anticipated. However, no attempt is made to argue for smooth, fixed transitions from one phase to the next. For a discussion of irregularity in sequences and regressions of the type anticipated above see Smelser, N. J., Social Change in the Industrial Revolution, London, Routledge and Kegan Paul, 1959, pp. 30-32.

The history of modernization and industrialization during the past 300 years provides ample evidence of the unevenness of this trend within the political boundaries existing at various points in time. As successive regions of polities become urbanized, industrialized and modernized the likelihood that they will seek separate sociocultural and political-operational integration is great, particularly if a past history of such separate integration exists or can reasonably be constructed. The past history of successive subdivisions of this kind and their subsequent rationalization is reviewed by Ronald F. Inglehart and Margaret Woodward, Language conflicts and political integration, Comparative Studies in Society and History 10, 27-45 (1967). The likelihood of future revisions of the current ethnically meaningless boundaries of many developing countries (should they undergo marked regionally discontinuous economic development) is discussed in Kapil, Raul L., On the conflict potential of inherited boundaries in Africa, World Politics 18, 656-673 (1966).

[11]"Indigenous or indigenized" is a necessary circumlocution if one wishes to cover national languages that are still intellectually recognized as imports from other locales but that have been so thoroughly influenced by local sociolinguistic forces as to be given an independent honorific name (Yiddish and not Judeo-German, Riksmaal and not Dano-Norwegian, Afrikaans and not Afrikaner Deutsch, Ukrainian and not Little Russian, etc.) and associated with indigenous historical experiences or integrative activity.

[12]The partial retraditionalization of hitherto Westernized elites in many nations where Type B decisions have recently been attained is a sign of their increasing self-redefinition. As long as they were oriented entirely toward the West, traditional foods, dress and pursuits could either be ridiculed, ignored or patronizingly

recognized at parties or other atypical occasions. With the growth
of national integrative processes (and pressures) more definite and
recurring realizations of national identification are called for and
become socially rather than idiosyncratically patterned.

[13]Karl Deutsch's preliminary draft on "Conditions for the
spread of inter-regional languages: the experience of medieval
Europe" (prepared for the SSRC Conference on Language Problems
of Developing Nations, Airlie House, Virginia, November 1966) is
an instructive introduction to the historical precursors of today's
Languages of Wider Communication. Deutsch points out how in the
great empires of bygone days Languages of Wider Communication
facilitated the introduction of new knowledge and "new skills with
relatively minimal disturbance of the traditional society. . . . Innovations are imported but contained. They are not infectious. They
overlay and mask local diversity but change it only very slowly, if
at all. Within limited sectors of each society their diffusion rates
are high, but the assimilation rates of the bulk of each society to
these new practices, culture patterns or languages are very small. . . .
Together, the gaps between rapid diffusion on the surface and among
the upper strata of a traditional agricultural society, and the slow
assimilation of its sedentary masses, produces the typical image of
a social layer cake. . . . Such societies do not teach the masses of their
people how to learn and innovate more quickly in the future."

Deutsch adopts the widespread American view that traditional
life and sociocultural diversity within national boundaries are undesirable. As a result, he fails to recognize that the problem—linguistically and behaviorally—is less often one of tradition or modernity
(indigenous language or Language of Wider Communication) than one
of tradition and modernity (indigenous language and LWC) in appropriate domains of social interaction.

[14] For a very able delineation of regional language planning,
on the one hand, and national language planning, on the other hand,
in a nation currently characterized by decisions of Type C, when
there is only a modicum of coordination between them, see Jyortirin-
dra Das Gupta, Language and politics in India, Ph. D. Dissertation,
University of California, Berkeley, 1967. For an indication of the
multiple diglossias that can exist in such nations see James W. Gater,
Sinhalese Diglossia, Anthropological Linguistics 10: 8, 1-15 (1968).

[15]It has been the purpose of this paper not merely to rationalize six dimensions that might be useful in differentiating between

the variety of elitist views and behaviors concerning the language
problems facing developing nations but also to indicate that these
dimensions themselves lend themselves to empirical study and revision. If language policy and language planning dimensions like those
suggested (together with other cross-polity dimensions like those
listed in such compendia as Rudolph J. Rummel's The dimensionality
of Nations Project, in Merritt and Rokkan, op. cit., footnote 3,
above) could be examined in an appreciable number of new nations
hypothesized as belonging to various types, then an R Factor by Q
Factor analysis could be attempted. An R analysis would tell us what
we can now only vaguely guess, namely, which dimensions are really
separate and which are primarily redundant. Such analysis would
enable us to determine how many orthogonal (i.e., clearly independent) dimensions there are in the measurement and description of
language problems and language policies in developing nations. Similarly, a Q analysis would tell us how many different types of developing nations there really are in conjunction with the language and
other dimensions utilized. Such an analysis would tell us, e.g.,
whether or not the hypothesized intermediate cases between Types A
and B are indeed a separate cluster.

As in all R by Q analysis few 1.00 loadings are expected.
If Table 1 can, for a moment, be considered the output of such an
analysis (whereas it is really only the hypothetical input) we would
expect each Q cluster of nations to have some loading on each R
dimension or measure. Nevertheless, we would also expect the Q
clusters to differ markedly in their relative loading patterns and
these profiles, then, would tell us which clusters of nations were
most similar and which were most dissimilar on which descriptive
dimensions. A pilot analysis of this kind could be undertaken even
now on the basis of a few expert judgments with respect to the six
dimensions suggested in Table 1 and selected dimensions from Rummel's studies.

For an example of how cross-polity data lend themselves
to sociolinguistic research see my Some contrasts between linguistically homogeneous and linguistically heterogeneous polities, Sociological Inquiry 36:2, 18-30 (1966). For several examples of how R
by Q factor analyses contribute to the compositing of sociolinguistic
data see Fishman, Joshua A., Robert L. Cooper and Roxana Ma,
Bilingualism in the Barrio, Bloomington, Indiana University Language
Sciences Monographs, 1971.

[16]Having carried my conceptual presentation this far purely
in theoretical terms it seems fitting to offer a few examples of how
I would currently characterize the language planning decisions of a
few nations with which I am somewhat familiar:

Type A		Type B	Type C
Cameroons	Philippines	Israel	India
Ghana	Indonesia	Thailand	Pakistan
Gambia	Tanzania	Somalia	Ceylon
		Ethiopia	Malaysia

The difficulties of utilizing the classification proposed in this
paper when proceeding non-quantitatively become apparent if we compare the position I have assigned to Tanzania with that assigned to
Ethiopia. Few Tanzanian leaders might agree that Tanzania still
lacks sufficiently integrating bonds to be classified as making Type
B decisions, particularly if Ethiopia, where native speakers of the
national language are also still a minority, can be so classified.
(For an example of a more intermediate view of Tanzanian integration
dated as recently as two years ago see M. Mosha, The role of language in nation building, EAIS and CA-EAA Conference on Mass Media
and Linguistic Communication in East Africa, March 31-April 3, 1967,
mimeo.). Of course, in the final analysis, phenomenological classifications must reveal the views of the beholders, because it is these
views that lead to subsequent actions. However, quantitative factor
loadings derived from such views and behaviors are also obtainable
and these would enable us to indicate the infinite degrees of similarity and difference that are actually provided for by the current conceptual approach in a fashion that simply cannot be matched by purely
nominal classifications based upon the judged resultant of forces.
        The problem of classifying Ireland presents us with another
opportunity for gauging the utility of the conceptual scheme advanced,
given the unusual case of a well nigh vanished vernacular that is still
governmentally termed to be the national language and "the first official language" (and, therefore, which is accorded every ceremonial
honor) while an erstwhile foreign colonialist Language of Wider Communication has, long since, become the actual mother tongue of the
vast majority of the population and the functional language of national
integration. Nevertheless, certain elites have set their sights on
Type B decision-making which would have Irish slowly but surely

destined to displace English (much like certain elites might plan to
have Arabic displace French in Tunisia). Most, however, claim (at
least in private) that Irish is an excessively deified corpse in honor
of which the nation has adopted Type C policies even though its population has—in the past 200 years—reestablished a new Type B integration and only one ethnic group and one integrating Great Tradition
are involved. The official position still maintains that Ireland consists of one people with two languages, each of which should be available to all for all national purposes and one of which requires substantial strengthening so that this goal may be attained. This official
position is difficult to classify within our conceptual framework since
it involves a functional duplication (which may, indeed, help explain
the singular lack of success in restoring Irish after 50 years of politically independent policy on behalf of that cause). The brunt of the
actions and decisions actually taken during this period seem to me to
be indicative of Type B decisions on behalf of a once foreign language
which has slowly been completely indigenized and associated with a
new indigenous Great Tradition while forcing the old vernacular into
being little but a vestigial rural marker, on the one hand (when spoken
conversationally), and a ceremonial marker on the other hand (when
printed or spoken on formal occasions).

10 | The Impact of Nationalism on Language Planning

Both modern nationalism as a mass movement and language planning as an aspect of national modernization are Western influences in South and Southeast Asia. At the same time, they are also reactions against Western influences. In either case they have been only selectively accepted or followed when compared to their original, European models. It is the purpose of this chapter to indicate the major similarities and differences between earlier European manifestations of nationalism and its impact on European language planning (these manifestations being themselves rather variegated and, therefore, ripe for picking and choosing on the part of Asian and African modernizers) and the subsequent recurrences of nationalism and language planning in South and Southeast Asia to this very day.

Nationalism

Three broad emphases characterize the manifestations of modern mass nationalism in Europe since the days of the French Revolution and its Napoleonic aftermath:

Unification

Nationalism as an integrative movement seeks to go beyond the primordial ties to family and locality (which defined the affiliative horizon of the common man in predominantly pre-industrial and pre-urban times) and to forge wider bonds that can draw the rural, the urban, and the regional into a broader unity: the nationality. In its birth throes nationalism stresses the inherent unity of populations that have never been aware of such unity before. In its further development nationalism may stress uniformation rather than unification alone.

Authentification

Nationalism is uniqueness-oriented. The avowed rationale for the unification of hitherto particularistic and diverse subgroups and the manifest dynamism both for the unificatory as well as for the purposive goals of nationalism are the ethnic uniqueness and cultural greatness of the nationality. This uniqueness, it is claimed, was, in the past, responsible for glorious attainments. If it can be recaptured in all of its authenticity, then, it is predicted, surely greatness will once again be achieved and, this time, permanently retained.

Modernization

Nationalism is a response to the problems and opportunities of modernity. Under the leadership of new proto-elites[1] that are oriented with respect to the challenges involved, nationalism brings to bear the weight of unified numbers and the dynamism of convictions of uniqueness upon the pursuit of organized cultural self-preservation, the attainment of political independence, the improvement of material circumstances, or the attainment of whatever other purpose will enhance the position of the nationality in a world in which social change is markedly rapid and conflictive.

All three ingredients mentioned above are essential for differentiating between nationalism and other social movements.[2] Without recognizing the ingredient of broader unification, nationalism cannot be differentiated from millenial sectarianisms, which, though alienated from most of their contemporaries, nevertheless, stress uniqueness as a response to the corruptions of modern life. Without recognizing the stress on ethnic or indigenous uniqueness, nationalism cannot be differentiated from cross-national movements for political, economic, or cultural planning, including international socialism and various regional confederations. Without recongizing the stress on accepting and overcoming the obstacles of modernization, nationalism

cannot be differentiated from nativistic and traditionalistic movements
that seek a genuine return to the ways of the past rather than (as in
the case of nationalism) a selective and purposive orientation thereto.[3]

Dialectic

It is quite apparent from the foregoing that there is a built-
in dialectic within nationalism, a quite inevitable tension between its
major components. Most obvious is the tension between the requirements of modernization and those of authentification. The one emphasizes the instrumental uniformities required by modern politico-
operational integration and is constantly straining toward newer,
more rational, more efficient solutions to the problems of today and
tomorrow. The other emphasizes the sentimental uniformities required by continuity based on sociocultural integration and is constantly straining towards purer, more genuine expressions of the
heritage of yesterday and of long ago.

A potential conflict also exists between the goal of authentification and that of unification since, in reality, pre-nationalist authenticity is highly localized. As a result, the supralocal authenticity
sought by nationalism must, to a large extent, be elaborated and
interpreted rather than merely returned to or discovered ready made.
The more stress on real authenticity, therefore, the more danger of
regionalism and ultimate secessionism. The more stress on unifica-
tion/uniformation, the less genuine authentification.

Even unification/uniformation and modernization are frequently at odds with each other. Some modern goals might well be
more fully or easily attained through the encouragement of diversity
(e.g., relations with important neighboring sources of supply might
well be improved if ethnic minorities speaking the same languages as
those used in the sources of supply were encouraged to maintain their
distinctiveness), while some pre-existing uniformities are actually
weakened rather than strengthened by industrialization, urbanization,
and other modernity tendencies (e.g., the weakening of religious
bonds).

It is part and parcel of the essence of nationalism to incorporate these potentially conflicting themes in its basic ideology.

Similarly, it is part and parcel of the essence of nationalism to engage the dialectic that is caused by the tension between these themes
and to derive from this dialectic a constant procession of solutions
to the problems engendered by its own ideological commitments. It
is this dialectic between potentially conflicting elements that constantly
recharges the dynamism of nationalist causes. Their business is
always unfinished because none of the goals of nationalist ideology
is ever fully attained or even substantially assured, not only because
of possible outside opposition, but also because of the internal insta-
bility of any resolution between its own contending components.

Types of European Nationalism

Modern European nationalisms were generally responses to
the same co-occurrences that prompted other major mass modernization movements of the past two centuries (widespread dislocations
and disorganization of recently urbanized populations brought on by
the impact of industrialization, the appearance of proto-elites offering action-oriented solutions to mass problems related to social
change, and the massification of political and cultural participation
in response to the pressures exerted by both the masses and elites
referred to). While nationalism proved to be combinable, perhaps,
in view of the similarity in its origins, with all major co-occurring
ideologies (viz., democratic nationalism, socialist nationalism, facist
nationalism, etc.), it contributed a very special emphasis of its own:
its stress on the ethnic authenticity of the nationality. This stress
appears to have been recognized in two different (but interrelated)
fashions throughout the course of the nineteenth century.

The State into Nationality Process

Nationality in the older and more firmly established European
states was considered to be a by-product of the common political-
operational institutions that had evolved in these states over the centuries. By the early nineteenth century, these states had already
gone through lengthy and successive processes of expansion and unification, which, on the one hand, had produced a rather widespread
sentiment of common nationality among their urban upper and middle

classes and which, on the other hand, made it easier for them to
cope with the problems of continued social change. These were the
so-called (and self-called) historic nations of Europe who could claim
in the nineteenth century that their primary institutions (their royal
houses, their governmental traditions, their educational systems,
their well established commercial and industrial patterns, and, above
all, their centuries of "shared experiences") had produced the unified
and authentic nationalities that populated them. Common nationality,
therefore, was a derivative, a by-product, of common institutions
rather than anything that could exist prior to or without such institutions. The "historic nations" of Europe were, by consensus, England,
France, Spain, Portugal, Holland, Denmark, and Sweden and, at
least potentially, also the Russian, Austro-Hungarian, and Ottoman
empires. The fact that these latter three were still digesting various
ethnic groups was well recognized, but it was assumed not only that
they would succeed in doing so but also that it was only natural and
proper that they continue to do so. Had not England digested the
Welsh, the Scots, and the Irish? Had not France digested the
Bretons, the Normans, the Gascons, the Occitans; and Spain the
Galicians, the Catalons, the Basques, and the like? The same process of unification and re-authentification on a broader base would
doubtlessly occur in the still multiethnic empires as well, given time
and the improvement of their primary institutions. This then became
the target of nationalism in the "historic nations" of nineteenth century Europe: the institutional liberalization and modernization of
the established states, for only such liberalization and modernization
could alleviate the suffering of the masses, could further the unity of
states, and could constructively harness the genius of nationalities
that the common institutions had created. The nationalism of the
"historic nations" of the early nineteenth century was, therefore,
liberal nationalism. It was the nationalism of those who already had
their own historically evolved and recognized states and state institutions. It was also the nationalism of the colonizers, for the "historic nations" of Europe were, simultaneously, the nations that held,
and were to continue to seek, political and economic colonies, both
close at hand as well as in new territories beyond the seas, in the
Americas, in Asia, and in Africa. It was this supralocal brand of
nationalism (with its stress on the integrative capacity of political-
operational institutions from which is derived a more abstract level
of sociocultural authenticity) that they exported willy-nilly to their
far-flung outposts.

Nationality into State Processes

The Napoleonic wars and the widespread but successful revolutions of 1830 and 1848 increased the awareness of European liberal intellectuals that there <u>were</u> apparently <u>some</u> nationalities who <u>were</u> such even in the absence of states of their own. Could anyone deny that the Greeks, the Poles, the Germans, the Italians, the Hungarians, and the Irish were nationalities? Although they had no states of their own at the time, and, therefore, no integrating state institutions under their own control, they nevertheless once had had them, long ago; and these, it was believed, had left such an imprint on the life of the people that they had continued as nationalities, as "defeated historic nationalities," on the strength of their common past memories.

The theory of the primacy of established institutions and of the derivative nature of nationality was salvaged by the subcategory of "defeated historic nations," and liberal nationalists of the "historic nations" frequently championed the causes of such nationalities, both for altruistic and for balance-of-power reasons.

The "Peoples without Histories"

Down to the very end of the nineteenth century and even into the twentieth, the intellectuals and spokesmen of the "historic nations" of the Atlantic coastline of Europe continued to argue, and then to plead, on behalf of the validity and the morality of the primacy of state-into-nationality process. Their efforts, however, were largely in vain because the very populations whom they sought to contain (and, in contrast, with whom they had termed themselves "historic nations") could not be contained.

The outmoded political-operational institutions of the multiethnic empires of Central, Eastern, and Southern Europe could not begin to fashion sufficiently integrative sociocultural bonds to compensate for the severe dislocation of their ethnically variegated rural populations. Proto-elites, trained in Western Europe, incessantly appeared to organize the mass demand for material improvement and for popular participation along ethnic lines. In organizing, in activating, and in focusing the masses, the proto-elites proceeded not only to capitalize and elaborate upon widespread sociocultural integrative themes of prior stability, justice, glory, and independence but also to fashion from them a view of nationality that was particularly appropriate for their own needs.

Among the submerged peoples of Europe, nationality was espoused as a primary, natural phenomenon, which, in turn, gave rise to the state as a secondary, instrumental by-product. Nationalities represented God-given demarcations or unities, and, as such, their uniqueness deserved to be prized, defended, liberated, and enhanced. These uniquenesses—and first and foremost among them, their respective vernaculars—were not only reflections of the limitless ingenuity and bounty of the Divine Force but also, each in its own right, directly responsible for the past period of greatness and glory that each submerged nationality had at one time experienced. The nationalist mission, therefore, was to recover or reconstruct the authentic uniqueness of the nationality (which had been contaminated by foreign models) and, thereby, to recover for the present as well as establish for the future the greatness that had existed in the past.

By means of this interpretation of nationality, the peoples of Central, Eastern, and Southern Europe sought to attain two goals. They did not want to be "peoples without histories" or even new nationalities; rather, they wanted to view themselves as continuations of old and once-illustrious traditions. However, neither they nor their leaders wanted to return to the past. Therefore, their slogan was "We must be ———and Europeans." The past was a key to the spirit of greatness, but, once unlocked, this spirit was to be used to overcome current hardships and to gain the good things of the world today. Thus, more recent European nationalism emphasized the ethnic uniqueness and authenticity of the nationality. Nationalities created states for their own protection and enhancement—for the recovery, cultivation, and enhancement of linguistic and cultural treasures. The nationality is primary and eternal. The state is derivative and unstable.[4]

Although their nationality-into-state view of nationalism contributed mightily to the trials and tribulations that destroyed the multiethnic empires of the Hapsburgs, the Czars, and the Sultans, it had but faint echoes throughout most of Africa and Asia. Between the two of them, however, the state-into-nationality processes and nationality-into-state processes reflect the two kinds of integrative bonds upon which all nations depend and which constantly reinforce each other, converge with each other, and give birth to each other. Just as the state-into-nationality nations stress(ed) their common sociocultural bonds, particularly in times of stress, so did (and do) the nationality-into-state nations stress politico-operational institutions as soon as they gain(ed) independence and face(d) the functional problems of modern nationhood.[5]

Two Examples of Language Planning in Europe

Even if (as would be useful for other purposes) we restrict language planning[6] to the elaboration, codification, and implementation that go on once language-policy decisions have been reached and, furthermore, even if we restrict our attention to language planning on behalf of varieties being put to newer and "higher" purposes than those to which they hitherto had normally been put, we nevertheless find ample illustrations of such planning in each of the two types of European nationalisms that we have reviewed.

In France

The classical example of language planning in the context of state-into-nationality processes is that of the French Academy. Founded in 1635—i.c., at a time well in advance of the major impact of industrialization and urbanization—the Academy, nevertheless, came after the political frontiers of France had long since approximated their current limits. Nevertheless, sociocultural integration was still far from attained at that time, as witnessed by the facts that in 1644 the ladies of Marseilles Society were unable to communicate with Mlle. de Scudéry in French; that in 1660 Racine had to use Spanish and Italian to make himself understood in Uzès; and that even as late as 1789 half of the population of the South did not understand French. The unparalleled literary creativity in French under the patronage of Louis IV could aim, at most, at a maximal audience of two million literates (out of a total estimated population of twenty

million). However, actually, no more than two hundred thousand
participated in the intellectual life of the country, and many of these
considered Italian, Spanish, and Occitan far more fitting vehicles for
cultured conversation, whereas for publications Latin, too, was a
common rival. All in all, the French Academy assumed an unenviable task—and one much ridiculed throughout the centuries—when it
presumed to codify French vocabulary, grammar, and spelling to
perfect refined conversation and written usage. [7]

Several aspects of the Academy's approach show its premod-
ernization goals and views. Far from seeking to provide technical
nomenclatures for industrial, commercial, and other applied pursuits, the Academy steadfastly refused to be concerned with such
"uncultured" and "unrefined" concerns. Instead of attempting to
reach the masses with its products, the Academy studiously aimed
its publications (at least for three centuries, if not longer) at those
already learned in the French language. Finally, in stead of appealing to anything essentially French in "spirit," in "genius," in "essence," or in "tradition," it defended its recommendations via appeals
to such purportedly objective criteria as euphonia, clarity, and necessity (redundancy). More than two hundred years after its founding,
when the Academy's continued lack of concern for the technical vocabulary of modernization had come to be accompanied by attacks on
anglomania and the tendency to angliciser, the worst that was said
about overly frequent English borrowings was that they were unnecessary rather than that they were un-French. [8]

From the point of view of its members, the Academy was an
institution—one of several—whose goal was to fashion and reinforce
French nationality. The Academy existed prior to, and independently
of, the French nationality. Indeed, French nationality was but a by-
product of the work of the Academy and of similar institutions and,
therefore, logically could not and morally should not be invoked to
carry out the Academy's goals. A similar disinclination to appeal to
nationalist authenticity marks the largely informal efforts on behalf
of language planning in England and the much more formal efforts
of the (Royal) Academy in Spain.

In the nationality-into-state context, the links between the
authenticity component of nationalism and language planning, on the

one hand, and the modernization-unification components of nationalism and language planning, on the other hand, are much more prominent and much more conscious. As a result, institutions and guidelines for language planning come into being very early in the mobilization process and remain in the foreground at least until authenticity, modernization, and unification seem reasonably assured. Here we are dealing with more highly pressured situations in which language planning is of high priority not only because of ideological considerations but also because without it the new elites can neither communicate with each other about specialized elitist concerns while remaining within the limits of authenticity nor move the masses towards greater unification, authentification, and modernization.

In Turkey

The case of Turkish language planning[9] is justifiably well known for the speed and the thoroughness with which it pursued modernization. As part of its over-all post World War I program of seeking a new Turkish identity (in contrast with its old Ottoman-Islamic identity), governmentally sponsored language planning conscientiously and vigorously moved to attain script reform (Roman in place of Arabic script), to attain Europeanization of specialized nomenclatures (rather than the Arabic and Persian loan words hitherto used for learned or cultured purposes), and to attain vernacularization or simplification of vocabulary, grammar, and phraseology for everyday conversational use (discarding the little understood and ornate flourishes patterned on Arabic or Persian).

Obviously, Turkish language planning was a part of Atatürk's over-all program of modernization. No nationalist movement, however, can continue to push modernization without regard for authenticity. Thus the break with the holy Arabic script soon came to be defended on the ground that it was unsuited for the requirements of authentic Turkish phonology. Since even the prophet had clearly been an Arab before he was a Mohammedan, he could hardly dispute the desire of Turks to put the needs of their Turkish authenticity first. The vast Europeanization of Turkish technical vocabulary had to be rationalized on the basis of the Great Sun Language theory. On the basis of this authenticity-stressing theory, .it was claimed that all

European languages were initially derived from Turkish. In that
case, all recent borrowings could be regarded as no more than re-
incorporations into the Turkish language of words or morphs that it
had originally possessed but lost under the foreign impact of Arabic
and Persian. Thus, the process of borrowing from European sources
was ultimately not rationalized as a modernizing step, but, rather
as an authenticating step! So, too, and even more clearly, was the
vernacularization and simplification of non-technical Turkish. Here
the language of the Anatolian peasant was held up as a model of purity
and authenticity on the ground that it had been least contaminated by
foreign influences and least corrupted by foreign fads.

Thus, on every front, decisions about language modernization in Turkey were finally rationalized and legitimatized through
sentiments of authenticity and a way was found for these two components of nationalist ideology to reinforce common nationalist goals
rather than to conflict with them or with each other. Such dialectic
skill is by no means rare in the annals of language planning within
highly nationalist contexts. On occasion, modernization may appear
to have the upper hand and, on other occasions, authentification is
stressed. In the longer run, however, what needs to be grasped is
not so much the seesawing back-and-forth as the need to retain both
components (actually all three components since uniformation, too,
must not be lost); and what needs to be found is a modus vivendi between them. Many examples of arriving at resolutions to the contradictory pressures built into nationalist language planning are to be
found in the Estonian, Czech, Ukrainian, Greek, Turkish, and other
relatively recent European language-planning experiences. These
examples deserve at least as much attention as do those drawn from
more uncompromising periods in which one or another component of
the "holy trinity" was stressed.

South and Southeast Asian Nationalism

If we review the past half century of South and Southeast
Asian nationalism[10] (combining approximately three decades of pre-
independence and two decades of post-independence history), we find
that it is overwhelmingly of the state-into-nationality variety. Its
emphases are still primarily instrumental, with a stress on the

building of modern and unified politico-operational institutions, out
of which, it is hoped, will develop a new and broader level of socio-
cultural integration and authenticity as Indians, as Pakistanis, as
Malaysians, as Indonesians, as Filipinos, and the like. In this sense,
South and Southeast Asian nationalisms follow directly in the tradition
of the nationalisms of their former colonial masters (as well as in the
footsteps of their own selectively reconstructed and interpreted
Great Traditions), although, of course, without anything like the long
experience with autonomous politico-operational integration available
to the Euro-American state-nationalities by the time they began to
face the stresses of modernization. As a result, South and Southeast
Asian nationalisms present a combination of state-into-nationality
ideologies plus nationality-into-state urgency and inexperience.

        Although South and Southeast Asian nationalism focuses upon
modernization and upon unification (the latter component requiring
particular attentions since the actual ethnic diversity encountered is
often far greater than that which existed in the multiethnic states of
pre-World War I Central, Eastern, and Southern Europe), there is,
nevertheless, attention to the rediscovery and re-creation of unifying
authenticity. To some extent, such authenticity is found in great pre-
Western traditions and glories; to some extent, it is found in more
recent experiences of struggling against political (pre-independence)
and economic (post-independence) colonialism. In either case, however, the authentification themes in South and Southeast Asian nationalism are supraethnic. Indeed, all attempts to revise the ethnically
meaningless political boundaries inherited from colonial rule (i. e. ,
all attempts to pursue nationality-into-state nationalism) have been
assiduously resisted and decried as "colonialism in disguise" and as
"artificially contrived by Western economic interests. "

        Had similar developments come to pass in Europe, then the
Austro-Hungarian, Russian, and Ottoman Empires not only would
have remained intact territorially but also would have converted into
new politico-operational structures in which ethnic Austrians (Germans), Hungarians, Russians, and Turks would no longer have been
undisputed masters relative to Czechs, Slovaks, Croates, Poles,
Ukrainians, Armenians, Arabs, and countless others. Instead, as
we know, these multiethnic empires were burst assunder, and their
fragmentation was legalized, justified, and protected by the Versailles
and Trianon treaties. In South and Southeast Asia, on the other hand,

as well as in all the other new nations of Africa and Asia, there has
been relatively little redrawing of colonial boundaries, either along
ethnic or other sociocultural integrative lines, neither at the time of
independence nor since. Save for Ceylon, Burma, Pakistan, Cambodia, Laos, and Vietnam, there have been no ethnic secessions or
divisions;[11] and save for the unification of West Irian with Indonesia
(and the unification of British and Italian Somaliland, as well as the
short-lived unification of Egypt and Syria, outside of the area that
we are discussing), there have been no (quasi-) ethnic unifications.

Certainly, this represents one of the major differences between the somewhat earlier national independence movements in
Europe and the somewhat later ones in Asia, a difference which harks
back to the differing models of nationalism under which they were
conducted.

Language Planning in South and Southeast Asia

The lesser stress on ethnic authenticity in South and Southeast Asian nationalism thus far is reflected in the correspondingly
greater roles of both indigenous and imported Languages of Wider
Communication (rather than of vernaculars alone) as languages of
central government and higher education. The well-nigh-complete
and rapid displacement of Latin, French, German, Russian, and
Arabic that marked the end of Austro-Hungarian, Czarist, and Ottoman hegemony in Central, Eastern and Southern Europe has had no
parallel in South and Southeast Asia.[12] Even the displacement of
Dutch in Indonesia was conducted with a regional Language of Wider
Communication in mind (a variety of Malay), rather than on behalf
of a vernacular. Although some vernaculars have gained a level of
recognition since independence that they never had in colonial days,
the positions of English and French, on the one hand, and of Hindi,
Urdu, Malay, Indonesian, and Pilipino, on the other hand, are definite signs of the continued supraethnic stress of South and Southeast
Asian language planning.

Indeed, the most central symbols and institutions of nationhood, the very processes of modernization and unification per se,
are generally not related to vernaculars at all. Thus, as the nations
of South and Southeast Asia progress along the path towards politico-

operational integration, we may expect that the new sociocultural
integration that they must seek to develop and the authenticity that
they must seek to stress will also be supraethnic. In the language-
planning field, this has taken the direction of protecting and increasing the authenticity of the non-Western Languages of Wider Communication that have come to be adopted for national unificatory purposes.
In this sense, the views of the language-planning agencies of South
and Southeast Asia[13] are constantly becoming more and more similar
to those of early twentieth century Central, Eastern, and Southern
Europe (even though they are not dealing as exclusively with vernaculars); and less and less like those of state-into-nationality contexts
that originally provided them with models.

Romanization of Script

Wherever classical literary traditions existed in pre-
independence South and Southeast Asia, Romanization of script has
usually been rejected. Although a modicum of Romanization is prac-
ticed in conjunction with highly technical and advanced scientific
work conducted in India, Pakistan, and Ceylon (e. g. , the proposals
to introduce Romanization of script of a wider front)—as an aid to
literacy, modernization, or interregional communication—it has
been resisted as vigorously in those countries as it has been in China,
Japan, or Israel outside of the area under consideration. The mass
ideologization of this resistance is consistently in terms of indigenous
authenticity as opposed to foreign artificiality.[14]

Purification

The tendency to reject European or, more generally, "international" lexical or morphological items, even for rather technical
scientific or governmental work, is increasing throughout South and
Southeast Asia. So, too, is the tendency to limit the various influences
of the vernacular on the national languages, even though such influences would tend to make these languages more widely understood.
With respect to Hindi, these tendencies take the direction successively
of more extreme Sanskritization, ignoring the pleas of educators and
statesmen alike that such treatment severely restricts the functional
utility of the language. A similar process of Arabo-Persianization

(and Islamization) is transforming High Urdu. In Malaysia, Indonesia, and the Philippines, it leads to a growing emphasis on Austronesian derivatives, rather than on Graeco-Latin roots, in developing the specialized nomenclatures that Malay, Indonesian, and Philipino increasingly require. In most of the earlier twentieth century European cases of language planning, the purification efforts were directed at one or another neighboring vernacular rather than at internationalisms as such. [15] In South and Southeast Asia, given the general identification of internationalisms with Euro-American colonialism, purification shows tendencies of combating "cultural colonialism" much more than neighboring vernaculars, all the more so, since the latter have little if any national significance. [16] The interest in indigenizing the national languages of South and Southeast Asia is a definite sign of the new and broader sociocultural integration that they must succeed in developing to the end that a new supraethnic authenticity will develop that will correspond to the new unification and modernization that has been emphasized thus far. [17]

Conclusions

South and Southeast Asian nationalism is slowly but predictably being transformed from complete reliance on state-into-nationality processes into increasing attention to (supraethnic) nationality-into-state processes as well. In this transition we may expect a growing ideologized stress on indigenousness in general and on the sociocultural integration evolved, during the period of independence, in particular. The national languages, although initially regional Languages of Wider Communications, are important symbols and media of the new authenticity of these states.

Language planning in South and Southeast Asia may be expected to be increasingly subjected to supraethnic authenticity goals on the part of governmental and intellectual elites. Whereas language planning thus far has been concerned primarily with such unification and modernization goals as mass literacy, participation, and productivity, the very focus on these goals has and must contribute, ultimately, to a redistribution of attention so that authenticity will also receive the recognition it has always required as one of the three equal-but-opposite partners in the inevitable triangle that nationalism represents.

NOTES

An abstract (prepared for the Proceedings of the Consultative Meeting
on Language-Planning Processes, East-West Center, Institute of
Advanced Projects, University of Hawaii, April 7-10, 1969) of a
forthcoming volume Language and Nationalism (Rowley, Mass.,
Newbury House, 1972). Detailed documentation of the historical processes and trends reviewed in this abstract will be found in the afore-
mentioned volume. Only a few bibliographic landmarks will be cited
in this abstract. This abstract was written while the author was a
Senior Specialist (1968-69) at the Institute of Advanced Projects, East-
West Center, University of Hawaii, Honolulu, Hawaii.

[1] Proto-elites: the leadership of nationalist groups in their
early and formative period, before they are fully and formally organized.

Elites: the leadership of later, more organized periods
in the history of nationalist movements.

[2] Of the huge literature on (European) nationalism the major
presentations which devote some attention to all three of these components are (Deutsch 1953, Gellner 1964, and Znaniecki 1952).

[3] Nationalism shares with all of the foregoing the characteristic of being a protest movement related to social change and the
dislocation resulting therefrom. It is illustrated by Despres (1967).

[4] The feverishness with which the so-called "peoples without
history" proceeded to recover, to reconstruct, and, where necessary,
to design their histories is interestingly reviewed in Jaszi (1929),
Kolarz (1946), and Kahn (1950).

[5] The distinction between the state-nationality and nationality-
state forms of nationalism is implicit in Zangwill (1917) and Talmon
(1965); and explicit in Pflanze (1966) and Rustow (1968). The cycli-
cal interaction between these two stages of nationalism is implicit
in Zangwill (1917) and explicit in Fishman (1968). By contrast, the
number of scholars who have argued that only one or another of these
processes is possible or desirable is extremely great and is reviewed
in my Language and Nationalism.

[6] For a brief but enlightening introduction to language planning, given these very restrictions, see Ferguson (1968). The basic
references are Haugen (1966a and 1966b).

only extensive account of the linguistic efforts of the French Academy
are those of Robertson (1910). For interesting and little-known facts
concerning the unenviable condition of French in France before the
revolution, no one can rival Brunot. The few illustrations cited here
are those recently enumerated by Gache (1969) in his review of the
changed relative strengths of English and French.

[8] The following poem of 1853 by Viennet is an example of
French elitist rejection of "anglomania," without nationalist animus
of any kind.

> On n'entend que des mots à déchirer le fer,
> Le railway, le tunnel, le ballast, le fender,
> Express, trucks, wagons; une bouche française
>   Semble broyer du verre ou mâcher de la braise...
> Certes, de nos voisins, l'alliance m'enchante,
> Mais leur langue, à vrai dire, est trop envahissante!
> Faut-il pour cimenter un merveilleux accord
> Changer l'arène en turf et le plaisir en sport,
> Demander à des clubs l'aimable causerie,
> Flétrir du nom de grooms nos valets d'écurie,
> Traiter nos cavaliers de gentleman-riders?
> Je maudis ces auteurs dont le vocabulaire
> Nous encombre de mots dont nous n'avons que faire
>   (cited by Gache, 1969)

[9] The most detailed account of Turkish language planning
under the impetus of the Atatürk revolution is that of Heyd (1954).
Less well known is Heyd's study of Gökalp—a somewhat earlier and
less revolutionary Turkish nationalist who more clearly indicated the
need to Europeanize certain domains of the national language and
culture—to Turkify other domains, while leaving a few relatively untouched in their pre-nationalist Perso-Arabic garb (Heyd 1950).
Gallagher indicates that such is currently the case, some forty years
after the modernizing excesses of Atatürk's reforms.

[10] Two informative introductions to Asian nationalisms and
to the differences and similarities that characterize them vis-à-vis
European nationalisms are those of Kautsky (1962) and Kennedy (1968).

[11] The recent secession of Singapore from Malaysia might be
considered another example of an ethnic secession, although economic
factors were probably more salient considerations.

[12] The reestablishment of Russian hegemony, first, in the
Soviet Union and, then, after World War II, in most of Eastern Europe,

has led to the reestablishment of Russian as a Language of Wider
Communication throughout the area. The point here, however, is the
extreme rapidity with which Russian vanished as a language of government and of higher education in Poland, the Baltic States, Bessa-
rabia and even the Ukraine after the defeat of the Czarist forces, as
opposed to the continued role of English in India, Pakistan, and the
Philippines and the continued role of French in Vietnam, Laos, and
Cambodia after independence from colonial rule was obtained.

[13] The most extensive list of the language-planning agencies
of Southeast Asia is that reported by Noss (1967), who also discusses
the language policies and problems of each country in the area. No
similar list or discussion is availably for South Asia.

[14] The rationales for suggesting—and for rejecting—the use
of a common Roman script in India are clearly and repeatedly presented in India (1963). Before their victory, Chinese communists
consistently espoused Romanization schemes. As late as 1958, this
was still official policy (Reform 1958), although it has since then been
quietly abandoned. In the Chinese case, Romanization would lead to
the loss of the unifying supraethnic (and supraphonic) written language
and to possibly dangerous encouragement to local vernaculars. Thus,
whereas Romanization would be a step away from (oft sanctified) indigenousness in India—and would render understandable written texts
that differ more in script than they do in vocabulary and grammar—
it would tend to have the opposite effect in China, where the common
supraphonic script makes the very great differences that exist between the various local languages.

[15] German is the prime European exception to this generalization, and even there the use of internationalisms continued down
into the Nazi period without being entirely displaced (Koppelman
1956). The origin of the antiinternationalist tendency in German language planning goes back to the violently anti-French sentiments of
Fichte, Herder, and even earlier fathers of German nationalism, all
of whom struggled against and suffered from the Francomania of
German princelings and courtiers (Kedourie 1961).

[16] For ample evidence of the ideologies of indigenization
effecting South and Southeast Asian language planning, see several
of the papers (other than those of the editor) in Alisjahbana (1971).
Very marked rationales of this kind are advanced and defended by
Del Rosario (1968).

[17] Sociocultural integration on the basis of post-independence
authenticity is also appealed to in campaigns that aim at decreasing

reliance on imported Languages of Wider Communication (such as English) in India, the Philippines, and elsewhere.

REFERENCES

Alisjahbana, S. Takdir, ed. 1971. The Modernization of the
    Languages of Asia. Kuala Lumpur.
Bright, William, ed. 1966. Sociolinguistics. Proceedings of the
    UCLA Sociolinguistics Conference, 1964. Janua Linguarum,
    Series Major, 20. The Hague: Mouton.
Brunot, Ferdinand. 1924-53. Histoire de la Langue Française des
    Origines à nos Jours. 1-9 (in 14 pts.). Paris: A. Colin.
Del Rosario, Gonsalo. 1968. A modernization-standardization plan
    for the Austronesian-derived national languages of South-
    east Asia. Asian Studies, 6:1:1-18.
Despres, Leo A. 1967. Cultural Pluralism and Nationalist Politics
    in British Guiana. Chicago: Rand McNally.
Deutsch, Karl W. 1966. Nationalism and Social Communication: An
    Inquiry into the Foundations of Nationality. 2nd ed. (revised
    tabular and bibliographic material). Cambridge, Mass.:
    MIT Press.
Ferguson, Charles A. 1968. Language development, in Fishman,
    Ferguson, and Das Gupta, 27-36.
Fishman, Joshua A.; Ferguson, Charles A.; and Das Gupta, Jyotirin-
    dra, eds. 1968. Language Problems of Developing Nations.
    New York: John Wiley and Sons.
Gache, Paul. 1969. Langue française et langue issue de l'Angle-
    terre. Le Travailleur, 39:15:1, 5.
Gellner, Ernest. 1964. Thought and Change. Chicago: University
    of Chicago Press.
Haugen, Einar. 1966a. Language Conflict and Language Planning:
    The Case of Modern Norwegian. Cambridge: Harvard
    University Press.
Haugen, Einar. 1966b. Linguistics and language planning, in Bright,
    50-71.
Heyd, Uriel. 1950. Foundations of Turkish Nationalism: The Life
    and Teachings of Ziya Gökalp. London: Luzac and Harvill.
    _____. 1954. Language Reform in Modern Turkey. Oriental
    Notes and Studies, 5. Jerusalem: Israel Oriental Society.
India. Ministry of Scientific Research and Cultural Affairs. 1963.

A Common Script for Indian Languages. Delhi: Republic of India.

Jazsi, Oscar. 1929. The Dissolution of the Habsburg Monarchy. Chicago: University of Chicago Press.

Kahn, Robert A. 1950. The Multinational Empire: Nationalism and National Reform in the Habsburg Monarchy, 1848-1918, 2 vols. New York: Columbia University Press. (Also note his one vol. abridgement, 1957. The Habsburg Empire: A Study in Integration and Disintegration. New York: Praeger.)

Kautsky, John H. 1962a. An essay in the politics of development, in Kautsky (1962b), 1-122.

_____, ed. 1962b. Political Change in Underdeveloped Countries: Nationalism vs. Communism. New York: John Wiley and Sons.

Kedourie, Elie. 1960. Nationalism (Rev. 1961). New York: Praeger.

Kennedy, Joseph. 1968. Asian Nationalism in the Twentieth Century. New York: Macmillan.

Kolarz, Walter. 1946. Myths and Realities in Eastern Europe. London: Lindsay Drummond.

Koppelman, Heinrich L. 1956. Nation, Sprache und Nationalismus. Leiden: Sijthoff.

Noss, Richard. 1967. Language Policy and Higher Education, Higher Education and Development in South-East Asia, 3:2. Paris: UNESCO and the International Association of Universities.

Pflanze, Otto. 1966. Characteristics of nationalism in Europe, 1848-1871. Review of Politics, 28:129-43.

_____. 1958. Reform of the Chinese Written Language. Peking: Foreign Languages Press.

Robertson, D. Maclaren. 1910. A History of the French Academy 1635 [1634]-1910. New York: Dillingham.

Rustow, Dankwart. 1968. Language, modernization and nationhood, in Fishman, Ferguson, and Das Gupta, 87-106.

Talmon, J. L. 1965. The Unique and the Universal. London: Secker and Warburg.

Zangwill, Israel. 1917. The Principle of Nationalities. London: Watts.

Znaniecki, Florian. 1952. Modern Nationalities. Urbana: University of Illinois Press.

Part V. General Sociolinguistic Theory

11 | The Relationship Between Micro- and Macro-Sociolinguistics in the Study of Who Speaks What Language to Whom and When

The Analysis of Multilingual Settings

        Multilingual speech communities differ from each other in so many ways that every student of societal multilingualism must grapple with the problem of how best to systematize or organize the manifold differences that are readily recognizable between them. This paper is directed to a formal consideration of several descriptive and analytic variables which may contribute to an understanding of who speaks what language to whom and when to those speech communities that are characterized by widespread and relatively stable multilingualism. It deals primarily with "within-group (or intragroup) multilingualism," rather than with "between-group (or intergroup) multilingualism," that is, it focuses upon those multilingual settings in which a single population makes use of two (or more) "languages" or varieties of the "same language" for internal communicative purposes (Fishman 1967). As a result of this limitation, mastery or control of mother tongue and other tongue (or, more generally, of the various languages or varieties constituting the speech community's linguistic repertoire [Gumperz 1962]) may be ruled out as a crucial variable since the members of many speech networks would find it possible to communicate with each other quite easily in any of their available codes or subcodes. It seems clear, however, that habitual language choice in multilingual speech communities or speech networks is far from being a random matter of momentary inclination, even under those circumstances when it could very well function as such from a purely probabilistic point of view (Lieberson 1964). "Proper" usage dictates that only one of the theoretically co-available languages or varieties will be chosen by particular classes of interlocutors on particular kinds of occasions to discuss particular kinds of topics.

What are the most appropriate parameters by which to describe these choice-patterns in order to maximize both factual accuracy and theoretical parsimony, and in order to facilitate the integration of small-group and large-group research rather than their further needless polarization? If we can clarify the problem of how to describe language choice in stable, within-group bilingual settings where the limits of language mastery do not intrude, we can then more profitably turn (or return) to the problem of choice determinants in less stable settings such as those characterizing immigrant-host relationships or between-group multilingual settings more generally (Fishman 1964).

A Hypothetical Example

American students are so accustomed to bilingualism as a "vanishing phenomenon," as a temporary dislocation from a presumably more normal state of affairs characterized by "one man, one language," that an example of stable intra-group bilingualism may help to start off our discussion in a more naturalistic and less bookish vein.

A government functionary in Brussels arrives home after stopping off at his club for a drink. He generally speaks standard French in his office, standard Dutch at his club and a distinctly local variant of Flemish at home. [1] In each instance he identifies himself with a different speech network to which he belongs, wants to belong, and from which he seeks acceptance. All of these networks—and more—are included in his over-arching speech community, even though each is more commonly associated with one speech variety than with another. Nevertheless, it is not impossible to find occasions at the office in which he speaks or is spoken to in one or another variety of Flemish. There are also occasions at the club when he speaks or is addressed in French; finally, there are occasions at home when he communicates in standard Dutch or even French.

Our hypothetical government functionary is most likely to use Flemish and get it in return at the office when he bumps into another functionary who hails from the very same Flemish-speaking town. The two of them grew up together and went to school together.

Their respective sets of parents strike them as being similarly "kind-but-old-fashioned." In short, they share many common experiences and points of view (or think they do, or pretend they do) and, therefore, they tend to speak to each other in the language which represents for them the intimacy that they share. The two do not cease being government functionaries when they speak Flemish to each other; they simply prefer to treat each other as intimates rather than as functionaries. However, the careful observer will also note that the two do not speak Flemish to each other invariably. When they speak about world affairs, or the worlds of art and literature, not to mention the world of government, they tend to switch into French (or to reveal far more French lexical, phonological or even grammatical influence in their Flemish), even though (for the sake of our didactic argument) the mood of intimacy and familiarity remains clearly evident throughout.

Thus, our overall problem is twofold: a) to recognize and describe whatever higher order regularities there may be in choosing among the several varieties that constitute the repertoire of a multilingual speech community (so that we need not always remain at an anecdotal and clinical level of analysis) and b) nevertheless, to recognize the interpersonal fluctuation (= lower order societal patterning) that remains even when higher order societal patterning is established.

Topic

The fact that two individuals who usually speak to each other primarily in X nevertheless switch to Y (or vacillate more noticeably between X and Y) when discussing certain topics leads us to consider topic per se as a regulator of language use in multilingual settings.

The implication of topical regulation of language choice is that certain topics are somehow handled "better" or more appropriately in one language than in another in particular multilingual contexts. However, this greater appropriateness may reflect or may be brought about by several different but mutually reinforcing factors. Thus, some multilingual speakers may "acquire the habit" of speaking about topic x in language X partially because that is the language in which they were trained to deal with this topic (e. g. , they received their university training in economics in French), partially because they (and their interlocutors) may lack the specialized terms for a satisfying discussion of x in language Y,[2] partially because language Y itself may currently lack as exact or as many terms for handling topic x as those currently possessed by language X, and partially because it is considered strange or inappropriate to discuss x in language Y. The very multiplicity of sources of topical regulation suggests that topic may not in itself be a convenient analytic variable when language choice is considered from the point of view of the larger societal patterns and sociolinguistic norms of a multilingual setting, no matter how fruitful it may be at the level of face-to-face interaction per se. What would be helpful for larger societal investigations and for inter-societal comparisons is an understanding of how topics reflect or imply regularities which pertain to the major spheres of activity in any society under consideration. We may be able to discover the latter if we inquire why a significant number of people in a particular multilingual setting at a particular time have received certain kinds of training in one language rather than in another; or what it reveals about a particular multilingual setting if language X is currently actually less capable of coping with topic x than is language Y. Does it not reveal more than merely a topic-language relationship at the level of particular face-to-face encounters? Does it not reveal that certain socio-culturally recognized spheres of activity are, at least temporarily, under the sway of one language or variety (and, therefore, perhaps, under the control of certain speech networks) rather than others? Thus, while topic is doubtlessly a crucial consideration in understanding language choice variance in our two hypothetical government functionaries, we must seek a means of examining and relating their individual, momentary choices to relatively stable patterns of choice that exist in their multilingual speech community as a whole.

Domains of Language Behavior

a) The concept of domains of language behavior seems to have received its first partial elaboration from students of language maintenance and language shift among Auslandsdeutsche in pre-World War II multilingual settings.[3] German settlers were in contact with many different non-German speaking populations in various types of contact settings and were exposed to various kinds of socio-cultural change processes. In attempting to chart and compare the fortunes of the German language under such varying circumstances Schmidt-Rohr seems to have been the first to suggest that <u>dominance configurations</u> needed to be established to reveal the overall status of language choice in various domains of behavior (1932). The domains recommended by Schmidt-Rohr were the following nine: the family, the playground and street, the school, the church, literature, the press, the military, the courts, and the governmental administration. Subsequently, other investigators either added additional domains (e.g., Mak [1935], who nevertheless followed Schmidt-Rohr in overlooking the work-sphere as a domain), or found that fewer domains were sufficient in particular multilingual settings (e.g., Frey [1945], who required only home, school and church in his analysis of Amish "triple talk"). However, what is more interesting is that Schmidt-Rohr's domains bear a striking similarity to those "generally termed" spheres of activity which have more recently been independently advanced by others interested in the study of acculturation, inter-group relations, and bilingualism (e.g., Dohrenwend and Smith 1962).

Domains are defined, regardless of their number,[4] in terms of <u>institutional contexts and their congruent behavioral co-occurrences.</u> <u>They attempt to summate the major clusters of interaction that occur in clusters of multilingual settings and involving clusters of interlocutors.</u> Domains enable us to understand that <u>language choice</u> and <u>topic</u>, appropriate though they may be for analyses of individual behavior at the level of face-to-face verbal encounters, are, as we suggested above, related to widespread socio-cultural norms and expectations. By recognizing the existence of domains it becomes possible to contrast the language of topics for individuals or particular sub-populations with the predominant language of domains for larger networks, if not the whole, of a speech community.

b) The appropriate designation and definition of domains of language behavior obviously calls for considerable insight into the socio-cultural dynamics of particular multilingual speech communities at particular periods in their history. Schmidt-Rohr's domains re-flect not only multilingual settings in which a large number of spheres of activity, even those that pertain to governmental functions, are theoretically open to both or all of the languages present, but also

those multilingual settings in which such permissiveness is at least
sought by a sizable number of interested parties. Quite different domains might be appropriate if one were to study habitual language use
among children in these very same settings. Certainly, immigrant-
host contexts, in which only the language of the host society is recognized for governmental functions, would require other and perhaps
fewer domains, particularly if younger generations constantly leave
the immigrant society and enter the host society. Finally, the domains of language behavior may differ from setting to setting not only
in number and designation but also level. Thus, in studying acculturating populations in Arizona, Barker (who studied bilingual Spanish
Americans [1947]) and Barber (who studied trilingual Yaqui Indians
[1952]) formulated domains at the level of sociopsychological
analysis: intimate, informal, formal and intergroup. Interestingly
enough, the domains defined in this fashion were then identified with
domains at the societal-institutional level mentioned above. The
"formal" domain, e.g., was found to coincide with religious-
ceremonial activities; the "intergroup" domain consisted of economic
and recreational activities as well as of interactions with governmental-
legal authority, etc. The interrelationship between domains of language behavior defined at a societal-institutional level and domains
defined at a socio-psychological level (the latter being somewhat
closer to topical-situational analyses discussed earlier) may enable
us to study language choice in multilingual settings in newer and more
fruitful ways.

c) The "governmental administration" domain is a social
nexus which normally brings certain kinds of people together primarily for a certain cluster of purposes. Furthermore, it brings them
together primarily for a certain set of role-relations (discussed below) and in a delimited environment. Thus, domain is a socio-cultural
construct abstracted from topics of communication, relationships between communicators, and locales of communication, in accord with
the institutions of a society and the spheres of activity of a speech
community, in such a way that individual behavior and social patterns
can be distinguished from each other and yet related to each other.[5]
The domain is a higher order summarization which is arrived at
from a detailed study of the face-to-face interactions in which language
choice is imbedded. Of the many factors contributing to and subsumed
under the domain concept some are more important and more accessible to careful measurement than others. One of these, topic, has

already been discussed. Two others, role-relation and locale remain to be discussed. Role relations may be of value to us in accounting for the fact that our two hypothetical governmental functionaries,
who usually speak an informal variant of Flemish to each other at the
office, except when they talk about technical, professional or sophisticated "cultural" matters, are themselves not entirely alike in this
respect. If one of the two tends to slip into French more frequently
than the other, it would not be surprising to discover that he is the
supervisor of the other.

Domains and Role-Relations

          In many studies of multilingual behavior the family domain
has proved to be very crucial. Multilingualism often begins in the
family and depends upon it for encouragement if not for protection.
In other cases, multilingualism withdraws into the family domain after
it has been displaced from other domains in which it was previously
encountered.   Little wonder then that many investigators, beginning
with Braunshausen several years ago (1928), have differentiated
"speakers" within the family domain. However, two different approaches have been followed with such differentiation. Braunshausen
and (much more recently) Mackey (1962, 1965, 1966) have merely
specified family "members": father, mother, child, domestic, governess and tutor, etc. Gross, on the other hand, has specified dyads
within the family (1951): grandfather to grandmother, grandmother
to grandfather, grandfather to father, grandmother to father, grandfather to mother, grandmother to mother, grandfather to child,
grandmother to child, father to mother, mother to father, etc. The
difference between these two approaches is considerable. The second
approach not only recognizes that interacting members of a family
(like the participants in most other domains of language behavior) are
hearers as well as speakers (i.e., that there may be a distinction
between multilingual comprehension and multilingual production),
but it also recognizes that their language behavior may be not merely
a matter of individual preference or facility but also a matter of
role-relations. In certain societies particular behaviors (including
language behaviors) are expected (if not required) of particular individuals vis-à-vis each other (Goodenough, 1965).

The family domain is not unique in its differentiability into role-relations. Each domain can be differentiated into role-relations that are specifically crucial or typical of it in particular societies at particular times. In those societies where religion can be differentiated from folkways more generally, the religious domain may reveal such role-relations as cleric-cleric, cleric-parishioner, parishioner-cleric, and parishioner-parishioner. Similarly, pupil-teacher, buyer-seller, employer-employee, judge-petitioner, all refer to specific role-relations in other domains. It would certainly seem desirable to describe and analyze language use or language choice in a particular multilingual setting in terms of the crucial role-relations within the specific domains considered to be most revealing for that setting. [6] The distinction between own-group-interlocutor and other-group-interlocutor may also be provided for in this way when intergroup bilingualism becomes the focus of inquiry.

Domains and Locales

Bock (1964), Ervin (1964) and Gumperz (1964) have presented many examples of the importance of locale as a determining component of situational analysis. If one meets his clergyman at the race track, the locale is likely to have a noticeable impact on the topics and role-relationships that normally obtain. However, we must also note that domains, too, are locale-related in the sense that most major social institutions are associated with a very few primary locales. Just as topical appropriateness in face-to-face language choice is indicative of larger scale societal patterns, and just as role appropriateness in face-to-face language choice is similarly indicative, so the locale constraints and locale appropriatenesses that obtain in face-to-face language choice have their large scale implications and extrapolations.

The Construct Validity of Domains

a) A research project dealing with Puerto Rican bilingualism in the Greater New York City Area has yielded data which may help clarify both the construct validity of domains as well as a procedure for their recognition. Since domains are a higher order generalization from congruent situations (i. e. , from situations in which

individuals interacting in appropriate role-relationships with each
other, in the appropriate locales for those role-relationships, engage
in discussing topics appropriate to their role-relationships) it was
first necessary to try-out and revise intuitive and rather clinical
estimates of the widespread congruencies that were felt to obtain.
After more than a year of participant observation and other data-
gathering experiences it seemed to Greenfield (1968) that five domains
could be generalized from the innumerable situations that he had encountered in the Puerto Rican speech community. He tentatively
labeled these "family," friendship," "religion," "education," and
"employment," and proceeded to determine whether a typical situation
could be presented for each domain as a means of collecting valid
self-report data on normative views regarding language choice. (For
a full report on his experiment, see Chapter 10, This Volume.)

        However, as Blom and Gumperz (1966), Fishman (1968 b)
and others have indicated, seemingly incongruent situations frequently
occur and are rendered understandable and acceptable (just as are
the seemingly ungrammatical sentences that we hear in most spontaneous speech). Interlocutors reinterpret incongruencies in order to
salvage some semblance of the congruency by which they understand
their social order and function within it. Were this not the case then
no seemingly congruent domains could arise and be maintained out of
the incongruencies of daily life. In order to test this assumption
Greenfield subsequently proceeded to present his subjects with two
incongruent components (e.g., with a person from one hypothetical
domain and with a place from another hypothetical domain) and asked
them a) to select a third component in order to complete the situation,
as well as b) to indicate their likelihood of using Spanish or English
in a situation so constituted. Greenfield found that the third component was overwhelmingly selected from either one or the other of
any two domains from which he had selected the first two components.
Furthermore, in their attempts to render a seemingly incongruous
situation somewhat more congruent, his subjects' language preferences
left the normal relationship between domains and language choice substantially unaltered (directionally) regardless of whether person,
places, or topics were involved. Nevertheless, all domains became
somewhat less different from each other than they had been in the
fully congruent situations. Apparently, when incongruencies appear,
both individual indecisiveness and sociolinguistic norms governing

domain regularity must be combined and compromised. In "usual" situations governed entirely by sociolinguistic norms of communicative appropriateness, language choice is much more clear cut and polarized than in "unusual" situations which must be resolved by individual interpretation (Table 2).

Greenfield's findings imply that the assumed relationship between face-to-face situations and larger scale societal domains obtains for self-report data. However, it remains necessary for other investigators to determine whether the domains adumbrated in this fashion have any validity in other speech communities they study.

b) A language census conducted among all 431 souls in a four-block Puerto Rican neighborhood in Jersey City yielded the data shown in Table 1.[7] Above and beyond examining the replies obtained to the individual census items the reader's attention is directed to the results of the factor analysis (shown below the Table). If domains are more than the investigator's etic reclassification of situations then they sould also become apparent from factor analysis which in essence asks: which items tend to be answered in a consistent fashion. Of the five domains extracted from this analysis, all four domains considered appropriate for census questioning (language in the context of family, education, work and religion) appeared as separate factors, namely, I. Spanish: Literacy (= education), II. Spanish: Oral (= family), IV. Spanish: at work, and V. Spanish: in religion. In addition, an English factor also appeared indicating that although English is not specifically domain associated for the population as a whole (although so associated for children, as we shall soon see) it is also not displacively or transitionally related to Spanish. An orthogonal English factor indicates that (as in other speech communities marked by relatively stable and widespread bilingualism) there is no need for one language to be learned or used at the expense of the other in the population under study.

c) A third indication of the construct validity of domains as analytic parameters for the study of large scale sociolinguistic patterns is yielded by Edelman's data (1968). Significant and instructive findings were obtained when the word naming responses of bilingual Puerto Rican children in Jersey City were analyzed in accord with the domains derived from Greenfield's and Fishman's data reported

Table 1. Language Census (Fishman, 1968 a)

Item	Yes*	Little*	No*	NP*
1. Can Understand Spanish conversation?	779	135	019	067
2. Can Speak Spanish (conversation)?	833	077	016	074
3. Can Read newspapers/books in Spanish?	397	049	318	237
4. Can Write letters in Spanish?	390	030	339	241
5. Can Understand English conversation?	571	176	183	070
6. Can Speak English (conversation)?	536	181	216	067
7. Can Read newspapers/books in English?	455	130	206	209
8. Can Write letters in English?	387	063	327	223

	Span*	Eng*	Both*	NP*
9. First language understood (conversation)?	886	002	039	072
10. First language spoken (conversation)?	884	---	023	093
11. First language read (newspapers/books)?	401	---	297	302
12. First language written (letters)?	383	002	276	339
13. Most frequently spoken at home?	657	088	183	072
14. Most frequently read at home?	267	051	357	325
15. Most frequently written at home?	339	014	255	392
16. Most frequently spoken with fellow workers?	137	049	137	677
17. Most frequently spoken with supervisor?	046	009	264	680
18. Most frequently spoken with clients/custs?	032	014	035	919
19. Language of instruction in school?	339	237	167	257
20. Language liked most (conversation)?	362	285	186	167
21. Language of priest's/minister's sermon?	452	137	193	206
22. Language of silent prayer?	469	123	151	257
23. Language of church service?	427	160	193	220

*Per cents carried to 3 places, decimals omitted.

Table 1 (continued)

On a re-interviewed sample of 124 cases the distributions obtained were practically identical to those shown above, indicating that the marginals reported are quite stable.

The language replies to the census have been subjected to a factor analysis (varimax orthogonal rotation). The following 5 factor solution appeared to be most revealing:

No.	Suggested factor name	Items (Loadings)
I	Spanish: literacy	4(93), 3(92), 15(89), 12(88), 11(87), 19(71), 14(70), 20(54)
II	English (oral and written)	7(89), 6(88), 5(84), 8(82)
III	Spanish: oral	9(78), 1(71), 2(66), 10(63), 13(38)
IV	Spanish: at work	18(79), 16(73), 17(55)
V	Spanish: in religion	21(93), 23(89), 22(40)

Table 2. Spanish and English Usage Self-Ratings in
Various Situations for Components Selected

I. Congruent Situations: Two "congruent" components presented; S selects
third congruent component and language appropriate to situation.

(1 = All in Spanish; 5 = All in English)

Congruent Persons Selected

	Parent	Friend	Total	Priest	Teacher	Employer	Total
Mean	2.77	3.60	3.27	4.69	4.92	4.79	4.81
S.D.	1.48	1.20	1.12	.61	.27	.41	.34
n	13	15	15	13	13	14	15

Congruent Places Selected

	Home	Beach	Total	Church	School	Work Place	Total
Mean	2.33	3.50	2.60	3.80	4.79	4.27	4.27
S.D.	1.07	1.26	1.10	1.51	.58	1.34	.94
n	15	6	15	15	14	15	15

Congruent Topics Selected

	Family	Friend-ship	Total	Religious	Educa-tion	Employ-ment	Total
Mean	1.69	3.30	2.64	3.80	4.78	4.44	4.38
S.D.	.92	1.20	.95	1.47	1.53	1.12	.73
n	16	18	18	15	18	18	18

Table 2 (continued)

II. Incongruent Situations: Two "incongruent" components presented; S selects third component and language appropriate to situation.

(1 = All in Spanish; 5 = All in English)

Incongruent Persons Selected

	Parent	Friend	Total	Priest	Teacher	Employer	Total
Mean	2.90	3.92	3.60	4.68	4.77	4.44	4.70
S.D.	1.20	.64	.70	.59	.48	.68	.52
n	16	16	16	14	15	9	15

Incongruent Places Selected

	Home	Beach	Total	Church	School	Work Place	Total
Mean	2.63	3.86	2.77	3.71	4.39	4.42	4.10
S.D.	.77	.94	.70	1.32	1.90	.96	.82
n	15	5	15	15	15	15	15

Incongruent Topics Selected

	Family	Friend-ship	Total	Religious	Educa-tion	Employ-ment	Total
Mean	2.83	3.81	3.26	3.07	3.66	3.81	3.49
S.D.	1.04	1.13	1.02	1.00	1.20	.85	.76
n	18	16	18	18	17	18	18

257

Table 3. Mean Number of Words Named by Young Schoolchildren
(Edelman, 1968)

(n – 34)

Age	Language	Domain				
		Family	Education	Religion	Neighborhood	Total
6–8	English	6.2	8.2	6.6	8.3	7.3
	Spanish	7.6	6.2	5.8	6.4	6.5
	Total	6.9	7.2	6.2	7.4	6.9
9–11	English	11.7	12.8	8.7	10.9	11.0
	Spanish	10.5	9.4	7.2	9.7	9.2
	Total	11.1	11.1	7.9	10.3	10.1
Total	English	9.0	10.5	7.7	9.6	9.2
	Spanish	9.0	7.8	6.5	8.0	7.8
	Total	9.0	9.1	7.1	9.0	8.5

Table 4. Analysis of Variance of Young
Schoolchildren's Word-Naming Scores

Source	df	ms	F
Between subjects	33		
C (age)	1	689.30	19.67**
D (sex)	1	15.54	.44
CD	1	87.87	2.51
error (b)	30	35.05	
Within subjects	235		
A (domain)	3	64.18	9.30**
B (language)	1	123.13	11.11**
AB	3	21.71	6.66**
AC	3	20.51	2.97*
AD	3	.96	.14
BC	1	16.50	1.49
BD	1	42.08	3.80
ABC	3	8.00	2.45
ABD	3	2.23	.68
ACD	3	4.51	.65
BCD	1	14.62	1.32
ABCD	3	2.66	.82
error (w)	207		
$error_1$ (w)	89	6.90	
$error_2$ (w)	29	11.08	
$error_3$ (w)	89	3.26	
Total	268		

*p < .05 level
**p < .01 level

259

above. For all children, the most Spanish domain was "family"
(Table 3), and the most English domain was "education." The analysis of variance (Table 4) indicates that not only did the children's responses differ significantly by age (older children giving more responses in both languages than did younger children), by language
(English yielding more responses than did Spanish), and by domain
(church yielding fewer responses than did any other domain), but that
these three variables interact significantly as well. This means that
one language is much more associated with certain domains than the
other is, and differentially so by age. This is exactly the kind of
finding for which domain analysis is particularly suited. Its utility
for inter-society comparisons and for gauging language shift would
seem to be quite promising.

The Integration of Macro- and Micro-Parameters

        The situational analysis of language and behavior represents
the boundary area between micro- and macro-sociolinguistics. The
very fact that a baseball conversation "belongs" to one speech variety
and an electrical engineering lecture "belongs" to another speech
variety is a major key to an even more generalized description of
sociolinguistic variation. The very fact that humor during a formal
lecture is realized through a metaphorical switch to another variety
(Blom and Gumperz, 1966) is undoubtedly indicative of an underlying
sociolinguistic regularity, which obtained before the switch occurred,
perhaps of the view that lecture-like or formal situations are generally associated with one language or variety while levity or intimacy
is tied to another. Without such a view, without a more general norm
assigning a particular topic or situation, as one of a class of such
topics or situations, to one language rather than to another, metaphorical purposes could neither be served nor recognized.

        As with all constructs (including situations, role-relationships
and speech events), domains originate in the integrative intuition of
the investigator. If the investigator notes that student-teacher interactions in classrooms, school corridors, school auditoriums and
school laboratories of elementary schools, high schools, colleges and
universities are all realized via H as long as these interactions are
focused upon educational technicality and specialization, he may begin

to suspect that these congruent situations all belong to a single (educational) domain. If he further finds that incongruent situations involving an educational and a non-educational component are, by and large, predictably resolved by use of H rather than L when the third ingredient is an educational time, place, or role-relationship, he may feel further justified in positing an educational domain. If informants tell him that the predicted language or variety would be appropriate in most of the examples he can think of that derive from his notion of the educational domain; assure him that it would not be as appropriate for examples that he draws from a contrasted domain; and finally, if the construct helps clarify and organize his data and, particularly, if it arises as a compositing feature out of his data—then with one major difference the construct is as usefully validated as is that of situation or event.

Whereas particular speech acts can be apportioned to the speech events and social situations in which they occur (Hymes, 1967), such acts cannot be so apportioned to societal domains. Domains are extra-polated from the data of "talk" rather than being an actual component of the process of talk. However, domains are as real as the very social institutions of a speech community, and, indeed, they show a marked paralleling with such major social institutions (Barker, 1947) and the somewhat varied situations that are congruent with them. There is an undeniable difference between "the family," the social institution, and any particular family, yet there is no doubt that the societal regularities concerning "the family" must be derived from data concerning many particular families. In the same way, once such societal regularities are formulated, they can be utilized to test predictions concerning the distributions of societally patterned variation in "talk."

Thus, domains and social situations reveal the links that exist between micro- and macro-sociolinguistics. The members of diglossic speech communities can come to have certain views concerning their varieties or languages because these varieties are associated (in behavior and in attitude) with particular domains. The H variety (or language) is considered to reflect certain values and relationships within the speech community, while the L variety is considered to reflect others. Certain individuals and groups may come to advocate the expansion of the functions of L into additional domains.

Others may advocate the displacement of L entirely and the sole use
of H. Neither of these revisionist views could be held or advocated
without recognition of the reality of domains of language-and-behavior
(in terms of existing norms of communicative appropriateness) on the
part of members of speech communities. The High culture values
with which certain varieties are associated and the values of intimacy
and folksiness with which others are congruent are both derivable
from domain-appropriate norms governing characteristic verbal
interaction.

There are several levels and approaches to sociolinguistic
description and a host of linguistic, sociolinguistic and societal constructs within each (Figure 1). Necessarily, the choice among them
depends upon the particular problem to be solved. Sociolinguistics
is of interest to students of small societies as well as to students of
national and international integration. It must help clarify the change
from one face-to-face situation to another. It must also help clarify
the different language-related beliefs and behaviors of entire social
sectors and classes. It must be as useful and as informative to sociologists pursuing inter-societal and intra-societal topics as it is to
linguists pursuing more contextualized synchronic description.

It would be foolhardy to claim that one and the same method
of data collection and data analysis should be utilized for such a
variety of problems and purposes. It is one of the hallmarks of
scientific social inquiry that methods are selected as a result of
problem specifications rather than independently of them. Sociolinguistics is neither methodologically nor theoretically uniform. Nevertheless, it is gratifying to note that for those who seek such ties
the links between micro- and macro- constructs and methods exist
(as do a number of constructs and methods that have wide applicability through the entire range of sociolinguistics). Just as there is no
societally unencumbered verbal interaction, so there are no large
scale relationships between language and society that do not depend
on individual interaction for their realization. Although there is no
mechanical part-whole relationship between them, micro- and macro-
sociolinguistics are both conceptually and methodologically complementary.

Figure 1. Relationships Among Some Constructs Employed
in Sociolinguistic Analysis*

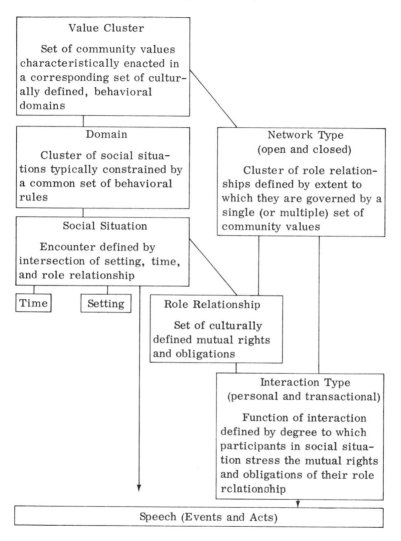

NOTES

A revision of "Who speaks what language to whom and when?" <u>La Linguistique</u>, 1965, 2, 67-88. In press, in <u>Directions in Sociolinguistics</u>, Dell Hymes and John J. Gumperz (eds.), New York, Holt, Rinehart and Winston.

[1] This example may be replaced by any one of a number of others: Standard German, Schwytzertutsch and Romansch (in parts of Switzerland); Hebrew, English and Yiddish in Israel; Riksmaal, Landsmaal and more local dialectal variants of the latter in Norway; Standard German, Plattdeutsch and Danish in Schleswig; French, Standard German and German dialect in Luxembourg, etc.

[2] This effect has been noted even in normally monolingual settings, such as those obtaining among American intellectuals, many of whom feel obliged to use French or German words in conjunction with particular professional topics. English lexical influence on the language of immigrants in the United States has also often been explained on topical grounds. The importance of topical determinants is discussed by Haugen (1953, 1956) and Weinreich (1953), and, more recently, by Gumperz (1962) and Susan Ervin (1964). It is implied as a "pressure" exerted upon "contacts" in Mackey's descriptions of bilingualism (1962, 1965, 1966).

[3] The study of language maintenance and language shift is concerned with the relationship between change or stability in habitual language use, on the one hand, and ongoing psychological, social or cultural processes of change and stability, on the other hand (Fishman, 1964, 1966; Nahirny and Fishman, 1965).

[4] We can safely reject the implication encountered in certain discussions of domains that there must be an invariant set of domains applicable to all multilingual settings. If language behavior is reflective of socio-cultural patternings, as is now widely accepted, then different kinds of multilingual speech communities should benefit from analyses in terms of different domains of language use, however defined and validated.

[5] For a discussion of the differences and similarities between "functions of language behavior" and "domains of language behavior" see (Fishman, 1964). "Functions" stand closer to socio-psychological analysis, for they abstract their constituents in terms of individual motivation rather than in terms of societal institutions.

[6] These remarks are not intended to imply that all role-relation differences are necessarily related to language-choice differences. This almost certainly is not the case. Just which role-relation differences are related to language-choice differences (and under what circumstances) is a matter for empirical determination within each multilingual setting as well as at different points in time within the same setting. In general the verification of significantly different clusters of allo-roles (as well as significantly different clusters of allo-topics and allo-locales) (see below) is a prerequisite for the empirical formulation of domains.

REFERENCES

Barber, Carrol. Trilingualism in Pascua; Social Functions of Language in an Arizona Yaqui Village, M.A. Thesis, University of Arizona, 1952.

Barker, George C. Social functions of language in a Mexican-American community, Acta Americana, 1947, 5, 185-202.

Blom, Jan-Petter and John J. Gumperz. Some social determinants of verbal behavior. Unpublished paper, presented at the 1966 Meeting of the American Sociological Association.

Braunshausen, Nicolas. Le bilinguisme et le famille, in Le Bilinguisme et l'Education, Geneva-Luxembourg, Bureau International d'Education, 1928.

Cooper, Robert L. How can we measure the roles which a bilingual's languages play in his everyday behavior?, in (Proceedings of The International Seminar on) "The Measurement and Description of Bilingualism," L. Kelley (ed.), Toronto, University of Toronto Press, 1969, pp. 192-239.

Dohrenwend, Bruce P. and Robert J. Smith. Toward a theory of acculturation, Southwest J. of Anthrop., 1962, 18, 30-39.

Edelman, Martin. The contextualization of children's bilingualism, in J. A. Fishman, R. L. Cooper, Roxana Ma, et al., Bilingualism in the Barrio. Final Report to DHEW under Contract No. OEC-1-7-062817-0297. New York, Yeshiva University, 1968. Also, revised (with R. L. Cooper and J. A. Fishman), Journal of Irish Education, 1969, 2, 106-111.

Ervin, Susan M.   An analysis of the interaction of language, topic
        and listener, American Anthropologist, 1964, 66, part 2,
        86-102.
Fishman, Joshua A.   Language maintenance and language shift as
        fields of inquiry, Linguistics, 1964, no. 9, 32-70.
        _____. Language Loyalty in the United States. The Hague:
        Mouton, 1966.
        _____. Bilingualism with and without diglossia; diglossia with
        and without bilingualism, Journal of Social Issues, 1967,
        23, no. 2, 29-38.
        _____. A sociolinguistic census of a bilingual neighborhood,
        in J. A. Fishman, R. L. Cooper, Roxana Ma, et al.,
        Bilingualism in the Barrio. Final Report to DHEW under
        Contract No. OEC-1-7-062817-0297. New York, Yeshiva
        University, 1968 a.
        _____. Sociolinguistic perspective on the study of bilingualism.
        Linguistics, 1968 b, 39, 21-49.
Frey, J. William.   Amish (triple talk), American Speech, 1945, 20,
        85-98.
Goodenough, Ward H.   Rethinking "status" and "role"; toward a
        general model of the cultural organization of social relation-
        ships, in Michael Banton (ed.), Relevance of Models for
        Social Anthropology. New York: Praeger, 1965.
Greenfield, Lawrence.   Spanish and English usage self-ratings in
        various situational contexts, in J. A. Fishman, R. L.
        Cooper, Roxana Ma, et al., Bilingualism in the Barrio.
        Final Report to DHEW under Contract No. OEC-1-7-062817-
        0297. New York, Yeshiva University, 1968; also, revised
        (with J. A. Fishman) and retitled, in Anthropos, 1970, 65,
        602-18.
Gross, Feliks.   Language and value changes among the Arapho,
        Intern. J. of Amer. Ling., 1951, 17, 10-17.
Gumperz, John J.   Types of linguistic communities, Anthropological
        Linguistics, 1962, 4, no. 1, 28-40.
        _____. Linguistic and social interaction in two communities,
        American Anthropologist, 1964, 66, part 2, 137-54.
Haugen, Einar.   The Norwegian Language in America (2 vols.).
        Philadelphia: University Of Pennsylvania Press, 1953.
        _____. Bilingualism in the Americas: A Bibliography and Re-
        search Guide. University (Alabama): University of Ala-
        bama Press, 1956.

Hymes, Dell. Models of the interaction of language and social setting, Journal of Social Issues, 1967, 23, no. 2, 8-28.

Kloss, Heinz. Sprachtabellen als Grundlage fur Sprachstatistik, Sprachenkarten and fur eine allgemeine Sociologie der Sprachgemeinschaften, Vierteljahrschrift fur Politik und Geschichte, 1929, 1 (7), 103-17.

Lieberson, Stanley. An extension of Greenberg's measures of linguistic diversity, Language, 1964, 40, 526-531.

_____. Language questions in censuses, Sociological Inquiry, 1966, 36, 262-79.

Mackey, William F. The description of bilingualism, Can. J. of Linguistics, 1962, 7, 58-85.

_____. Bilingual interference: its analysis and measurement, Journal of Communication, 1965, 15, 239-49.

_____. The measurement of bilingual behavior, The Canadian Psychologist, 1966, 7, 75-90.

Mak, Wilhelm. Zweisprachigkeit und Mischmundart in Oberschlesien, Schlesisches Jahrbuch fur deutsche Kulturarbeit, 1935, 7, 41-52.

Nahirny, Vladimir C. and Joshua A. Fishman. American immigrant groups: ethnic identification and the problem of generations, Sociological Review, 1965, 13, 311-26.

Schmidt-Rohr, Georg. Mutter Sprache. Jena: Eugen Diederichs Verlag, 1963. (Title of first edition: Die Sprache als Bildnerin der Völker, Munich, 1932).

Weinreich, Uriel. Languages in Contact: Findings and Problems. The Hague: Mouton, 1953 (second printing, 1963).

12 | Problems and Prospects of the Sociology of Language

In a time when anyone over 20 is considered to be "suspiciously old" it may come as no surprise that a field as young as the sociology of language (whose rebirth occurred in the summer of 1964, at an eight week seminar of linguists and social scientists; see Ferguson 1965) should already have developed several internal divergent emphases. By attending in some detail to these various "streams" (for briefer attention in the past see Fishman 1967, 1970, and 1971) we may benefit both the sociology of language and the sociology of knowledge, particularly if the future resultant of current intellectual forces comes into being as a result of a more thorough awareness and evaluation of the past.

What's in a Name?

The above-mentioned summer seminar at Indiana University (sometimes referred to as "the Bloomington Seminar") was sponsored by the Committee on Sociolinguistics of the (American) Social Science Research Council and took place within the general framework of the annual (summer) Linguistic Institute. This may help explain why the label "sociolinguistics" was so readily adopted by all concerned as a proper and adequate name for their joint field of inquiry. However, it was evident from the very outset that the name covered a variety of differing emphases.

At the time of the seminar I was still putting the finishing touches on my Readings in the Sociology of Language (Fishman 1968a), the release of which was subsequently delayed for four years by the publisher. I certainly had enough time during that summer, as well as in the years immediately thereafter, to retitle the volume <u>Readings</u> <u>in Sociolinguistics</u>, and yet I did not do so even then, when the label sociolinguistics appealed to me more than it did subsequently (and certainly more than it has in the past few years). It smacked to me of linguistic priority, if not of linguistic imperialism. The field that focused upon the interpenetration between language behavior and other social behavior appeared to me then, as it does now, to be broader than and different from the focus implied by even the most benevolently hyphenated kind of linguistics. Nevertheless, I used the term "sociolinguistics," together with the other seminar participants, and tried to broaden its interpretation to include behavior toward language (language attitudes, language movements, language planning) and the language concomitants of social processes large and small (including societal formation and reformation, societal interaction and societal change and dislocation). For approximately five years after the Bloomington Seminar I continued to employ the label "sociolinguistics" in connection with interests such as these (see, e.g., Fishman 1968b and 1970) and have only recently ceased to do so, in favor of an almost exclusive return to <u>The Sociology of Language</u>.

Since I was not the only sociologist (social psychologist, political scientist, social anthropologist) to adopt the label "sociolinguistics," and since I am by no means the only one to eschew this label today, I suggest that it is as worth while to look into <u>why</u> the label had some appeal initially, as it is to examine <u>why</u> this was always a conflicted label from which most of the appeal has now departed.

"Sociolinguistics" for the sociologist

I will be very frank and admit that much of the initial appeal of "sociolinguistics" lay in my dissatisfaction with the state of the "sociology of language" at that time. At worst, "the sociology of language" reminded me of the capitulations of German <u>Sprachwissen-</u> <u>schaftliches Minderheitenforschung</u> (and <u>Auslandsdeutsche Volksfor-</u> <u>schung</u>) on the one hand, and of Soviet <u>Lingvatekhnika</u> on the other hand, when each was faced by the demands and by the opportunities of violent totalitarianisms. At best—which was none too good—it reminded me of countless hortatory, non-rigorous, non-empirical "do-gooder" articles and texts which endlessly "made the point" that language was "important indeed" in social behavior and in societal affairs. The label "sociolinguistics" was relatively fresh and unencumbered. It made it possible to stress new beginnings and by implication, to dissociate oneself from certain undesirable if not unsavory overtones of the past. Now, after more than six years of new work in "the sociology of language," I and others no longer react to this label in term of the old associations with it. The term now stands in my mind for the reborn field, the revitalized field, whereas "sociolinguistics" has increasingly come to stand for a "kind of linguistics" and, therefore, for a possibly important preoccupation, but for one with which I do not and cannot fully identify.

Sociolinguistics for the Linguist

The term "sociolinguistics" has fared somewhat better in the hands of linguists, but not much better. From the very first discussions in Bloomington some seminar participants held, with Labov, that sociolinguistics was not and should not be a field of specialization in its own right. Whatever insights it possessed were, by right, they claimed, contributions to linguistics more generally and, if these contributions were really as central as they were made out to be, they would soon be adopted by and integrated into linguistics more generally. From this point of view the stage in which an identifiable specialty and a separate label were needed was definitely a transitional one. Like the "withering away of the state," it would be replaced by a new and final stage, marked by far greater blessings, at which time general linguistics and sociolinguistics would be fully integrated. Thus, from this point of view, sociolinguistics leads to the broadening of linguistics, but it is nevertheless linguistics and not society that remains at the center.

On the other hand, there have been linguists, like Hymes, who have viewed sociolinguistics as merely part of the etkhalta d'geula (beginnings of deliverance) by means of which linguistics itself would be transformed into a general science or interscience (superscience?) of communication. Hymes had argued much before Bloomington (and also since) that the destiny of linguistics was to

become a corner stone of the more encompassing ethnography of
speaking (or of the ethnography of communication). This future
queen of the human sciences would be interested in more than code
and parole. It would be proudly and sensitively and exhaustively ethnographic. It would arrive at generalizations on the basis of detailed
cases, occasions and acts of communication. It would attend to
written and to other signaled and symbolized communication rather
than merely to spoken communication. It would draw upon psychology
and sociology and other social sciences but it would principally draw
upon anthropology, ethnography and linguistics. In this new sum-
total, sociolinguistics, as an identifiable and permanent "something,"
is not of great theoretical or practical moment.

Labov's position and Hymes' position may be essentially
similar, the latter's views being primarily a topical extension and
elaboration of the former's (although they were obviously first advanced by Hymes). Labov sees sociolinguistics as a passing stage
in the "maturation" of linguistics. Hymes sees it as a passing stage
in the "transformation" of linguistics and in its (linguistic's) ascen-
dancy to the apex of the communication sciences.

Will the term "sociolinguistics" soon disappear as a designation for a field of interest of sociologists and/or linguists? Perhaps, but probably not. It is too catchy a term, particularly in its
adjectival and adverbial uses in English, to be easily displaced. Nevertheless, it does not seem to be the most preferred designation of
the field as conceptualized by its various major protagonists. It
does not accurately designate the particular interests and emphases
that are currently being developed most intensively. As a result,
it may tend to become more and more a catch-all term and more and
more associated with critical reviews to the effect that such and such
is "not really sociolinguistics" or is only "so called sociolinguistics."
It is a term that has quickly become old, perhaps because it "masks"
the active differences in theory, method, data and purpose that compete with each other underneath the surface.

Putting aside all concern with respect to matters of relative
emphasis in connection with such compound terms as "sociolinguistics" (some native speakers of English seem to interpret these as

emphasizing their <u>first</u> component, while others interpret them as emphasizing their <u>second</u> component), I admit to a basic convinction (an intuition, if you will) that the sociology of language must be much more vigorously in touch with social and comparative history, with social geography and with political science than with linguistics. I view linguistics as one of many crucial methodological laboratories into which the sociologist of language must have ready access. However, I view social history, e.g., as one of the many crucial conceptual laboratories into which he must not only have ready access but from which he must ultimately derive his worthiest hypotheses, his most fundamental substantive problems, his basic orientation toward society. Society itself, however, exists at many levels and in manifold processes. It is to a consideration of the differences between these levels and processes (and to their implications for the future of the field) that I now turn, using the recently concluded four-day-long program of the Research Section on Sociolinguistics of the International Sociological Association (Seventh World Congress of Sociology, Varna, Bulgaria, September 14-19, 1970) as the immediate focus of discussion.

The Study of Micro-Processes

In order to appreciate some of the excitement and the disappointment at Varna one must first go back to Bloomington.

Among the Bloomington "refounding fathers" of sociolinguistics John Gumperz immediately appeared as the champion of micro-process analysis. In retrospect his contribution appears to be, at one and the same time, fundamental, programmatic and non-transmittable (or, at least, neglected). Its fundamental nature derives from Gumperz's simultaneous orientation to speech processes and other interpersonal processes, all of which are viewed as constantly intertwined and, therefore, necessarily analyzable in similar conceptual terms. (Gumperz 1964, Blom and Gumperz 1972). Speech repertoire/role repertoire, variety access and role access, variety compartmentalization and role compartmentalization, speech network and role network, these are not only heuristically useful and parsimonious at the micro-level, but they are also tantalizingly promising for the clarification of processes underlying macro-structures as well.

Yet, Gumperz's contribution still must be characterized as programmatic due to the fact that the empirical confirmation or revision of the parameters that he has suggested is not substantially further along today than it was in 1965. To some extent this is due to the fact that Gumperz himself has been less concerned with these parameters—at either a theoretical or an empirical level—than might have been expected or hoped for. In part it is due to the nature of evidence or confirmation that is recognized as such by differing disciplines. Perhaps Gumperz and others consider the self-evident symmetry and sensibility of the parameters that have been proferred as tantamount to (if not superior to) evidential confirmation. Perhaps the few brief situational examples cited and the few brief lexical, grammatical and phonological examples provided are considered evidential confirmation. Others, however, may view them as no more than part of "putting the case" (and the case is, admittedly, often very well put) rather than as part of "proving the case."

The non-transmittable nature of Gumperz's admittedly stimulating contributions is deducible from the reaction that it has elicited among other major cultivators of the micro-process vineyard. Neither Garfinkle nor Sacks, among the stricter ethno-methodologists (Garfinkle 1967; Garfinkle and Sacks in press; Sacks, mimeo. notes), nor Rose, nor Kjolseth, nor Schegloff, nor Cicourel, among the revisionists (Rose 1967; Kjolseth 1969, 1972; Cicourel in press; Schegloff 1968), nor Hymes (1967), nor Hammer (1969), nor Helmer (ms.), nor Janousek (ms.), to mention the two major micro-process papers at Varna, nor any others of the many who have more recently turned to the study of the understandings and misunderstandings in actual ("natural") conversations, gives more than a passing nod (and usually less than that) to Gumperz's dimensions. Yet there is a great deal that unites them all and it seems to me that Gumperz represents a very possible link between their work and other ongoing work in the sociology of language. Gumperz and Gumperzian micro-process analysis were sorely missing at Varna and that was sad for, better by far than other micro-process analysts, Gumperz's system links to a higher societal level and, therefore, to large scale social problems and processes.

For one who was socialized in the tradition of "scientific social psychology" of the late forties and early fifties much of the current work on micro-processes in the sociology of language prompts feelings of déjà vu and discomfort. The phenomenological and functional emphases, the stress on the non-qualitative, immediate, naturalistic, genuine experience, the emphatic recognition of truth and beauty and relevance, are all honorable parts of the age-old see-sawing relationship between variegated attempts to understand man, to explain him, to predict him and to control him. In its current "coming" micro-process analysis, of whatever persuasion (and there are many orthodoxies competing with each other), has about it an aura of bringing salvation, jargons shared only by small circles of those who are "in," deprecation of the establishment, and expectations of great advances in the future.

The Chomskian revolution in linguistics has prompted an expectation of a forthcoming revolution in the social sciences in general and in the study of language in society in particular. Indeed, there is much that is Chomskian about the new micro-process emphases in the sociology of language. Both are equally enamoured of "because that is the way man (or society) basically is" as an adequate answer to certain problems that are recognized but that are currently not answerable in satisfying detail. Both are inordinately fond of difficult cases or exceptional examples or little bits of text to be explicated as ways of tackling the basically "universal" and "natural" phenomenon and process to which they attend. Both seem to be singularly incapable of communicating in a simple fashion with those so benighted as to be outside their fold. And yet they differ greatly as well. Unlike the Chomskians, the micro-process analysts have not yet formulated an exhaustive set of propositions nor even of analytic procedures. Nor have they formalized much as yet, either in terms of hypotheses, analyses or conclusions. If a hallmark of science is that theory is much briefer than and different from the data, then generative-transformational linguistics stands closer to a recognizable model of science than does micro-process analysis in the sociology of language. But, on the other hand, the latter is much younger than the former and may yet settle down to a less wordy, less opaque, less argumentative, less informal relationship between theory and data. Part of its difficulty in doing any of this is that it is not only (or, perhaps, not basically) a sociology of language that is being fashioned but a much more general sociology of everyday understandings and interactions of all kinds. It is social man and social communication in toto that are being rediscovered, and rescued, if you please, from the oblivion to which they have been assigned by the establishment social science forces.   This is, of course, a fundamental task with which one must sympathize and which one must even admire, even while attempting to understand it and to cope with it.

Macro-Structure Analysis

The extreme of macro-structure orientation in current sociology of language was revealed by the Soviet papers presented at Varna (where, by the way, the major portion of the program was closer to macro-structure analysis than to micro-process analysis precisely because of the unprecedented Soviet participation).   With the exception of the paper by Gubolgo (a recapitulation of his paper of 1969 which provided language census figures and correlational analyses between these and other types of census data) all of the Soviet papers were socio-historical summaries at best and journalistic-ideological exercises at worst.   (For names of authors and titles of papers see Program of the Congress).   In either case they dealt with entire languages and national or regional communities, as well as with the large scale changes that characterize them, particularly when pre-revolutionary and current statuses are compared.   As with the micro-process papers at the same meetings the Soviet papers were generally devoid of hard-data-subjected-to-formal-analysis (as distinct from running interpretive commentary), but at a completely opposite level of abstraction.   Whereas the micro-analysts never mentioned countries, nor centuries, nor social classes, nor languages, nor formal institutions, nor established societal domains, the Soviets never mentioned listeners, nor speakers, nor understandings, nor metaphors, nor situations, nor varieties, nor role relation.   Let it be perfectly clear.   I do not object here to the particular social bias revealed by those papers; I object to their unwillingness to pursue their social bias by the carefully measured and difficult steps of empirical social science.

My decided impression is that the Varna papers on micro-process analysis were much better representatives of "their kind" than were the Soviet papers vis-à-vis macro-structural analyses. I would like to pause to explain why this is my impression, admitting

at the outset that I may be more severe with the Soviets precisely
because I feel a greater relationship between their work and my own.

What is it that was lacking in the thirty some Soviet papers
on sociolinguistics presented in Varna? I have already mentioned the
relative absence of data and formal analysis and the superabundance
of social history and social philosophy (the latter, in the place of
scientific hypotheses and theory). The upshot of all of this is that
no parameters are isolated, their separate relevance is never determined, their combined and interactional significance is not considered,
and local as well as cross-national or comparative importance is
assumed or argued rather than examined and demonstrated. Thus,
as far as macro-structure analysis is concerned (whether Soviet or
capitalist), I object not to the problems selected for examination, nor
to the conclusions arrived at, as much as I object to the avoidance of
precise problem definition, data collection, data analysis and data
interpretation, or to their presence merely as ideological rather than
as scientific exercises. I do not mean to imply that science and ideology are ever free of each other. I merely mean to claim that there
is a difference between the residual interpenetration of the one by the
other and a total disregard for the degree of this interpenetration or,
indeed, its maximization.

As one who has engaged in macro-structure analysis, is
engaged in it, and probably will continue to be engaged in it during
the years ahead, I have certain favorites in mind when I consider
this level appropriate for a particular problem at hand. One such
favorite is definitely Haugen's The Norwegian Language in America
(vol. I). Here we find a constant marshalling of demographic and
other quantitative data, together with the judgments and evaluations
that are necessarily the author's, and, therefore, outside of the data.
Here we find not only a chronological and a topical progression but
also a constant relationship to the theories and findings of other
researchers. The whole is not only rigorous but also lively, since
there are many passages from diaries, interviews, previous publications, etc. In the 1950s this was truly an unbeatable macro-example
of sociology of language and, as such, I was delighted to use it as the
required text in what was certainly one of the first courses in the
sociology of language to be given in the USA (1958-1959 academic

year, University of Pennsylvania). Methodologically, my own
Language Loyalty in the United States (1966) does not constitute a
major advance beyond Haugen's volume, even though it does represent a substantive updating and major expansion relative to his earlier
study focused on a single immigrant group.

In this same tradition of data oriented and theory related
macro-level sociology of language I would include Kloss's Volksgruppenrecht in den Vereinigten Staaten (1942), Rubin's National Bilingualism in Paraguay (1968), Lieberson's studies of linguistic diversity in
Canada and elsewhere (1965, 1970), Deutsch's justly famous Nationalism and Social Communication (1966) and Tabouret-Keller's comparisons of earlier European and current West African language shift
trends (1964, 1968). If I turn to work of either a more historical or
a more integrative (i.e. basically theoretical) nature at this level I
strongly admire Kloss's Entwicklung neuer germanischen Kultursprachen (1952), Ferguson's "Diglossia" (1959), DeFrancis' history
of attempts to revise the Chinese writing system (1950, 1968), Das
Gupta's account of group politics and language policy in India (1970),
Clough's concise and classic history of the Flemish movement in
Belgium (1930), and, quite definitely, Haugen's truly thrilling account
of the Riksmål-Landsmål struggle in Norway (1966). These are all
works of truly broad conceptualization and their significance is fully
consonant with their scope. They are addressed to real social problems (which are always larger in scope than the comfortable boundaries of disciplines) and to their examination at the level of complete
functional communities and, often, over extensive time periods. Yet,
although they are all favorites of mine and I refer to each and every
one of them extensively when teaching the sociology of language, there
is good reason, I think, why none of them could be used today as a text
for the purpose of introducing students to the sociology of language
as a whole, or for the purpose of reviewing the basic theories and
concepts of the field (not to mention its major findings). As I see it,
this is because this cannot be done on the basis of work at the macro-
level alone, anymore than it can be done by work which is narrowly
focused on the micro-level alone. It is well and good for the sociology
of language to contribute to and draw upon social history, but if it is
not itself to be synonymous with social history it must have a very
definite linguistic component as well.

And Never the Twain Shall Meet?

Is it possible to so develop the sociology of language that
the micro-level processes and the macro-level structures are not
only present but are bridged? Before this question can be answered
it is probably wise to ask whether it is desirable to do so. My bias
is that it is desirable, indeed, that the field is stunted or artificially
segmented without such a bridging effort.

There is no conflict between examining small events or subtle
processes and investigating large-scale structures or widespread
regularities. The two levels may not both be visible at one and the
same time; particularly, they may not be "writable about" or
"reportable upon" at one and the same time. However the fact that
so much of our social science is a written tradition (and, therefore,
suffers from the restrictions of all writing upon the ongoing interpenetration of viewing, reporting and evaluating) should not make it necessary for the sociology of language to recapitualte within its own
slender ranks the entire structuralist-functionalist controversy, or
the painful resolution to that controversy evidenced both within
anthropology and sociology as well as in part, between them. Must
phylogeny recapitulate ontogeny in intellectual pursuits as well? Such
a prospect would make me infinitely sad.

Of course, each level or focus may well have problems and
concepts that are peculiarly its own, but I am even surer that there
should be strong links between them. It is odd to have to defend this
point of view to some who have only so recently castigated others
for pretending that there could be either grammars without societies
or societies without speech. However, it seems equally fallacious
to me to pretend that socially patterned language processes have no
differential representation in social classes, social groups or social
sectors, or that all of the latter are in someway less real than the
former (the process). Similarly, it seems undiscerning to speak
generally of entire languages, countries, classes, etc. , when there
is obviously so much socially patterned variation below these levels
of analysis that are equally reflective of educational, economic, religious, political or other experiential differences. It seems obvious
to me that while some investigators may (from time to time, generally or always) be interested in micro-level phenomena and others

may (from time to time, generally or always) be more interested in macro-level phenomena, that all should at least see the need for bridging these levels, for the sake of the field as a whole as well as for the sake of broadening the significance of their own work.

However, not all that is desirable is possible, and, therefore, I return to the question of whether such bridges are possible, either at this time or in the foreseeable future. I think so, even though their precise and ultimate number and nature are not yet entirely clear. Nevertheless, there are already examples of studies that have within them the bridges that I am looking for. One such is the classic Brown and Gilman study (1960) which started the tu-vu series on its merry chase. Here we find, even more fully than in most of the subsequent studies of this kind, not only a concern with the message form, and not only a concern with social-psychological parameters (power and solidarity) that bridge the gap between the linguistic form and the role relationships and status differentials involved, but, also, above and beyond all of the foregoing, a sense of larger history, of cross-national differences and similarities over countries, and of the elegant and esthetic parsimony which is the hallmark of deep structured explanation.

There are other examples of bridges between the data of speech (or writing) per se and data of real social problematics. Perhaps the most quantitative example of this kind is Ma and Herasim-chuk's demonstration (1971) that phonological data can be factor analyzed into speech varieties (or patterned speech co-occurrences) and that social background data can be factor analyzed into social networks (or patterned social co-occurrences) and, finally, that these two different kinds of factors can be interrelated to the greater clarification of both. At a less ambitious level Fishman and Herasim-chuk have provided a similar demonstration (1969) of the very tight dovetailing that exists between linguistic data of a very precise and situationally delimited variety and the broad gauged data of social class, education, geographic region, etc. There are other studies that make the same general point: it is no longer necessary or de-sirable (at least, not at the conceptual level) to divide the sociology of language into two separate volumes, one on the linguistic facts and theories and the other on the societal facts and theories. Nor is it necessary to approach language behavior and other social behavior as

two clearly separate orders of "things" that can merely be correlated
with each other. It is now possible to go beyond such correlation to
the demonstration of interpenetration while yet keeping the societal
vision, urgency, problematics, and vitality primary.

Susan Ervin-Trip has done this in her studies of Japanese
war-brides in the USA (1964), William Labov has done this in his
studies of Lower East Side New Yorkers (1966), Martha's Vineyard
residents (1963), and Black and Puerto Rican adolescents in New
York (1968). Kimple and Cooper have kept language data, societal
data and attitudinal data in constant touch (1969), as have (in many
instances) Fishman, Cooper, Ma and their associates (1971). The
above studies do not exhaust the list of what I would like to call
"middle ground studies," i.e. studies that are neither so focused on
the linguistic act or on the social world that the one is present without
the other or as a mere correlate of the other. I am not trying to list
all such studies here. On the other hand I am trying not to list studies
that merely talk about linguistic data but do not operate with it, or
that talk about social relevance but do not try to capture it in terms
of formally analyzed and publicly replicable data.

Hopes and Fears

I am neither a prophet nor the son of a prophet but I do
know what my "druthers" are and which are so fanciful as to be best
kept to myself. I hope that the links between micro and macro will
become ever stronger, to the point that they will be viewed much like
the links between organic and inorganic chemistry: important and
self evident rather than dubious or controversial. I consider this to
be a first order priority. Without bridges the gap between micro and
macro will grow, as will the gap between sociolinguistics and the
sociology of language, and these gaps are essentially fruitless and
nonproductive ones, while the middle ground is both fertile in itself
as well as stimulating to those on either side. The middle ground
is represented by the vision that calls for the relationship between
small events or processes and large scale aggregates or structures,
for the natural and the formalized, for the empirical as well as for
theoretical parsimony. I suspect that this is what the future will
bring increasingly.

There are other hopes which I think are equally well based. The current interest in applied concerns and in social problems (education, language learning—including second language and second dialect, language policy, language planning, literacy, translation programs, etc.) is a healthy one (both for the field as well as for society) and I am quite sure it will develop further without becoming little more than either feasibility or developmental work. "The coming crisis of Western Sociology" (Gouldner 1970) cannot and will not hit the sociology of language because it has always been value conscious and socially "involved." The current concern for improving the linguistic training of sociologists and the social research training of linguists must soon break through the "pious wish (that someone else will do something about it) barrier" and be implemented at institutional and organizational levels that can sponsor summer seminars, post-doctoral training fellowships, and regular year academic courses and field experiences. Certainly, I expect the trend to organize the field (via texts, journals, societies, regular meetings, special conferences and committees) to continue for a while longer but to taper off before it either suffocates us or bankrupts us. I think that our most rapid growth is behind us but that our most stable and vital maturation is now about to begin.

Ultimately, my faith in the viability of "the sociology of language" derives not from my faith in particular methods (since all methods are needed at some point in the research process), nor in any faith in particular levels of analysis, nor in any faith in the overriding worth of particular substantive foci, nor in any faith in disciplinary or interdisciplinary links of one kind rather than another. My basic faith is that an immensely powerful and innovative orientation vis-à-vis the social history of mankind and vis-à-vis the basic social problems of mankind can be advanced from the point of view of the sociology of language. Great problems make for great disciplines. If we still but keep after the great problems of language in society, letting methods and levels of analysis flow therefrom, we cannot but succeed in the more minor tactical tasks that also lie ahead.

NOTE

I would like to express my thanks to Lluis V. Aracil, Robert L. Cooper, Dell Hymes and Joan Rubin for their helpful comments on an earlier draft of this paper.

REFERENCES

Blom, Jan-Petter and Gumperz, J. J. 1972. Some social deter-
    minants of verbal behavior, in Directions in Sociolinguistics,
    ed. by J. J. Gumperz and D. Hymes (New York: Holt,
    Rinehart and Winston).
Brown, R. and Gilman, A. 1960. The pronouns of power and soli-
    darity, in Style in Language, ed. by T. A. Sebeok (Cambridge,
    Mass.: M. I. T. Press), pp. 253-76. Also in Fishman
    (1968a).
Cicourel, A. In press. The acquisition of social structures: to-
    wards a developmental sociology of language and meaning,
    in Contributions in Ethnomethodology, ed. by H. Garfinkel
    and H. Sacks (Bloomington: Indiana University Press).
Clough, S. B. 1930. A History of the Flemish Movement in Belgium:
    A Study in Nationalism (New York: Smith).
Cooper, R. L. et al. 1971a. Degree of bilingualism, in J. A.
    Fishman et al., Bilingualism in the Barrio.
_____. 1971b. Bilingual comprehension, interpretation and
    perception, in J. A. Fishman et al., Bilingualism in the
    Barrio.
Das Gupta, J. 1970. Language Conflict and National Development
    (Berkeley: University of California Press).
De Francis, J. 1950. Nationalism and Language Reform in China
    (Princeton: Princeton University Press).
_____. 1968. Language and script reform (in China), Current
    Trends in Linguistics 2, 130-50.
Deutsch, K. L. 1966. Nationalism and Social Communication, 2nd
    ed. (Cambridge, Mass.: M. I. T. Press).
Ervin-Tripp, S. 1964. An analysis of the interaction of language,
    topic and listener, AA 66, 86-102.
Ferguson, C. A. 1959. Diglossia, Word 15, 325-40.
_____. 1965. Directions in sociolinguistics, SSRC Items 19,
    1-4.
Fishman, J. A. 1966. Language Loyalty in the United States (The
    Hague: Mouton).
_____. 1967. Review of Hertzler, A sociology of language,
    Language 43, 586-604.
_____. 1968a. Readings in the Sociology of Language (The
    Hague: Mouton).
_____. 1968b. Sociolinguistics and the language problems of

developing countries, in J. A. Fishman et al., Language
Problems of Developing Countries (New York: Wiley), pp.
3-16.

Fishman, J. A. 1970. Sociolinguistics: A Brief Introduction
(Rowley, Mass.: Newbury House).

_____. 1971. Advances in the Sociology of Language I (The
Hague: Mouton).

_____. 1972. Advances in the Sociology of Language I (The
Hague: Mouton).

_____. f. c. The Sociology of Language: An Interdisciplinary
Social Science Approach to Sociolinguistics, Current Trends
in Linguistics 12, ed. by T. A. Sebeok (The Hague: Mouton).

_____ and Cooper, R. L. 1969. Alternative measures of bilingualism, Journal of Verbal Learning and Verbal Behavior 8,
260-82.

_____ and Herasimchuk, E. 1969. The multiple prediction of
phonological variables in a bilingual speech community, AA
71, 648-57.

_____ and Terry, C. 1969. The validity of census data on bilingualism in a Puerto Rican neighborhod, American Sociological Review 34, 636-50.

_____, Cooper, R. L., Ma, Roxanna et al. 1971. Bilingualism
in the Barrio (Bloomington: Indiana University Language
Sciences Monographs).

Garfinkel, H. 1967. Studies in Ethnomethodology (Englewood Cliffs,
N.J.: Prentice-Hall).

_____ and Sacks, H. In press. On formal structures of prac-
tical actions, in Theoretical Sociology: Perspectives and
Developments, ed. by J. C. McKinney and E. Tiryakin
(New York: Appleton-Century-Crofts).

Gubologo, M. N. 1969. O vliyanii rassyelenya na yazikoviye
protsyessi, Sovyetskaya Etnografia 5, 16-30.

Gumperz, J. J. 1964. Linguistic and social interaction in two communities, AA 66, 37-53.

Hammer, M. et al. 1969. Speech predictability and social contact
patterns in an informal group, Human Organization 28, 235-
47.

Haugen, E. 1953. The Norwegian Language in America: A Study in
Bilingual Behavior (Philadelphia: University of Pennsylvania
Press/Oslo: Gyldendal Norsk Forlag). 2 vols.

_____. 1966. Language Planning and Language Conflict (Cambridge, Mass: Harvard University Press).

Helmer, J. 1970. Saying and meaning: reference in sociolinguistic theory, Papers presented at the Seventh World Congress of Sociology. Varna, Bulgaria, September 14-19, 1970.

Hymes, D. 1967. Models of interaction of language and social setting, Journal of Social Issues 23, 8-28.

Janousek, J. 1970. Social psychological problems of dialogue in cooperation, Papers presented at the Seventh World Congress of Sociology. Varna, Bulgaria, September 14-19, 1970.

Kjolseth, R. 1969. We the Gods: The Members' Natural Constitutive Account of Creation, Evolution and Revolution in Their Small Language Community (Davis: University of California Department of Sociology).

_____. 1972. Making sense: natural language and shared knowledge in understanding, in J. A. Fishman (1972).

Kloss, H. 1952. Die Entwicklung neuer germanischer Kultursprachen (Munich: Pohl).

_____. 1940-1942. Volksgruppenrecht in den Vereinigten Staaten von Amerika, Also abbreviated and/or translated as Das Nationalitaetenrecht der Vereinigten Staaten von Amerika (Wien: Braumüller, 1963) and Excerpts from the National Minority Laws of the United States of America (Honolulu: Institute of Advanced Projects, East-West Center, 1963).

Kimple, J., Jr. et al. 1969. Language shift and the interpretation of conversations, Lingua 23, 127-34.

Labov, W. 1969. The social motivation of sound change, Word 19, 273-309.

_____. 1966. The Social Stratification of English in New York City (Washington: Center for Applied Linguistics).

_____ et al. 1968. A Study of the Non-Standard English of Negro and Puerto-Rican Speakers in New York City (Final Report of Cooperative Research Project no. 3288) (New York: Columbia Universtiy).

Lieberson, S. 1965. Bilingualism in Montreal: a demographic analysis, American Journal of Sociology 71, 10-25.

_____. 1970. Language and Ethnic Relations in Canada (New York: Wiley).

Ma, R. and Herasimachuck E. 1971. Linguistic dimensions of a bilingual neighborhood, in J. A. Fishman et al., Bilingualism in the Barrio.

Rose, E. 1967. A Looking-glass Conversation in the Rare Languages of Sez and Pique (= Program on Cognitive Processes, Report No. 102) (Boulder: University of Colorado Institute of Behavioral Sciences).

Rubin, J. 1968. National Bilingualism in Paraguay (The Hague: Mouton).

Schegloff, E. A. 1968. Sequencing in conversational openings, AA 70, 1075-95.

Tabouret-Keller, A. 1964. A contribution to the sociological study of language maintenance and language shift, in Proceedings of the Ninth International Congress of Linguists (The Hague: Mouton), pp. 612-19. Revised and expanded for J. A. Fishman (1972). Advances in the Sociology of Language II (The Hague: Mouton).

_____. 1968. Sociological factors of language maintenance and language shift: a methodological approach based on European and African examples, in J. A. Fishman et al., Language Problems of Developing Nations (New York: Wiley).

13 | Sociocultural Organization:

Language Constraints and Language Reflections

One of the major lines of social and behavioral science interest in language during the past century has been that which has claimed that the radically differing structures of the languages of the world constrain the cognitive functioning of their speakers in different ways. It is only in relatively recent years—and partially as a result of the contributions of psycholinguists and sociolinguists—that this view (which we shall refer to as the linguistic relativity view) has come to be replaced by others: (a) that languages primarily reflect rather than create socio-cultural regularities in values and orientations and (b) that languages throughout the world share a far larger number of structural universals than has heretofore been recognized. While we cannot here examine the work related to language universals (Greenberg 1966; Osgood 1960), since it is both highly technical and hardly sociolinguistic in nature, we can pause to consider the linguistic relativity view itself as well as the linguistic reflection view which is increasingly coming to replace it in the interests and in the convictions of social scientists. It is quite clear why so much interest has been aroused by the question of language as restraint and language as reflection of socio-cultural organizations. Both of these views are undirectional. One posits that language structure and language usage are fundamental and "given" and that all behavior is influenced thereby. The other claims that social organization and behavior are prior and language merely reflects these. A position on one side or another of this argument must be taken by those who are interested in changing or influencing the "real world" of behavior.

Grammatical Structure Constrains Cognition

The strongest claim of the adherents of linguistic relativity—whether by Whorf (1940, 1941), Hoijer (1951, 1954), Trager (1959),

Kluckhohn (1961), or by others—is that cognitive organization is directly constrained by linguistic structure. Some languages recognize far more tenses than do others. Some languages recognize gender of nouns (and, therefore, also require markers of gender in the verb and adjective systems) whereas others do not. Some languages build into the verb system recognition of certainty or uncertainty of past, present, or future action. Other languages build into the verb system a recognition of the size, shape and color of nouns referred to. There are languages that signify affirmation and negation by different sets of pronouns just as there are languages that utilize different sets of pronouns in order to indicate tense and absence or presence of emphasis. Some languages utilize tone and vowel length in their phonological systems whereas English and most other modern European languages utilize neither. There are languages that utilize only twelve phonemes while others require more than fifty. A list of such striking structural differences between languages could go on and on—without in any way denying that each language is a perfectly adequate instrument (probably the most adequate instrument) for expressing the needs and interests of its speakers. That the societies using these very different languages differ one from the other in many ways is obvious to all. Is it not possible, therefore, that these sociocultural differences—including ways of reasoning, perceiving, learning, distinguishing, remembering, etc.—are directly relatable to the structured differences between the languages themselves? The Whorfian hypothesis claims that this is indeed the case (Fishman 1960).

Intriguing though this claim may be it is necessary to admit that many years of intensive research have not succeeded in demonstrating it to be tenable. Although many have tried to do so no one has successfully predicted and demonstrated a cognitive difference between two populations on the basis of the grammatical or other structural differences between their languages alone. Speakers of tone languages and of vowel length languages and of many-voweled languages do not seem to hear better than do speakers of languages that lack all of these features. Speakers of languages that code for color, shape and size in the very verb form itself do not tend to categorize or classify a random set of items much differently than do speakers of languages whose verbs merely encode tense, person and number (Carroll and Casagrande 1958). Whorf's claims (namely,

that "...the background linguistic system [in other words, the gram-
mar] of each language is not merely a reproducing instrument for
voicing ideas, but rather is itself the shaper of ideas, the program
and guide for the individual's mental activity, for his analysis of
impressions, for his synthesis of his mental stock in trade. Formulation of ideas is not an independent process, strictly rational in the
old sense, but it is part of a particular grammar and differs, from
slightly to greatly, between grammars," 1940) seem to be overstated
and no one-to-one correspondence between grammatical structure
and either cognitive or socio-cultural structure measured independently of language has ever been obtained. Several of the basic principles of sociolinguistic theory may help explain why this is so, although the psychological maxim that most men think about what they
are talking about (i.e., that language structure is always being
struggled with via cognitive processes) should also be kept in mind.

        In contrast with the older anthropological-linguistic approach
of Whorf, Sapir, Kluckhohn, Korzybski and others who pursued this
problem during the first half of the twentieth century, sociolinguistics
is less likely to think of entire languages or entire societies as cate-
gorizable or typable in an overall way. The very concepts of linguistic repertoire, role repertoire, repertoire range and repertoire compartmentalization argue against any such neat classification once
functional realities are brought into consideration. Any reasonably
complex speech community contains various speech networks that
vary with respect to the nature and ranges of their speech repertoires.
Structural features that may be present in the speech of certain interaction networks may be lacking (or marginally represented) in the
speech of others. Structural features that may be present in certain
varieties within the verbal repertoire of a particular interaction network may be absent (or marginally represented) in other varieties
within that very same repertoire. Mother-tongue speakers of language X may be other-tongue speakers of language Y. These two
languages may co-exist in a stable diglossic pattern throughout the
speech community and yet be as structurally different as any two languages chosen at random.

        Certainly, all that has been said above about the difficulty
in setting up "whole-language" typologies is equally true when we turn
to the question of "whole-society" typologies. Role repertoires vary

Schematic Systemization of the Whorfian Hypothesis
(Fishman 1960)

	Data of (Cognitive) Behavior	
Data of Language Characteristics	Language data ("cultural themes")	Non-linguistic data
Lexical or "semantic" characteristics	Level 1	Level 2
Grammatical characteristics	Level 3	Level 4

Level 1 of the Whorfian ("linguistic relativity") hypothesis predicts that speakers of languages that make certain lexical distinctions are enabled thereby to talk about certain matters (for example, different kinds of snow among speakers of Eskimo and different kinds of horses among speakers of Arabic) that cannot as easily be discussed by speakers of languages that do not make these lexical distinctions. Similarly, Level 3 of the Whorfian hypothesis predicts that speakers of languages that possess particular grammatical features (absence of tense in the verb system, as in Hopi, or whether adjectives normally precede or follow the noun, as in English vs. French) predispose these speakers to certain cultural styles or emphases (timelessness; inductiveness vs. deductiveness). These two levels of the Whorfian hypothesis have often been criticized for their anecdotal nature as well as for their circularity in that they utilized verbal evidence for both their independent (causal) and dependent (consequential) variables. Level 2 of the Whorfian hypothesis predicts that the availability of certain lexical items or distinctions enables the speakers of these languages to remember, perceive, or learn certain non-linguistic tasks more rapidly or completely than can the speakers of languages that lack these particular lexical items or distinctions. This level of the Whorfian hypothesis has been demonstrated several times—most recently and forcefully in connection with the differing color terminologies of English and Zuni—but it is difficult to argue that the absence of lexical items or distinctions in a particular language is more a cause of behavioral differences than a reflection of the differing socio-cultural concerns or norms of its speakers. As soon as speakers of Zuni become interested in orange (color) they devise a term for it. Language relativity should be more stable and less manipulable than that! Level 4 of the Whorfian hypothesis is the most demanding of all. It predicts that grammatical characteristics of languages facilitate or render more difficult various non-linguistic behaviors on the part of their speakers. This level has yet to be successfully demonstrated via experimental studies of cognitive behavior.

from one interaction network to the next and roles themselves vary
from one situation to the next within the same role-repertoire. Distinctions that are appropriately made in one setting are inappropriate
in another and behaviors that occur within certain interaction networks
do not occur in still others within the same culture. The existence of
structured biculturism is as real as the existence of structured bilingualism and both of these phenomena tend to counteract any neat and
simple linguistic relativity of the kind that Whorf had in mind.

Nevertheless, there are at least two large areas in which a
limited degree of linguistic relativity may be said to obtain: (a) the
structuring of verbal interaction and (b) the structuring of lexical components. The first area of concern points to the fact that the role of
language (when to speak, to whom to speak, the importance of speaking per se relative to inactive silence or relative to other appropriate
action) varies greatly from society to society (Hymes 1966). However,
this type of relativity has nothing to do with the structure of language
per se in which Whorf was so interested. The second area of concern
deals with lexical taxonomies and with their consequences in cognition
and behavior. However, these border on being linguistic reflections
of socio-cultural structure rather than being clearly and solely linguistic constraints that inevitably and interminably must bring about
the particular behaviors to which they are supposedly related. It is
to a consideration of these lexical taxonomies that we now turn.

Lexical Structure Constrains Cognition

For many years it was believed that the only tightly structured levels of language were the grammatical (morphological and
syntactic), on the one hand, and the phonological, on the other.
These two levels certainly received the brunt of linguistic attention
and constituted the levels of analysis of which linguists were most
proud in their interactions with other social and behavioral scientists.
By contrast, the lexical level was considered to be unstructured and
exposed to infinite expansion (as words were added to any language)
and infinite interference (as words were borrowed from other languages). A small but hardy group of lexicographers (dictionary
makers) and etymologists (students of word origins) continued to be
enamoured of words per se but the majority of linguists acted as

though the lexicon was the black sheep, rather than a bona fide member in good standing, of the linguistic family. The discovery of structured parsimony in parts of the lexicon has done much to revive linguistic interest in the lexical level of analysis. The discovery as such is one in which psychologists, anthropologists and sociologists were every bit as active as were linguists themselves (if not more so). This may also explain why the interrelationship between lexical organization and behavioral organization has been so prominent in conjunction with the investigation of lexical structure.

The psychological contributions to this area of analysis take us back to one level of the Whorfian hypothesis (see level 2 in Figure 1). Psychologists had long before demonstrated that the availability of verbal labels was an asset in learning, perception and memory tasks (see, e.g., Carmichael et al. 1932; Lehmann 1889; Maier 1930). A new generation of psychologists has recently set out to determine whether this could be demonstrated both interlinguistically (i.e., by comparing different languages) as well as intralinguistically (i.e., within a given language) on a structured set of behaviors that corresponded to a structured portion of lexicon.

They chose the color spectrum to work with because it is a real continuum that tends to be environmentally present in all cultures. Nevertheless, the investigators hypothesized that language labels for the color spectrum are culturally idiosyncratic. These labels not only chop up the color continuum into purely conventional segments in every language community, but they probably do so differently in different language communities. By a series of ingenious experiments, Brown and Lenneberg (1954), Lenneberg (1953, 1957), Lantz and Stefflre (1964) and others have demonstrated that this was indeed true. They have demonstrated that those colors for which a language has readily available labels are more unhesitatingly named than are colors for which no such handy labels are available. They have shown that the colors for which a language has readily available labels (i.e., highly codable colors) are more readily recognized or remembered when they must be selected from among many colors after a delay subsequent to their initial presentation. They have demonstrated that somewhat different segments of the color spectrum are highly codable in different language communities. Finally, they have shown that the learning of nonsense-syllable

associations for colors is predictably easier for highly codable colors
than for less codable colors that require a phrase—often an individually formulated phrase—in order to be named.

All in all, this series of experiments has forcefully shown
that the availability of a structured set of terms has both intralinguis-
tic as well as interlinguistic consequences. However, in addition,
it has underscored the equally important fact that every speech community has exactly such terms for those phenomena that are of concern to it. Certainly, artists, painters, and fashion-buyers have a
structured color terminology that goes far beyond that available to
ordinary speakers of English. The relative absence or presence of
particular color terms in the lexicon of a given speech network is
thus not a reflection of the state of that network's code per se as
much as it is a reflection of the color interests, sensitivities and conventions of that network at a particular time in its history.

A color terminology is merely one kind of folk-taxonomy,
i.e., it is an example of the many emic semantic grids that are contained in the lexicons of all speech communities. Other such examples are the kinship terminologies of speech communities, their
disease or illness terminologies, their plant terminologies, their
terms of address, etc. (Basso 1967; Conklin 1962; Frake 1961, 1962;
Pospisil 1965; Friederich 1966; Metsger and Williams 1966; Price
1967; Wittermans 1967; etc.). In each of these instances the particular lexicons involved constitute "un systeme on tout se tient."

Each such system is considered by its users to be both literally exhaustive and objectively correct. Nevertheless, each system is socially particularistic, i.e., for all of its self-evident
objectivity ("what other kind of kinship system could there possibly
be?"—we can imagine the average member of each of the scores of
such systems asking himself), it is a reflection of locally accepted
conventions rather than a necessary reflection either of nature or of
language per se. This last is particularly well demonstrated in the
work of Friederich (on Russian kinship terms), Wittermans (on
Javanese terms of address), and Basso (on Western Apache anatomical terms and their extension to auto parts; see Figure 1).

The Russian revolution brought with it such fargoing social
change that the kinship terms in use in Czarist days had to be changed

Figure 1. Lexical Structure and Social Change (Basso, 1967)

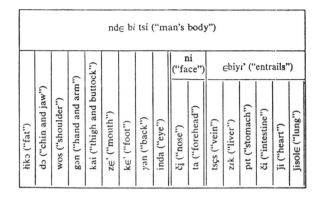

ndɛ bi tsi ("man's body")									ni ("face")		ɛbiyɪ' ("entrails")					
łikɔ ("fat")	dɔ ("chin and jaw")	wos ("shoulder")	gɔn ("hand and arm")	kai ("thigh and buttock")	zɛ' ("mouth")	kɛ' ("foot")	yɔn ("back")	inda ("eye")	či ("nose")	ta ("forehead")	tsɣs ("vein")	zɪk ("liver")	pɪt ("stomach")	či ("intestine")	ji ("heart")	jisolɛ ("lung")

Note: Black bars indicate position of additional (unextended) anatomical terms.

Figure 1a. Taxonomic Structure of Anatomical Set

Western Apache

nałbil bɪ tsi ("automobile's body")									nia		ɛbiyɪ' ("machinery under hood")					
łikɔ ("grease")	dɔ ("front bumper")	wos ("front fender")	gɔn ("front wheel")	kai ("rear fender")	zɛ' ("gas pipe opening")	kɛ' ("rear wheel")	yɔn ("bed of truck")	inda ("headlight")	či ("hood")	ta ("front of cab," "top")	tsɣs ("electrical wiring")	zɪk ("battery")	pɪt ("gas tank")	či ("radiator hose")	ji ("distributor")	jisolɛ ("radiator")

[2] "Area extending from top of windshield to bumper"

Figure 1b. Taxonomic Structure of Extended Set

to some degree. In contrast with the refined stratificational distinctions that existed in Czarist days—distinctions that recognized gradations of power, wealth and proximity within the universe of kin, not unlike those that were recognized in the larger universe of social and economic relationships—Soviet society stressed far fewer and broader distinctions. As a result, various kinship terms were abandoned entirely, others were merged and others were expanded. A very similar development transpired in Javanese with respect to its highly stratified system of terms of address. The impact of post-war independence, industrialization, urbanization and the resulting modification or abandonment of traditional role-relationships led to the discontinuation of certain terms of address and the broadening of others, particularly of those that implied relatively egalitarian status between interlocutors. Howell's review of changes in the pronouns of address in Japan (1967) also makes the same point, as did his earlier study of status markers in Korean (1965). Not only does he indicate how individuals change the pronouns that they use in referring to themselves and to each other, as their attitudes and roles vis-a-vis each other change, but he implies that widespread and cumulative changes of this kind have occurred in Japan since the war, to the end that certain pronouns have been practically replaced by others. Certainly the best known study of this kind is Brown and Gilman's review of widespread Western European social change with respect to the use of informal (T) vs. formal (V) pronouns and verb forms for the third person singular (1960). Feudalism, renaissance, reformation, the French Revolution, 19th century liberalism and 20th century democratization each had recognizable and cumulative impact. As a result, both T and V forms were retained in interclass communication (except in the case of English) but their differential use came to indicate differences primarily in solidarity or differences in solidarity and in power rather than differences in power alone as had been the case in the early middle ages (see Figure 2).

Note that the complexities of the pre-revolutionary kinship taxonomies in Russia did not keep Russians from thinking about or from engaging in revolution. Note also that the revolution did not entirely scrap the pre-existing kinship taxonomy. Similarly, the Apache anatomical taxonomy did not preclude (but rather assisted) taxonomic organization of automobile parts. Thus, while we are clearly indicating the untenability of any strong linguistic relativity

Figure 3. The Two-Dimensional Semantic (a) in Equilibrium and
(b) under Tension (Brown and Gilman 1960)

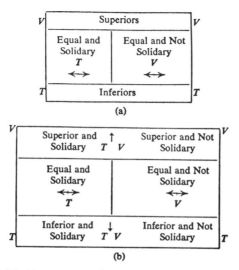

(a)

(b)

Solidarity comes into the European pronouns as a means of
differentiating address among power equals. It introduces a second
dimension into the semantic system on the level of power equivalents.
So long as solidarity was confined to this level, the two-dimensional
system was in equilibrium (see Figure 3a), and it seems to have remained here for a considerable time in all our languages. It is from
the long reign of the two-dimensional semantic that T derives its common definition as the pronoun of either condescension or intimacy and
V its definition as the pronoun of reverence or formality. These definitions are still current but usage has, in fact, gone somewhat beyond
them.

The dimension of solidarity is potentially applicable to all
persons addressed. Power superiors may be solidary (parents, elder
siblings) or not solidary (officials whom one seldom sees). Power in-
feriors, similarly, may be as solidary as the old family retainer and
as remote as the waiter in a strange restaurant. Extension of the
solidarity dimension along the dotted lines of Figure 3b creates six
categories of persons defined by their relations to a speaker. Rules
of address are in conflict for persons in the upper left and lower right
categories. For the upper left, power indicates V and solidarity T.
For the lower right, power indicates T and solidarity V.

Well into the nineteenth century the power semantic prevailed
and waiters, common soldiers, and employees were called T while
parents, masters, and elder brothers were called V. However, all
our evidence consistently indicates that in the past century the
solidarity semantic has gained supremacy. The abstract result is a
simple one-dimensional system with the reciprocal T for the solidarity
and the reciprocal V for the nonsolidarity.

position when we show that semantic taxonomies are subject to change, expansion and contraction as the socio-cultural realities of their users change, we are also demonstrating that their linguistic reflection of social reality is also likely to be both slow and partial. Nevertheless, as between the two, the taxonomic reflection of socio-cultural reality is more likely to have widespread heuristic utility at any given time, however much the existence of such taxonomies is likely to be constraining in the momentary cognitive behavior of individual members of socio-cultural systems.

The emic distinctions which underlie these taxonomies are differentially constraining for various interaction networks within any speech community. Some networks (e.g., the networks of quantitative scientists) can repeatedly rise above the cognitive constraints of the taxonomies current in their speech communities. These networks are likely to be the ones that are most actively engaged in social change and in taxonomic change as well. Other networks are unable to break out of the socio-cultural taxonomies that surround them. In such cases, as, e.g., in connection with Kantorowitz' race relations taxonomy among White and Negro prison inmates (1967; see Figure 4), or Price's botanical taxonomies among the Huichols (1967), these taxonomies may be taken not only as useful reflections of the cognitive world of the speech community from which they are derived but also as forceful constraints on the cognitive behavior of most, if not all, of the individual members of these networks.

Lexical Structure Reflects Social Organization

There are, however, more pervasive (and, therefore, seemingly less systematic) ways in which lexicons in particular and languages as a whole are reflective of the speech communities that employ them. In a very real sense a language variety is an inventory of the concerns and interests of those who employ it at any given time. If any portion of this inventory reveals features not present in other portions this may be indicative of particular stresses or influences in certain interaction networks within the speech community as a whole or in certain role-relationships within the community's total role-repertoire. Thus, Epstein's study of linguistic innovation on the Copperbelt of Northern Rhodesia (1959) revealed that the English

and other Western influences on the local languages were largely
limited to matters dealing with urban, industrial and generally non-
traditional pursuits and relationships. Similarly, M. Weinreich's
meticulous inquiry into the non-Germanic elements in Yiddish (1953)
sheds much light on the dynamics of German-Jewish relations in the
11th century Rhineland.

Like all other immigrants to differently-speaking milieus,
Jews, learning a variety of medieval German in the 11th century,
brought to this language learning task sociolinguistic norms which incorporated their prior verbal repertoire. In this case the repertoire
consisted of a vernacular (Loez, a variety of Romance) and a set of
sacred languages (Hebrew-Aramaic). However, the pre-existing
sociolinguistic norms did not impinge upon the newly acquired Germanic code in either a random fashion or on an equal-sampling basis.
Quite the contrary. Both the Romance and the Hebraic-Aramaic elements in Yiddish were overwhelmingly retained to deal with a specific
domain: traditional religious pursuits and concerns. The Christo-
logical overtones of many common German words, for example
lesen (to read) and segnen (to bless), were strong enough to lead to
the retention of more neutral words of Romance origin (leyenen and
bentshn) in their stead. Similarly, Hebrew and Aramaic terms were
retained not only for all traditional and sanctified objects and ceremonies but also in doublets with certain Germanic elements in order
to provide contrastive emphases: bukh (book) vs. seyfer (religious
book, scholarly book); lerer (teacher) vs. melamed or rebi (teacher
of religious subjects), etc. Thus, Yiddish is a wonderful example of
how all languages in contact borrow from each other selectively and
of how this very selectivity is indicative of the primary interests and
emphases of the borrowers and the donors alike (for examples pertaining to early Christianity see Knott 1956, Mohrman 1947, 1957).
Indeed, M. Weinreich has conclusively demonstrated (1953, 1967,
etc.) that a language not only reflects the society of its speakers but,
conversely, that societal data per se is crucial if language usage and
change are to be understood.

Findling's work too (1969) is interpretable in this fashion,
demonstrating as it does that Spanish and English among Puerto Rican
youngsters and adults in the Greater New York Metropolitan area reflect different psycho-social needs and conflicts. In word-association

Figure 4. Selected Examples of Vocabulary Used Differently
by White and Negro Prison Inmates
(N. Kantrowitz, American Dialect
Society, Chicago, 1967)

Concepts or names Used Exclusively by Negroes	names Used in Common by Both Negroes and Whites	Concepts or names used Exclusively by Whites

A white man who does not discriminate against Negroes

↓

free thinker

A Negro who believes whites are superior, and acts subservient to them

jeff, jeffer, jeff-davis, jeff artist, charlie mccarthy, chalk eyes, renegade, shuffler, sometimer, uncle tom, devil lover, stays in uncle tom's-cabin, hoosier lover

A Negro who constantly tells both Negroes and whites that Negroes must be accorded the same status and rights as whites

aggressive man, free-speaker, man of-reasoning

sander, smoke-blower, easy going black slave

civil rights man, race-man, mau mau, equal rights man

A white man who associates with Negroes

↓

nigger lover

A Negro who is not aggressive or does not insist on his equal rights with whites

↓

free thinker

A Negro who hates whites, and expresses it vehemently and freely among Negroes

civil rights nigger, freedom rider, little-rocker, lumumba, a-martin luther king, mau mau preacher, muslim, pale hater, tom tom guy

tasks Findling found his subjects mentioning humans more frequently
in English than in Spanish and more frequently in the work and education domains than in the home and neighborhood domains (Table 1a
and 1b). According to various previous studies in the area of personality theory, the prevalence of human terms in such unstructured tasks
is indicative of "need affiliation," that is, the need to be accepted into
positive relationships with others. Findling therefore maintains that
the language of Puerto Ricans in New York reveals this need to be
stronger (because less gratified) in English interactions and in Anglo-
controlled domains than in Spanish interactions and Puerto Rican
controlled domains. Knowing, or suspecting, as we do from other
sources, that Puerto Ricans in New York are struggling for acceptance in an Anglo-dominated world, Findling's interpretations seem
reasonable and intriguing indeed.

Language Behavior and Societal Behavior: A Circular Process of Mutual Creations

The difference between the language constraint view and the
language reflection view is related to the difference between being
interested in language as langue and language as parole. It is also
related to the difference between being interested in inter-cultural
variation and being interested in intra-societal variation. Obviously,
the sociology of language is more fully at home with the latter level
of analysis, in both cases, than with the former. However, the latter
level too can be overstated, particularly if it is claimed that not only
is language behavior a complete index to social behavior, but, also,
that it is nothing more than an index of such behavior. While indices
are merely passive, language behavior is an active force as well as
a reflective one. Language behavior feeds back upon the social reality
that it reflects and helps to reinforce it (or to change it) in accord
with the values and goals of particular interlocutors.

When Weinreich relates that Yiddish (then Judeo-German)
came to be the vernacular of Rhineland Jewry because Jews and non-
Jews on the eastern shore of the Rhine shared open networks and because higher status in these Jewish-Gentile networks also came to
provide Jews with higher status in their own closed networks, he is
saying much more than that language usage reflects social interaction.

Table 1a. Analysis of Variance of Human Ratio
(Need Affiliation) Scores
(Findling 1969)

Source of Variance	Sum of Squares	df	Mean Square	F	F_{95}	F_{99}
Between subjects	19,573.09	31				
Occupation (C)	110.73	1	110.73	.17	4.17	7.56
Error (b)	19,463.08	30	648.77			
Within subjects	65,904.10	288				
Language (A)	701.69	1	701.69	3.78*	4.17	7.56
Domain (B)	12,043.27	4	3,010.82	12.10**	2.44	3.47
AB	239.49	4	59.87	.48	2.44	3.47
AC	181.84	1	181.84	.98	4.17	7.56
BC	1,855.50	4	463.87	1.86	2.44	3.47
ABC	446.16	4	111.54	.89	2.44	3.47
Error (w)	50,436.15	270				
$Error_1$ (w)	5,571.17	30	185.71			
$Error_2$ (w)	29,851.83	120	248.77			
$Error_3$ (w)	15,013.15	120	125.11			
Total	85,477.19	319				

*p>.07
**p>.01

Table 1b. Mean Need Affiliation Ratio Scores
by Language and Domain
(Findling 1969)

	Domain					
Language	Work	Education	Religion	Neighborhood	Home	Total
English	33	24	20	17	14	22
Spanish	28	23	17	13	14	19
Total	30	23	18	15	14	20

Of course, Judeo-German was a reflection of the fact that Jews and Gentiles participated in common open networks. However, Judeo-German also helped implement and reinforce these networks, and, thus, became a co-participant in creating or preserving the social reality that it reflected. Similarly, when Weinreich tells us that Judeo-German became increasingly more indigenously normed (and therefore increasingly more Yiddish and less Judeo-German) he is referring to much more than a linguistic reflection of the primacy of its closed networks for this Jewish community. He is also telling us that the uniquely Jewish aspects of Yiddish (in phonology, lexicon and grammar) also helped foster the primacy of Jewish closed networks for its speakers. As a result, Yiddish not only reflected (as it does today) the cohesiveness and separateness of its speakers, but it helped to preserve and to augment these characteristics as well.

Thus, both unidirectional views are outgrowths of an artificial search for independent variables and original causes. The original cause of any societal behavior may well be of some interest but it is a historical interest rather than a dynamic one with respect to life as it continues round about us. If we can put aside the issue of "what first caused what" we are left with the fascinating process of ongoing and intertwined conversation and interaction. In these processes language and societal behavior are equal partners rather than one or the other of them being "boss" and "giving orders" to the other.

REFERENCES

Basso, Keith H. Semantic aspects of linguistic acculturation. American Anthropologist, 1967, 69, 471-477.

Brown, Roger W. and Gilman, Albert. The pronouns of power and solidarity, in Sebeok, Thomas A. (ed.), Style in Language. Cambridge, M.I.T. Press, 1960, 253-276.

Brown, Roger W. and Lenneberg, Eric H. A study in language and cognition. Journal of Abnormal and Social Psychology, 1954, 49, 454-462.

Carmichael, L., Hogan, H. P., and Walter, A. A. An experimental study of the effect of language on the perception of visually perceived form. Journal of Experimental Psychology, 1932, 15, 73-86.

Carroll, John B. and Casagrande, J. B. The function of language classifications in behavior, in Maccoby, E. , Newcomb, T. , and Hartley, E. (eds.), Readings in Social Psychology, New York, Holt, 1958, pp. 18-31.

Conklin, Harold C. Lexicographic treatment of folk taxonomies, in Householder, Fred W. and Saporta, Sol (eds.), Problems in Lexicography, Bloomington, Research Center in Anthropology, Folklore and Linguistics, Indiana University, Publication 21, 1962, pp. 119-141.

Epstein, A. L. Linguistic innovation and culture on the Copperbelt, Northern Rhodesia. Southwestern Journal of Anthropology, 1959, 15, 235-253.

Findling, Joav. Bilingual need affiliation and future orientation in extragroup and intragroup domains. Modern Language Journal, 1969, 53, 227-231.

Fishman, Joshua A. A systematization of the Whorfian Hypothesis. Behavioral Science, 1960, 8, 323-339.

Frake, Charles O. The diagnosis of disease among the Subanun of Mindanao. American Anthropologist, 1961, 63, 113-132.

Frake, Charles O. The ethnographic study of cognitive systems, in Gladwin, T. and Sturtevant, William C. (eds.), Anthropology and Behavior, Washington, D. C. , Anthropological Society of Washington, 1962, pp. 77-85.

Friederich, Paul. The linguistic reflex of social change: from Tsarist to Soviet Russian kinship. Sociological Inquiry, 1966, 36, 159-185.

Greenberg, Joseph R. Universals of Language, 2nd ed. Cambridge, Mass., M.I.T. Press, 1966.

Hoijer, H. Cultural implications of the Navaho linguistic categories. Language, 1951, 27, 111-120.

Hoijer, H. The Sapir-Whorf hypothesis, in Hoijer, H. (ed.), Language in Culture. American Anthropological Association, Memoir No. 79, Chicago, University of Chicago Press, 1954, pp. 92-104.

Howell, Richard W. Linguistic status markers in Korean. Kroeber Anthropological Society Papers, 1965, 55, 91-97.

Howell, Richard W. Terms of address as indices of social change. Paper presented at American Sociological Association Meeting, San Francisco, Sept. 1967. 1967.

Hymes, Dell H. Two types of linguistic relativity, in Bright, William (ed.), Sociolinguistics. The Hague, Mouton, 1966, pp. 114-157.

Kantrowitz, Nathan. The vocabulary of race relations in a prison. Paper presented at American Dialect Society Meeting, Chicago, Dec. 1967.

Kluckhohn, Clyde. Notes on some anthropological aspects of communication. American Anthropologist, 1961, 63, 895-910.

Knott, Betty I. The Christian "special language" in the inscriptions. Vigiliae Christianae, 1956, 10, 65-79.

Lantz, De lee, and Stefflre, Volney. Language and cognition revisited. Journal of Abnormal and Social Psychology, 1964, 49, 454-462.

Lehmann, A. Uber Wiedererkennen. Philosophical Studies, 1889, 5, 96-156.

Lenneberg, Eric H. Cognition in ethnolinguistics. Language, 1953, 29, 463-471.

Lenneberg, Eric H. A probabilistic approach to language learning. Behavioral Science, 1957, 2, 1-12.

Maier, Norman R. F. Reasoning in humans. I. On direction. Journal of Comparative Psychology, 1930, 10, 115-143.

Metzger, Duane and Williams, Gerald E. Some procedures and results in the study of native categories: Tzeltal "firewood." American Anthropologist, 1966, 68, 389-407.

Mohrmann, Christine. Le latin commun et le latin des Chretiens. Vigiliae Christiannae, 1947, 1, 1-12.

Mohrmann, Christine. Linguistic problems in the Early Christian Church. Vigiliae Christiannae, 1957, 11, 11-36.

Osgood, Charles E. The cross-cultural generality of visual-verbal-synesthetic tendencies. Behavioral Science, 1960, 5, 146-149.

Pospisil, Leopold. A formal semantic analysis of substantive law: Kapauku Papuan laws of land tenure. American Anthropologist, 1965, 67, part 2, 186-214.

Price, P. David. Two types of taxonomy: a Huichol ethnobotanical example. Anthropological Linguistics, 1967, 9, no. 7, 1-28.

Trager, George L. The systematization of the Whorf hypothesis. Anthropological Linguistics, 1959, 1, no. 1, 31-25.

Weinreich, Max. Yidishkayt and Yiddish: on the impact of religion on language in Ashkenazic Jewry, in Mordecai M. Kaplan Jubilee Volume. New York, Jewish Theological Seminary of America, 1953.

Weinreich, Max. The reality of Jewishness versus the ghetto myth: the sociolinguistic roots of Yiddish, in To Honor Roman Jacobson. The Hague, Mouton, 1967, 2199-2211.

Whorf, Benjamin L. Science and linguistics. Technology Review, 1940, 44, 229-231, 247-248.

Whorf, Benjamin L. The relation of habitual thought to behavior and to language, in Speier, L. (ed.), Language, Culture and Personality. Menasha (Wisc.), Sapir Memorial Publication Fund, 1941, 75-93.

Wittermans, Elizabeth P. Indonesian terms of address in a situation of rapid social change. Social Forces, 1967, 46, 48-52.

Part VI. Applied Sociology of Language

14 | The Uses of Sociolinguistics

       It may be difficult for some of those reading these remarks who were not themselves involved in the Bloomington Seminar of the Committee on Sociolinguistics, held during the Linguistic Institute of summer 1964, to believe that only five years have elapsed since there took place the first prolonged attempt of a group of American linguists and American sociologists and other social scientists to try simultaneously to understand each other and the field of sociolinguistics. I say this because it is often difficult for those of us who <u>were</u> there, who grappled with each other and with each other's facts, faults and fidelities, to believe that only five years have transpired since then. Much more has happened to the offspring specialty-field of that seminal encounter than was anticipated even by those who saw themselves in the light of its benign parents (or fairy godparents), and the very topic of this paper is itself a sign of how robust and unafraid that offspring has become, how eagerly it has been welcomed by many who only a few years ago were unaware of its existence.

Sociolinguistics: the outer trappings

       Those of us who have ever tried to modify the course of academic life, to alter university programs, to change departmental offerings, to redirect journal "tendencies," to influence the agendas of professional society meetings and to obtain financial support for new directions and emphases, know how heartbreakingly difficult this can be when attempted prematurely, before there is a groundswell of almost overpowering dimensions. On the other hand, those of us who have also tried to contain fads, to limit stylish distortions, to rebalance the warped and biased by-products, human and literary, of

overzealous and oversuccessful innovation, know how heartbreakingly
difficult it is to slow down a galloping trend that has found its stride.
There were certainly many lean, dry years when the study of societally patterned language behaviors and behaviors toward language
seemed to be blocked by ignorance and apathy on every side. How
fitting, therefore, that we now review the few fat and sleek years, to
see whether or not their contributions appear relatively stimulating
and useful, after the first flush of their exuberance has passed.

In 1964 there were no collections of diversified readings that
instructors could assign and that students could pursue in conjunction
with sociolinguistics. Today there are six in English and Spanish one
in preparation. In 1964 there were no courses or programs of study
leading to graduate specialization in sociolinguistics. Today there are
several officially designated as such and many times that number of
departments where such study is welcome and encouraged, even if,
at times, under other more traditional names. In 1964 the literature
that would now be recognized as sociolinguistic was sparse, and much
of it was by no means recent (since new additions to that literature
were few and far between). Today the annual yield in articles and
books is great enough and sufficiently sought after to prompt commercial publishers to plan specialized journals and series in sociolinguistics. In 1964 there were no specially organized groups meeting regularly on sociolinguistic research or theory. Today there are at least
four such, a fifth being planned,[1] and the frequency of sociolinguistic
conferences or sociolinguistic sessions at conferences on more general topics is increasing at American universities. The outer trappings of success are certainly all there and it is high time to look to
the inner man, to the inner field, to the inner yield as well.

Application as a theory of knowledge

I do not propose to make a ringing declaration to the effect
that the only true test of knowledge is application or applicability.
I will only say that my background in social psychology has long since
convinced me—as has yours in linguistics and in other language studies—that there is indeed truth in Kurt Lewin's claim that "nothing
is as useful as a good theory," just as much as it has convinced me
that there is nothing as theoretically provocative as effective practice.

However, I do not propose to judge sociolinguistics only by the degree
to which it can be or has been put to use. Older and much more entrenched disciplines cannot (yet) afford to be evaluated in such terms.
Therefore I merely propose to examine the extent to which sociolinguistics is germane to linguistic applications and the extent to which
applied linguistics is in touch with the universe of societal discourse,
of societal concern, of societal inquiry and of societal danger that is
associated with societal application. I propose to do so because I
see the interaction between science and society, the mutual correction of theory and use, as a measure of each, as a never-ending process of influence, correction, overcorrection and redirection, and
therefore, as one legitimate measure of sociolinguistics, if only because it is an inevitable one, a necessary one, and one already being
applied to both linguistics and sociology.

The uses of sociolinguistics for applied linguistics

My comments on the uses of sociolinguistics will keep in
mind four separate categories of actual and potential users, namely,
linguists and socilogists on the one hand, and the users of linguistics
as well as the users of sociology on the other hand. Sociolinguistics,
as a hybrid or bridge-building specialization, is useful not only as it
pertains to the front line of contact between science and society but
also as it enables those in theoretical heartlands to understand their
basic fields afresh and in refreshing ways. Application and applicability are themselves an endless array of concentric circles that
surround all immediate problems in an ever-widening and interlocking flow. It is never wise to rigidly declare some knowledge "useful"
and other "useless," for neither knowledge nor usefulness (nor even
the very problems to which both are referred) hold still long enough
for such judgments to be more than myopic indicators of how near or
far we stand with respect to a particular and often fleeting goal. All
knowledge is useful, and if at any point in time we nevertheless grope
toward a consideration of the "uses of X," it is merely because for
some particular proposals at some particular time some knowledge
may seem more useful than others.

Since it must be obvious to all that I can neither review all
of sociolinguistics nor all of applied linguistics in the space at my

disposal, I have decided to orient my comments toward a few recognized topics within applied linguistics and to do so, quite openly, in
order to illustrate and document a point of view. My point of departure in relating sociolinguistics to applied linguistics is Charles A.
Ferguson's ten-year-old effort to divide the latter into its six most
common American branches: the creation and revision of writing
systems, literacy efforts, translation work, language teaching efforts,
and language policy efforts.[2] My basic questions will be: what has
this work accomplished <u>without</u> formal socilinguistic awareness or
sophistication? what has socilinguistics <u>contributed</u> to more recent
applied efforts in these topical areas? finally, what more <u>could</u> sociolinguistics contribute to these (and even to other) applied linguistic
concerns if its practitioners were to really take <u>both</u> parts of this
hybrid field with <u>equal seriousness</u> and with the deep technical and
theoretical proficiency that they <u>both</u> require.

Creation of writing systems

        The sophistication of phonological theory, both that of the
early part of this century as well as that of very recent years, and
the recent linguistic interest in theories of writing systems and in
the relations between such systems and spoken language are, and
have long been, powerful linguistic contributions to the worldwide
efforts to create writing systems for preliterate peoples. However,
the very sophistication of the linguist's professional skills in code
description and code creation (e.g., Pike 1947 and Ray 1963) merely
intensified the separation trauma when it became increasingly obvious that it was necessary to go outside the code and to confront the
real world if writing systems were not only to be devised but employed. The first steps in this direction were moderate indeed.
These consisted of Vachek's (1945/49 and 1948) and Bolinger's (1946)
protests (among others) that the writing system must be viewed separately from the spoken code, i.e. that it could not properly be viewed
as merely the phonetic transcription of the spoken code, and that it
was basically a "visual system" with regularities all its own.

        The reverberations of these early protests are still with us.
As Berry has pointed out (1958), new alphabets have merely become
less purely phonemic and more inclined to the "use of reason and

expedience" (rather than to rely on phonemicization alone) in their
pursuit of acceptance. Indeed, the latter concern, that of acceptance,
has tended to replace the former, that of "reduction to writing, " and,
as a result, arguments pertaining to intra- (writing) code phenomena
have tended to recede evermore into the background. While "phonetic
ambiguity" is still considered a "bad" thing and while it is generally
agreed that "words pronounced differently sould be kept graphically
apart" (Bradley 1913/14), it is considered to be an even "worse
thing" if alphabets of exquisite perfection remain unused or unaccepted.
More and more the creation of writing systems has shown awareness
of the fact that such non-acceptance is only to a relatively minor
degree governed by intra-code ambiguities, inconsistencies or irrel-
evancies (all of these being rampant characteristics of the most
widely used writing systems today and throughout history). Time and
again in recent years the greater importance of extra-code phenomena
has been hinted at (Gelb 1952, Bowers 1968), pointed to (Sjoberg
1964, 1966) and, finally, even catalogued (Smalley 1964).

Desired similarity and dissimilarity

        Perhaps because their attention is basically directed toward
intra-code factors, linguists and applied linguists were quickest to
notice those extra-code factors in the adoption or rejection of writing
systems which indicated societal preferences or antipathies for
writing conventions associated with some other language or languages.
Thus, among the "practical limitations to a phonemic orthography"
Nida (1953) discussed the fact that both the Otomi and the Quechua
"suffer from cultural insecurity" and want their writing systems not
only to "look like Spanish" but to operate with the same graphematic
alternances as does Spanish, whether these are needed or not in terms
of their own phonemic system. [3] In a related but crucially different
vein Hans Wolff recommended (1954) that Nigerian orthographies be
created not only in terms of tried and true technically linguistic criteria (such as "accuracy, economy and consistency") but that "similarity to the orthographies of related languages" also be used as a
guide. Of course, Wolff was merely following in the footsteps of the
Westermann Script, of the late twenties, which, in its fuller, more
generally applicable form, became the All-Africa Script of the International African Institute (Anon. 1930). However, he was also

following in the tradition that placed the linguist or other outside expert in the position of judging not only which languages were sufficiently related in order to deserve a common writing system, but that placed them in the position of deciding whether such similarity in writing system was or was not a "good thing" and whether it was or was not desired by the speech communities involved.

However, once having stepped outside of the charmingly closed circle of intra-code considerations, Pandora's box had been opened never again to be shut. In very recent days, to mention only such examples, Serdyuchenko has assured us that the Cyrillic alphabet is used as the model in "the creation of new written languages in the U.S.S.R." only because of the widespread and still growing interest in subsequently more easily learning Russian. More recently the Bamako Meeting on the Use of the Mother Tongue for Literacy (28 February-5 March, 1966, UNESCO sponsored) went a step further. It not only recommended that new writing systems be similar to those of unrelated but important languages for the learners (Bowers 1968) but it also warned of "possible repercussions of a technical and economic nature" following upon the adoption of non-European diacritics and special letters in the standard transcriptions of West African languages (Ferru 1966). Such letters and diacritics, it is pointed out, increase the cost of printing and typing, as well as the cost of manufacturing printing and typing equipment, and do so at the time when the per capita cost of printed or typed material is already likely to be troublesomely high in view of the limited number of consumers available for them in newly literate societies.

The obverse case has been less fully documented, namely, that in which newly literate communities have desired a more distinctive writing system, one that they could call their own or one that would more effectively differentiate their language from others with which they did not seek similarity but rather dissimilarity. Dickens' (1953) discussion of the Ashante rejection of the Akuapem-based writing system for standard Twi (in the late thirties and early forties) is one such case. Another is Ferguson's reference (1967) to the fact that St Stefan of Perm (fourteenth century) purposely created a separate alphabet for the Komi (giving "some of the letters an appearance suggestive of the Tamga signs in use among the Komi as property markers and decorations") "so that the Komi could regard the writing

system as distinctively theirs and not an alphabet used for another
language." There must be many examples of this kind, e.g. St
Mesrop's creation of the Armenian alphabet in the fifth century
(Ferguson 1967), but little detailed evidence concerning them is
available in the scholarly literature dealing with contemporary societies.[4] The reluctance to document such cases is probably not unrelated to the more general reluctance of those who practice applied
linguistics upon others to recognize the frequent desires of non-
literate peoples to be themselves (albeit "in a modern way") rather
than merely to be imitative copies of ourselves (whether we be Chinese, Russian, French, British, American, Spanish, or Portuguese).

    A little more complicated than that. If economics answers
all questions with "supply and demand," and psychology with "it all
depends," then the first contribution of sociolinguistics to linguistics
is doubtlessly to make us aware of the fact that the relations and inter-
penetrations between language and society are "a little more complicated than that," whatever that may be. Indeed, although it is nearly
half a century since Radin first implied that the adoption (actually,
the borrowing) of an alphabet by an aboriginal people was a fascinat-
ingly complex and internally differentiated chain of social processes,
we have not to this very day seriously followed up this seeming complexity, let alone tried to reduce it to some underlying set of basic
dimensions. Our technical expertise and theoretical sophistication
lead us more readily to agree with Burns' (1953) early conclusion,
based on sad experience with the failure of "linguistics without sociology" in Haiti, that the choice of an orthography has widespread
social and political implications. They also lead us to continually
admire Garvin's accounts (1954, also see 1959) of his attempts to
achieve consumer consensus and participation in the creation of a
standard orthography for Ponape, and to share his disappointment
that even this was not enough to assure the use of that orthography.
Beyond such agreement and admiration, however, we can only suggest that the process of gaining acceptance for technically sound writing systems is even "a little more complicated than that."

    Basically what is it that sociolinguistics could contribute to
future studies of the acceptive creation of writing systems? As I
see it, being almost entirely an outsider to the area of endeavor,
modern sociolinguistics can contribute most by linking this branch

of applied linguistics with the body of theory and practice that has
grown up in connection with the acceptance of other systematic innovations, the planning of social change more generally, and the ameli-
oration of the inevitable dislocations that follow upon the introduction
of innumerable innovations and changes of which new writing systems
are merely symptomatic.

The creation of writing systems is itself necessarily an out-
growth of culture contact, if not of political and economic domination
from outside. Thus, the creation of a writing system is singularly
unlikely to be viewed dispassionately and its propagation and acceptance by indigenous networks are necessarily viewed as having implications for group loyalty and group identity. Latinization, Cyrilli-
zation or Sinoization are not merely far-going indications of desired
(and frequently of subsidized or directed) social change and cognitive-
emotional reorganization, but they have immediate consequences for
the relevance of traditional elitist skills and implications for the distribution of new skills and statuses related to literacy and to the
philosophy or ideology which is the carrier of literacy.

The creation of writing systems is significant only insofar
as it leads to the acceptance and implementation of writing systems.
The latter are revolutionary rather than narrowly technical acts.
They succeed or fail far less on the basis of the adequacy of their
intra-code phonological systems or on the basis of their fidelity to
model systems than on the basis of the success of the larger revolutions with which they are associated: revolutions in the production
and consumption of economic goods (leading to new rural-urban populations distributions, new jobs, new training programs, new avoca-
tions, new pastimes, and new purposive social groups) and revolutions
in the distributions of power and influence. All of these both lead to
and depend upon an increasing number of new texts and new written
records. Thus, when sociolinguistic attention is finally directed to
the creation of writing systems it will be focused upon the organization, functioning and disorganization of an increasingly literate society. This is potentially a very useful addition to the linguist's disciplinary focus because even more than writing changes speech (via
"spelling pronunciations") literacy changes speakers and societies.
It is this perspective on the creation of writing systems—as always,
a perspective which is outside of the linguistic system alone—that is

part of the programmatic promise of the sociolinguistics of writing systems.

How will such attention improve or alter the creation of writing systems? Precisely by relating the problem of creation to the problem of acceptance, of impact, of possible dislocation, of possible manipulation, of possible exploitation, of possible redistribution of power and of studied awareness of the interdependency of the very best writing system on revolutionary processes at their most pragmatic as well as at their most symbolic. Of course, it will require a far greater liberation of sociolinguistics from disciplinary linguistics and its far greater immersion in societal processes and problems before sociolinguistics can be broadly useful in these respects rather than merely descriptively "helpful" on the one hand or diffusely "stimulating" on the other.

Orthographic reform. To some extent such liberation and immersion are more advanced with respect to the study and planning of orthographic reforms, perhaps because the truly vast amount of technical linguistic effort invested in these reforms has yielded such meager results. Even though orthographic reform may be so sweeping as to involve the complete replacement of one writing system by another (and, in that sense, it may be viewed as a subcategory of the topic just reviewed), it deals with already literate networks and, as a result, more clearly reveals the societal ramifications and reverberations of seemingly technical linguistic adjustments.

If the introduction of a newly created writing system easily threatens to change established lines of relative advantage and disadvantage, practical and symbolic, the revision of traditional orthographies often attempts to do so. Orthographic change represents the abandonment of written tradition and as such it must cope with the gatekeepers of written tradition, the poets, priests, principals and professors, with the institutions and symbols that they create and serve, or be destined to oblivion. Indeed, the greater and grander the tradition of literacy, literature and liturgy in an orthographic community, the less likely that even minor systematic orthographic change will be freely accepted and the less likely that any orthographic change will be considered minor.

In this connection we have a larger number of rather detailed and, to some extent <u>sociolinguistically oriented</u> descriptions,
than is the case for the creation of writing systems, but, as yet we
have no sociolinguistic analyses or hypotheses <u>per se</u>. The socioculturally contextualized descriptions of orthographic reforms in the
U. S. S. R. (Orenstein 1959, Quelquejay and Bennigsen 1961, Sedyu-
chenko 1965, Weinreich 1953, Winner 1952), Turkey (Rossi 1927,
1929, 1935, 1942, 1953; Heyd 1954; Ozmen 1967; Gallagher 1967
and 1969), Norway (Haugen 1966, which contains an exhaustive bibliography of other studies) and Vietnam (Haudricourt 1943, Sheldon
1946) again point to the literally revolutionary nature of the societal
processes that have often accompanied system-wide orthographic
change. On the other hand, the available descriptions of less successful attempts to bring about orthographic changes under less dramatic
circumstances, e. g. in Japan (DeFrancis 1947, Holton 1947, Meyenberg 1934, Scharshmidt 1924), Haiti (Valdman 1968, Burns 1953) and
Israel (Rabin 1969), or to bring about the orthographic unification of
closely related languages in the absence of accompanying societal
unification, e. g. in India (Anon. 1963, Jones 1942, Ray 1960), Africa
(Dickens 1953, Ward 1945) and Indonesia-Malaysia (Alisjahbana 1969
and in press) all indicate the difficulties encountered and the failures
experienced thus far.

However, there is no justification for interpreting the above
cited investigations as implying "revolutionary success and non-
revolutionary failure" as the proper summation of experience with
orthographic reform. In earlier centuries a great deal of orthographic
reform seems to have been accomplished both quietly and successfully, essentially without the involvement of mobilized populations or,
indeed, of any other population segments than "the authorities" whose
business it was to make wise decisions for the community. The initial
orthographic distinctions between Serbian and Croatian or between
Ruthenian (Ukrainian) and Polish were decided upon by representatives of God and Caesar who sought to cultivate <u>ausbau</u> differences
between speech communities that were "in danger" of religious,
political and linguistic unification. The restoration of written Czech
(and Slovak) in Latin script was engineered by Count Sednitzsley, the
administrative director of the Austro-Hungarian police and one of the
most influential officials under the Emperor Francis (early nineteenth
century), by subsidizing the publication of the Orthodox prayer book

in Latin letters as "an important device to fight the political danger
of the Pro-Russian Pan-Slav movement (Fischel 1919, p. 57)." The
Roumanian shift from Cyrillic to Latin script in 1863 was accomplished
by a painless edict which sought to further that nation's self-defined
Latinizing and Christianizing role in the heathen "Slavo-Moslem"
Balkans (Kolarz 1946). In more recent days Irish orthography has
been changed without arousing great interest (Macnamara 1969)—
indeed, the ease of the change being a reflection of the lack of widespread Irish interest or concern for the Revival—as have the orthographies of other small speech communities.

Not only has there been much successful orthographic reform
without revolutionary change (particularly where mass mobilization
along language-related lines was absent for one reason or another),
but there has also been a good bit of unsuccessful orthographic reform
even when these have been accompanied by revolutionary social
changes. Thus, the Soviet "rationalization" of Yiddish orthography
initially aimed at both the phonetization of words of Hebrew-Aramic
origin, as well as at the discontinuation of the special final letters of
the traditional Hebrew alphabet. However, twenty-five years after
the October revolution, the names of the grandfathers of modern Yiddish literature were neither spelled:

מענדעלע מויכער ספֿאָרים, צֿכאַק לײבוש בעדעצ אוֹן
שאָלעם אַלײכעם

(as they had been throughout the twenties and thirties), nor were they
spelled:

מענדעלע מוכר ספרים, יצהק לײבוש ברץ און שלום עליכם

(as they had been before the Revolution and continued to be everywhere
outside of the Soviet Union), but, rather, in an attempt to reach a
compromise that would maximize the propaganda value of the few
permitted Yiddish publications primarily distributed to and published
for readers outside of the U.S.S.R.: [5]

מענדעלע מויכער ספֿאָרים, צֿכאַק לײבוש בערעץ און
שאָלעם אַלײכעם

However, even in its heyday the Soviet revolution in Yiddish orthography could not entirely overcome the visual traditions of the orthographic community. The initial silent aleph at the beginning of words
that would otherwise begin with the vowels י and ו was never dropped,
regardless of its phonemic uselessness, perhaps because the initial

silent aleph in such cases was considered to be too strong a visual
convention to be tampered with (Hebrew writing itself—i.e. the visual
precursor to Yiddish—never beginning words with vocalic ז or ן).

      A far more widely renowned revolutionary attempt at ortho-
graphic reform which has failed (certainly thus far) is the once promised phonetization of (Northern Mandarin) Chinese. While the basic
sources available to us in English (DeFrancis 1950 and 1968, Mills
1956 and Hsia 1956) all agree that the Latinized New Writing was
abandoned sometime late in the fifties, the reason for this abandonment can still only be surmised. By 1956 it had become necessary to
defend the "Han (Chinese) language phonetization draft plan" as being
concerned with an alphabet (Latin) which was truly progressive and
international rather than necessarily related to any anti-proletarian
class (Chinese Written Language Reform Committee 1956, Wu Yu-
chang 1956). By 1959 Chou En-lai had officially demoted phonetization from its original goal of immediate "liberation and development
of the whole Chinese language from the shackles of the monosyllabic
Chinese characters (Ni Hai-shu 1949, cited by DeFrancis 1968)" to
third place and the indefinite future, after both simplification of the
traditional characters and adoption of a spoken standard for "Common
Speech" had been attained (Chou En-lai 1965). While work on the first
two tasks is constantly going on in a very direct fashion (see, e.g.,
Anon. 1964 and Wu Yu-chang 1965) work on the latter is primarily
nominal (i.e. phonetization is kept alive as a distant goal but is not
substantively advanced) and indirect (i.e. phonetization is utilized for
subsidiary purposes, such as annotating novel or complex Chinese
characters in technical texts, furthering instruction in the Common
Speech among speakers of other regional languages, or creating
"initial alphabetic scripts" for illiterate non-Chinese-speaking minorities). Indeed, while phonetization has recently been reported to be
superior for such special purposes as telegraphic communication
(Wu Yu-chang 1964) and minority group initial literacy (Li Hui 1960),
the traditional characters have again been proclaimed as superior in
connection with general education for the bulk of the population among
whom these characters are viewed as symbolic of education and the
standard pronunciation (Serruys 1962). The goal of phonetization is,
seemingly, still a long way off and may or may not be reached any
more rapidly than the withering away of the state.

From the foregoing examples it is clear that if we but dichot-
omize "success" (acceptance) and "revolutionary social change" we
have examples of all four possible types of co-occurrences: successful orthographic revision with and without revolutionary social change
and revolutionary social change with and without successful follow-
through of planned orthographic revision. The discussions of revolutionary social change thus far encountered in studies of either the
creation of writing systems or the revision of orthographies is still
far too crude to be considered as more than rough labeling. As sociolinguistic description it is regrettably out of touch with the sizable
modernization literature in economics, political science, sociology
and anthropology. It lacks either the concepts or the technical data
collection methods and data analysis skills needed to inquire into intensity, extensity or continuity of the change forces and processes or
counterchange forces and processes that it notices.

It is also unfortunate that here are so few localized case
studies of variation in sub-group reactions to new writing systems or
to revised orthographies and, conversely, proportionally so many
commentaries, studies, evaluations, and recommendations that deal
with entire countries, continents, and even the world at large. The
result is an imbalance with respect to the usual mutual stimulation
between micro-analysis and its emphases on process and function concerns, on the one hand, and macro-analysis and its emphases on structure, quantification, compositing and weighting of parameters on the
other hand. Either type of study, when pursued too long without correction from the other, becomes myopic and, therefore dangerous
for theory as well as (or even more so) for application.

Language planning

Perhaps the area of applied linguistics which most clearly
illustrates the full complexity of societal phenomena which sociolinguistics may some day enable us to understand is that which is concerned with language planning. Just as sociolinguistic inquiry into
the creation of writing systems and into the revision of orthographies
permits us to first recognize and to then refine our appreciation of
the magnitudes of social change and social planning (if not social dislocation) with which such activities are commonly associated, so the

systematic sociolinguistic study of language <u>planning</u> as a whole
(incorporating the creation of writing systems and the revision of
orthographies, but going beyond them to the conscious governmental
efforts to manipulate both the structure and the functional allocation
of codes within a polity) enables us to appreciate the societal complexity impinging on the determination, implementation and evaluation of
language <u>policy</u> as a whole. The study of language planning is the
study of organized efforts to find solutions to societal language problems (Jernudd and Das Gupta 1969). As such, it is necessarily most
dependent—of all the fields of applied language concerns—on sociolinguistics and on the social sciences as a whole in order to move
from theory to informed practice.

Language planning studies recently or currently underway
have dealt with the cost-benefit analysis of alternative or hypotheti-
cally alternative decisions between which governmental or other
bodies must choose (Jernudd 1969, Thorburn 1969). Others have discussed the pressure functions focused upon decision making and decision implementary bodies in the language field (whether the latter
be legislative-executive within government or political-religious-
literary-academic outside of government) from a variety of special
interest groups running the gamut from professional associations of
educators, to manufacturers of typewriters and publishers of text-
books, to spokesmen for literary, journalistic and ideological groupings, etc. (Das Gupta 1969). There are now several theoretical
models (happily commensurable) of the interaction of sentimental and
instrumental integrative and disintegrative forces in the language
planning process (Kelman 1969). There is a recent critique and integration of the literature on the evaluation of planned change in education, industry, agricultural and other areas of conscious societal
planning, in an effort to suggest evaluative methods that might be
most fruitfully adopted for the evaluation of success or failure in
language planning (Rubin 1969). Finally a five-country study has just
gotten underway (involving linguists, anthropologists, political scientists, sociologists, psychologists and educationists) in order to obtain
roughly comparable data concerning the processes of language planning
<u>per se</u> in each of the above contexts (decision making, pressure func-
tions, national integration, implementation and evaluation).

Several nations throughout the world are currently engaged
in language planning without anything like the information available

to them in other areas of planning. Sociolinguistic research on language planning aims to first locate and then to apportion the variation in behavior toward language which is to be observed in language planning contexts. It seeks detailed knowledge of how orthographic decisions (or script decisions, or national language decisions, or nomenclature decisions, etc.) are arrived at, how they are differentially reacted to or followed by agencies inside and outside government, how they are differentially accepted or resisted by various population segments, how they are differentially evaluated and how subsequent policies and plans are differentially modified as a result of feedback from prior policy and planning. Sociolinguistics is just now beginning to describe the variation that constantly obtains in all of these connections. After this has been done sufficiently well and in sufficiently many contexts it should begin to successfully account for this variation and, at that point, be able to offer suggestions that are useful from the point of view of those seeking to influence, implement or evaluate language planning in the future.

Some straws in the wind

However, even in the absence of the amount of detail and sophistication that is needed before practical information becomes available, "sociolinguistically oriented" and "sociolinguistically motivated" changes in applied linguistics are clearly on the increase. Not only are such topics as the creation of writing systems, the reform of orthographies and language planning more generally marked (as we have seen) by a constantly increasing awareness of societal interpenetration and of the need for truly professional competence (which is more than simply being either critical or admiring) if one is to understand, let alone influence, the societal forces at work, but such awareness is growing in most other fields of applied linguistics as well.

The planning, implementation and evaluation of literacy campaigns increasingly ceased being merely applied linguistics plus education (pedagogy) plus ethnography as the period of immediate post World War II exuberance was left behind (Smith 1956). What is currently being developed in this field goes beyond advice on how to establish proper local contacts and obtain official co-operation (Young

1944, Russell 1948), important though such advice undoubtedly is.
It goes beyond care to adapt programs to local needs (Jeffries 1958),
to utilize a variety of methods on a variety of fronts (Ivanova and
Voskresensky 1959), or to evaluate outcomes broadly enough to include
health, economic and other pertinent indices (UNESCO 1951). Current
efforts to advance literacy are increasingly based upon efforts to more
fully understand the meaning and impact of literacy via small pilot
studies which seek to recognize and weigh alternatives (Correa and
Tinbergen 1962, Lewis 1961, McClusker 1963) and clarify the societal dimensions of literacy enterprises in different contexts (Goody
1968, Hayes 1965, Nida 1967, Schofield 1968, Wurm 1966).

        A similar systematic intrusion of societal considerations
has become noticeable in the field of translation. It is here, in particular, that sociolinguistic differentiation of language into varieties
and of speech communities into situations is beginning to be felt,
perhaps more so than in any other field of applied linguistics. One
cannot read Catford's Linguistic Theory of Translation (1965) without
being delighted by the fact that it is far broader than immaculate linguistics alone, and one cannot read Wonderly's Bible Translation for
Popular Use (1968) without wishing that its sensitivity to social varieties and social occasions were part of the professional orientation of
translation for far more worldly purposes as well. Certainly the
deep concern with recognizing the significance of functional variation
in language variety use, the sensitivity shown with respect to the
situational analysis of repertoires of social and linguistic behavior—
viewing Bible reading and listening as kinds of situations that may
require particular kinds of language—and the repeated attention given
to the contextual-functional differences between written and spoken
language (and the multiple varieties of each) must sooner or later
feed back into religious work on the creation of writing systems and
on literacy more generally. This is, indeed, the beginning of technical sociolinguistic utility for an applied field. Having once embarked
along the path of recognizing that all of the factors influencing communicative appropriateness in a particular speech community also
influence the acceptability and the impact of translations in that community the probability of mutual enrichment between application and
theory for both fields of endeavor (translation and sociolinguistics)
is indeed very great.

The same may yet be the case for the huge field of language teaching, where the contacts with sociolinguistics are still far more tenuous, if only because the contacts between an elephant and a sparrow must always be rather incomplete. Nevertheless, although the problems and prospects of language teaching could easily swallow up or trample underfoot not only all of sociolinguistics but even all of linguistics per se, first the latter (linguistics) and now the former (sociolinguistics) have had some impact on the beast. A valuable introduction to sociolinguistics has been presented to language teachers generally by Halliday, McIntosh and Strevens (1964). In this introduction teachers are urged to recognize the different uses (and, therefore, the different varieties) of language that co-exist within speech communities, rather than, as has usually been the case thus far, to persist in the erroneous and deadening fiction that there is always only one (and always the same one) correct variety. More recently we have witnessed a deluge of "sociolinguistically oriented" interest in the language of disadvantaged speakers of non-standard English with Bernstein's work (e.g. 1964) being best known in England and Labov's (1965) or McDavid's (1958) in the U.S.A. Most of the products of this interest seek to contrastively highlight the basic structure of the speech of such communities so that teachers may be able to more successfully recognize and overcome the difficulties that learners will encounter when confronted with the phonological and grammatical structures of standard (school) English (Labov 1965, 1966; Shuy 1966; Wolfram 1969; Baratz and Shuy 1969). "Sociolinguistically oriented" advice is now also being directed toward the teacher of bilinguals (Troike 1968). In the latter case teachers are admonished that learners should be encouraged to have repertoires (incorporating several varieties) in each of their languages—rather than to displace all non-standard varieties in favour of one standard version of each—as well as to select from each repertoire in accord with the norms for communicative appropriateness of the particular networks with which they seek mutually accepting interaction. Of course the distance is still considerable between "sociolinguistically oriented" advice or sensitivity training for teachers and any more complete interrelationship between teaching-methodology and sociolinguistics. The historical dimension and the cross-national one are also obviously still lacking in the contacts between sociolinguistics and language teaching. The education of bilinguals is still viewed primarily within the context of disadvantaged and dislocated minorities (whose lot in life will be far easier if only they learn English, French, Russian, etc.) rather than within the broader context of world wide experience with bilingual education—including elitist bilingualism, traditional bilingualism and, more generally widespread and stable (i.e. non-dislocated) bilingualism. As a result the education of speakers of non-standard English is being pondered, e.g., without awareness of the fact that most students entering German, French, Italian, and other schools during the past century have also been speakers of non-standard varieties of their respective languages. A true meeting of education and sociolinguistics will enable both to discover why proportionally so many dialect speakers do and did become readers and speakers of the standard in Germany and elsewhere whereas so few seem to accomplish this in the U.S.A. today.

NOTES

Preparation of this paper was made possible by the Institute of Advanced Projects, East-West Center, University of Hawaii, where the author spent the 1968-9 academic year as Senior Specialist.

[1]I am aware of the following: the American Social Science Research Council's Committee on Sociolinguistics, the Working Group on Sociolinguistics of the International Sociological Association, the Sociolinguistics Group of the Luigi Sturzo Institute, Rome, and the British Social Science Research Council's recent decision to bring sociolinguistics within its purview. I know of no organizational provision for sociolinguistics within any of the farflung outcroppings of worldwide linguistics.

[2]See Charles A. Ferguson and Raleigh Morgan, Jr., "Selected readings in applied linguistics," Linguistic Reporter, 1959, Supplement 2, 4 pp. This presentation is currently being revised as part of the forthcoming report of the Linguistics Panel of the Behavioral and Social Sciences Survey Committee of the National Research Council and the Social Science Research Council. There are, of course, other definitions and demarcations of the field of applied linguistics, e.g. G. Kandler, "Zum Aufbau der angewandten Sprachwissenschaft," Sprachforum, 1955, I, 3-9, and N. D. Andreev and L. R. Zinder, "Osnovnye problemy prikladnoj lingvistiki," Voprosy Jazykoznanija, 1959, 4, 1-9.

[3] The unpopularity of "hooked letters" in written Hausa (ɗ, ɓ, ƙ) is said to reflect a desire among its users that it look as much like English as possible. A similar desire has led to several other orthographic differences between modern Hausa as written in Nigeria and as written in Francophone Niger. The Yiddish Scientific Institute's recommendations that the conventional ﬢ for /v/ be written װ and that the conventional ﬢ, ﬢ and ﬢ, ﬢ distinctions be rendered as ﬡ, ﬡ and ﬡ, ﬢ have found little acceptance, largely on the ground that no change is needed but, in part, also on the ground that it would tend to make Yiddish "look different" than the traditional alphabet for Hebrew (an attempt which is also associated with early Soviet attempts to "declericalize" Yiddish).

[4] Kolarz (1967) refers briefly to the reformed Arabic alphabet adopted by the Volga Tatars in the early twenties prior to central Soviet concern for their writing system. Henze (1956) comments that "the practicality and popularity of this reformed alphabet made the Soviet introduction of the Latin alphabet among the Tatars very difficult. Even Tatar Communists at first opposed it." As with many other brief references it is difficult to determine whether the creation adoption of a new writing system or the reform of an existing one was primarily involved or, if both problems were involved for various segments of the population, when and for whom the problem ceased to be primarily the former or the latter or shifted from being one to being the other. The Chinese government's claim (Anon. 1964) that it would "help create written languages for those nationalities having no written languages of their own and improve existing written languages of others (pp. 67-8)" is another example of the lack of detail that makes sociolinguistic documentation in this area difficult.

[5] A parallel example of retreating from the internal Soviet orthography for the purposes of external propaganda has occurred in conjunction with Uiger (Vigur). Whereas publications for the Uigers living in Soviet Central Asia have been completely Cyrillicized since 1941 the Uiger-Russian and Russian-Uiger dictionaries of 1955 and 1956 employ the Arabic script. The impression that these publications are intended for the Uigers in Sinkiang is reinforced by the fact that the textbook includes a short dictionary of "new words" encountered in Soviet political and economic writings (Najip, Uigurski Yazyk, Moscow, 1954).

REFERENCES

Alisjahbana, S. Takdir (ed.). The Modernization of the Languages of
        Asia. In press.
_____. Some planning processes in the development of the Indo-
        nesian-Malay language, in Rubin and Jernudd (eds.), Can
        Language Be Planned? (1971), pp. 179-88.
Alitto, Susan Biele. The language issue in Communist Chinese educa-
        tion. Comp. Educ. Review, 1969, 13, 43-60.
Anon. A Common Script for Indian Languages. Delhi, Ministry of
        Scientific Research and Cultural Affairs, 1963.
Anon. Continue to promote reform of the written language. Selections
        from Mainland China Magazines, 1964, No. 411 (6 April).
Anon. Practical Orthography of African Languages. International
        Institute of African Languages and Cultures, Memorandum
        I, Oxford, Oxford University Press, 1930, revised edition.
Anon. Policy Towards Nationalities of the People's Republic of China.
        Peking, Foreign Language Press, 1953.
Baratz, Joan and Shuy, Roger W. Teaching Black Children to Read.
        Washington, CAL., 1969.
Bernstein, Basil. Elaborated and restricted codes: their social ori-
        gins and some consequences. Amer. Anthrop., 1964, 66,
        No. 6, Part 2, 55-69.
Berry, Jack. The making of alphabets, in Proceedings of the Eighth
        International Congress of Linguists (Oslo, 1957). Oslo,
        Oslo University Press, 1958, pp. 752-64; also reprinted in
        J. A. Fishman (ed.), Readings in the Sociology of Language,
        The Hague, Mouton, 1968, pp. 737-53.
Bolinger, D. L. Visual Morphemes. Language, 1946, 22, 333-40.
Bowers, John. Language problems and literacy, in J. A. Fishman,
        C. A. Ferguson and J. Das Gupta (eds.), Language Problems
        of Developing Nations. New York, Wiley, 1968, pp. 381-401.
Bradley, Henry. On the relation between spoken and written language.
        Proceedings of the British Academy, 1913/14, 6, 212-32.
Burns, Donald. Social and political implications in the choice of an
        orthography. Fundamental and Adult Education, 1953, 5 (2),
        80-85.
Chinese Written Language Reform Committee. Several points con-
        cerning the Han language phoneticization plan (draft) explained.
        Current Background, 1956, 380 (15 March), 4-13.

Chou En-lai. Current tasks of reforming the written language, in
    Reform of the Chinese Written Language. Peking, Foreign
    Language Press, 1965.
Correa, Hector and Tinbergen, Jan. Quantitative adaptation of educa-
    tion to accelerated growth. Kyklos, 1962, 15, 776-85.
Das Gupta, Jyotirindra. Religion, language, and political mobiliza-
    tion, in Rubin and Jernudd (eds.), Can Language Be Planned?
    (1971), pp. 53-64.
DeFrancis, John. Japanese language reform: politics and phonetics.
    Far Eastern Survey, 1947, 16, No. 19, 217-20.
_____. Nationalism and Language Reform in China. Princeton,
    Princeton University Press, 1950.
_____. Language and script reform [in China]. Current Trends
    in Linguistics 2. The Hague, Mouton, 1968, pp. 130-50.
Dickens, K. J. Unification: The Akan dialects of the Gold Coast, in
    The Use of the Vernacular Languages in Education. Paris,
    UNESCO, 1953, pp. 115-23.
Ferguson, Charles A. St. Stefan of Perm and applied linguistics, in
    To Honor Roman Jakobson. The Hague, Mouton, 1967. Also
    in J. A. Fishman, C. A. Ferguson, J. Das Gupta (eds.),
    Language Problems of Developing Nations. New York, Wiley,
    1968.
Ferru, Jean Louis. Possible repercussions of a technical and eco-
    nomic nature of the adoption of particular letters for the
    standard transcription of West African languages. Bamako
    [Mali] Meeting on the Standardization of African Alphabets
    February 28-March 5, 1966. UNESCO/CLT, Baling.
Fischel, A. Der Panslawismus bis zum Weltkrieg. Stuttgart/Berlin,
    Cotta, 1919.
Franke, Wolfgang. Die Möglichkeiten einer Schriftreform in Japan.
    Ostasiatische Rundschau, 1935, 16.
Gallagher, Charles F. Language rationalization and scientific prog-
    ress. Paper prepared for Conference on Science and Social
    Change, California Institute of Technology, 18-20 October,
    1967.
_____. Language reform and social modernization in Turkey,
    in Rubin and Jernudd (eds.), Can Language Be Planned?
    (1971), pp. 159-78.
Garvin, Paul L. Literacy as problem in language and culture.
    Georgetown University Monograph Series on Language and
    Linguistics, 1954, 7, 117-29.

Garvin, Paul L. The standard language problem—concepts and methods. Anthropological Linguistics, 1959, 1 (3), 28-31.

Goody, Jack. Literacy in Traditional Societies. London, Cambridge University Press, 1968.

Halliday, M. A. K., McIntosh, Angus and Strevens, Peter. The Linguistic Sciences and Language Teaching. London, Longmans, 1964.

Haudricourt, A. G. De l'origine des particularités de l'alphabet Vietnamien. Dan Vietnam, 1943, No. 3.

Haugen, Einar. Language Conflict and Language Planning: The Case of Modern Norwegian. Cambridge, Harvard University Press, 1966.

Hayes, Alfred S. Recommendations of the Work Conference on Literacy. Washington, CAL, 1965.

Henze, Paul B. Politics and alphabets. Royal Central Asian Society Journal, 1956, 43, 29-51.

Heyd, Uriel. Language Reform in Modern Turkey. Oriental Notes and Studies No. 5. Jerusalem, The Israel Oriental Society, 1954.

Holton, Daniel C. Ideographs and ideas. Far Eastern Survey, 1947, 16, No. 19, 220-23.

Hsia, Tao-tsi. China's Language Reforms. New Haven, Yale University Press, 1956.

Ivanova, A. M. and Voskresensky, V. D. Abolition of adult illiteracy in USSR, 1917-1940. Fundamental and Adult Education, 1959, 11 (3), 131-86.

Jeffries, W. F. The literacy campaign in Northern Nigeria. Fund. and Adult Educ., 1958, 10 (1), 2-6.

Jernudd, Bjorn. Notes on economic analysis for solving language problems, in Rubin and Jernudd (eds.), Can Language Be Planned? (1971), pp. 263-76.

_____ and Das Gupta, Jyotirindra. Towards a theory of language planning, in Rubin and Jernudd (eds.), Can Language Be Planned? (1971), pp. 195-216.

Jones, D. Problems of a National Script for India. Hartford, HSF, 1942.

Kelman, Herbert C. Language as an aid and barrier to involvement in the national system, in Rubin and Jernudd (eds.), Can Language Be Planned? (1971), pp. 21-52.

Kohn, Hans. Nationalism: Its Meaning and History. Princeton, Van Nostrand, 1955.

Kolarz, Walter. Myths and Realities in Eastern Europe. London, Lindsay Drummond, 1946.

_____. Russia and her Colonies. Hamden (Conn.), Archon Books, 1967.

Labov, William. The Social Stratification of English in New York City. Washington, CAL, 1965.

_____. Stages in the acquisition of standard English, in Roger W. Shuy (ed.), Social Dialects and Language Learning. Champaign, NCTE, 1966.

Lewis, W. Arthur. Education and economic development. Social and Economic Studies, 1961, 10, No. 2, 113-27.

Li Iiui. The phonetic alphabet—short cut to literacy. Peking Review, 1960, 13, No. 28 (12 July).

Macnamara, John. Successes and failures in the movement for the restoration of Irish, in Rubin and Jernudd (eds.), Can Language Be Planned? (1971), pp. 65-94.

McClusker, Henry F., Jr. An Approach for Educational Planning in the Developing Countries. Menlo Park, Stanford Research Institute, 1963.

McDavid, Raven I. The dialects of American English, in W. N. Francis (ed.), The Structure of American English. New York, Ronald, 1958.

Meyenberg, Ervin. Der heutige Stand der Romazi-Bewegung in Japan. Forschungen und Fortschritte, 1934, No. 10, 23-24.

Mills, H. Language reform in China. The Far Eastern Quarterly, 1956, 15, 517-40.

Nida, Eugene. Practical limitations to a phonemic orthography. Bible Translator, 1953, 5.

_____. Sociological dimensions of literacy and literature, in Shacklock, Floyd, et al. (ed.), World Literacy Manual, ch. 11. New York, Committee on World Literacy and Christian Literature, 1967.

Orenstein, Jacob. Soviet language policy: theory and practice. Slavic and East European Journal, 1959, 17, 1-24.

Ozmen, Yucel. A Sociolinguistic Analysis of Language Reform in Turkey 1932-1967, with Special Reference to the Activities of the Turk Dil Kurumu. MS Thesis, Georgetown University, 1967. (Unpublished)

Pike, Kenneth L. Phonemics: A Technique for Reducing Languages to Writing. Ann Arbor, University of Michigan Press, 1947.

Quelquejay, C. and Bennigsen, A. The Evolution of the Muslim Na-
    tionalities of the USSR and Their Linguistic Problems. Lon-
    don, Central Asian Research Centre, 1961.
Rabin, Chaim. Spelling reform—Israel 1968, in Rubin and Jernudd
    (eds.), Can Language Be Planned? (1971), pp. 95-122.
Radin, Paul. The adoption of an alphabet by an aboriginal people.
    Cambridge University Reporter (Proceedings of the Cam-
    bridge Philological Society), 1924, 25 November, 27-34.
Ray, Punya Sloka. A Single Script for India. Seminar, 1960 (July).
    Language Standardization (ch. 9: Comparative description and
    evaluation of writing systems, pp. 106-20). The Hague,
    Mouton, 1963.
Rossi, Ettore. La questione dell'alfabeto per le lingue turche.
    Oriente Moderno, 1927, 7, 295-310.
_____. Il nuovo alfabeto latino introdotto in Turchia. Oriente
    Moderno, 1929, 9, 32-48 (note: for text of the statute
    changing the alphabet for various types of publications by
    specific dates, see pp. 41-42).
_____. La riforma linguistica in Turchia. Oriente Moderno,
    1935, 15, 45-57.
_____. Un decennio di riforma linguistica in Turchia. Oriente
    Moderno, 1942, 22, 466-77.
_____. Venticinque anni di rivoluzione dell'alfabeto e venti di
    riforma linguistica in Turchi. Oriente Moderno, 1953, 33,
    378-84.
Rubin, Joan, and Jernudd, Bjorn (eds.). Can Language Be Planned?
    Honolulu: University Press of Hawaii, 1971.
Russell, J. K. Starting a literacy campaign. Books for Africa, 1948,
    18 (2), 17-20.
Scharshmidt, Clemens. Schriftreform in Japan: Ein Kulturproblem.
    Mitteilungen des Seminars für Orientalischen Sprachen, 1924,
    26/27, No. 1, 183-86.
Schofield, R. S. The measurement of literacy in pre-industrial
    England, in Jack Goody (ed.), Literacy in Traditional Socie-
    ties. London, Cambridge University Press, 1968.
Serdyuchenko, G. P. The eradication of illiteracy and the creation of
    new written languages in the USSR. Intern. J. of Adult and
    Youth Education, 1962, 14 (1), 23-29.
_____. Elimination of Illiteracy among the People Who Had No
    Alphabets. Moscow, U.S.S.R. Commission for UNESCO,
    Ministry of Education, RSFSR, 1965, 16pp.

Serruys, Paul L-M. Survey of the Chinese Language Reform and the
    Anti-Illiteracy Movement in Communist China (Studies in
    Communist Chinese Terminology, No. 8). Berkeley, Center
    for Chinese Studies, Institute of International Studies, UC-B,
    1962.
Sheldon, George. Status of the Viet Nam. Far Eastern Survey, 1946,
    15, No. 25, 373-77.
Shuy, Roger W. (ed.). Social Dialects and Language Learning. Cham-
    paign, NCTE, 1966.
Sjoberg, Andrée F. Socio-cultural and linguistic factors in the devel-
    opment of writing systems for preliterate peoples, in
    William Bright (ed.), Sociolinguistics. The Hague, Mouton,
    1966, pp. 260-76.
_____. Writing, speech and society: some changing interrela-
    tionships, in Proceedings of the Ninth International Congress
    of Linguists. The Hague, Mouton, 1964, pp. 892-97.
Smalley, William A. Orthography Studies: Articles on New Writing
    Systems. London, United Bible Societies, 1964 ("Help for
    translators," vol. 6).
Smith, Alfred G. Literacy Promotion in an Underdeveloped Area.
    Ph.D. Thesis, University of Wisconsin, 1956.
Thorburn, Thomas. Cost-benefit analysis in language planning,
    in Rubin and Jernudd (eds.), Can Language Be Planned?
    (1971), pp. 253-62.
Troike, Rudolph C. Social dialects and language learning: implica-
    tions for TESOL. TESOL Quarterly, 1968, 2, 176-80.
UNESCO. The Haiti Pilot Project. Paris, UNESCO, 1951.
Vachek, Josef. Written language and printed language. Recueil
    Linguistique de Bratislava, 1948, I, 67-75; reprinted in
    J. Vachek (ed.), A Prague School Reader in Linguistics.
    Bloomington, Indiana University Press, 1964, pp. 453-60.
Vachek, Joseph. Some remarks on writing and phonetic transcrip-
    tion. Acta Linguistica (Copenhagen), 1945-49, 5, 86-93.
Valdman, Albert. Language standardization in a diglossia situation:
    Haiti, in J. A. Fishman, C. A. Ferguson and J. Das Gupta,
    Language Problems of Developing Nations. New York,
    Wiley, 1968, 313-26.
Ward, Ida C. Report of an Investigation of Some Gold Coast Language
    Problems. London, Crown Agents for the Colonies, 1945.

Weinreich, Uriel. The Russification of Soviet minority languages.
    Problems of Communism, 1953, 2 (6), 46-57.
Winner, T. G. Problems of alphabetic reform among the Turkic
    peoples of Soviet Central Asia. Slavonic and East European
    Review, 1952, 132-47.
Wolff, Hans. Nigerian Orthography. Zaria, Gaskiya Corp., 1954.
Wolfram, Walter A. A Sociolinguistic Description of Detroit Negro
    Speech. Washington, CAL, 1969.
Wu Yu-chang. Concerning the draft Han language phonetization plan.
    Current Background, 1956, No. 380, 15 March, 14-20.
    _____. Widening the use of the phonetic script. China Recon-
    structs, 1964, 13, No. 6, 29-31.
    _____. Report of the current tasks of reforming the written lan-
    guage and the draft scheme for a Chinese phonetic alphabet, in
    Reform of the Chinese Written Language. Peking, Foreign
    Language Press, 1965.
Wurm, S. A. Language and literacy, in E. K. Fish (ed.), New
    Guinea on the Threshold. Canberra, ANU, 1966, pp. 135-48.

15 | Bilingual and Bidialectal Education:

An Attempt at a Joint Model for Policy Description

A basic conceptual premise of modern sociology of language/
sociolinguistics is that the functional diversification of the language
repertoire of a speech community can be analyzed along essentially
identical dimensions regardless of the societal views or the nature
of the codes or varieties involved therein. Thus, whether it consists
of several "languages," or whether it consists of several "dialects"
or "sociolects," or whether it consists of both different "languages"
and different "dialects/sociolects," the functional allocation of varieties within the community is felt to be describable in much the same
way. Whether the analysis is in terms of situations and their counterparts or in terms of domains and their counterparts is related
not to any distinction between "languages" on the one hand and "dialects" on the other, but, rather, at best, to the level of analysis required by the researcher for the particular problem under study, or,
at worst, to the level indicated by the limits of his own professional
indoctrination. In either case the distinction between "languages"
and "dialects" is considered to be basically a within-community
functional-evaluative distinction, rather than one that can be made
primarily on the basis of objective external criteria. Certainly a
diachronic view amply supports this approach (revealing any number
of once "mere" dialects, that were subsequently functionally, evalu-
atively and structurally "elevated" to the position of languages, as
well as many cases of the reverse progression), however much a
synchronic view may reveal objective differences between coexisting
languages and dialects with respect to such matters as extent of
elaboration and codification.

Given the foregoing view that all varieties in a community's
repertoire can be subjected to sociolinguistic analysis along identical

dimensions—regardless of the functional-evaluative-structural differences that may characterize them—this paper attempts to examine
the further question as to whether a single integrative model is also
possible with respect to educational policy description when such
policy deals with separate languages on the one hand and with separate
dialects on the other.

A model for bilingual policy description will be examined
first, namely that derived from my paper on "National languages
and languages of wider communication in the developing nations"
(Fishman, 1969). In its initial formulation the model proved to be
useful to me and to some others (Kelman, 1971; Whiteley, 1970) for
the purpose of discussing national language policies in general. On
further examination, this model may hold forth some promise also
for the purposes to be discussed here.

Type A policy formulations with respect to bilingual education transpire in those settings in which educational authorities feel
compelled to select for educational use a language which is not a
mother-tongue within the administrative unit of educational policy
decision (a country, a region, a district, etc.). This is done when
none of the varieties natively available within such units is considered
to be integratively school-worthy, i.e. to correspond to a great tradition of past, present and future integrative authenticity and integrative greatness. Under such circumstances an outside Language of
Wider Communication is selected (at times by popular demand) to
fulfil most educational functions.

The immediate practical consequences of conducting a
school-system in a language which is not the mother tongue of (the
vast majority of) the students are many. The first consequence is
that the Type A policy itself must initially be set aside for the earliest period of education, no matter how brief this may be, so that at
least a minimum of one-way communication (from pupils to teachers)
is possible from the outset. A frequent further consequence is that
teachers too must begin by using the MT of their pupils, or at least,
by being receptively familiar with it and with some of its contrastive
features vis-a-vis the LWC which they must implement. All in all,
however, the bilingual education that results from Type A policy
decisions is minimal and transitional. Even if this stage is recognized

in teacher training or in the preparation of learning and teaching materials the goal is to leave bilingualism behind as soon as possible
in order to transfer all educational efforts to the selected external
LWC. Several countries of West Africa (e.g. Gambia, Sierra Leone)
have made national policy decisions of this type, as have Latin American countries with respect to the education of indigenous regional
Indian populations, as have most host countries with respect to the
education of regionally concentrated immigrant groups, particularly
those of low social standing.

  Further consequences of Type A policy decisions regarding
bilingual education also inevitably flow from the adoption of an external LWC. Since the language adopted is a mother tongue elsewhere
(outside of the administrative unit under consideration), it must be
decided whether the curriculum and standards in effect "there"
should also be implemented "here," or whether indigenously determined content, methods and standards are to be employed. Frequently the former view has prevailed at the outset and the latter
view has been accepted only later and reluctantly. Finally the consequences for adult literacy of Type A policy decisions are clearly
fargoing. Those beyond school age have even greater difficulty in
achieving and retaining literacy in a foreign language than do those
who are still of school age. Even the latter experience difficulty in
both of these respects given the high drop-out rates and the lack of
post-school functional exposure to or reliance upon the school language which mark most settings in which Type A policy decisions are
reached.

  Do Type A policies (which, in effect, restrict bilingual education to the barest minima consistent with transitional goals) have
their counterparts in the area of bi-dialectal education? Obviously
there are many similarities, particularly where social mobility is
low and role repertoires are narrow. Under such circumstances
dialects/ sociolects that are common in other parts of the country/
region/ district may be generally unmastered and non-functional
within particular administrative units. To the extent that the transition to the school variety (D) is unreasonably hurried, and to the
extent that use of other varieties (d1, d2, d3) are considered contra-
educational (contra-cultural, contra-integrative), at the same time
that role expansion is restricted or non-existent, then obviously, an

educational burden is being placed upon those least equipped to carry
it and a barrier to future mobility is being erected against those least
likely to scale it successfully. Such an approach to "non-standard"
dialects is still common in connection with the view of Black English
and Chicano Spanish held by many American school districts, as well
as the views of non-standard French, Spanish, Russian, Hebrew, and
Arabic still common in the countries for which the standard (or classical) versions of these languages are the only ones administratively
recognized.

In none of the above cases is the view widespread that
whereas all schools should teach all students something in D and
some students many things in D, there are also at least some things
that should be taught to all students in d and some students most of
whose education may well be in d rather than in D. The insistence
on D and D only (for all students for all subjects) is potentially non-
functional even though it may be a widely shared view rather than
one imposed from without in many ways. It artificializes education
to the extent that it identifies it with a variety that is not functional
in the life of the community. It threatens the viability of the student's
primary community and of its primary networks to the extent that it
implies that only by leaving his native speech repertoire behind can
the student enter a new role repertoire (and a new reward schedule).
It often causes education to depend upon outsiders to the community—
a veritable army of occupation and pacification on occasion—rather
than permitting it to be a partially shared function across communities or a community controlled function. It tends to impose educational content and methods and standards upon communities that are
not as meaningful or as indigenous or as appealing to pupils as would
be the case if the native life patterns (including the native speech) of
the community were also viewed as school-worthy.

All in all, the similarities between Type A policies when
L1, L2, L3 and LWC are concerned, and Type A policies when d1,
d2, d3 and D are concerned are both great and disturbing. In both
cases local populations are relatively unconsulted and decisions are
commonly made for them by elites marked by broader integrative
philosophies but also by self-status protective interests.

Type B policies at the inter-language level pertain to bilingual education of a somewhat more permissive sort. Type B
policies hold that an internally integrative great tradition does

exist at the unit level. Nevertheless, for one reason or another additional traditions too must be recognized. On the one hand, there may be smaller traditions (i.e. smaller than those that are unit-wide) one or more of which are believed to have their own place and deserve some acknowledgement in the cultural-educational sphere. On the other hand there may (also) be certain larger traditions than those that are unit-wide and these (too) may require (or demand) recognition. All in all, therefore, Type B policies obtain where administrative units do recognize an overriding and indigenous integrative principle, but yet provide for local variation under and beneath or over and above it.

Such might be considered the between-language situation in the Soviet Union (vis-a-vis Russian and, at least, the larger local republic languages), in Mainland China (vis-a-vis common spoken and written Mandarin and at least larger regional languages), in Yugoslavia (vis-a-vis Serbian and the various larger regional languages), in the Philippines (vis-a-vis Tagalog/ Pilipino and the various larger regional languages), and, perhaps, within time, in the USA (vis-a-vis English and the more entrenched minority languages). Certainly such policies result in a series of practical problems of their own. How many and which languages should be recognized and what should be taught in them and for how many years? The fact that bilingualism is not viewed as being merely transitional in nature does not, in and of itself, provide a single answer to such questions. As indicated elsewhere, bilingual education in the monocentric context (and, therefore, normally, for the minority child alone) may still be merely oral or partial rather than full (Fishman and Lovas, 1970).

At the level of between-dialect policy decisions Type B policies certainly also obtain. Once again these policies have a distinct similarity to those that exist at the between language level. Once again there is one variety (D) which is viewed as having indigenous cross-unit validity. Some subjects, it is believed, should be taught in this variety everywhere and to everyone. However, in addition, and particularly in the elementary grades, it is believed that there are also other subjects that may well be taught in various parts of the polity in the local d's that parents, children and school-teachers alike share as the everyday varieties of various social

functions.[1] Only in the upper grades—in schools which are likely
to be regional rather than local in nature—is it expected that almost
everything will be taught in D, but, then, such schools are either not
expected to serve everyone to begin with or, in addition, by the time
students reach them, they will have had eight or more years of time
to master D, at least in writing if not fully in speech.

    The foregoing approaches to bidialectal education is encoun-
tered in most parts of Germany (see Fishman and Lueders, in press),
in most parts of Italy, in most parts of the Netherlands, in many
parts of Norway and Great Britain, in various sections of German-
Switzerland and elsewhere. The burden of acquiring and mastering
D is primarily reserved for the written language and falls primarily
upon those best able to handle it, namely, those with the most education and, therefore, with the expectation of the widest role-repertoire
and with the best chances for real social as well as geographic mobility. Teachers (particularly elementary school teachers) and pupils
are commonly members of the same speech community. The school
is not viewed as a foreign body thrust upon an unwilling local populace, but, rather, as a place in which local speech, local folklore,
local history and local authenticity have their rightful place. However, the local who aspires to the wider role repertoire that is the
mark and the distinction of the professional and the intellectual must
also prepare to rub shoulders with peers from other localities than
his own, and, therefore, he must master D, as well as d1 (or socially
differentiated d1, d2, d3). All communities recognize and respect
D, but all communities also feel themselves to be respected and con-
sulted partners in the overall enterprise which D symbolizes.

    Finally we come to Type C policies with respect to between-
language relationships. In this connection we find that no single
integrating indigenous tradition exists, but, rather, several competing great traditions, each with its numerous and powerful adherents.
Thus, regional differences, far from needing protection or recognition, need, instead, to be bridged or momentarily set aside if the
polity is to survive. It is well recognized that pupils will be educated
in their own mother tongues. The only question is whether they will
also be sufficiently educated in some other tongue that they can use
for communicating with fellow citizens of another mother tongue.

Here bilingual education is of two kinds: sometimes in one or another of the several coequal (and often mutually sensitive) regional languages, and sometimes in an exterior LWC that may appear nonthreatening to all concerned. Such bilingual education is common in Belgium, in Canada, in Switzerland, in India. Sometimes such polities lack a real link language and only a small bilingual elite exists to hold together their multicentricity. Switzerland is an example of how stable even such arrangements can be (although German probably functions as an overall link language more frequently than is officially recognized to be the case).

Type C polities also have their counterparts at the between-dialect level, although these are few in number. Just as there are several polities with locally well entrenched languages, such that each locality must be educationally concerned with teaching a link language for communication with the other localities of the same polity, so there are (or, at least, have been) counterparts of this situation at the between-dialect educational policy level. There are, of course, also polities in which each region teaches in its own dialect without any concern at all for a link-dialect, due to the fact that the dialects themselves are of high mutual understandability and of roughly similar social standing. The United States and several Latin American countries may be said to be in this situation.

In recent years, a noteworthy Type C policy at the inter-dialectal level existed at the height of Norway's efforts to link Riksmål and Landsmål via a manufactured Samnorsk. However, if we go back earlier in history we can find a few more instances of this same type. These are instances from settings in which language standardization was not yet well advanced and vernacular education was primarily regional rather than national. Indeed, wherever vernacular education became well established in advance of unifying political or industrial development (Germany, Italy, Ireland) it was the unifying standard that had to fight for a place in education rather than the regional variant. Nevertheless, such cases tend to be self-liquidating in developing settings. Where a single standard becomes accepted it tends to lead to Type B policies in the bidialectal education field. Where no such standard becomes accepted bidialectalism in education is not a meaningful problem.

Conclusions

        Generally speaking, the same theoretical model of educational
policy decisions may be said to be useful for the description of bilingual as well as for bidialectal education. Indeed, use of such a model
indicates that the same administrative units may well vary with respect to their policies at these two levels. Some units may be very
permissive at one level but entirely non-permissive at others. Thus,
some units are more permissive with respect to dialects than they
are with respect to languages (e. g. German-Switzerland, Italy),
whereas others are more permissive with respect to languages (e. g.
India, where only standard Hindi may be taught even though there are
tens of millions of speakers of regional varieties of Hindi). In addition, the use of a similar model for both kinds of variation renders
more easily comparable any data pertaining to questions regarding
degree (e. g. number of years), curricular content, etc. Once again,
educational units vary widely in these respects when their bilingual
and bidialectal policies are compared. Finally, the use of a single
model for both levels of analysis facilitates comparisons at differing
administrative levels and may make it possible to more quickly compare not only polities with polities and districts with districts, but
also to undertake simultaneous between polity and within polity studies
in order to compare both of these sources of policy variations.

NOTES

This paper was prepared for the Conference on Child Language,
Chicago, November 1971.
        [1] The rejection of this belief underlies all decisions on behalf
of exclusively monodialectal education.

REFERENCES

Fishman, Joshua A. National languages and languages of wider com-
        munication in the developing nations. Anthropological Lin-
        guistics, 1969, 11, 111-35. [In this volume, 191-223.]

Fishman, J. A. and Lovas, John. Bilingual education in socio-
        linguistic perspective. TESOL Quarterly, 1970, 4, 215-22.
_____ and Lueders, Erika. What has the sociology of language
        to say to the teacher? (On teaching the standard variety
        to speakers of dialectal or sociolectal varieties). The Func-
        tions of Language, ed. by Courtney B. Cazden, Vera John
        and Dell Hymes. New York: Teachers College Press, in
        press. [In this volume, pp. 340-55.]
Kelman, Herbert C. Language as aid and barrier to involvement in
        the national system. Can Language Be Planned? ed. by
        Joan Rubin and Bjorn Jernudd, pp. 21-51. Honolulu: East-
        West Center and University of Hawaii Press, 1971.
Whiteley, W. H. Language Use and Social Change. London: Oxford
        University Press, 1970.

16 | What Has the Sociology of Language to Say to the Teacher?

(On Teaching the Standard Variety to Speakers of Dialectal or Sociolectal Varieties)

In Collaboration with Erika Luders

The major focus of American linguistic and sociolinguistic attentions vis-à-vis the American educational scene has recently gravitated toward the problems of teaching standard English to speakers of Black English. Whereas the frontier scholars and teachers in this undertaking are engaged in structural and historical studies of Black English and White English, those who are closer to the barricades of daily classroom instruction are largely involved in two other pursuits. On the one hand, instructional materials must be prepared for students of varying ages, abilities and degrees of distance from standard English (and teachers and parents must be taught how to use and evaluate these materials). On the other hand, parents, teachers and administrators, Black and White, must be prepared, cognitively and emotionally, to handle the very concepts of "Black English" and "White English" and to consider their implications for our schools and our society.

In the latter connection an aspect of American provincialism that bars our way toward intelligent decision making is our abysmal ignorance with respect to the sociology of language in general and toward its international and diachronic manifestations in particular. Our problems always strike us as so unparalleled that we rarely grasp their general significance, their general position in human experience, and, as a result, we rarely understand the answers to our problems even when we are fortunate enough to find such.

Cross-national perspective

Having smugly cut ourselves off from our immigrant origins
and from our religious and ethnic roots, the rest of the world has a
benighted existence for us, at best, when we are faced with an educational problem which has international significance. Given a moment's thought it is quite apparent that most of the world's schoolchildren (rather than our Black children alone) are not taught to read
and write the same language or language variety that they bring with
them to school from their homes and neighborhoods. Indeed, if this
phenomenon is viewed historically, then the discrepancy between
home language and school language increases dramatically the further
we go back in time into periods that predate the vernacularization
of education and mass education itself. And yet, no American educational scholar or planner or leader seems to have shown any curiosity
about this at all.

Given our current failure to teach Black children to read or
write or speak standard English is there anything to be learned from
the German experience of teaching standard German to speakers of
regional German varieties? Is there anything to be learned from
similar experiences with non-standard speakers—many of them obviously socially and culturally disadvantaged—that typify Italian education, Spanish education, Chinese education, Soviet Education, etc?
Whereas we have only discovered our speakers of Black English a
few years ago—when their needs could no longer be ignored and their
anger could no longer be contained—other countries have been aware
of their regionally/socially different students for generations. Is
there nothing that we can learn from their experiences? Let us
briefly examine one such case, the German, and see.

For a German who grew up in the 50's speaking a dialect it
would sound strange to note several aspects of the discussion of
Black English that has been carried on so heatedly during the past
several years by language scholars and language teachers in the
United States. Even though the complaints against the German school
system were and are at least as manifold as are the complaints
against the American school system in the USA, the category "com-
plaint about dialect-only speaking graduates" is and was almost

entirely absent in Germany. This might lead to the impression that
all or most German youngsters, after eight or nine years of schooling
can speak an acceptable High German, i.e., at least High German
with no more than a minor local accent. If this is really the case the
comparison to Black ghetto youth who after ten years of schooling
cannot speak standard English would justifiably prompt the question:
"Why do we accomplish so much less with our dialect speakers here
in the USA?"

    First of all, let us ask, if it is true, that all or most German
students can speak High German with "no more than a minor local
accent" by the time they graduate from elementary school.

The Schwaben region and the Schwaebisch varieties

    We will mainly consider the area around Stuttgart called
Schwaben, where the schwaebische (Swabian) dialect is spoken. If
we are to compare ghetto Black students with the Swabian students
around Stuttgart with any degree of validity we must, of course,
attempt to hold constant various variables that pertain to language
learning, e.g., social class and overall scholastic achievement. If
we look for a comparable sample in Schwaben, we find it most easily
in the small rural villages. Narrowing our comparison down to this
subsample of students, one quickly becomes uncertain about the general impression reported above, that most German students who
have completed elementary school speak an acceptable High German.

    What is the criterion for "acceptable"? Even today we still
meet a small percentage of young people in the Swabian villages who
can speak their local dialect only and who become mute and embarrassed if they are requested to speak High German. If it is absolutely
required, their speech becomes slow and very artificial with much
functional and structural hypercorrection. If this population is examined as carefully as the Black ghetto youngster has been in the USA
it is very doubtful that the German school system is more successful
in teaching High German to disadvantaged speakers of regional German than the US system is in teaching standard English to its disadvantaged pupils.

Nevertheless, the schwäbische dialect speaking children—even those in rural villages—are eventually able to express themselves in a higher dialect (H) than that which they originally learned at home, from family and friends. However, a small minority of Schwäbisch speaking people ever reach the point where they can hide their Swabian background. This statement (based upon our own observations) is in direct contrast to Leopold who claims that: "now it is often difficult or impossible to detect which region an educated speaker comes from" (1968, p. 362). Leopold may have been unduly influenced by dislocated German speakers or by German speakers stemming from northern rather than southern regions. Rahn, on the other hand, does not hesitate to write: "Man wird behaupten koennen, dass kein Schwabe, der nicht eine gruendliche Spracherziehung genossen hat, in der Lage ist, Woerter wie 'Undank, Anbetung, ausreiten'.... so zu sprechen, dass man nicht sogleich den Schwaben in ihm erkennt" (1962, p. 28). Indeed, we find in Schwaben a <u>continuum</u> of different varieties of Schwäbisch, whereas there seems to be much more of a break between, for example, the Black English spoken in the Oakland ghetto and the English of native white Californians in the same city.

Rahn (1962), and most others, distinguishes five varieties of Schwäbisch, namely:
1. Grundschicht: Bauernsprache (p. 86)
2. Obere Grundschicht: Provinzielle Umgangssprache (p. 12)
3. Mittlere Städtische Sprachschicht: württembergische Umgangssprache (p. 21)
4. Obere städtische Sprachschicht: Honoratiorenschwäbisch (p. 18)
5. Einheitssprache: Schwäbisch getoentes Hoch- oder Schriftdeutsch (which is quite close to 6. Hochsprache: mundartfreie Bühnensprache, p. 8).
With these five varieties (examples of which have been reproduced in the appendix) it is easier to indicate what one means by "poor High German" or "acceptable High German."

Somewhat in accord with Leopold's observations is our own that variety one seems to be dying out slowly. But varieties two to five are still very much alive. Nor should these be viewed as merely minor departures from standard German for the following reasons:

1. A visitor from North Germany would not be able to understand
when the Schwaben talk variety two or three to each other.
2. The appendix examples of the different varieties demonstrate
clearly enough that their pronounciation is very different from that of
standard German.
3. There are many lexical and grammatical differences which must
confuse every outsider. A little poem expresses this nicely:

> Wer ist das ?
> Er hat keine Beine, bloss Fuesse.
> Wenn er geht, dann lauft er.
> Wenn er lauft, dann springt er.
> Wenn er springt, dann hopft er.
> Und wenn er rennt, dann saut er... (Rahn 1962, p. 29)

How are the more formal varieties of Schwäbisch acquired ?
How is standard German acquired ? There is among the Schwaben
a very small minority of highly educated and peripatetic individuals
(by no means a speech community) who can, if they want to, disguise
in their speech their schwäbisch background. A much larger group
are those in business, education, administration and so forth, who
can easily speak variety five, a "schwäbisch getoentes Hoch- oder
Schriftdeutsch." However, these people usually fall back to variety
four when they are among friends or at home. Honoratiorenschwäbisch is also the variety that most people, who usually speak variety
one, two or three, can speak if they are in a sufficiently demanding,
formal situation. And then we have, especially in the rural area, a
small minority who cannot speak anything but the local variety one or
two of Schwäbisch. Generally speaking, there is little overt educational concern about these limited-repertoire speakers.

This leaves us with two questions to raise if we compare the
Swabian situation to that in the USA.
1. Why is there almost no concern over the minority group which
cannot switch into any higher variety of Schwäbisch ?
2. How are the majority of Swabian children (who come from variety
one, two or three homes and communities) taught to speak the higher
varieties of Schwäbisch and standard German as well ?

Question one is fairly easy to answer. Most of the students
who are not able to speak Honoratiorenschwäbisch are to be found in

the small villages. These students are the most likely to learn a
simple trade or go into farming and to stay in the general area in
which they were born. In this way they are perfectly capable of supporting themselves and, later on, of supporting a family. Their dialect is no social barrier since it is the local dialect, generally used
and respected by all. The situation for the ghetto boy is quite different. Since there are not enough jobs in the ghetto he has to go outside in order to be self-supporting—and, thus, is immediately outside of his home dialect. The dialect speaker in Germany on the
other hand, finds himself as one of a large "Gemeinschaft" of people
who all speak the dialect to each other in at least some contexts. The
sophistication of a speaker is indicated not by whether he speaks dialect but by the ease and the completeness with which he switches to a
higher variety in appropriate contexts. The speaker of Black English
however speaks an outcast's variety as soon as he steps across the
boundary of the ghetto. Since many Black students are aware of the
fact that their dialect is not accepted in the white community, one can
in turn understand their growing hostility towards standard English
and their growing ideological defense of Black English.

In Schwaben it is considered very desirable to be able to
speak High German. Students know that they need to be able to read
and write High German in order to get a good job. They also know
that the more honored people in the community don't speak variety
one Schwäbisch—but these same honored people still speak Schwäbisch
rather than standard German! It is only recently that Black English
has gotten this same recognition from more successful sectors of the
Black community and, indeed, has begun to be acknowledged for general instructional purposes in some ghetto schools. All in all, however, Black English is still often a sign of rebellion or of identity-
manifestation whereas Schwäbisch is a much more ordinary aspect of
every day school life.

Regional German and Standard German in the classroom: the theory

Being in front of a class of Schwäbisch speaking children,
interspersed here and there with a foreign child and with a few children
speaking other dialects, what does the teacher do to make the children
comfortable in speaking Honoratiorenschwäbisch? A pattern is

346 Language in Sociocultural Change

followed which does not at all involve a stagewise progression from
regional Schwäbisch material to standard texts (one suggestion currently espoused by some American students of Black English) but,
rather, which involves the recognition of diglossia and of the functional differences between regional and standard German. This may
be illustrated by quoting from a teacher training text which is a century old and has a chapter entitled "Das Hochdeutsch sollte gelehrt
werden im Anschluss an die Volkssprache oder Haussprache." In
this chapter the author compares High German to Latin and continues:
"Ganz so ist aber das alte Verfahren beim deutschen Unterrichte
noch heutzutage, und wo man davon abweicht und zu einer Beachtung
der Volkssprache sich herbeilaesst, da geschieht es wie dort durch
den Zwang der Verhältnisse oder aus einer Anwandlung des Gefühls,
oft wohl widerwillig und unwillig, aber nicht aus Grundsatz und
geflissentlich. So tritt dann auch das Hochdeutsch den Kindern nicht
als etwas entgegen, das die von ihnen mitgebrachte Sprache aufheben,
bei Seite schieben, sich an ihre Stelle setzen soll—oder eigentlich
noch schärfer: selbst eine Beziehung zwischen beiden ist so zu
sagen amtlich nicht anerkannt in der Schule, Denn das Hochdeutsche
ist ja eine Schriftsprache, sie schreiben zu können das höchste Ziel
des Schülers; was hat aber die Mundart mit der Schrift zu tun! das
wäre ja, wenn sichs um vollen Ernst handelte, eine Entweihung der
edlen Buchstaben, mögen auch vornehme Leute sich hie und da den
Spass machen. ...Einem Dorfschullehrer ist das Hochdeutsch sein
Latein und er steht damit dem Deutsch, das seine Buben reden, in
demselben ueberlegenen Hochgefühl gegenüber wie der Lateinlehrer
früher seinen Elementarschülern. ...das Hochdeutsch darf nicht als
ein Gegensatz zur Volkssprache gelehrt werden, sondern man muss
es dem Schüler aus dieser hervorwachsen lassen; das Hochdeutsch
darf nicht als verdrängender Ersatz der Volkssprache auftreten,
sondern als eine veredelte Gestalt davon, gleichsam als Sonntagskleid
neben dem Werktagskleid" (Hildebrand 1903, pp. 67-68).

Hildebrand's four principles of teaching German are still
taught to teachers today:

> 1. Der Sprachunterricht soll mit der Sprache zugleich
> den Inhalt der Sprache, ihren Lebensgehalt voll und
> frisch und warm erfassen. 2. Der Lehrer des Deutschen
> soll nichts lehren, was die Schüler selbst aus sich finden
> können, sondern alles das sie unter seiner Leitung

finden lassen. 3. Das Hauptgewicht soll auf die ges-
prochene und gehörte Sprache gelegt werden, nicht auf
die geschriebene und gesehene. 4. Das Hochdeutsch
als Ziel des Unterrichts soll nicht als etwas für sich
gelehrt werden, wie ein anderes Latein, sondern im eng-
sten Anschluss an die in der Klasse vorfindliche Volkssprache oder Haussprache. (Rutt 1963, p. 222).

Long before Hildebrand the demand was made clear by various German educators, especially by Lorenz Kellner, that German
should only be taught in connection with the spoken language. Indeed,
after the influence of Hildebrand the formal teaching of German was
abolished completely for a while by Gansberg and Scharrelmann who
cared about content only. The formal teaching of German recovered
quickly however with Seidemann who prepared the first complete
methods series on teaching standard German for the grades one to
ten. However, he ignored the dialects almost completely. The only
times "Mundart" is mentioned in his book is where he says: "Jeder
beherrscht einen andern Abschnitt aus der gemeinsamen Muttersprache,
hat je nach Altersatufe, Bildungsgrad und landschaftlicher Zugehörig-
keit seine besondere 'Mundart' " (Seidemann 1963, p. 36) and "Der
Sprachunterricht muss das Kind frei machen von der Sprache des
Herkommens, die ihm gleichwohl seinen Wortschatz liefert" (Seidemann 1963, p. 37).

The idea that the child had to be freed from the language so
that he would be the master of the language has been carried on by
Weisgerber. He states several times that the teacher must guard
against producing a student..."der sich vorwiegend passiv von der
Muttersprache prägen lasst" (Weisgerber 1950, p. 92). But he
acknowledges that..."Beherrschtwerden durch die Muttersprache
liegt dem Beherrschen der Muttersprache zugrunde" (Weisgerber
1964, p. 145). He warns with strong works against any forcing of
the child as far as his language is concerned..."Einbruch in das
muttersprachliche Wachstum" (Weisgerber 1964, p. 154). Mastery
of the language cannot be forced. He demands of the school: "Was
der Sprachunterricht dabei soll, ist dem Grundsatz nach ganz offen-
sichtlich: aus der doppelten Einsicht in den Aufbau des muttersprach-
lichen Weltbildes und in die geistige Entwicklung des Kindes die
Sprachmittel bereitstellen, die dem Kinde zu seinem sprachlichen

Wachstum jeweils notwending und förderlich sind; sie dem Kinde so
nahe bringen, dass es sie in einem echten Nachaffen sich aneignet;
das Ergebnis des natürlichen Sprachwachsens an der rechten Stelle
so klären und ergänzen, dass diese Sprachmittel nun wirklicher
Besitz sind" (Weisgerber 1950, p. 31). Weisgerber doesn't give concrete examples, but based on his principles one can justify dialect in
the classroom, since this is where the child is. From here, largely
through fun and games, the vocabulary is to be slowly enlarged and
the child guided to the standard variety. Thus, the emphasis on the
spoken word over reading and writing has been a constant in German
education for at least the past century.

Regional German and Standard German in the classroom: from theory into practice

Even the strictest teachers in Schwaben never push students
to speak High German in class discussion. However, there are quite
a few drills in speaking High German through many recitations of
proverbs, songs and poems. In such a literary context standard
German does not sound "phony" to the child but "in place." Young
children also play at "being building blocks for a story." Here each
child is responsible for adding one sentence to a story in High German. In this way the child learns to use High German—but doesn't
have to employ it in spontaneous speech.

High German is also constantly taught when the child learns
how to read, since none of the German primers are in dialect. Actually it is quite hard for any German to read little stories written in
dialect. The naturally spoken language just isn't the written one.
The junior author of this paper learned most of her best High German
pronounciation when she started to sing in a choir. Again, here the
participants had fun pronouncing the words correctly, since to their
own ears a choir, singing in dialect, just didn't sound right. Low
ability students caught on to this very quickly too. It was usually
enough to sing once demonstratively "...es druckten ihn die die Sorga
schwär, ar suchte neies Land em Mär" to have them all unified in
correct "...es drükten ihn die Sorgen schwer, er suchte neues Land
im Meer."

It does not seem necessary for a teacher in Schwaben to speak the dialect herself but, rather, merely to accept the children's spontaneous speech for the above result to obtain. Of course, it does not <u>harm</u> the quality of her student's speech if she speaks Honoratiorenschwäbish most of the time. However, she should also be able to speak variety five—and do so from time to time as appropriate—so that the students have a proper model to follow in their repertoire acquisition.

Repertoire expansion and repertoire retention

Most Swabian students who do not go to the Gymnasium (and fewer than half do) never experience any conflict between regional and standard German. They are well accepted with no higher variety than Honoratiorenschwäbisch. The only ones that <u>do</u> experience any such conflict are the better educated students. Most of them finally manage variety five, but they rarely feel fully comfortable in it. They usually fall back into Honoratiorenschwäbisch when they are among friends. Thus, it is not the ordinary student who faces a problem but, rather, the more accomplished one. However, he is also more able to handle this problem, if it really becomes serious, via special courses, travel, etc. Finally, it should be clear that the regional varieties remain both strong as well as functionally differentiated themselves. Varieties two and three particularly are surrounded by emotional and primary experiences and relationships that none would forego. Certainly the Black ghetto child should not have to forego his verbal links to spontaneity and familiarity. If other Americans can learn to accept him as he is linguistically and socioculturally there is no reason why he should not be able to learn other varieties of English as well for particular functions and relationships. The learning gap is on <u>both</u> sides of the ghetto wall, rather than merely on one or the other.

Verbal repertoire and functional differentiation

Clearly, one of the central notions that is required in order to ponder the foregoing discussion of regional German-standard German experience is that of <u>verbal repertoire.</u> In the broader

Swabian area a five (or six) variety repertoire exists and all of the varieties in this repertoire are considered "OK" by the larger speech
community, provided each is kept by and large in its own place. American teachers are still largely innocent of this elementary fact of the
sociology of language, namely, that speech communities characteris-
tically exhibit verbal repertoires and that the varieties in these repertoires are functionally differentiated—rather than merely linguistically so—in accord with societally established and reinforced norms
of communicative appropriateness. Indeed, American teachers (and
parents and administrators) are by and large still mesmerized by the
fiction that there is only one proper kind of English for all purposes
and that it alone should be allowed to cross the threshold of the classroom. American teachers still insist that they themselves only talk
one kind of English, the right kind, and that this is the only kind to
which their charges should be exposed.

Written language—spoken language

     The distinction between the written language and the spoken
language is obviously easier to grasp in a context such as the German
(where the varieties involved are so different from each other) than
in the white American. Nevertheless, that alone does not explain the
German willingness to accept the spoken language for most school
discussion purposes, nor does it explain the widespread American
insistence on the written language as the proper model for communications to and from the teacher. Of course, both these matters can
be explained as a result of particular socio-historical experiences
but that is not our task here. It should be sufficient here to say that
German regional approach not only reveals more sociolinguistic
sensitivity and toleration on the part of teachers but that it seems to
foster such as well. The child and the adult deserve to have and to
hold their home speech. The home and regional speech can be used
for many purposes in school as well. The standard language has
serious functions, but it can be enjoyably learned and unashamedly
restricted to its prescribed prerogatives.

Regional is neither wrong nor funny

     Not only is regional or non-standard "schoolworthy" but it
has several varieties itself. Thus, the distinction is not between two

straw men, an exaggeratedly pure or correct standard on the one hand
and an impossibly gross and barbarous non-standard on the other.
Indeed, regional speech can boast varieties which are more frequently
associated with local formal events, ceremonies and interactions
than can the standard. The mayor, the priest, the doctor and the
teacher utilize the highest forms of the regional speech in their
formal capacities and in their official roles, thereby placing the regional repertoire within the pale of sanctity rather than reserving
that pale for the standard alone. Indeed, more opprobrium would be
attached to a would-be local dignitary who could not command variety
four or five than to be one who could not control variety six in speech.
Thus, the respect attached to varieties of regional speech makes it
easier to avoid pressures to necessarily read and write the regional
varieties—or to start with primers in these varieties—in order to
either defend regional dignity or to recognize the child as he is or to
making learning easier.

Contextual markers vs. demographic stereotypes

In White eyes Black English not only stamps one as Black
but as lower class Black. It is taken to be a demographic marker of
basically one-variety speakers. It does not occur to the teacher that
the speakers of Black English may really control other varieties of
English as well or that Black English itself is subdivisible into several varieties. Thus Black English is a stereotype that represents
a certain kind of person, all of him, all of the time. Regional German on the other hand is not a demographic stereotype at all, certainly not within the area of its use. Rather, it is a contextual marker
standing for a particular kind of situational or metaphorical content,
depending on the particular regional variety being employed from one
speech act or event to another. Whites in general and White teachers
in particular are not accustomed to viewing speakers of Black English
in anywhere near such subtle, contextual terms.

Speech community

Contextual shifting from one variety to another within a verbal repertoire and the correct and effortless interpretation of the

communicative significance of such switching is the undeniable sign
of the existence and the functional operation of a speech community.
Teachers and pupils in regional Germany are usually co-members of
the same speech community. They accept and implement common
norms of communicative appropriateness, whether these pertain to
the use of regional variety three, regional variety four or standard
German itself. Teachers and pupils in our Black ghetto school are
most often not members of the same speech community. They do not
share common norms of communicative appropriateness. They do
not engage in or even fully recognize each other's verbal repertoires.
They do not have common norms vis-à-vis the use of standard English
on the one hand or of Black English on the other. What is a contextual marker for the one is a demographic stereotype for the other and
vice versa. One imposes communications upon the other rather than
engage in joint contextual shifting.

Should Black children be taught to read and write Black English ?

         If the parallel question were asked in regional Germany the
answer would be "no." Regional German is not for reading and writing, as far as the indigenous diglossia system is concerned. Over a
period of years a variety of German that no one uses conversationally
is slowly and enjoyably learned so that it can be used for reading and
writing (and certain singing and reciting), and those who go higher in
society learn this variety better than do others. Throughout the
school experience, however, more attention is given to educating
children and to encouraging them to express themselves clearly,
forcefully and effectively than to standard German reading and writing
or formal language skills as a whole. Seemingly "getting educated"
and "learning standard German" are not considered to be one and the
same.

         Would such an approach to standard and non-standard lan-
guage varieties work in our ghetto schools ? Perhaps so, if teachers
and students and parents and administrators more frequently constituted a single speech community and, furthermore, if substantial role
relationships and networks involving standard English were really
available to ghetto adolescents and adults, either within their own
speech communities or in neighboring ones. Under such circumstances

it would obviously be disfunctional to teach reading and writing of Black English. Instead of sharing a variety with the White world and instead of using this variety for some of the same functions as it has in the White world the Black and the White verbal repertoires would become even more discontinuous, linguistically and functionally, than they are today. The interacting relationship between language and social behavior being what it is, such discontinuity would not only reflect the social distance between Blacks and Whites but it would further reinforce and extend this distance as well. Perhaps this is the ultimate lesson that we must derive from the cross-national examination of sociolinguistic processes: if we are to foster a broader speech community we must safeguard not only the internal vitality and legitimacy of its smaller sub-communities but also their links with each other (Fishman, in press).

REFERENCES

Fishman, Joshua A. The sociology of language: an interdisciplinary social science approach to sociolinguistics, Current Trends in Linguistics 12, ed. by T. A. Sebeok, The Hague, Mouton, in press.

Hildebrand, Rudolf. Vom deutschen Sprachunterricht in der Schule. Verlag von Julius Klinkhardt, Leipzig, 1903, Achte, durchgesehene Auflage.

Leopold, Werner. The decline of German dialects, in Fishman, J. A., ed., Readings in the Sociology of Language. The Hague: Mouton, 1968, pp. 340-364. Originally published in Word, 1959, 15, 130-153.

Rahn, Fritz. Der schwäbische Mensch und seine Mundart. Hans E. Günther Verlag Stuttgart, 1962.

Rutt, Theodor. Didaktik der Muttersprache. Verlag Moritz Diesterweg Frankfurt, Berlin, Bonn, 1963.

Seidemann, Walther. Der Deutschunterricht als innere Sprachbildung. Quelle und Meyer, Heidelberg, 1963, sechste Auflage.

Weisgerber, Leo. Das Tor zur Muttersprache. Pädagogischer Verlag Schwann, Düsseldorf, 1950.

Weisgerber, Leo. Das Menschheitsgesetz der Sprache. Quelle und Meyer, Heidelberg, 1964, zweite, neubearbeitete Auflage.

APPENDIX

Examples of Varieties of Schwäbisch

All examples are from Rahn (1962)

I, p. 86:   (Bauer und Bäuerin unterhalten sich über die Werbung des
            Jungbauern Karl um ihre Tochter)
            Bauer: Om s Kathrele hot er gfroget, der Karl.
            Bäuerin: I hao s no ghairt. —Om s Kathrele! —Dussa
            stohts ond heulet, —so graoss es isch.
            Bäuerin: Brauchscht e Weib, Karl—s ischt wohr.
            Brauchscht naitech e Weib. —Aber was soll mer sa:—
            zwenga ka' mer s et.

II, p. 12:   (Becka ond Becka)
            Wo em Becka Schlumberger sei' Denschtmädle gmerkt hot,
            dass ihr Bauch jeden Tag a bissle dicker wird, hot se dr
            Schlumberger an dr Hand gnomma ond hot so tröschtet:
            "Butz dei' Na's, Luisle! Du brauchsch koi Angscht hau.'
            I zahl alles. Bloss muescht mr versprecha, dass de koim
            Mensche saisch, wer dr Vatter isch."
            Ond wie s no ghoissa hot, dass s Luisle en Buebe kriegt
            hab, isch dr Beck en d Fraueklinik nuff ond hot se bsuecht,
            Aber glei zairscht hot er se gfrogt, ob se au gwiiss neamer
            gaait hab... se wiss scho' was. Aber s Luiale hot bloss
            gschluchzt: "O moischtr, uf Ehr ond Seligkeit, i hau's
            koim Menscha gsait, aber di Herra wisset halt alles. Die
            sehets de Kender von ausse-n-a', wer dr Vatter isch."
            "Domms Zeug," sait dr Beck, "bild dr no'nex ei'. Woher
            sollet s au die Herra wissa, wenn du nex gsait hosch!"
            "Doch, se wisset s! I hau' s selber ghairt. Wo dr Pro-
            fesser zu Visitt komme-n-isch, hot ehn dr Oberazt: glei
            an der Tür zu mir gwiesa ond hot gsait: Do henta leit des
            Madle mit dem kloina Becka. Ond no haun-e au nemme
            verleugna-kenna."

III, p. 21:   (Schiffsschaukel)
            Meire' Lebtag han-e d Tante in Keire' so Aufregugn gsehe'
                Wia an sellem Mittag, an eme' Johrmarkt isch gwä:
            Alles hot zitteret an re' bis nauf zu der Feder am Hüatle,

Ond noch Luft hot se geschnappt wia e' heniger Fisch.
"Jesesmariaondjosef! was ist den passiert ond was fehlt
dr?"—"I ka' nemme, i muass zersto' verschnaufe' e'
Weil...Wisseter, wer in der Stadt ist: der Fritz! Mit
eigene Auge'

Han-e se gsehe' dia Schand, drausse' beim Turnhalle-
platz: Mittle' onter de Bude'—ond Karre'leut hot r sei'
Schaukel

Ond auf em Schild an der Kass ausgschemmt de' Name
debei!

IV, p. 18:   (Der Traum)
D Frau Pfarrer hat emal Bsuch kriegt von dr Bachbäure.
Die hat sich ebe immer so scheniert bei de bessere Leut.
Aber d Pfarrerfrau hat ihr a Gläsle Wei hi'gstellt und hat
so e recht freundliches Gespräch mit ihr a'gfanga:

"Heut nacht hat mr s übrigens von Ihne träumt, denket
Se nur!"

"Oms Himmels Wille, Frau Pfarrer! Dees war aber
doch <u>mei</u> Plicht ond Schuligkeit gwä...!"

Author's Postscript

The appearance of a volume such as this provides an opportunity for personal reflection ("stock-taking" would be a more mundane term for what I have in mind), not unlike the personal soul-
searching at the time of the annual High Holidays. Having devoted so
much time and effort to the sociology of language during the past
decade, time and effort taken from my family, my friends and my
associates in other than sociolinguistic pursuits, it is fitting to pause
to ask: "What has it all amounted to, and has it really been worthwhile?" Such questions, particularly when put in public, are likely
to prompt answers which are either heavy with sentiment or self-
congratulatory. I would like to avoid both of these pitfalls, and yet
not avoid either the questions themselves or the feeling-dimension
to which they obviously pertain.

I consider it to be the profoundest good fortune that the
sociology of language arose as a serious interest within a sector of
the American social science scene at exactly the time that it did. I
had been searching for it, thirsting for it, during my undergraduate,
graduate and early professional years, and, all of a sudden, there it
was. After the loneliness of giving a course in the sociology of language (University of Pennsylvania, 1959-60) and seeming to be the
only person in the country to be doing so at that time, after the an-
xiety of directing a major research project in the sociology of language (The Language Resources Project, 1960-63) and finding that
co-fellows at the Center for Advanced Study in the Behavioral Sciences
still "couldn't quite figure it out" in terms of where it (and I) belonged
academically, there it was, practically full-blown. The Social Science Research Council's Committee on Sociolinguistics, its summer
seminar at Indiana University (1964), the fellowship of colleagues
and students, a plentitude of research grants, conferences and study

leaves, all of these appeared at exactly the right time for me—intellectually, emotionally and professionally. Today, in a vastly different period of American and world-wide academic opportunity, I cannot help but look back in amazement at what the past decade was like, and in humility, at what more it might have been. But, by any odds, it was a good decade in which to be a young American social science professor interested "in something new. "

The interest started much earlier, of course. It started with a childhood as a member of a family and of a struggling speech community to which few things mattered as much as keeping the Yiddish language alive, and well, enriching it, ennobling it, liberating it of the linguistic and social impediments set up against it by conscious and unconscious enemies and opponents, at home and abroad. It started, even more germanely for academic work, with parents and teachers who encouraged me to intellectualize and extrapolate from the daily pains and pleasures of the all-engrossing struggle for creative Yiddish-English societal bilingualism to more generally relevant theoretical questions and answers. Starting from such origins it is no longer any wonder that "small languages" everywhere are my particular passion and that their stable functional complimentarity with "wider languages" (yes, even with the very widest) is my particular joy. Neither the doubts of advisors as to whether "any such field" existed, nor the concern of friends as to whether one could really "make one's way" under such a flag, ever succeeded in making me doubt that I and the sociology of language were created for each other.

The past decade has witnessed many striking successes in revising general understanding of language in society. I have been privileged, indeed, to be associated with a cadre of brilliant and dedicated colleagues and students whose work essentially underlies and leads to these revisions. Thus, instead of fixing our gaze upon languages per se, we now recognize language use as the variable of primary interest. We recognize the concurrent variability in such use as underlying both the functional change and the structural change which diachronic study reveals across periods of sociocultural flux. We recognize that speech networks organize on behalf of those particular functional and structural designata that they favor on cognitive and affective-symbolic grounds. What's more we recognize that such

activity, far from being without issue, frequently succeeds, both
linguistically and socioculturally. Thus, in the period of a decade,
we have come to see that language behavior is social behavior, both
in its pattern and in its variability; that language change can often be
observed in operation (or, at least, that its catalytic change-agents
can be specified linguistically and socially); indeed, that such change
is often desired, planned and effectuated. All in all, these revisions
amount to a major reformulation of what language is as a societal
variable and of what society does to it and with it. I am grateful
indeed (and particularly to those who have previously been honored
by volumes in the LRGP Language Science and National Development
Series) for the inspiration and the forbearance of many associates
in the common struggle (sometimes with each other, and sometimes
with traditional orthodoxies) that we have waged so that these newer
views might become more generally known, demonstrated and accepted.

        And yet, some of the successes that were dreamed about
during this formative decade have eluded us. We have not succeeded
in making linguistic training a part of the general preparation of
social scientists, nor in making social science training part of the
general preparation of linguists. Thus, the generation of our students,
and of theirs, will have to struggle with each other out of partial
ignorance of their joint patrimony, very much as we did ourselves.
That struggle adds insight and poignancy and even depth to that which
is ultimately learned, of course, but it is often a pity none the less.
The truly interdisciplinary sociolinguistic scholar will ultimately
arise, because he must, and will be no more considered an "odd-ball"
when he appears than does the biochemist, the astrophysicist or the
social psychologist. My experience in the Language and Behavior
Ph.D. program at Yeshiva University (1966-1972) has convinced me
of the soundness of such a goal, as well as of its reasonable attaina-
bility, given the genuine good will of the parent disciplines and scholars devoted to it.

        I view with even greater regret the lack of impact that the
sociology of language has had on sociology as such. The ultimate
preparation of genuinely interdisciplinary specialist cannot come from
one discipline alone and as long as sociology fails to see language
behavior (its dimensions, processes and problems) as fundamental

aspects of society's dimensions, processes and problems, we are all definitely the weaker, linguists, sociologists and hybrids alike. Certainly, were I more of a teacher, more of an organizer of academic efforts beyond the cultivation of the research and theory dear to me, I would dedicate myself to this particular task during the decade ahead with more confidence than I can now muster.

As it is, I must appeal to colleagues and students, particularly those in sociology, to carry the brunt of this burden. Now that we have breached the fortress of linguistics, to the point that it recognizes socialized speech (rather than the abstractly perfect code-structure it so loved to envisage) we must now organize a full-fledged attack on sociology in order to cause it to recognize the role of speech in the basic stuff of all social processes. If we will but note how psycholinguistics has contributed to and become part and parcel of psychology during the past two decades we cannot help but realize how far we are still from such a state of affairs vis-à-vis the relationship between the sociology of language and sociology proper. This I consider to be the primary task of the decade ahead. Unless it is attained our accomplishments of the past decade will soon be doubly shallow. If the present collection will have any impact in so far as interesting students of sociology in the sociology of language, then I will consider this to be an achievement of particular note. Actually, only if sociologists of various "persuasions" (topical and methodological) are attracted to the field will the sociology of language truly come of age and claim its birthright. Whereas "Sociolinguistics" may be satisfied with either reforming (Labov) or with revolutionizing (Hymes) linguistics, the sociology of language is after quite different goals. It seeks to understand society and societal processes, and to reveal such processes and language behavior as inextricably intertwined. Because that has been my goal I am all the more sensitive to the distance that still separates me from it and the sociological comradeship that I require if it is ever to be reached.

As far as this volume itself is concerned, I am, of course, indebted to Anwar Dil for having conceived of it and for seeing it through to completion. It mirrors, far better than I would have imagined possible within a restricted number of pages, my interests and efforts during the past decade. If there are any areas which remain somewhat neglected (for example, the area of Jewish concern,

which, frankly, is always creatively strong in all of my thinking and
in much of my writing as well, as well as the preference for empirical data quantitatively analyzed, which has always been fundamental
to my social-psychological conceptualization of research data and
research demonstration) these can be reconstituted from my bibliography that Dr. Dil has kindly appended. I owe him a debt of gratitude,
for his friendship and his zeal. It is no mean thing for any scholar
to receive as a gift a published selection of his central writings. It
is particularly touching for me to receive such a gift from a Pakistani
scholar and from the Linguistic Research Group of Pakistan. It is
all the more meaningful for it to come to pass in conjunction with
Stanford University, where I have repeatedly formed such deep bonds,
both with colleagues, students and nature itself. Perhaps, then, it
is more than my admitted penchant for unity in science and in all of
life to hope that this bringing together of so many meaningful ingredients in one whole is a sign that the sociology of language, per se, is
a superbly integrating and fraternalizing experience. I certainly have
found it to be so, while, at the same time, it has never asked me to
surrender the treasured social identity that originally brought me to
its threshold.

A few major systematic preoccupations have undergirded
much of my work of the past decade and Anwar Dil has very cleverly
delineated them via the titles that he has used for the six clusters of
papers selected for this volume. It is quite obvious that I have been
fascinated by social settings marked by widespread and relatively
stable bi-(multi-)lingualism (see section III). The delicate intra-code
balance of complementary functions, the compartmentalization of
role and verbal repertoires, and the institutionally-related, compos-
ited, views concerning all of the above in the minds of speech community members, these have elicited my attention again and again.
They are for me, the basic dimensions of the sociology of language,
and ones to which one must constantly bring both greater interdisciplinary integration and greater ingenuity. The fact that I find it
most gratifying to study these matters in settings of widespread and
relatively stable societal multilingualism is, in part, an accident of
personal interest, and in part, a justifiable preference from the
point of view of research parsimony. More important, perhaps, is
my conviction that every study, even one presumably concerned with
other substantive issues, should also try to contribute to basic

concerns, theoretical or methodological, that have wider implications for the entire field.

If stable societal multilingualism is the "steady state" from which I frequently gain perspective on basic issues and dimensions in the sociology of language, then two other major foci of my attention deal with the erosion of that state. In the study of language maintenance and language shift (section II) I have tried to delineate the large scale forces of sociocultural change that have acted mightily against previously established patterns of societal bilingualism, particularly as they involve the "smaller languages" of intimacy and the "greater languages" of wider communication. In section IV, dealing with the study of language planning (an aspect of which is my current major preoccupation), I have been concerned with the more localized, concrete and conscious steps that language antagonists and protagonists take when they try to reverse shift processes, or indeed, when they try to hurry them along. All in all, I have found the confrontation between my "stable state" concerns (recognizing, of course, that any societal state can never really be fully stable) and my "unstable state" concerns (recognizing, similarly, that every speech community must reveal a normative consensus with respect to communicative appropriateness, however shaky this consensus may be) to be a most provocative and productive one. It is my hope that others may also come to regard it as "a healthy conflict of interests."

The apparent conflict (or, at least, tension) between the relative demands of theory and practice (sections V and VI) has also been a stimulating one for me. It has been and is one that I not only would not be without, but one to which I expect to devote increasing amounts of time in the years ahead. Although I was academically socialized at a time when applied social concerns were not generally looked upon with favor, my whole background was such as to stress the view that without practical issue all knowledge was both barren and irresponsible. Through early participation in SPSSI (The Society for the Psychological Study of Social Issues), and in its Journal of Social Issues (which I edited from 1965 through 1968), I was enabled to nurture this conviction until, today, I find that it is the dominant view, particularly among students and younger colleagues. Indeed, the spirit of the times may have passed me by in this respect, for, rather than pleading that there is a benefit-to-theory from applied efforts,

I now find myself stressing that there is a benefit-to-application from sound theory. Just as my <u>Language Loyalty in the United States</u> helped bring about the Bilingual Education Act, on the one hand, and the theoretical systematization of language maintenance and language shift as a field study, on the other hand, so I am hopeful that my future work will have all the more practical value because of its theoretical grounding and ever greater theoretical significance because of its applied implications.

I am constantly amazed at how much more than I now know or understand must still be mastered if the application of the sociology of language is to lead to desired results. I am also frequently reminded of the obvious and dreadful misuse of the applied sociology of language by totalitarian regimes, not only yesterday but also today. Thus, my conviction that knowledge must and will be used is increasingly tempered by concerns with philosophical, esthetic and religious pursuits quite far from the sociology of language per se. Finally, then, this is another healthy tension, one between useful knowledge and basic human values, a tension which must be far better resolved in the near future than it has been in the past if man himself is to survive.

Bibliography of
Joshua A. Fishman's Works

Compiled by Anwar S. Dil

1949 a. Bilingualism in a Yiddish school; some correlates and
non-correlates. [Unpublished prize-winning monograph].
New York: Yiddish Scientific Institute. 125 pp.
 b. Review of A treasury of Jewish folklore, ed. by N.
Ausubel Crown. Yivo Bleter 33.195-204.

1951 a. Tsveyshprakhikeit in a yidisher shul. Bleter far Yidisher Dertsiung 4.32-34.
 b. Testing—its relationship to teaching and learning. JEC
Bulletin 76.8-10.
 c. Review of Standard dictionary of folklore, mythology,
and legend, ed. by M. Leach. Yivo Bleter 35.264-72.

1952 a. Degree of bilingualism in a Yiddish school and leisure
time activities. Journal of Social Psychology 36.155-
65.
 b. How safe is psychoanalysis? Jewish Education 23.45-
48.
 c. How long should the lesson be? (Massed vs. spaced
learning in the classroom). The Synagogue School 10:
3.5-9.

1954 a. Evaluation of results in current American Jewish education. Jewish Education 24:3.22-28.
 b. Patterns of American "self-identification" among children of an American minority group; preliminary ex-
ploration of hypotheses via interview data. Yivo Annual
of Jewish Social Science 10.212-66.
 c. Comment. Additions to Guides to psychological literature. American Psychologist 9.159.

d. (With Irving Lorge). The role of the culture-group
affiliation of the "Judge" in Thurstone Attitude-Scale
Construction. American Psychologist 9.368-69.

1955 a. Negative stereotypes concerning Americans among
American-born children receiving various types of
minority-group education. Genetic Psychology Monographs 51.107-82.

b. (With Ruth E. Hartley). The acceptance of new reference groups, exploratory phase. Annual Technical
Report 1. New York: The City College.

c. Comment. Suggestions on the reading of papers.
American Psychologist 10.174.

d. The roots of hatred. Review of Christianity and anti-
Semitism, by N. A. Berdyaev. The Humanist 15.284.

e. The study of language—a critical review. Journal of
Social Psychology 41.169-79.

f. Comment. On Hildebrand's The social responsibility
of scientists. American Scientist 43.90-92.

g. What's happening to SPSSI today? SPSSI Newsletter,
April 2 and 4.

1956 a. A review of the research activities of the College Entrance Examination Board, 1952-1955. New York:
College Entrance Examination Board. 90 pp.

b. Supplement (1955-56) to the review of the research activities of the College Entrance Examination Board.
New York: College Entrance Examination Board. 10 pp.

c. An examination of the process and function of social
stereotyping. Journal of Social Psychology 43.27-64.

d. General semantics through the "language, meaning,
and maturity" looking glass. A "Loyal Opposition" view.
Etc., A Review of General Semantics 13.225-31.

e. A note on Jenkins' "Improved method for tetrachoric r."
Psychometrika 21.305.

f. The MTAI in an American minority-group school setting:
I. Differences between test characteristics for norm
and non-norm populations. Journal of Educational
Psychology 48.41-51.

1957 a.   The 1957 supplement to College Board Scores 2. New
          York: College Entrance Examination Board.   204 pp.
     b.   The use of quantitative techniques to predict college
          success. Admissions Information 1. 49-61.
     c.   New directions in College Board research. College
          Board Review 33. 9-12.
     d.   (With R. E. Morris). Witnesses and testimony: a
          social problem in need of social research. Journal of
          Social Issues 13: 2. 3-5.
     e.   Some current research needs in the psychology of tes-
          timony. Journal of Social Issues 13: 2. 60-67.
     f.   The use of tests for admission to college: the next 50
          years. Long range planning for education, ed. by
          Arthur Traxler, pp. 74-79. Washington, D. C. : Amer-
          ican Council on Education.
     g.   Comments. College Board Research notes. College
          Board Review 31. 3-4; 32. 3; 33. 2-3.

1958 a.   The research activities of the College Entrance Exami-
          nation Board, 1952-1957. New York: College Entrance
          Examination Board. 120 pp.
     b.   Social science research relevant to American Jewish
          education: first annual bibliographic review. Jewish
          Education 28: 2. 49-60.
     c.   The MTAI in an American minority-group school setting:
          II. Indirect validation as a test of pupil directedness.
          Journal of General Psychology 59. 219-27.
     d.   Improving criteria for educational and psychological
          measurement: remarks of the Chairman. Proceedings
          of the 1957 Invitational Conference on Testing Problems
          11-12 and 30-32. Princeton: Educational Testing
          Service.
     e.   Educational evaluation in the context of minority-group
          dynamics. Jewish Education 29. 17-24.
     f.   Unsolved criterion problems in the selection of college
          students. Harvard Educational Review 28. 340-49.
     g.   Comments. College Board Research Notes. College
          Board Review 34. 2; 35. 2-3.
     h.   Review of Doctor and patient in Soviet Russia. Ameri-
          can Scientist 46. 152A-54A.

1959 a.   Social science research relevant to American Jewish
           education. Jewish Education 29.64–71.
      b.   (With G. S. Fishman). Separatism and integrationism:
           a social-psychological analysis of editorial content in
           New York newspapers of three American minority
           groups. Genetic Psychology Monographs 59.219–61.
      c.   Publicly subsidized pluralism: the European and the
           American contexts. School and Society 87:2154.246–48.
      d.   The American dilemmas of publicly subsidized plural-
           ism. School and Society 87:2154.264–67.
      e.   (With Irving Lorge). The influence of judge's character-
           istics on item judgments and on Thurstone scaling via
           the method of ranks. Journal of Social Psychology
           49.187–205.
      f.   American Jewry as a field of social science research.
           Yivo Annual of Jewish Social Science 12.70–102.
      g.   (With E. Leacock and M. Deutsch). The Bridgeview
           Study: a preliminary report. Journal of Social Issues
           15.30–37.
      h.   Non-intellective factors as predictors, as criteria, and
           as contingencies in selection and guidance. Selection
           and Educational Differentiation. Berkeley: Field
           Service Center and Center for the Study of Higher Educa-
           tion, University of California.
      i.   The American Jewish family today. The Jewish Family.
           New York: Anti-Defamation League, 2–6.
      j.   Review of Destiny and motivation in language, by A. A.
           Roback. Etc., A Review of General Semantics 16.250–
           51.
      k.   Review of SRA tests of educational ability. Fifth mental
           measurements yearbook, ed. by Oscar Buros, pp. 510–
           11. Highland Park, N.J.: Gryphon Press.
      l.   Review of Thurstone test of mental alertness. Fifth
           mental measurements yearbook, ed. by Oscar Buros,
           pp. 529–30. Highland Park, N.J.: Gryphon Press.

1960 a.   A systematization of the Whorfian hypothesis. Behav-
           ioral Science 5.323–39. [Reprinted several times,
           e.g., as item A414 in The Bobbs-Merrill Reprint
           Series in Social Science.]

b. (With A. Passanella). College admission-selection studies. Review of Educational Research 30.298-310.

c. American higher education in current social perspective. Teachers College Record 62.95-105.

d. New York's non-English dailies and the deliverymen's strike. Journalism Quarterly 37.241-54.

e. The emerging picture of modern American Jewry. Journal of Jewish Communal Service 37.21-33.

f. (With Philip E. Jacob). Social change and student values. Educational Record 41.338-46.

1961 a. Social-psychological theory for selecting and guiding college students. American Journal of Sociology 66. 472-84.

b. Childhood indoctrination for minority group membership. Daedalus (Spring issue), 329-49. [Reprinted in Minorities in a changing world, ed. by M. L. Baron, pp. 177-200. New York: Knopf, 1967.]

c. Some social-psychological theory for selecting and guiding college students. The American College, ed. by Nevitt Stanford, pp. 666-89. New York: John Wiley,

d. Some social and psychological determinants of intergroup relations in changing neighborhoods. Social Forces 40.42-51.

e. Flies in the psychometric ointment. Teachers College Record 62.595-601.

f. Southern City. Midstream 7:3.39-56.

g. From language to communication. Review of The process of communication, by D. K. Berlo. Contemporary Psychology 6.248-49.

1962 a. Higher education in megalopolis. Journal of Higher Education 33.72-76.

b. Amerikaner yidntum vi an obyect fun sotsial-visnshaftlekher forshung: dergreykhungen un problemen. Yivo Bleter 42.35-67. [Translation of 1959 f]

c. The "language situation" in the United States. Hachinuch 34.274-78. [In Hebrew]

d. Yiddish in America. Heritage (Fall issue), 5-12.

e. How have Franco-Americans fared in preserving the French language in the United States? Les Conferences

de l'Institut Franco-Americain de Bowdoin College,
Deuxieme Serie. pp. 44-77.

f.   Cops, robbers and psychology. Review of Legal and
     criminal psychology, by H. Toch. Contemporary Psy-
     chology 7.292.

g.   Review of The larger learning, by M. Carpenter. Per-
     sonnel and Guidance 40.746-47.

h.   Review of The sociometry reader, by J. J. Moreno.
     Psychometrika 27.216-18.

1963 a.   Natsionale shprakhn in Amerike. Tsukunft 68.212-16.

b.   (With Paul L. Clifford). The impact of testing programs
     on college preparation and attendance. The impact and
     improvement of school testing programs, ed. by Warren
     A. Findley, pp. 82-102. Chicago: University of
     Chicago Press.

c.   Megalopolis: the urbanized northeastern seaboard of
     the United States. Journal of Higher Education 34.176-
     78.

1964 a.   Language loyalty in the United States. 3 vols. New
          York: Yeshiva University. (Mimeographed report to
          DHEW-OE)

b.   What can mass-testing programs do for-and-to the
     pursuit of excellence in American education? Harvard
     Educational Review 34.63-79.

c.   (With Martin Deutsch, Leonard Kogan, Robert North
     and Martin Whiteman). Guidelines for testing minority
     group children. Journal of Social Issues 20:2.129-45.

d.   (With V. Nahirny). The ethnic group school and mother
     tongue maintenance in the United States. Sociology of
     Education 37.306-17.

e.   Language maintenance and language shift as a field of
     inquiry. Linguistics 9.32-70.

1965 a.   (With M. Deutsch and E. Leacock). Toward integration
          in suburban housing: the Bridgeview study. New York:
          Anti-Defamation League.

b.   (Ed. with L. Davidowicz, E. Ehrlich, S. Ehrlich).
     For Max Weinreich on his seventieth birthday. The
     Hague: Mouton.

c. U. S. Census data on mother tongues: review, extrapolation and prediction. For Max Weinreich on his seventieth birthday, pp. 51-62. The Hague: Mouton.

d. Yiddish in America. Bloomington: Research Center in Anthropology, Folklore and Linguistics, Indiana University.

e. The status and prospects of bilingualism in the United States. Modern Language Journal 49.143-55.

f. Bilingualism, intelligence and language learning. Modern Language Journal 49.227-37.

g. Language maintenance and language shift; the American immigrant case within a general theoretical perspective. Sociologus 16.19-38.

h. Varieties of ethnicity and varieties of language consciousness. Georgetown University Monograph Series on Languages and Linguistics 18.69-79. [Reprinted in Georgetown University Round Table Selected Papers on Linguistics, 1961-1965, ed. by J. Alatis, pp. 91-101. Washington, D. C.: Georgetown University Press, 1968.]

i. Who speaks what language to whom and when? Linguistique 2.67-88.

j. (With Peter Hesbacher). Language loyalty: its functions and concomitants in two bilingual communities. Lingua 13.145-65.

k. (With Vladimir Nahirny). American immigrant groups: ethnic identification and the problem of generations. Sociological Review 13.311-26.

l. Language maintenance and language shift in certain urban immigrant environments: the case of Yiddish in the United States. Europa Ethnica 22.146-58.

1966 a. Language loyalty in the United States. The Hague: Mouton.

b. Hungarian language maintenance in the United States. Bloomington: Indiana University Uralic-Altaic Series. [= The Hague: Mouton.]

c. Bilingual sequences at the societal level. On teaching English to speakers of other languages 2.139-44.

d. The implications of bilingualism for language teaching and language learning. Trends in language teaching, ed. by A. Valdman, pp. 121-32. New York: McGraw-Hill.

e. Some contrasts between linguistically homogeneous and linguistically heterogeneous polities. Sociological Inquiry 36.146-58. [= in Explorations in Sociolinguistics, ed. by Stanley Lieberson; IJAL, Publication no. 44, Research Center for Anthropology, Folklore and Linguistics, Indiana University, 1967.]

f. Italian language maintenance efforts in the United States and the teacher of Italian in American high schools and colleges. The Florida FL Reporter 4:3.3, 6, 26.

g. Review of The ethnography of communication, ed. by J. J. Gumperz and D. Hymes. IJAL 32:2.193-95.

1967 a. The breadth and depth of English in the United States. University Quarterly (England), March, 133-40. [Reprinted in Language and language learning, ed. by Albert H. Marckwardt, pp. 43-53. Champaign, Ill.: National Council of Teaching English, 1968.]

b. (With Neal Gross). The management of educational establishments. The uses of sociology, ed. by P. Lazarafeld, W. H. Sewell and H. L. Wilensky, pp. 304-58. New York: Basic Books.

c. Cross-cultural perspective on the evaluation of guided behavioral change. The evaluation of teaching, pp. 9-31. Washington, D. C.: Pi Lambda Theta.

d. Bilingualism with and without diglossia; diglossia with and without bilingualism. Journal of Social Issues 23:2. 29-38.

e. Review of Bilingualism and primary education, by John Macnamara. The Irish Journal of Education 1.79-83.

f. Review of The sociology of language, by J. Herzler. Language 43.586-604.

1968 a. (Ed.). Readings in the sociology of language. The Hague: Mouton.

b. (Ed. with C. A. Ferguson and J. Das Gupta). Language problems of developing nations. New York: Wiley. [Includes the following papers by Fishman: (1) Sociolinguistics and the language problems of developing countries, pp. 3-16; (2) Nationality-nationalism and nation-

nationism, pp. 39-52; (3) Some contrasts between linguistically homogeneous and linguistically heterogeneous
polities, pp. 53-68; (4) Language problems and types of
political and sociocultural integration: a conceptual
summary, pp. 491-98.]

c. (With R. L. Cooper, Roxana Ma, et al.). Bilingualism
in the Barrio. 2 vols. New York: Yeshiva University.
(Mimeo.)

d. What can mass-testing programs do for—and to—the
pursuit of excellence in American education? Problems
and Issues in Contemporary Education. Glenview, Scott
Foresman. pp. 150-66.

e. Problems of research collaboration and cooperation.
Journal of Social Issues 24:2.235-41.

f. Sociolinguistics and the language problems of the developing countries. International Social Science Journal
20.211-25. [Also appeared in the French edition of
this journal.]

g. Sociolinguistics and national development. Language
Development, pp. 3-14. New York: The Ford Foundation.

h. (With T. D. Berney and R. L. Cooper). Semantic
independence and degree of bilingualism in two Puerto
Rican communities. Revista Interamericana de Psicologia 2.289-94.

i. (With M. Edelman and R. L. Cooper). The contextualization of school children's bilingualism. Irish Journal
of Education 2.106-11.

j. Sociolinguistic perspective on the study of bilingualism.
Linguistics 39.21-50.

k. Review of Sociolinguistics, ed. by W. Bright. Lingua
19:4.428-32.

1969 a. Language maintenance and language shift: Yiddish and
other immigrant languages in the United States. Yivo
Annual of Jewish Social Science 16.12-26.

b. National languages and languages of wider communication in the developing nations. Anthropological linguistics 11.111-35. [Revised version in Language use and
social change, ed. by W. H. Whiteley, pp. 27-56.
London: Oxford University Press, 1970.]

c. (With Heriberto Casiano). Puerto Ricans in our press.
    Modern Language Journal 53.157-63.
d. (With J. Ronch and R. L. Cooper). Word naming and
    usage scores for a sample of Yiddish-English bilinguals.
    Modern Language Journal 53.232-35.
e. (With Sheldon Fertig). Some measures of the interaction
    between language domain and semantic dimension in
    bilinguals. Modern Language Journal 53.244-50.
f. (With Eleanor Herasimchuk). The multiple prediction
    of phonological variables in a bilingual speech commun-
    ity. American Anthropologist 71.648-57.
g. (With Robert L. Cooper). Alternative measures of bi-
    lingualism. Journal of Verbal Learning and Verbal Be-
    havior 8.276-82. [Revised version: The interrelation-
    ships and utility of alternative bilingual measures.
    Language use and social change, ed. by W. H. Whiteley,
    pp. 126-42. London: Oxford University Press, 1970.]
h. Bilingual attitudes and behaviors. Language Sciences
    5.5-11.
i. Chairman's summary. The description of societal bi-
    lingualism. The description and measurement of bi-
    lingualism, ed. by L. G. Kelly, pp. 275-81. Toronto:
    University of Toronto Press. [Also "comments,"
    pp. 223, 224, 264, 265, etc.]
j. (With J. Kimple and R. L. Cooper). Language switching
    and the interpretation of conversations. Lingua 23.127-
    34.
k. Puerto Rican intellectuals in New York: some intra-
    group and intergroup contrasts. Canadian Journal of
    Behavioral Sciences 1.215-26.
l. (With C. Terry). The validity of census data on bilin-
    gualism in a Puerto Rican neighborhood. American
    Sociological Review 34:5.636-50.
m. A sociolinguistic census of a bilingual neighborhood.
    The American Journal of Sociology 75:3.323-39.
n. (With Y. Findling). Review of International encyclope-
    dia of the social sciences. Language 45.458-63.
o. Literacy and the language barrier. Science 165.1108-9.

1970 a. Sociolinguistics; a brief introduction. Rowley, Mass.:
          Newbury House. [Dutch version: Taalsociologie.
          Labor-Brussel, Steppe-Ninove, 1970; French version:
          Sociolinguistique. Labor-Brussel, Steppe-Ninove,
          1971.]

      b. Intellectuals from the Island. La Monda Lingvo-
          Problemo 2:4.1-16.

      c. (With Rebecca Agheyisi). Language attitude studies.
          Anthropological Linguistics 11.137-57.

      d. The politics of bilingual education. Georgetown Univer-
          sity Monograph Series on Languages and Linguistics 23.
          47-58.

      e. Sociolinguistic perspective on internal linguistic ten-
          sions and their impact on external relations. Transac-
          tions of the Sixth World Congress of Sociology, Vol. 3,
          pp. 281-89. Milan: International Sociological Associa-
          tion.

      f. (With L. Greenfield). Situational measures of normative
          language views in relation to person, place and topic
          among Puerto Rican bilinguals. Anthropos 65.602-18.

      g. Bilingual education in sociolinguistic perspective.
          TESOL Quarterly 4.215-22.

      h. Yiddish for the people! Judaism 20:2.216-22.

      i. Di yidishe svive un di internatsionale akademishe svive.
          [The Jewish milieu and the international academic
          milieu.] Khesed L'avrahom, ed. by M. Shtarkman,
          pp. 741-48. Los Angeles: A. Golumb Jubilee Commit-
          tee.

1971 a. (With R. L. Cooper, Roxana Ma, et al.). Bilingualism
          in the barrio. Bloomington: Research Center for the
          Language Sciences, Indiana University.

      b. (Ed.). Advances in the sociology of language I. The
          Hague: Mouton.

      c. The sociology of language. Pensiero e Linguaggio
          Operazioni 2.99-122. [Reprinted in Language and social
          context, ed. by P. P. Giglioli, pp. 45-58. Harmond-
          worth, Eng.: Penguin Books, 1972.]

d. Preface. International Migration Review 5.121-24.
    [= Special issue: Migration and language shift, ed. by
    J. A. Fishman.]
e. (With Jyotirindra Das Gupta). Inter-state migration
    and subsidiary-language claiming: an analysis of
    selected Indian census data. International Migration
    Review 5.227-49.
f. The impact of nationalism on language planning. Aspects
    sociologiques du plurilinguisme. Bruxelles: AIMAV,
    pp. 15-34. [Revised version in Can language be planned?
    ed. by J. Rubin and B. Jernudd, pp. 3-20. Honolulu:
    University Press of Hawaii, 1971.]
g. Attitudes and beliefs about Spanish and English among
    Puerto Ricans. Bulletin of the School of Education
    (Indiana University) 47:2.51-72.
h. Life in the neighborhood. International Journal of Com-
    parative Sociology 12.85-100.
i. Jewish language and Jewish identity. The study of Jew-
    ish identity; issues and approaches, pp. 18-21. Jeru-
    salem: The Insitute of Contemporary Jewry, Hebrew
    University.
j. The uses of sociolinguistics. Applications of linguis-
    tics, selected papers of the Second International Con-
    gress of Applied Linguistics, ed. by G. E. Perren and
    J. L. M. Trim, pp. 19-40. Cambridge: Cambridge
    University Press.
k. Review of Language and poverty, ed. by F. Williams.
    Social Forces 49.641.
l. Die Soziologie der Sprache auf dem 7 Weltkongress für
    Soziologie. Zür Sociologie der Sprache, ed. by Rolf
    Kjolseth and Fritz Sack, pp. 33-35. Koelner Zeitschrift
    für Sociologie und Sozialpsychologie, Sonderhefte 15,
    Opladen, Westdeutscher Verlag.
m. Ein Mehrfaktoren- und Mehrebensatz zum Studium von
    Sprachplanungsprozessen, in Zür Sociologie der Sprache,
    ed. by Rolf Kjolseth and Fritz Sack, pp. 206-213.
    Koelner Zeitschrift für Sociologie und Sozialpsychologie,
    Sonderhefte 15, Opladen, Westdeutscher Verlag.

n. (With J. Das Gupta, B. Jernudd and Joan Rubin). Research outline for comparative studies of language planning. Can language be planned? ed. by Joan Rubin and Bjorn Jernudd, pp. 293-305. Honolulu: University Press of Hawaii.

1972 a. The sociology of language. Rowley, Mass.: Newbury House.

b. Language and nationalism. Rowley, Mass.: Newbury House.

c. Domains and the relationship between micro- and macrosociolinguistics. Directions in sociolinguistics, ed. by J. J. Gumperz and D. Hymes, pp. 435-53. New York: Holt, Rinehart and Winston.

d. Bilingual and bidialectal education: an attempt at a joint model for policy description. In this volume, pp. 331-39. [To appear in Proceedings of the 1971 conference on child language, ed. by T. Anderson, in press.]

e. Problems and prospects of the sociology of language. In this volume, pp. 268-76. [To appear in Einar Haugen Festschrift, ed. by N. Hasselmo, et al. The Hague: Mouton, in press.]

f. (With Erica Lueder). What has the sociology of language to say to the teacher? (On teaching the standard variety to speakers of dialectal or sociolectal varieties). In this volume, pp. 340-55. [To appear in The functions of language, ed. by C. B. Cazden, V. John and D. Hymes. New York: Teachers College Press, in press.]

g. Author's postscript. In this volume, pp. 356-62.

h. Joshua A. Fishman on language in sociocultural change. Perspectives in Linguistic Education: Conversations with Language Scholars, by Anwar S. Dil. Abbottabad: Linguistic Research Group of Pakistan, in press.

Fishman, Joshua A.   1926-
        Language in sociocultural change:
essays by Joshua A. Fishman. Selected and
Introduced by Anwar S. Dil. Stanford, California:
Stanford University Press [1972]
        xvi, 376 p. 24cm.
(Language science and national development series,
Linguistic Research Group of Pakistan)
        Includes bibliography.
I. Dil, Anwar S., 1928-   ed.
II. (Series) III. Linguistic Research Group of Pakistan

Language in Sociocultural Change

Essays by Joshua A. Fishman
Selected and Introduced by Anwar S. Dil

Sociocultural change, both planned and un-planned, is viewed by the author as the dominant social process of our age, and, therefore, as the most fitting context in which to view language in society. Addressed to both students of language and students of society, this collection of sixteen papers by a leading authority in the field of sociolinguistics demonstrates the importance of language-related concerns for modern social science.

The papers are divided into six major sections. The first and fifth present the author's general approach to the sociology of language —theoretically, topically, and methodologically. The second is concerned with language maintenance and language shift, both as a field of study and as a field of social action and responsibility. The third focuses upon societal bilingualism as the most fruitful basis for sociolinguistic research and theory. The fourth is devoted to language planning, conscious efforts to influence the structure and function of language varieties. The last section stresses the applications of the sociology of language, actual as well as potential. The book concludes with an "Author's Postscript" and a complete bibliography of the author's work to date.

LANGUAGE SCIENCE AND NATIONAL DEVELOPMENT SERIES

Joshua A. Fishman is Distinguished University Research Professor of Social Sciences at Yeshiva University. Anwar S. Dil is Director of the Linguistic Research Group of Pakistan.